R. Gupta's®

Logical and Analytical Reasoning

Useful for All Competitive Exams

Edited by

A.K. Gupta

Ramesh Publishing House, New Delhi

Published by

O.P. Gupta *for* Ramesh Publishing House

Admin. Office

12-H, New Daryaganj Road, Opp. Officers' Mess,
New Delhi-110002 ✆ 23261567, 23275224, 23275124

E-mail: info@rameshpublishinghouse.com
Website: www.rameshpublishinghouse.com

Showroom

• Balaji Market, Nai Sarak, Delhi-6 ✆ 23253720, 23282525
• 4457, Nai Sarak, Delhi-6, ✆ 23918938

Book Code: R-273

35th Edition: 1901

ISBN: 978-93-5012-776-6

HSN Code : 49011010

CONTENTS

1

RELATIONSHIP AND ANALOGY

Questions on relationship and analogy cover almost all types of commonality that one can think of. This is a process of reasoning based on similar feature of two things. In this type of questions a set of two words is given in which the two words are related through a specific relationship with each other. A third word, and a question mark followed by a set of alternatives, is also given. Candidates are asked to identify the relationship between the given two words and then to select one alternative out of the given set of alternatives. The selected answer should bear the same relationship with the third word as exists between the two words given in the beginning.

Example 1: MAN : WALK : : FISH : ?

A. Swim B. Run
C. Eat D. Fly
E. Live

Explanatory Answer: As man walks for going from one place to another place, fishes swim.

So alternative 'A' is the correct answer

Example 2: Glove : Hand :: Hat : ?

A. Cap B. Cloth
C. Head D. Eyes
E. Hair

Explanatory Answer: Glove is a covering for the hand whereas hat is a covering for the head. Therefore here C is the correct answer.

Example 3: In the following example, suggest a suitable substitute in place of question mark (?).

(?) is related to Gall in the same way as Gland is related to (?)

A. Liver, Hormone
B. Gall bladder, Urine
C. Kidney, Blood
D. Spleen, Phlegm
E. None of the above

Explanatory Answer (A): As Gall is secreted from the liver, Hormone is secreted from Gland.

Example 4: If PRLN : XZTV : : JLFH : ? then select the correct set of letters from the following five alternatives to replace the question mark (?)

A. NRPT B. NTRP
C. NPRT D. RTNP
E. RPNT

Explanatory Answer: In each set of letters, first and the third letters are two steps behind of the second and the fourth letters. First letter of the set is two steps ahead of the fourth letter. Letters in the other sets also bear the same relationship. Therefore (D) is the correct alternative.

Example 5: If FRIEND is related to FRIENDLY then OPPONENT is related to which of the following?

A. CONTEST B. DEFEAT
C. HOSTILE D. ENEMY
E. None of these

Explanatory Answer (A): Here the word OPPONENT is most nearly opposite in meaning of the word FRIEND. So one word is antonym of the other word. Therefore antonym of FRIENDLY is HOSTILE which is the correct alternative.

Example 6: If (?) is related to vegetable in the same way as wheat is related to (?), then which of the following group of words will suitably replace the question mark?

A. Leaves, Rice
B. Barley, Flour
C. Cabbage, Cereal
D. Plant, Bread

Explanatory Answer (C): Cabbage is a type of vegetable and wheat is a type of cereal. Therefore C is the correct alternative.

Example 7: In this question three problem figures and a question mark (?) are given in which first two figures are related in some way. The same relationship holds between the third question figure and the answer figure which should replace (?). Identify that figure from the answer figures (A), (B), (C) and (D).

Problem Figures:

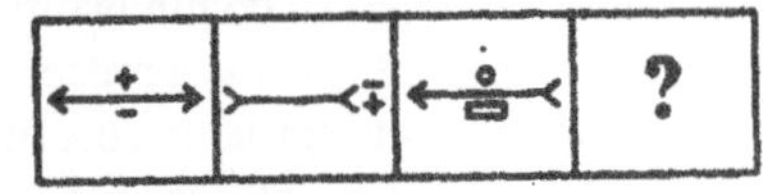

Answer Figures:

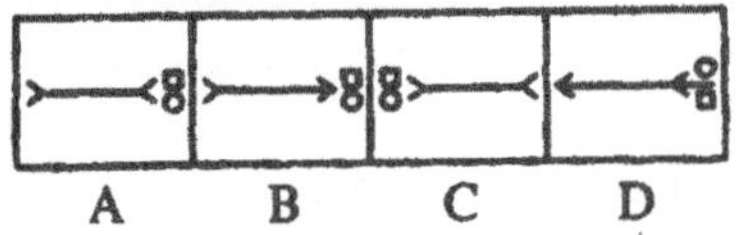

A B C D

Explanatory Answer (B): Arrow marks at the two ends of the line in first figure are reversed in the second figure. In addition the + and – signs on either side of the line in the first figure come at one end of the line in the second figure and sign of '–' which was below the line in the first figure, comes above the + sign in the second figure. The same relationship holds in the third problem figure and the second answer figure. Therefore (B) is the correct answer.

EXERCISE - 1

Directions (Qs. 1 to 41): *In each of the following questions a set of two words is given on the left side of sign (: :). These two words are related through a specific relationship with each other. A third word followed by a set of alternatives is given on the right of the sign (: :). You are to identify the relationship and choose the alternative which expresses the same relationship with the third word and should replace (?).*

1. Mountain : Valley : : Light : ?
A. Sun B. Morning
C. Night D. Dark
E. Shadow

2. Plant : Tree : : Girl : ?
A. Lady B. Girl Friend
C. Sister D. Wife
E. Mother

3. Procession : Way : : Earth : ?
A. Highway B. Sky
C. Sun D. Revolution
E. Orbit

4. Flower : Bouquet : : Player : ?
   A. Captain B. Play
   C. Group D. Team
   E. Playground
5. Carpenter : Wood : : Tailor : ?
   A. Furniture B. Dress
   C. Cloth D. Textile
   E. Sewing
6. High : Low : : Sky : ?
   A. Ground
   B. Stars
   C. Nether region
   D. Ocean
   E. None of these
7. Light : Rays : : Sound : ?
   A. Sound B. Audible
   C. Tune D. Listen
   E. Wave
8. Bulb : Candle : : Motorcar : ?
   A. Mobil Oil
   B. Motorcycle
   C. Scooter
   D. Bullock Cart
   E. Aeroplane
9. Water : Life : : Spirituality : ?
   A. Difficult B. Death
   C. Disease D. Peace
   E. Unrest
10. South : North-west : : West : ?
   A. South-west B. South
   C. East D. North-east
   E. North
11. Water : Ocean : : Air : ?
   A. Sky
   B. Moon
   C. Atmosphere
   D. Ocean
   E. Land
12. Parrot : Cage : : Man : ?
   A. Life B. Road
   C. House D. Prison
   E. Forest
13. Bird : Aeroplane : : Fish : ?
   A. Sailor B. Swim
   C. Eat D. Ship
   E. Water
14. Man : Walk : : Fish : ?
   A. Swim B. Eat
   C. Run D. Water
   E. Live
15. Hat : Head : : Spectacles : ?
   A. Eyes B. Textile
   C. Mouth D. Hat
   E. Hair
16. Umbrella : Rain : : Coat : ?
   A. Winter B. Summer
   C. Light D. Dust
   E. Sun
17. Sympathy : Ill-will : : Hatred : ?
   A. Affection B. Love
   C. Simplicity D. Attachment
   E. Anger
18. Horse : Hair : : Ewe : ?
   A. Wool B. Fur
   C. Lambkin D. Milk
   E. Meat
19. Chapter : Book : : Flower : ?
   A. Garden B. Pollen
   C. Plant D. Bouquet
   E. Lotus
20. Poison : Death : : Medicine : ?
   A. Decay B. Weak
   C. Disease D. Life
   E. Relief
21. Day : Night : : ? : Evening
   A. Sun B. Star
   C. Light D. Sky
   E. Morning
22. Day : Week : : Week : ?
   A. Year B. Hour

C. Month D. Day
E. Second

23. Feather : Bird : : ? : Fish
A. Scale B. Tail
C. Fin D. Swim
E. Mouth

24. House : Wall : : Wall : ?
A. Plaster B. Sand
C. Brick D. Roof
E. Cement

25. Hunger : Food : : Syntax : ?
A. See B. Speak
C. Give D. Listen
E. Feel

26. Ornament : Beauty : : Colour : ?
A. Wall B. Building
C. Painting D. Room
E. Decoration

27. Cardboard : Opaque : : Glass : ?
A. Shiny B. Transparent
C. Brittle D. Hard
E. Smooth

28. Petrol : Engine : : ? : Body
A. Medicine B. Water
C. Heat D. Food
E. Cloth

29. Leg : Man : : Hoof : ?
A. Fish B. Rabbit
C. Dog D. Cat
E. Cow

30. Factory : Production : : School : ?
A. Descipline B. Building
C. Teacher D. Student
E. Education

31. Examinee : Examination : : Traveller : ?
A. Experience
B. Ability
C. Travel
D. Recreation
E. Train

32. Soft : Sponge : : Sharp : ?
A. Knife B. Cut
C. Blunt D. Drill
E. None of these

33. Child : Mother : : Mars : ?
A. Sun B. Light
C. Earth D. Ray
E. Daughter

34. Marriage : Function : : Separation : ?
A. Failure B. Punishment
C. Success D. Sadness
E. Playful

35. Walk : Run : : Wind : ?
A. Air B. Fast
C. Cold D. Storm
E. Respiration

36. Water : Snow : : Water-vapour : ?
A. Hot B. Steam-Engine
C. Water D. Gas
E. Cold

37. Narrow : Broad : : Thin : ?
A. Fat B. Small
C. Long D. Dwarf
E. None of these

38. Person : Society : : Book : ?
A. Study B. Author
C. Library D. Page
E. None of these

39. Monday : Wednesday : : January : ?
A. March B. April
C. Friday D. Thursday
E. Sunday

40. Food : Hunger : : Water : ?
A. Wash B. Drink
C. Swim D. Thirst
E. Sweet

41. Book : Author : : Newspaper : ?
A. Library B. Printing press
C. Reporter D. Editor
E. Magazine

EXERCISE - 2

1. IDOL is related to SIZE in the same way as SONG is related to:
   A. NOTE B. POET
   C. WORD D. POEM
   E. SINGER
2. SMOKE is related to POLLUTION in the same way as WAR is related to:
   A. VICTORY B. ENEMY
   C. ARMY D. DEATH
   E. TREATY
3. COAL is to MINE as WATER is to:
   A. WELL B. POND
   C. RAIN D. WATER
   E. RIVER
4. KANGAROO is related to AUSTRALIA in the same way as GIRAFFE is related to:
   A. ANTARCTICA
   B. INDIA
   C. JAPAN
   D. AFRICA
   E. PAKISTAN
5. MARCH is to YEAR as SUMMER is to:
   A. SPRING B. HOT
   C. COLD D. WINTER
   E. SEASON
6. OCEAN is to POND as DEEP is to:
   A. CLEAN B. SHALLOW
   C. CHANNEL D. TRENCH
   E. RIVER
7. ACCIDENT is related to CARE in the same way as DISEASE is related to:
   A. BACTERIA
   B. CLEANLINESS
   C. GERM
   D. WATER
   E. WINE
8. CARE is related to ELATION in the same way as ATTENTION is related to:
   A. CAUTIOUS
   B. DISRESPECT
   C. DISREGARD
   D. DISTURBED
   E. REQUIREMENT
9. CLEANLINESS is related to CONTAMINATION in the same way as HEALTH is related to:
   A. AGONY
   B. POLLUTION
   C. THERAPEUTIC
   D. GENEROSITY
   E. MENTAL DISEASE
10. PLAYFUL is related to STEADY in the same way as CHANGE is related to:
    A. PERMANENCE
    B. REGULAR
    C. PERIODICITY
    D. DIFFERENCE
    E. SWIFTNESS
11. HONEYBEE is related to STING in the same way as SNAKE is related to:
    A. POISON B. RATS
    C. FANG D. SLIP
    E. SCORPION
12. WATCH is related to SECOND in the same way as CALENDAR is related to:
    A. DAY B. MONTH
    C. YEAR D. DATE
    E. WEEK

13. TIREDNESS is related to HARDWORK in the same way as DISPLACEMENT is related to:
   A. MOVEMENT
   B. WEAKNESS
   C. MUSCLE
   D. FATIGUE
   E. LETHARGY
14. SKIN is related to ANIMAL in the same way as HUSK is related to:
   A. ORANGE B. BARLEY
   C. PEA D. MANGO
   E. BANANA
15. INFANT : INFANCY : : YOUNG-MAN : ?
   A. ADULTHOOD
   B. OLDAGE
   C. YOUTH
   D. CHILDHOOD
   E. None of these
16. FINGER is to ARM as TOE is to:
   A. KNEE B. CALF
   C. LEG D. FOOT
   E. HEAD
17. CAPTAIN is to SOLDIER as LEADER is to:
   A. GROUP B. SEAT
   C. MINISTER D. VOTE
   E. FOLLOWER
18. THEFT is related to POVERTY in the same way as EXERCISE is related to:
   A. MUSCLES B. WEAKNESS
   C. HEALTH D. FATIGUE
   E. GAME
19. What is related to NATION in the same way as GOVERNOR is related to STATE?
   A. JUDGE
   B. PRESIDENT
   C. PRIME MINISTER
   D. FATHER OF THE NATION
   E. CHIEF MINISTER
20. BOTANY is related to plant in the same way as HYGIENE is related to:
   A. DISEASE
   B. PHYSIOLOGY
   C. DISINFECTION
   D. HEALTH
   E. CLEANLINESS
21. FIRST is to LAST as FAITHFUL is to:
   A. OPPONENT
   B. GENTLE
   C. TRAITOR
   D. TRUTHFUL
   E. DISOBEDIENT
22. What is related to FLOWER in the same way as SENTENCE is related to WORD?
   A. PETAL
   B. GARDEN
   C. GARLAND
   D. TREE
   E. BUD
23. UMBRELLA is to RAIN as QUININE is to:
   A. CHEMIST
   B. MEDICINE
   C. MALARIA
   D. DOCTOR
   E. AIDS
24. LATHER is to FOAM as PROFIT is to:
   A. CAPITAL B. GAIN
   C. LOSS D. EARNING
   E. BUSINESS
25. MECHANIC is to ENGINEER as STENO-TYPIST is to:
   A. TYPIST B. SHORTHAND

C. SPEED D. SKILL
E. TYPEWRITER

26. Which of the following is related to NECK in the same way as WAIST is related to BELT?
A. SHIRT B. TIE
C. COLLAR D. NECKER
E. PANTALOON

27. Which of the following is related to SNAKE in the same way as ELEPHANT is related to IVORY?
A. RAT
B. SNAKE-CHARMER
C. PREY
D. SLOUGH
E. CAT

28. BROOM is related to FLOOR in the same way as SPOON is related to:
A. PLATE B. KNIFE
C. TABLE D. FORK
E. KITCHEN

29. TELEPHONE is to SOUND as LETTER is to:
A. DATE
B. POST OFFICE
C. ENVELOPE
D. WRITING
E. JOURNALIST

30. COUNTRY is related to PRESIDENT in the same way as STATE is related to:
A. STATE MINISTER
B. PRIME MINISTER
C. GOVERNOR
D. CHIEF MINISTER
E. LT. GOVERNOR

31. PAGE is to BOOK as WATER is to:
A. BOTTLE B. BUCKET
C. TRAY D. SPOON
E. LAKE

EXERCISE - 3

Directions (Qs. 1 to 22): *In each question there are two words to the left of sign : : and one word and a question mark to the right of sign : : . The question mark is to be replaced by one of the words given below each question. The selected answer should bear the same relation with the word given to the right of the sign as exists between the two words to the left.*

1. Bird : Aves : : Man : ?
A. Mammal
B. Homo sapiens
C. Horse
D. Holothuroidea
E. Lizard

2. Teaching : Learning : : Treatment : ?
A. Disease B. Medicine
C. Wound D. Doctor
E. Cure

3. Skrmish : War : : Disease : ?
A. Doctor B. Hospital
C. Epidemic D. Injection
E. Pain

4. Fossils : Creatures : : Mummies : ?
A. Dead Bodies
B. Human beings
C. Caves
D. None of these
E. Mothers

5. Labourer : Wages : : Entrepreneur : ?
A. Department B. Salary

C. Bonus D. Proprietorship
E. Profit

6. Procession : Route : : Earth : ?
A. Space B. Rotation
C. Ether D. Orbit
E. Revolution

7. Sun : Candle : : Ocean : ?
A. Water tank B. Water
C. River D. Sea
E. Pond

8. Telephone : Cable : : Radio : ?
A. Microphone
B. Television
C. Wireless
D. Plug
E. Diode

9. Guilt : Past : : Hope : ?
A. Success
B. Life
C. Imagination
D. Future
E. Tomorrow

10. Doctor : Patient : : Teacher : ?
A. Ignorance
B. Student
C. Knowledge
D. School
E. Principal

11. President : Republic : : King : ?
A. State B. Kingdom
C. Monarchy D. Country
E. Continent

12. Outright : Secret : : Public : ?
A. Personal B. Open
C. Private D. Known
E. Secret

13. Nothing : Something : : All : ?
A. Much B. Little
C. Less D. None
E. Many

14. Blood : Heart : : Air : ?
A. Nose B. Breathing
C. Nostrills D. Lungs
E. Hand

15. Hot : Oven : : Cold : ?
A. Pitcher
B. Air-Conditioner
C. Refrigerator
D. Ice
E. Cooler

16. Watch : Second : : Calendar : ?
A. Period B. Desk
C. Year D. Date
E. Week

17. Cobbler : Shoe : : Carpenter : ?
A. Furniture B. Paintings
C. Wood D. Clothes
E. Art

18. Squint : Vision : : Stammering : ?
A. Memory B. Tongue
C. Speech D. Hearing
E. Blind

19. Save : Rescue : : Seldom : ?
A. Frequently B. Often
C. Rare D. Usually
E. Mostly

20. Ancient : Modern : : Often : ?
A. Frequent B. Regular
C. Always D. Never
E. Seldom

21. Ornithologist : Bird : : Anthropologist : ?
A. Sound B. Diseases
C. Animals D. Man
E. Plants

22. Step : Staircase : : Soldier : ?
A. Gun B. Victory
C. Army D. Battle
E. Fleet

23. With which of the following CLOTH is related in the same way as NEWSPAPER is related to PRESS ?

A. COTTON B. MILL
C. MARKET D. TAILOR
E. THREAD

24. WAITING is to BOREDOME as EDUCATION is to:

A. SYLLABUS
B. ENTHUSIASM
C. ENLIGHTENMENT
D. SCHOOLING
E. BOOKS

25. DAWN is to DUSK as LIGHT is to:

A. ELECTRICITY
B. TORCH
C. SUN
D. HEAVY
E. NOON

26. With which of the following OPERATION is related in the same way as PUNISHMENT is related to PRISONER?

A. DISEASE
B. OPERATION THEATRE
C. PATIENT
D. HOSPITAL
E. DOCTOR

27. WELL is to DEPTH as OFFICER is to:

A. PAY
B. AUTHORITY
C. EFFICIENCY
D. SUBORDINATE
E. PROMOTION

28. PLAYER is to TEAM as SHIP is to:

A. WATER B. HARBOUR
C. FLEET D. SEA
E. SAILOR

29. DRAMA : DIRECTOR : : MAGAZINE : ?

A. PRODUCER
B. READER
C. WRITER
D. PUBLISHER
E. EDITOR

30. DISEASE : PATHOLOGY : : PLANET : ?

A. ORBIT
B. ASTROLOGY
C. ASTRONOMY
D. SATELLITE
E. SUN

EXERCISE - 4

Directions: *In each of the following question, identify the relationship between the two words given on the left of the sign (: :) and then select a word from the alternatives given below each question. The selected answer should bear the same relationship with the word given to the right of the (: :) sign as exists between the two words to the left.*

1. CVUB : BUVC : : QJOI : ?

A. IPQT B. IOJQ
C. IDQU D. IOJU
E. IQOJ

2. TFOEFX : SGNFEY : : ? : OFNKBZ

A. PDOLCA B. DEOMO
C. NEMJAY D. PGOLCA
E. PEOJCY

3. OPJUBL : POKTAK : : NFDFEA : ?
A. MECGOZ B. OGEEDZ
C. MGCFFZ D. MELGEB
E. OGEFDZ

4. YeWG : hVFX : : SkQM : ?
A. nPLR B. qMOO
C. IuGW D. kSIU
E. nYLR

5. ZADC : BCFE : : ? : TUHC
A. RTKH B. SKHV
C. UVGI D. RSFE
E. RFSE

6. TPVOE : UOWNF : : POISE : ?
A. QNHTF B. QPJTY
C. QNJRF D. QPHTD
E. QJNRF

7. PCWL : REXM : : THNY : ?
A. PMKZ B. UVXZ
C. VJOZ D. OZPL
E. VKOZ

8. ? : WIUH : : ZKXJ : CMAL
A. FIKT B. FRTK
C. TFEM D. TGRE
E. TGRF

9. ACFJ : OUBJ : : SUXB : ?
A. GORC B. GKPY
C. GMTB D. GNSA
E. ECUB

10. BZDX : FVHT : : JRLP : ?
A. NMLR B. MNPT
C. NNPL D. NNLO
E. NPPJ

11. YAWC : UESG : : QIOK : ?
A. KOME B. LIME
C. MINC D. MMKO
E. MNKO

12. FED : MKI : : PON : ?
A. TSQ B. XVU
C. WUS D. IHG
E. WSU

13. ZXYW : USTR : PNOM : ?
A. KIJH B. JHKI
C. KHIJ D. IHKJ
E. KJHI

14. BACE : ONPR : : JIKM : ?
A. XYWZ B. WVXZ
C. UZYW D. WVZY
E. WXVZ

15. PSQR : CFED : : JKML : ?
A. WYXZ B. UVXZ
C. WZYX D. YZXW
E. WXYZ

16. BDCE : GIHJ : : QSRT : ?
A. VZXY B. VXYZ
C. UYXZ D. VXWY
E. VUWX

17. MILD : NKOH : : GATE : ?
A. HCWI B. HCWT
C. HWCT D. EYRC
E. HICW

18. NAMO : OCPS : : GODS : ?
A. HPFV B. HQSX
C. HQGW D. NQES

19. ZY : ? : : UT : NM
A. DB B. DO
C. QR D. NL
E. ED

20. ABE : EFI : : STW : ?
A. VWX B. WXZ
C. VWZ D. WXA
E. WAX

21. LXNU : NYPV : : QTBR : ?
A. SRUD B. RUSD
C. SUDS D. RSUD
E. SURD

22. NUMBER : UNBMRE GHOST : ?
A. HGOST B. HOGST
C. HGSOT D. HOGTS
E. HGTSO

23. Aab : aAB : : Pqr : : ?
A. PqR B. PQR
C. pQr D. pQR
E. pRQ

24. ACE : HIL : : MOQ : ?
A. XVT B. TUX
C. WUS D. SUW
E. TXU

25. ABC : ZYX : : CBA : ?
A. XYZ B. BCA
C. XZY D. YZX
E. XZY

26. OYGO : SAIQ : : UCKS : ?
A. WFMU B. VEMU
C. WEMU D. WDLU
E. WDMU

EXERCISE - 5

Directions: *In each of the following questions there are three numbers. The first two numbers on the left of sign (: :) are related in some way. The same relationship is obtained between the number to the right of the sign (: :) and one of the alternatives given below each question. Select the right alternative.*

1. 6 : 35 : : 11 : ?
A. 120 B. 121
C. 115 D. 122
E. 124

2. 5 : 26 : : 7 : ?
A. 50 B. 26
C. 55 D. 19
E. 28

3. 6 : 24 : : 5 : ?
A. 26 B. 19
C. 23 D. 20
E. 22

4. 3 : 9 : : 8 : ?
A. 25 B. 64
C. 24 D. 14
E. 20

5. 5 : 8 : : 15 : ?
A. 17 B. 21
C. 18 D. 20
E. 22

6. 08 : 09 : : 64 : ?
A. 32 B. 25
C. 125 D. 20
E. 16

7. 08 : 28 : : 15 : ?
A. 26 B. 124
C. 65 D. 126
E. 63

8. 11 : 17 : : 19 : ?
A. 29 B. 23
C. 25 D. 27
E. 21

9. 01 : 04 : : 08 : ?
A. 72 B. 81
C. 64 D. 96
E. 49

10. 3 : 10 : : 08 : ?
A. 16 B. 14
C. 17 D. 10
E. 13

11. 12 : 20 : : 30 : ?
A. 35 B. 48
C. 15 D. 42
E. 32

12. 01 : 08 : : 16 : ?
A. 64 B. 125
C. 81 D. 25
E. 27

13. 42 : 56 : : 110 : ?
A. 132 B. 149

C. 136 D. 156
E. 144

14. 3 : 16 : : 7 : ?
A. 81 B. 73
C. 64 D. 52
E. 49

15. 122 : 170 : : 290 : ?
A. 332 B. 362
C. 315 D. 344
E. 299

16. 7 : 11 : : 31 : ?
A. 45 B. 43
C. 37 D. 36
E. 39

17. 01 : 08 : : 09 : ?
A. 49 B. 36
C. 16 D. 25
E. 64

18. 01 : 04 : : 05 : ?
A. 25 B. 16
C. 24 D. 36
E. 06

19. 09 : 25 : : 49 : ?
A. 64 B. 100
C. 63 D. 81
E. 36

20. 1/2 : 1/8 : : 2/3 : ?
A. 2/6 B. 1/3
C. 1/6 D. 1/4
E. 2/7

21. 4 : 9 : : ? : 27
A. 8 B. 15
C. 6 D. 13
E. 16

22. 15 : 25 : : 45 : ?
A. 65 B. 95
C. 80 D. 70
E. 75

23. 12 : 35 : : 16 : ?
A. 40 B. 64
C. 62 D. 63
E. 53

24. 3 : 10 : : 5 : ?
A. 16 B. 26
C. 27 D. 2
E. 25

25. 1/4 : 1/8 : : 1/3 : ?
A. 2/6 B. 2/7
C. 1/6 D. 1/7
E. 1/3

EXERCISE-6

Directions (Qs. 1 to 25): *In the questions given below establish the relationship between the two words. Then from the given options select one, the words given in which bear the same relationship as exists between the two words given in the beginning.*

1. TREE and PLANT bear the same relationship as is there between:
A. RIVER and FOUNTAIN
B. TREE and FURNITURE
C. BUD and FLOWER
D. HORSE and MARE

2. Which of the following bear the same relationship as exists between BUNCH and KEY?
A. HORSE and STABLE
B. EXAMINATION and SUBJECT
C. HIVE and BEE
D. BOUQUET and FLOWER

3. Which of the following bear the same relationship as exists between ART and BEAUTY?
A. VOWEL and CONSONANT
B. MANGO and SWEETNESS
C. SCHOLAR and LITERATE
D. MUSIC and MELODY

4. Which of the following bear the same relationship as exists between INTELLIGENCE and NATURAL BORN?
A. CURD and MILK
B. AGE and LABOUR
C. EDUCATION and SCHOOL
D. EXPERIENCE and EDUCATION

5. Which of the following bear the same relationship as exists between KING and EMPEROR?
A. GOD and TEMPLE
B. TEACHER and STUDENT
C. PRIME MINISTER and COUNTRY
D. STATE and EMPIRE

6. Which of the following bear the same relationship as exists between HOUSE and RENT?
A. DEBTOR and CREDITOR
B. LABOURER and LABOUR
C. ABILITY and INCOMPETENCE
D. CAPITAL and INTEREST

7. Which of the following bear the same relationship as exists between GOOD FORTUNE and MISFORTUNE?
A. GLAD and HAPPY
B. ACCURATE and CORRECT
C. SLAVERY and FREEDOM
D. ANIMAL and MAN

8. Which one of the following pairs of words bears the same relationship as exists between WORD and SENTENCE?
A. LETTER and WORD
B. VOWEL and CONSONANT
C. BEE and HIVE
D. PROSE and SENTENCE

9. Which one of the following pairs of words bears the same relationship as exists between CLASS and TEACHER?
A. SCHOOL and COLLEGE
B. LIBRARY and LIBRARIAN
C. PEN and WRITER
D. BOOK and COLLEGE

10. Which of the following bear the same relationship as exists between DROP and OCEAN?
A. TREE and FOREST
B. CROP and FARM
C. LETTER and DICTIONARY
D. TOOTH and MOUTH

11. CARPENTER and WOOD bear the same relationship as is there between :
A. HORSE and STABLE
B. TAILOR and SEWING MACHINE
C. PAINTER and BRUSH
D. GOLDSMITH and SILVER

12. Which one of the following pairs of words bears the same relationship as exists between VAPOUR and BOIL?
A. CRACK and BREAK
B. CLOTH and STITCH
C. SWIMMING and TO SWIM
D. JUICE and SQUEEZE

13. Which one of the following pairs bears the same relationship as exists between PULP and PAPER?
A. WOOD and SAW DUST
B. CLOTH and SHIRT
C. THREAD and CLOTH
D. IRON and STEEL

14. Which one of the following pairs bears the same relationship as exists between VISITOR and WELCOME?
A. HUNGRY and BEGGAR

B. WATCH and THEFT
C. WORSHIP and GOD
D. CRIMINAL and PROSECUTE

15. Which one of the following pairs bears the same relationship as exists between EARTH and MOON?
A. SCHOOL and CLASSROOM
B. SHIP and BOAT
C. ASIA and INDIA
D. SUN and URANUS

16. Which one of the following pairs bears the same relationship as exists between EFFORT and SUCCESS?
A. ENJOY and DRAMA
B. HEALTHY and VITAMIN
C. READING and KNOWLEDGE
D. PLAY and CRICKET

17. THIRST : WATER : :
A. HUNGER : FOOD
B. ICE : COLD
C. POISON : DEATH
D. MEAL : APPETITE

18. Which one of the following pairs of words bears the same relationship as exists between SUCCESS and FAILURE?
A. PLAYING and LOSING
B. HAPPY and SAD
C. READING and WRITING
D. PROFIT and LOSS

19. From the given alternatives, select the word to replace question mark in the third pair below which should bear the same relationship as exists between the first two pairs —
WATER : FLUID, STONE : SOLID, AIR : ?
A. ATMOSPHERE
B. VAPOUR
C. AIR
D. GAS

20. From the given alternatives, select the word to replace question mark in the third and last pair below which should bear the same relationship as exists between the first two pairs
CAT : RAT, TIGER : LAMB, LIZARD : ?
A. SPIDER B. POISON
C. NECTAR D. CROW

21. TREE : FOREST : :
A. HOUSEFLY : MILK
B. WATER LEVEL : SHIP
C. BOOK : LIBRARY
D. YOUTHFUL LADY : GARDEN

22. CORRUGATED : STRIPED : :
A. BOX : ZEBRA
B. PAINT : CRAYON
C. ROUGHNESS : SMOOTHNESS
D. PIT : DOT
E. SAND : GRAINY

23. AUTHOR : POET : :
A. BOOK : POEM
B. WRITER : ARTICLE
C. AUTHOR : BOOK
D. PROSE : POETRY

24. CHEMISTRY : SCIENCE : :
A. PAINTING : ART
B. SURGERY : MEDICINE
C. PLEADING : PLEADER
D. SKETCHING : SCIENCE

25. From the given options below select one which bears the same relationship with the third word as exists between the given two words at the left of sign : :
GOLDSMITH : GOLD : LEATHER : ?
A. PIGMENT B. CLEANER
C. DYER D. COBBLER

Directions (Qs. 26 to 35): *In each of the questions given below two words followed by eight alternatives are given. The two words are related through a specific relationship with each other. You are to select a pair of two alternatives out of the given set of alternatives. The selected words should bear the same relationship with each other as exists between the two words given in the beginning.*

26. NEAT and CLEAN
A. Dirty B. Root
C. White D. Water
E. Beauty F. Plain
G. Unclean H. Prudent

27. OXYGEN and MAN
A. Driver B. Wood
C. Carpenter D. Sky
E. Petrol F. Stool
G. Water H. Fish

28. HAND and FINGER
A. Nose B. Stomach
C. Hat D. Tooth
E. Head F. Eyes
G. Leg H. Hair

29. CAR and GARAGE
A. Horse B. Hive
C. Animal D. Grass
E. Man F. Stable
G. Bird H. Water

30. FAILURE and LETHARGY
A. Pin B. Success
C. Game D. Lazy
E. Labour F. School
G. Study H. Guilelessness

31. HIGH and LOW
A. Far B. Fair
C. Distance D. Near
E. Last F. Clean
G. Next H. Fare

32. COLD and HOT
A. January B. August
C. March D. June
E. Year F. Thursday
G. Month H. Monday

33. BROTHER-IN-LAW and SISTER-IN-LAW
A. My
B. Young man
C. I
D. Sister-in-Law
E. Girl Friend
F. Beautiful Woman
G. Youthful Lady
H. Wife

34. CONSTABLE and POLICE
A. Girl
B. Medical Department
C. File
D. House
E. Drug
F. Doctor
G. Clerk
H. Mother

35. TREE and FOREST
A. Teacher B. Ship
C. Books D. Study
E. Library F. Paper
G. Ocean H. Study Classes

EXERCISE - 7

Directions (Qs. 1 to 5): *In each of the following two columns five groups have been given. Each group contains three elements. In the questions (1 to 5) based on these groups, four alternatives each comprising of two* *groups of elements have been given. You have to compare these two columns and find out whether the elements of the one group of any alternative are related in the same way as the elements of the other group of that alternative are related. Mark your answer as alternative (A), (B), (C) or (D).*

Column - 1

A. Cereal, Wheat, Tomato
B. Seed, Apple, Fruit
C. Mother, Sister, Female
D. Teacher, Writer, Speaker
E. Stool, Furniture, Table

Column - 2

P. Apple, Banana, Fruit
Q. Wheat, Barley, Cereal
T. Army, Soldier, Civilian
R. Doctor, Painter, Father
S. Cow, Mammal, Animal

1. A. AQ B. BP
   C. CR D. EP
2. A. AT B. BR
   C. CS D. DP
3. A. BR B. DR
   C. ET D. CS
4. A. AQ B. AT
   C. BS D. DQ
5. A. BQ B. CR
   C. EQ D. DS

Directions (Qs. 6 to 10): *Find out the correct answer out of the four alternatives in each of the following questions.*

6. Cheese, Ghee and Butter are most commonly related to:
   A. Butter milk
   B. Curd
   C. Cream
   D. Milk
7. Regulation, Coordination and Circulation are most commonly related to:
   A. Give direction
   B. Support
   C. Drive
   D. Publicity
8. Which of the following is just the same as Pink, Yellow and Red?
   A. Flower B. Flag
   C. Blood D. Blue
9. Which of the following is just the same as Kidney, Brain and Lungs?
   A. Ear B. Eyes
   C. Liver D. Nose
10. Which of the following is just the same as undisturbed, unprevented and unobstructed?
    A. Uncertain
    B. Unobviated
    C. Unlimited
    D. Unrelieved

Directions (Qs. 11 to 21): *In each of the following questions, there are three words at the top which have some characteristics common to them. Of the four alternatives given under these words one has the same characteristics or tells the characteristics common to the three words at the top. Find the correct alternative in each question.*

11. Sitar, Lyre, Flute
    A. TambourineB. Musical note
    C. Song D. Tune
12. Milk, Curd, Butter
    A. She-buffaloB. Cow
    C. White D. Ghee

13. Eye, Ear, Nose
A. Hair B. Finger
C. Tongue D. Hand

14. Mumbai, Kolkata, Delhi
A. Chennai B. Nagpur
C. Cochin D. Allahabad

15. Why, How, Where
A. Here B. When
C. Then D. Now

16. Guava, Apple, Orange
A. Leaf B. Seed
C. Mango D. Tree

17. Sledge, Bullock cart, Tonga
A. Cycle-rickshaw
B. Scooter
C. Car
D. Motorcycle

18. Ox, Cock, Lion
A. Cow B. Horse
C. Bitch D. Mare

19. Iron, Copper, Gold
A. Coal B. Fossil
C. Manganese D. Brass

20. Chair, Stool, Sofa
A. Almirah B. Table
C. Bed stead D. Bench

21. Mars, Jupiter, Saturn
A. Galaxy B. Venus
C. Sun D. Moon

Directions (Qs. 22 to 26): *Below are given three capitalised words followed by a set of alternatives, one of which expresses most effectively the general characteristics of the three capitalised words. Select that word and mark your answer.*

22. DAISY, PANSY, ROSE
A. Red B. Violet
C. Plant D. Lotus

23. LIBERATE, ACQUIT, FREE
A. Depart
B. Forgive
C. Not bound
D. To be obstinate

24. BASKET, BUCKET, COOKER
A. Tong B. Knife
C. Spoons D. Bowl

25. COAL, EMBERS, LAMP BLACK
A. Rust B. Iron
C. Ash D. Teak Wood

26. MUMBAI, KOLKATA, COCHIN
A. Sholapur B. Kanpur
C. Chennai D. Delhi

Directions (Qs. 27 to 31): *Choose the correct alternative in the qeustions that follow underneath.*

27. LOCK : SHUT : : FASTEN : ?
A. Iron B. Window
C. Block D. Door

28. LUNGS : LIVER : : KIDNEY : ?
A. Intestines B. Heart
C. Neck D. Testicle

29. YELLOW is related to ORANGE in the same way as GREEN is related to:
A. Leaf B. Purple
C. Tree D. Grass

30. GRAND-FATHER : FATHER : : BROTHER : ?
A. Son-in-law B. Baby
C. Son D. Father-in-law

31. Which one of the following alternatives have a common characteristic as exists among ARID, PARCHED and DROUGHT?
A. Dry B. Cow
C. Draft D. Earth

EXERCISE - 8

Directions (Qs 1 to 10): *In each of the following questions, two question marks are given in the statement at the top of which one is in the beginning of the statement and other is in the last of the statement. Select a pair of words from the given alternatives to replace question marks.*

1. (?) is related to TOUCH in the same way as EAR is related to (?)

A. HAIR, DIRT
B. HAND, KNOW
C. SKIN, HEAR
D. EXPERIENCE, FEELING

2. (?) is related to BRAIN in the same way as MOUTH is related to (?)

A. SKULL, TONGUE
B. TURBAN, SALIVA
C. HAT, LIPS
D. HAIR, TUNE

3. (?) is related to SUN in the same way as RAIN is related to (?).

A. DAY, NIGHT
B. LIGHT, CLOUD
C. SKY, WET
D. MOON, RAINBOW

4. SUGAR is related to (?) in the same way as THICKENED MILK is related to (?).

A. WHITE COLOUR, SWEET
B. SWEETNESS, SOUR
C. SUGARCANE, MILK
D. POWER, MACHINE

5. TABLE is related to (?) in the same way as CUP is related to (?)

A. STUDENT, HORSE
B. WOOD, HOT
C. FURNITURE, TEA
D. CHAIR, PLATE

6. (?) is related to IVORY in the same way as DEER is related to (?)

A. COSTLY, RARE
B. ELEPHANT, HORN
C. BIG, RARE
D. WHITE, PREY

7. (?) is related to SRI LANKA in the same way as DELHI is related to (?)

A. COLOMBO, INDIA
B. INDIA, PARIS
C. KATHMANDU, CAPITAL
D. ISLAND, PORT

8. (?) is related to UNCLE in the same way as MOTHER is related to (?)

A. FATHER, WIFE OF FATHER'S ELDER BROTHER
B. BROTHER, FOSTER
C. COUSIN, BEAUTIFUL
D. AUNT, FATHER

9. (?) is related to SKY in the same way as FISH is related to (?)

A. TREE, COLOUR
B. BIRD, WATER
C. BLUE, SWIMMING
D. OPEN, FINS

10. (?) is related to MASCULINE in the same way as FEMALE is related to (?)

A. POWERFUL, MISTRESS
B. DISGUISE, SHY
C. MALE, FEMININE
D. STRENGTH, LADY

EXERCISE - 9

Directions (Qs. 1 to 15): *In each of the following questions, two groups of figures are given in which first group contains question figures and the second group contains answer figures. In the first group three question figures and a question mark (?) are given in which first two figures are related in some way. The same relationship holds between the third question figure and the answer figure which should replace sign of interrogation (?). Identify that figure from amongst the Answer figures and mark your answer.*

1. Question Figures:

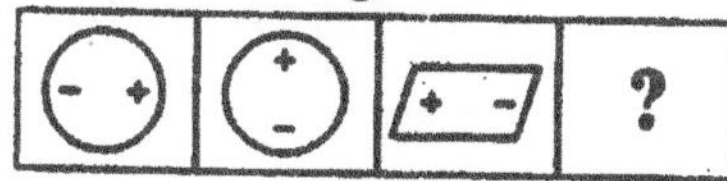

Answer Figures:

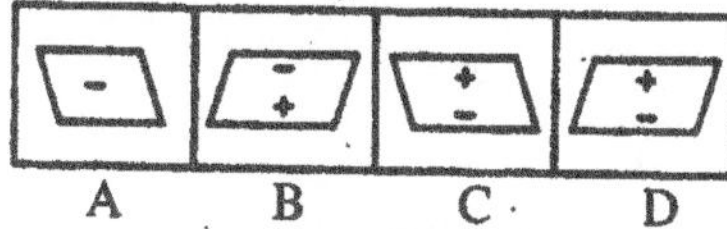

2. Question Figures:

Answer Figures:

3. Question Figures:

Answer Figures:

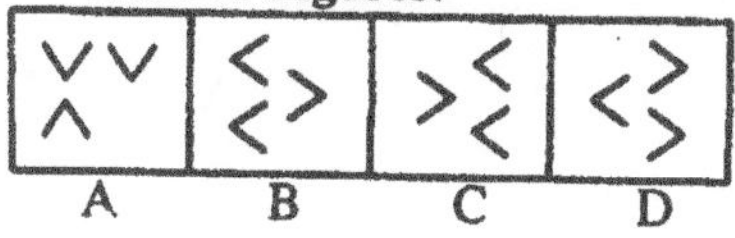

4. Question Figures:

Answer Figures:

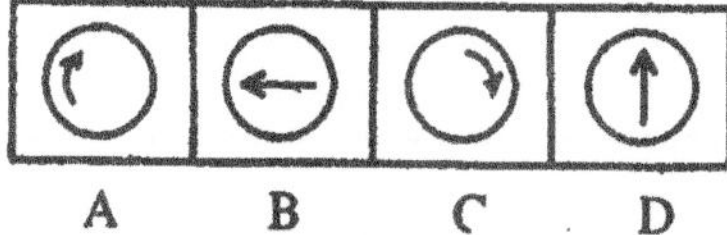

5. Question Figures:

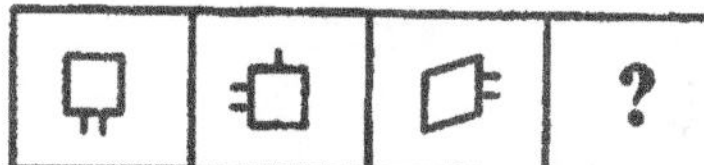

Answer Figures:

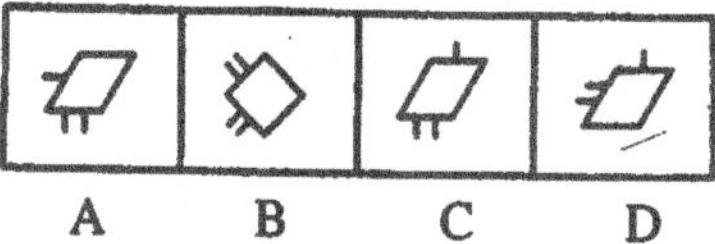

6. Question Figures:

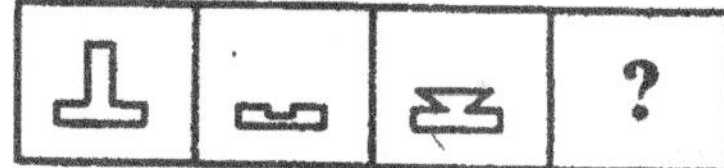

Answer Figures:

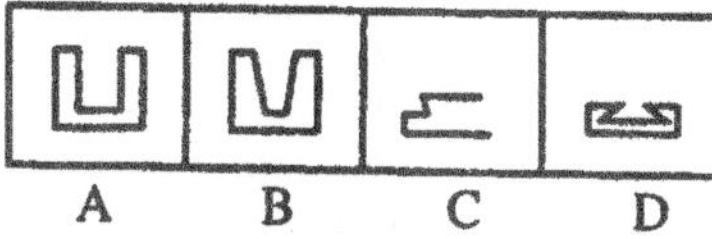

7. Question Figures:

Answer Figures:

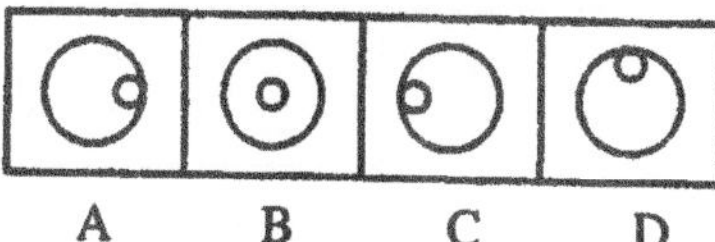

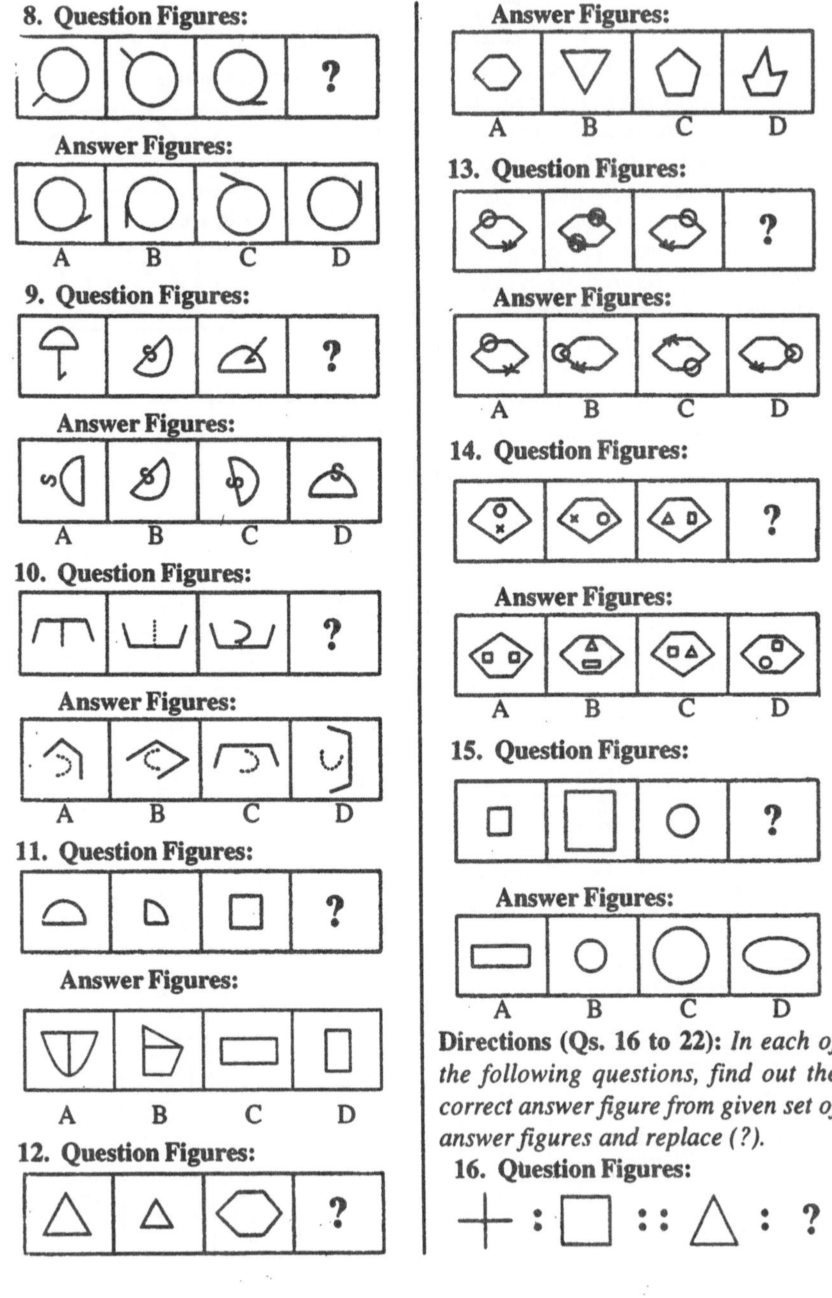

8. Question Figures:

Answer Figures:

A B C D

9. Question Figures:

Answer Figures:

A B C D

10. Question Figures:

Answer Figures:

A B C D

11. Question Figures:

Answer Figures:

A B C D

12. Question Figures:

Answer Figures:

A B C D

13. Question Figures:

Answer Figures:

A B C D

14. Question Figures:

Answer Figures:

A B C D

15. Question Figures:

Answer Figures:

A B C D

Directions (Qs. 16 to 22): *In each of the following questions, find out the correct answer figure from given set of answer figures and replace (?).*

16. Question Figures:

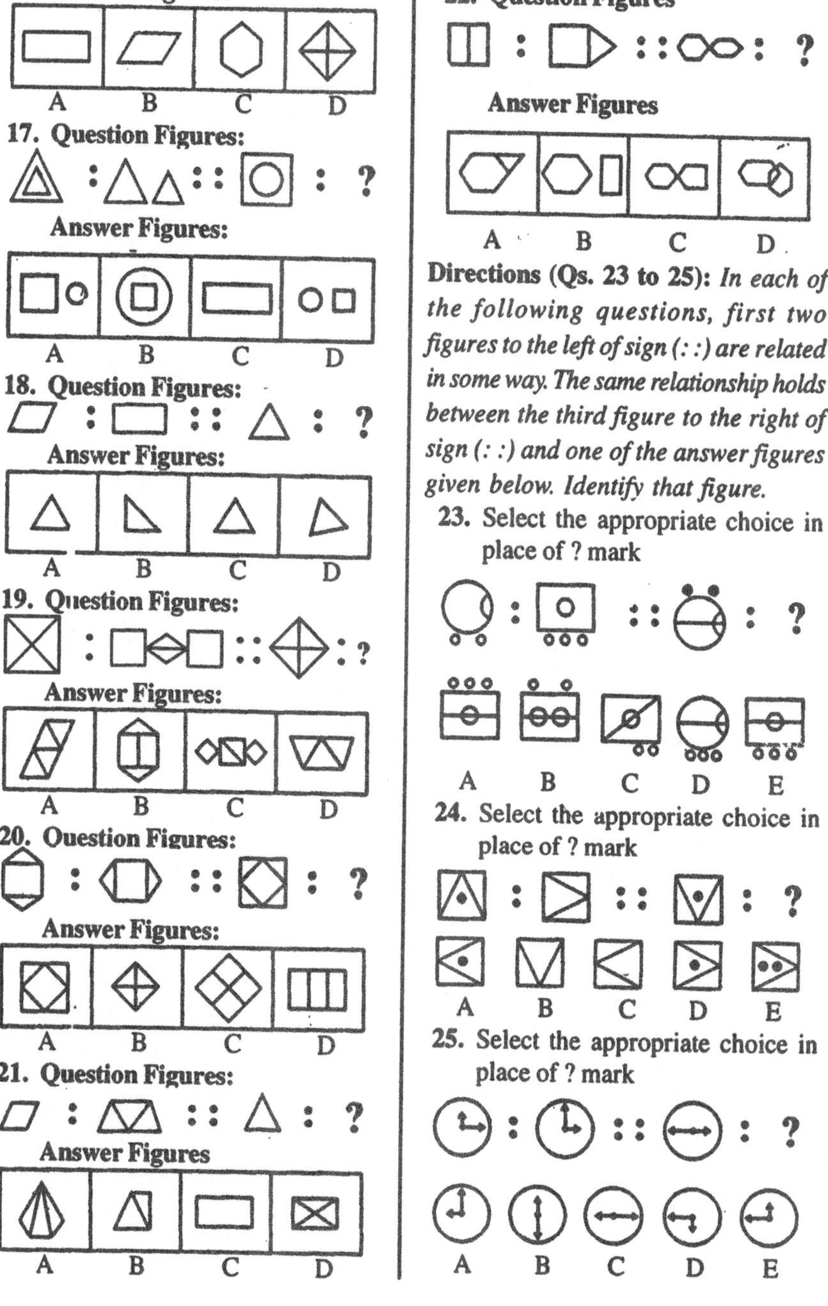

Answer Figures:

A B C D

17. Question Figures:

Answer Figures:

A B C D

18. Question Figures:

Answer Figures:

A B C D

19. Question Figures:

Answer Figures:

A B C D

20. Question Figures:

Answer Figures:

A B C D

21. Question Figures:

Answer Figures

A B C D

22. Question Figures

Answer Figures

A B C D

Directions (Qs. 23 to 25): *In each of the following questions, first two figures to the left of sign (: :) are related in some way. The same relationship holds between the third figure to the right of sign (: :) and one of the answer figures given below. Identify that figure.*

23. Select the appropriate choice in place of ? mark

A B C D E

24. Select the appropriate choice in place of ? mark

A B C D E

25. Select the appropriate choice in place of ? mark

A B C D E

Directions (Qs. 26 - 32): *In each of the following questions, two sets of figures are given. One set is called problem figures while the other set is called answer figures. Each problem figure consists of four elements numbered I, II, III and IV. These are followed by five answer figures marked A, B, C, D and E. Problem figures numbered I and IV contains question marks. From the set of answer figures, you have to select a figure the elements of which when placed at question marks in the problem figures may indicate the same relation between I and II as between III and IV.*

26. ? : : : : ? I II III IV

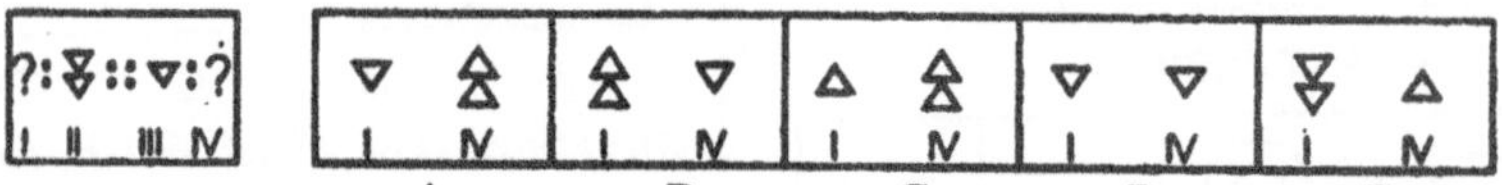

I IV I IV I IV I IV I IV
A B C D E

27. ? : : : : ? I II III IV

I IV I IV I IV I IV I IV
A B C D E

28. ? : : : L : ? I II III IV

L K I IV I IV K L I IV K I IV L I IV
A B C D E

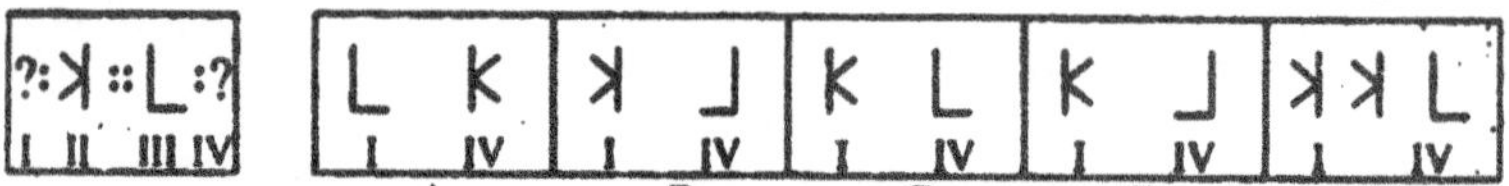

29. ? : △ : : : ? I II III IV

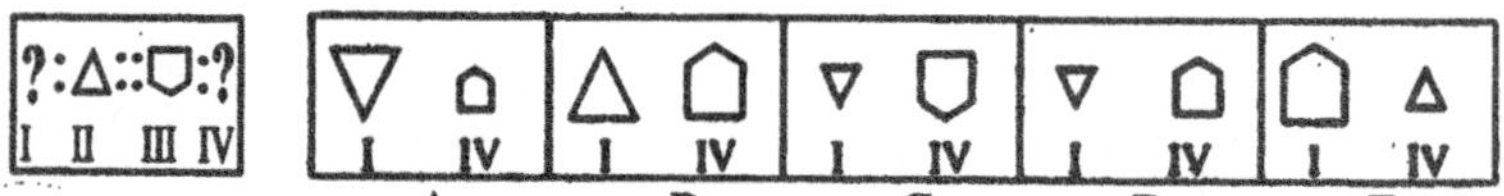

I IV I IV I IV I IV I IV
A B C D E

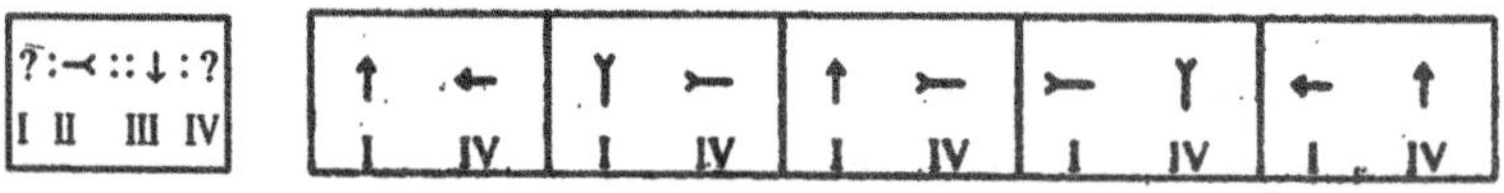

30. ? : : : : ? I II III IV

I IV I IV I IV I IV I IV
A B C D E

31. ? : : : : ? I II III IV

I IV I IV I IV I IV I IV
A B C D E

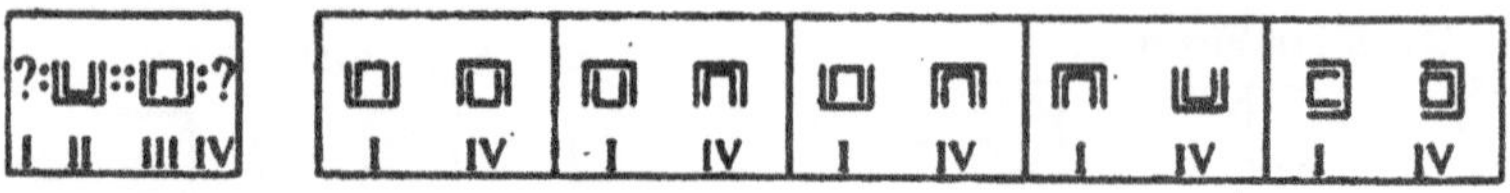

32. Find out the figure in place of question mark (?) from amongst the alternatives given.

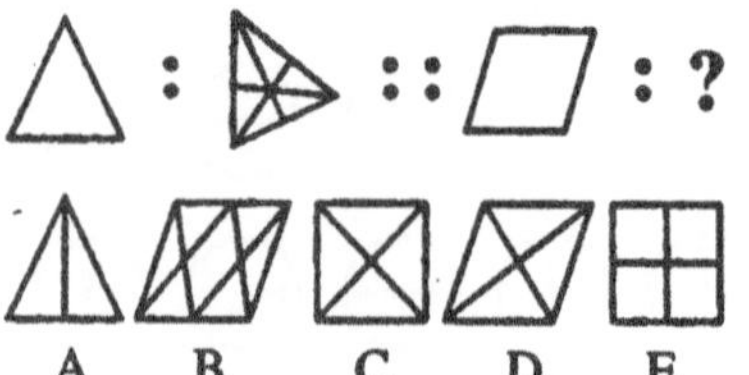

Directions (Qs. 33 to 36): *In each of the questions there are two sets of figures. First set of figures contains three figures and one question marked space and these are indicated by numbers 1, 2, 3 and 4. The second set of figures are the set of answer figures marked by A, B, C, D and E. In question figures 1 and 2 bear the same*

relationship as exists between 3 and 4. You have to establish the analogy and find out the correct answer to replace question mark.

33.

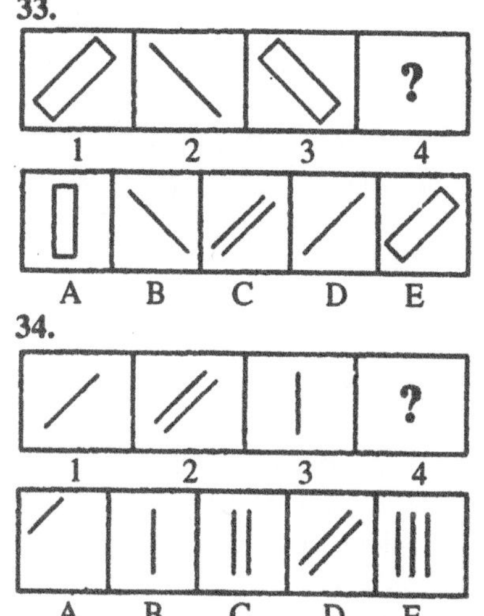

35.

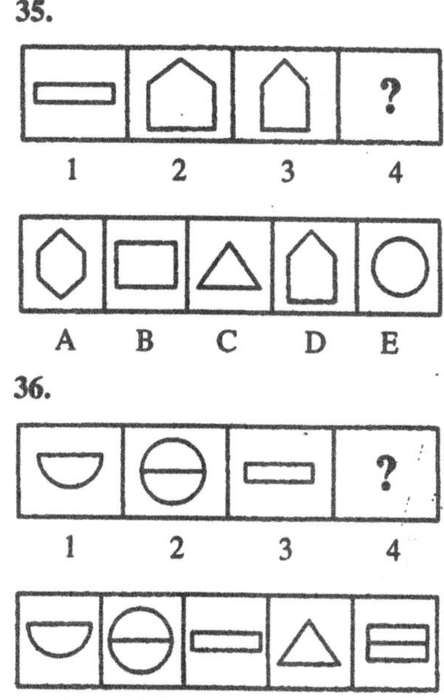

EXPLANATORY ANSWERS

EXERCISE - 1

1. D: 'Valley' is opposite of 'Mountain'. So the word opposite in meaning of 'Light' is 'Dark'.

2. A: 'Plant' grows into a 'Tree' and 'Girl' grows into a 'Lady'.

3. E: As 'Procession' moves on the 'way' so the 'Earth' moves round the sun on its 'Orbit'.

4. D: There are many 'Flowers' in a 'Bouquet' and a 'Team' consists of many 'Players'

5. C: 'Carpenter' makes many items using 'Wood' while 'Tailor' makes dresses using 'Cloths.'

6. C: As 'High' and 'Low' are antonymous to each other, so are the words 'Sky' and 'Nether region'.

7. E: 'Light' emits 'Rays' and 'Sound' travels in 'Waves'.

8. D: 'Bulb' and 'Motor Car' are associated in the way that both these are outcome of modern scientific inventions and for the operation of boh electricity is required whereas 'Candle' and 'Bullock Cart' are the traditional source of light and transportation respectively.

9. D: We say water is life. Similarly 'Spirituality' gives us 'Peace'.

10. D: Hand of a clock moves by 135°

in reaching from 'South' to 'North-West.' Similarly on moving 135° it will reach from 'West' to 'North-east.'

11. C: As 'Ocean' is full of 'Water,' so 'Air' is present in the 'Atmosphere.'

12. D: 'Parrot' is kept in 'Cage'. Similarly 'man' is kept in 'Prison'.

13. D: 'Aeroplane' flies in air like 'Bird.' Similarly 'Ship' swims in water like 'Fish'.

14. A: Man 'walks' and Fish 'swims'.

15. A: 'Hat' is a cover of 'Head' and 'Spectacles' are cover of 'Eyes'.

16. A: 'Umbrella' protects from 'Rain'. Similarly 'Coat' protects our body during 'Winter'.

17. D: 'Ill-will' is antonym of 'Sympathy' similarly antonym of 'Hatred' is 'Love'.

18. A: 'Horse' bears 'Hair' on its body while 'Ewe' bears 'Wool'.

19. D: There are many 'Chapters' in a 'Book'. Similarly many 'Flowers' are contained in a 'Bouquet'.

20. D: 'Poison' can bring 'Death' while 'Medicine' can bring 'Life'.

21. E: 'Day' is opposite in meaning of 'Night'. In the same way the word opposite in meaning of 'Evening' is 'Morning'.

22. C: 'Week' is bigger unit of time than day. Similarly 'Month' is bigger unit of time than week.

23. C: Birds fly with the help of their 'wings' and Fishes swim with the help of their 'Fins'.

24. C: 'Houses' are made of 'Walls' and 'Walls' are made of 'Bricks'.

25. B: We eat 'Food' to satiate 'Hunger'. Similarly 'Speaking' improves our syntax.

26. E: 'Ornament' enhances 'Beauty' and for 'Decoration' colour is used.

27. B: Cardboard is opaque while 'Glass' is 'Transparent'.

28. D: 'Engine' gets energy from 'Petrol', similaly 'Body' gets energy from 'Food'.

29. E: As 'man' has 'leg', so 'cow' has 'Hoof'.

30. E: 'Production' is achieved in 'Factory', similarly 'Education' is imparted in 'School'.

31. C: 'Examinee' take an 'Examination' and 'Traveller' goes for a Travel.

32. A: 'Sponge' is 'Soft' and 'Knife' is 'Sharp'.

33. A: 'Mother' gives birth to her child. Similarly 'Mars' has come into existence after it got separated from the 'Sun'.

34. D: As 'Marriage' is associated with 'Function' so 'Separation' is associated with 'Sadness'.

35. D: Swift 'walk' is called 'Run'. Similarly swift 'wind' is called 'storm'.

36. C: As snow is formed on cooling 'water', so water is formed on cooling 'water vapour'.

37. A: 'Broad' is opposite in meaning of 'Narrow', similarly opposite of 'Thin' is 'Fat'.

38. C: As 'Person' is a part of 'Society', so 'Book' is a part of 'Library'.

39. A: 'Wednesday' is one day ahead

of Monday, similarly 'March' is one month ahead of 'January'.

40. A: We eat 'Food' to satiate our 'Hunger', similarly we drink 'water' to satiate our 'Thirst'.

41. D: 'Book' is written by the 'Author' while 'Newspaper' is finalized by the 'Editor'.

EXERCISE - 2

1. A: Elegance of 'Idol' depends on its 'Size' while elegance of 'Song' depends on its note.

2. D: 'Smoke' adds to 'Pollution' while 'war' adds to 'Death'.

3. A: 'Coal' is extracted from 'Mine' while 'water' is extracted from 'Well'.

4. D: 'Kangaroo' is found in 'Australia' while 'Giraffe' is found in 'Africa'.

5. E: As 'March' is part of 'year' so 'summer' is part of 'season'.

6. B: As 'Pond' is the small form of 'Ocean', so the small form of 'Deep' is 'Shallow'.

7. B: 'Care' can avert 'Accidents' and 'Cleanliness' can avert 'Diseases'.

8. C: As 'Care' is opposite in meaning of 'Elation', so the word opposite in meaning of 'Attention' is 'Disregard'.

9. B: As 'Contamination' creates an adverse effect on 'Cleanliness', so 'Pollution' creates an adverse effect on 'Health'.

10. A: Antonym of 'Playful' is 'Steady' and antonym of 'Change' is 'Permanence'.

11. C: As 'sting' is protective organ of 'Honey bee', so the protective organ of 'Snake' is 'Fang'.

12. A: 'Second' is the smallest unit of time indicated by 'Watch'. Similarly 'Day' is the smallest unit of time indicated by 'Calendar'.

13. A: On doing 'Hardwork', we feel 'Tiredness', similarly 'Displacement' occurs on 'Movement.'

14. B: As the body of an 'Animal' is covered with 'Skin', so Barley is covered with 'Husk'.

15. C: As "Infancy' is adjective of 'Infant', so 'Youth' is the adjective of 'Young man'.

16. D: As 'Finger' is the hindmost part of 'Arm', so 'Toe' is the hindmost part of 'Foot'.

17. E: As 'Captain' leads 'Soldiers', so 'Leader' leads his 'Followers'.

18. B: As occurrence of 'Theft' is related with increase in 'Poverty', so is related the extent of 'Exercise' with 'Weakness'.

19. B: As Governor is constitutional head of the state, so the President is constitutional head of the country.

20. D: As Botany is the science of study of 'Plants', so 'Hygiene' is the science of study of 'Health'.

21. C: As 'First' is antonym of 'Last', so antonym of 'Faithful' is 'Traitor.'

22. C: As a number of 'words' combine to make a 'sentence', so a number of 'Flowers' combine to make a 'Garland'.

23. C: As 'Umbrella' protects from 'Rain', so 'Quinine' protects from 'Malaria'.

24. B: 'Lather' is synonym of 'Foam', similarly 'Profit' and 'Gain' are synonymous to each other.

25. A: As 'Mechanic' provides subservice to Engineer, so 'Typist' provides subservice to 'Steno-typist'.

26. B: 'Belt' is a wearing of 'Waist', Similarly 'Tie' is wearing of 'Neck'.

27. D: 'Ivory' is an organ of 'Elephant', similarly 'Slough' is an organ of 'Snake'.

28. A: 'Broom' is worked on 'Floor', similarly 'Spoon' is worked on 'Plate'.

29. D: 'Sound' is heard on 'Telephone' while 'Writing' can be seen on 'Letter'.

30. C: As 'President' is paramount of a 'Country', so state's paramount is 'Governor'.

31. E: 'Book' is the collection of 'Pages' while 'Water' is collected in 'Lake'.

EXERCISE - 3

1. A: 'Birds' belong to the class of 'Aves'. Similarly 'Man' belongs to the class of "Mammal".

2. E: 'Learning' is the outcome of 'Teaching', similarly 'Cure' is the outcome of 'Treatment'.

3. C: Widespread form of 'Skirmish' is 'War', similarly widespread form of 'Disease' is 'Epidemic'.

4. A: 'Fossils' are the trace of former living 'Creatures', similarly 'Mummies' are the embalmed 'Dead bodies'.

5. E: As 'Labourer' gets 'Wages', so 'Entrepreneur' gets 'Profit'.

6. D: 'Procession' moves on 'Route' while 'Earth' moves on its 'Orbit'.

7. D: 'Sun' and 'Ocean' are natural objects while 'Candle' and 'Water-tank' are man made objects.

8. C: 'Telephone' works through 'Cable' while 'Radio' works 'Wireless'.

9. D: 'Guilt' is the state of having done something wrong in the 'Past' while 'Hope' pertains to 'Future'.

10. B: A 'Doctor' cures the 'Patient' while a 'Teacher' teaches the 'Student'.

11. C: 'President' is related to 'Republic' in the same way as 'King' is related to 'Monarchy'.

12. C: Words in the both sides of sign (: :) are antonymous to each other.

13. A: 'Nothing' is most nearly opposite in meaning of the word 'All'. Similarly 'something' and 'Much' are antonymous to each other.

14. D: As in Circulatory System 'Blood' enters into 'Heart', so in respiratory system 'Air' enters into 'Lungs.'

15. C: We make things 'Hot' in 'Oven' and 'Cold' in 'Refrigerator'.

16. D: 'Second' is the smallest unit of

time indicated by 'Watch'. Similarly 'Date' is the smallest unit of time indicated by 'Calendar'.

17. A: 'Cobbler' mends 'Shoes' while 'Carpenter' works on 'Wood' to make furniture.

18. E: 'Squint' is the error of 'Vision' while 'Stammering' is the error of 'Speech.'

19. C: As the synonym of 'Save' is 'Rescue', so the synonym of 'Seldom' is 'Rare'.

20. E: As the antonym of 'Ancient' is 'Modern', so the antonym of 'Often' is 'Seldom'.

21. A: 'Ornithologists' study about 'Birds' while 'Anthropologists study about 'Man'.

22. C: As 'Step' is a part of 'Staircase', so 'Soldier' is a part of 'Army'.

23. B: 'Newspaper' is printed in 'Press' while 'Cloth' is manufactured in 'Mill'.

24. C: 'Waiting' creates 'Boredom' while 'Education' brings 'Enlightenment'.

25. D: As antonym of 'Dawn' is 'Dusk' so the antonym of 'Light' is 'Heavy'.

26. C: 'Punishment' is given to 'Prisoner' while 'Operation' is a surgical performance which is carried out to cure a 'Patient'.

27. B: Significance of 'Well' increases with its 'Depth' while significance of an 'Officer' increases with the 'Authority' he possesses.

28. C: As 'Team' is a group of 'Players', so 'Fleet' is a group of 'Ships'.

29. E: As 'Drama' is directed by the 'Director', so 'Magazine' is published in the direction of an 'Editor'.

30. C: As the study of 'Diseases' is called 'Pathology', so the study of 'Planets' is called 'Astronomy'.

EXERCISE - 4

1. B: Letters in the second group have been arranged in reverse order from that in the first group. Therefore 'B' is the correct answer.

2. E: The first, third and fifth letters of the second group are one step behind the corresponding letters of the first group and second, fouth and sixth letters of the second group are one step ahead of the corresponding letters of the first group.

3. B: The first and third letters of the second group are one step ahead of the corresponding letters of the first group and second, fourth, fifth and sixth letters of second group are one step behind the corresponding letters of the first group.

4. A: The first letter of the second group is small letter and it is one step ahead of the fourth letter of the first group. Second letter of the second group is one step behind the third letter of the first group. The same relation exists between other two letters of both the groups.

5. D: The all four letters of the first group are two steps behind the corresponding letters of the second group.

6. C: The first, third and fifth letters of the second group are one step ahead of the corresponding letters of the first group. The second and fourth letters of the second group are one step behind the corresponding letters of first group.

7. E: The first and second letters of the second group are two steps ahead of the corresponding letters of thc first group. The third and fourth letters of the second group are one step ahead of the corresponding letters of the first group.

8. E: The four letters of the first set of letters in either side of sign (: :) are moved +2, +1, +2 and +1 step respectively.

9. E: The first three letters of the first set of letters on either side of sign (: :) are moved +14, +18 and +3 steps respectively. Fourth letter of each set of letters on either side of sign (: :) is same.

10. E: First and third letters of the second group are four steps ahead of the corresponding letters of the first group. Second and fourth letters of the second group are four steps behind the corresponding letters of the first group.

11. D: First and third letters of the second group are four steps behind the corresponding letters of the first group. Second and fourth letters of the Second group are four steps ahead of the corresponding letters of the first group.

12. C: All the three letters of the first group are in reverse order. The three letters of the second group are also in reverse order but skip one letter in between.

13. A: In each set of letters, fourth and second letters and third and first letters are in natural order.

14. B: In each set of letters, second, first and third letters are in natural order and the fourth letter is two steps ahead of the third letter.

15. C: In the first group first, third, fourth and second letters are in natural order while in the second group first, fourth, third and second letters are in natural order.

16. D: In each set of letters, first, third, seccnd and fourth letters are in natural order.

17. A: In the second group, first, second, third and fourth letters are +1, +2, +3 and +4 steps ahead of the corresponding letters of first group.

18. C: In the second group, first, second, third and fourth letters are +1, +2, +3 and +4 steps ahead of the corresponding letters of the first group.

19. A: In each set, the given two letters are in reverse order.

20. D: In each set, first two letters are in natural order. Also the third letter of the first set is kept as first letter of the second set.

21. C: First and third letters of the second group are two steps ahead of the corresponding letters of first group. Second letters of the first and second groups and third letters of these two groups are in natural order.

22. C: First and second letters of first group have become second and first positioned letters in the second group. Similarly third and fourth leters of the first group have become fourth and third positioned letters in the second group. This relation holds in next pair of words also.

23. D: Capital letter of the first group becomes small letter in the second group and small letters of the first group becomes capital letters in the second group.

24. B: In the first group, letters are in natural order and skip one letter in between while in second group, first two letters are in natural order but two letters have been left in between second and third positioned letters.

25. A: In the first group, letters are in natural order while in second group, order of the letters has been reversed.

26. C: First, Second, third and fourth letters of the second group are two letters ahead of their corresponding letters of the first group.

EXERCISE - 5

1. A: The second number is square of first number minus 1.

2. A: The second number is one more than the square of first number.

3. D: The second number is four times the first

4. B: The second number is square of first number.

5. C: The second number is 3 more than the first number.

6. B: In the left side of sign (: :), first number is cube of 2 and second number is square of 3. Now as the first number in the right side of sign (: :) is cube of 4, so the second number in the right side of sign (: :) will be square of 5.

7. C: In the left side of sign (: :), first number is 1 less than the square of 3 and second number is 1 more than the cube of 3. Using this very relationship between the numbers at the right side of sign (: :), we see that the first number is 1 less than the square of 4. So here at the place of question mark, the second number will be 1 more than the cube of 4.

8. A: First number is prime number (11). Second number is a prime number leaving one prime number (13) in between 11 and 17. The third number (19) is a prime number next to 17. So the fourth number *i.e.*, the second number in the right side of sign (: :) will be the prime number (29) leaving one prime number in between 19 and 29.

9. B: 1 is added to the first number and then squared to get the second number in the left side of sign (: :). The same relationship is applied to get the second number in the right side of sign (: :).

10. C: First number in the left side is $2^2 - 1 = 3$ and the second number is $3^2 + 1 = 10$. Here the first number in the right side of the sign (: :) is $3^2 - 1 = 8$, so the second number at the place of question mark will be $4^2 + 1 = 17$.

11. D: First number is $3^2 + 3 = 12$, second number is $4^2 + 4 = 20$, third number is $5^2 + 5 = 30$. So the fourth number will be $6^2 + 6 = 42$.

12. B: First number is square of 1, second number is cube of 2, third number is square of 4. So the fourth number will be cube of 5.

13. A: First number is $6^2 + 6 = 42$ and second number is $7^2 + 7 = 56$. since the third number is $10^2 + 10 = 110$, hence fourth number will be $11^2 + 11 = 132$.

14. C: First number is 1 less than the square of 2 and the second number is square of 4. Since the third number is 1 less than the cube of 2, hence the fourth number will be cube of 4.

15. B: First, second, third and fourth numbers are one more than the square of consecutive prime numbers starting from 11. Fourth number at the place of question mark will be $19^2+1 = 362$.

16. C: First number in the left side of sign (: :) is prime number (7) and the second number (11) is also a prime number which is next to 7. Therefore number at question mark will also be the prime number next to prime number 31.

17. E: First number is square of 1, second number is cube of 2. Again third number is square of 3. Therefore the fourth number will be cube of 4.

18. D: 1 is added to the first number and then squared to get the second number in the left side of sign (: :). Similarly 1 will be added to the third number (5) and then squared to get the fourth number.

19. D: First number is square of 3. Second number is square of 5 and the third is square of 7. Therefore the fourth number will be square of 9.

20. C: First number is four times the second number. Thus fourth number will be $\frac{2}{3} \times \frac{1}{4} \times \frac{1}{6}$.

21. A: 4 and 9 are squares of 2 and 3 respectively. Similarly 8 and 27 are the cubes of 2 and 3 respectively.

22. E: 5/3 times 15 is 25. Similarly 5/3 times 45 is 75.

23. D: Second number is obtained by subtracting 1 from the square of half of the first number.

24. B: Square of first number plus 1 is the second number.

25. C: First number is two times the second number. Thus fourth number will be $\frac{1}{3} \times \frac{1}{2} = \frac{1}{6}$.

EXERCISE - 6

1. C: As 'Plant' grows into 'Tree', so 'Bud' grows into 'Flower'.

2. D: 'Bunch' contains a number of 'Keys', similarly 'Bouquet' contains a number of 'Flowers'.

3. D: 'Art' is associated with 'Beauty' while 'Music' is associated with 'Melody'.

4. C: 'Inelligence' is 'Natural born' characteristic while 'Education' can be achieved in 'School' only.

5. D: King has not very wide territory under his possession but Emperor rules over a very wide territory. Similarly territory under rein of a king is called 'State' and that under an Emperor is called 'Empire'.

6. D: As 'Rent' is earned from 'House', so 'Interest' is earned from 'Capital.'

7. C: 'Good fortune' and 'Misfortune' are antonymous to each-other. Similarly 'Slavery' and 'Freedom' are antonymous to each other.

8. A: 'Sentence' is the combination of a number of 'Words', similarly 'Word' is the combination of a number of 'Letters'.

9. B: 'Teacher' teaches in the 'Class' and 'Librarian' regulates the 'Library.'

10. C: 'Ocean' contains innumerable 'Drops' of water. Similarly innumerable 'Letters' are present in 'Dictionary'.

11. D: 'Carpenter' works on 'Wood' while 'Goldsmith' works on 'Silver'.

12. D: 'Vapour' is formed when we 'Boil' water. Similarly on squeezing lemon 'Juice' is extracted out.

13. C: 'Paper' is made from 'Pulp', similarly 'Cloth' is made from 'Thread'.

14. D: 'Visitors' are 'Welcome' while 'Criminals' are 'Prosecuted'.

15. D: As the 'Moon' moves round the 'Earth', so the 'Uranus' moves round the 'Sun.'

16. C: 'Success' can be achieved by making 'Efforts', similarly 'Knowledge' is gained by 'Reading'.

17. A: 'Water' satiates 'Thirst', similarly 'Food' satiates 'Hunger'.

18. B: 'Success' and 'Failure' are antonymous to each other. Similarly 'Happy' and 'Sad' are also antonymous to each other.

19. D: 'Water' is liquid, 'stone' is solid and 'Air' is Gas.

20. A: In each pair one is the prey of other.

21. C: Plenty of 'Trees' are present in 'Forest'. Similarly plenty of 'Books' are kept in 'Library'.

22. D: Relationship of structure and design.

23. D: 'Author' writes 'Prose' and 'Poet' writes 'Poetry'.

24. A: 'Chemistry' is a branch of 'Science', similarly 'Painting' is a branch of 'Art'.

25. D: 'Goldsmith' works on 'Gold', similarly 'Cobbler' works on 'Leather'.

26. A, G: These are synonymous to each other.

27. G, H: 'Man' lives on 'Oxygen', similarly Fish lives in 'Water'.

28. E, H: 'Hands' bear 'Fingers' and 'Head' bears 'Hairs'.

29. A, F: 'Car' is kept in 'Garage', similarly 'Horse' is kept in 'Stable'.

30. B, E: 'Lethargy' brings 'Failure' while 'Success' can be achieved by doing 'Labour'.

31. A, D: These are antonymous to each other.

32. A, D: 'January' is the month of cold winds while 'June' is the month of hot winds.

33. B, G: 'Sister-in-Law' is opposite of 'Brother-in-Law', similarly 'Youthful Lady' is opposite in meaning of 'Young man'.

34. B, F: 'Constable' works under 'Police' Department, similarly a 'Doctor' works under the 'Medical Department'.

35. C, E: Numerous 'Trees' are present in 'Forest', similarly numerous 'Books' are present in 'Library'.

EXERCISE - 7

1. D: E contains Furniture and its two names. Similarly P contains Fruit and its two names.

2. C: C contains Mother who is sister as well as 'Female'. Similarly S contains Cow who is a 'Mammal' as well as 'Animal'.

3. B: Teacher may be writer and speaker also. Similarly a Doctor might be a 'Painter' and a 'Father' also.

4. B: 'A' contains Cereal and it also contains a type of Cereal, *i.e.*, wheat. It also contains an other different name, *i.e.*, Tomato. Similarly T contains Army, a rank in Army, *i.e.*, soldier and another different name, *i.e.*, Civilian.

5. C: E contains Furniture and its two names. Similarly Q contains Cereal and its two names.

6. D: All these items are made of milk.

7. A: All these are related with administration.

8. D: All these are names of various colours.

9. C: These are the names of internal organs of body.

10. B: All these words are most nearly indicative of "obstruction free".

11. A: All are musical instruments.

12. D: All are the names of milk products.

13. C: All these are sense organs present on the face.

14. A: All these are Metropolitan Cities of India.

15. B: All these are interrogative words.

16. C: All these are names of fruits.

17. A: All these are names of carts which are pulled by one or other means.

18. B: All these are Masculine words.

19. C: All these are names of metals.

20. D: All these are used for sitting.

21. B: All these are planets of Solar system.

22. D: All these are names of flowers.

23. C: All these give indication of freedom.

24. D: All these are utensils used in kitchen.

25. C: All these are produced after burning.

26. C: These all are Port cities.

27. D: We fasten the lock and shut the door.

28. A: Lungs and Kidney are responsible for purifying the petrified blood while Liver and Intestine are engaged in digestion of food.

29. D: Orange has the colour between red and yellow. Grass has green colour.

30. C: Father and Grand-father have the same generation gap as is between brother and son.

31. A: All these give a sense of moisturelessness.

EXERCISE - 8

1. C:

2. A:

3. B:

4. C:

5. D:

6. B:

7. A:

8. D:

9. B:

10. C:

EXERCISE - 9

1. B: From first figure to second figure, one design is rotated 90° anticlockwise.

2. D: From first figure to second figure all the curves are reversed.

3. B: From first unit to second unit the direction of arrow heads is reversed.

4. B: From first figure to second figure, the arrow line is rotated 180° clockwise.

5. A: From first figure to second figure, the design is rotated 90° clockwise and one dot is added in the next arm in clockwise direction.

6. D: In the first figure a small structure is shown extruding out of the rectangle. The extruded part in the first figure goes in the inside of rectangle in the second figure.

7. C: From the first figure to second figure, the small circle inside the design is rotated 180° clockwise.

8. B: Coming from first figure to second figure the dot attached with the circle moves 90° clockwise.

9. B: From first figure to second figure, the semicircle rotates 135° clockwise and the vertical line and curved dash attached to the semi circle in first figure changes into S-form.

10. C: From first figure to second figure, the design rotates 180° clockwise and the vertical line in the middle of the design changes into dotted line.

11. D: From first figure to second figure, design diminishes to half.

12. A: From first figure to second figure, the design decreases in size.

13. C: From first figure to second figure, the design is rotated 90° clockwise.

14. B: From first figure to second figure, the signs of cross and circle are moved 90° clockwise.

15. C: Size of the design in the first figure enhances in second figure.

16. C: There are two lines which cross each other perpendicularly in the first figure while in the second figure number of lines becomes double, *i.e.*, 4 and these form a closed design.

17. A: In the first set, there are 2 figures of which one is within the other. In the second set the figures are placed separately. The same relationship holds in the set of figures at the right side of sign (: :).

18. B: Parallelogram of the first figure becomes rectangle in the second figure. Similarly equilateral triangle at the right side of (: :) will become right angled triangle.

19. C: In the second figure, the design of the first figure is rotated 90° and one square each at the either side of square comes.

20. A: From first figure to second figure, the design it rotated 90° clockwise.

21. B: From first figure to second figure, one line in between the design and one triangle in the side are increased.

22. C: From first figure to second figure, design at the left side of the figure remains unchanged while in the right side of the figure, one line deminishes.

23. A: From first figure to second figure, circle changes into square and one small circle comes at the centre and at the outside of design number of small circles increases by one. In addition to this, the arc in the first figure disappeares in the second figures. From first figure to second figure small circles remain in the same side.

24. C: From first figure to second figure the triangle within the square is rotated 90° clockwise and dot inside the triangle has disappeared.

25. C: From first figure to second figure, the small and big arrow lines mutually interchange their positions.

26. C: In problem figures, figure at number I, becomes double in figure II and overturns.

27. D: In problem figures, figure at number I, overturns in figure II and gets shaded.

28. D: The problem figures, figure at number I, which is K-shaped, is rotated 180° clockwise in figure II.

29. A: In problem figures, the big triangle of figure at number-I is diminished in figure II.

30. C: In problem figures, arrowhead of figure numbered I is inverted and it is rotated 90° clockwise in figure II.

31. B: From problem figure number I to problem figure number II, direction of outer ⊓-shaped design is overturned while the inside ⊔-shaped design remains unchanged.

32. B: From first problem figure to second problem figure, three more lines are inserted inside the triangle. Similarly from the figure at the right side of sign (: :), which is a parallelogram, to second figure at the right side of (: :) four more lines will be inserted inside the parallelogram.

33. D: From first figure to second figure, rectangle is diminished to a line which is inclined at 90° with the rectangle.

34. C: From first figure to second figure, one more line is added which is drawn in the direction of the line of the first figure.

35. A: From first figure to second figure, one more side is added to the design. So in the fourth figure, there should be six lines in the design.

36. E: From the first figure to the second figure one semicircle is added to the opposite side of diameter. Therefore in the fourth figure also, above one side of the figure, there should be a design as is below that side (line).

2

CLASSIFICATION OR ODD ONE OUT

Classification means to assort or classify the items of a given group in accordance with certain common quality or qualities possessed by them and then to spot the odd one out. In this section, the given question bears a number of items out of which all excepting one are similar to one another in a certain way or they bear certain relationship among themselves. Candidates are asked to select the item which does not belong to the given group. In other words, which does not bear the same characteristic` as is borne by other items of the group. In this context, it is pertinent to note that the candidates must be well acquainted with the types of similarities whieh can possibly exist among the given items.

Example 1: Four of the following five are alike in a certain way and so they form a group. Which is the one that does not belong to that group?

A. Apple
B. Grape
C. Brinjal
D. Pomegranate
E. Mango

Explanatory Answer (C): Except Brinjal, which is name of a vegetable, all others are names of fruits. So Brinjal given at item 'C' is the correct answer.

Example 2: In the following pairs, select the pair from among the given five alternatives which is different from other four.

A. Cow and she-buffalo
B. Cock and Hen
C. Horse and Mare
D. Dog and Bitch
E. Peacock and Peahen.

Explanatory Answer (A): Except A, all other pairs are the pairs of masculine and Feminine of the same species.

Example 3: Find the group of letters which is different from the other groups

A. ONMLK
B. XWVUY
C. EDCBA
D. TSRQP
E. JIHGF

Explanatory Answer (B): In all other groups, Except B, letters are in reverse order. In group B, first four letters are in reverse order while the fifth and last letter is different.

Example 4: Four of the following five figures are alike in a certain way and hence they form a group. Find out the figure which does not belong to the group for lack of common characteristics

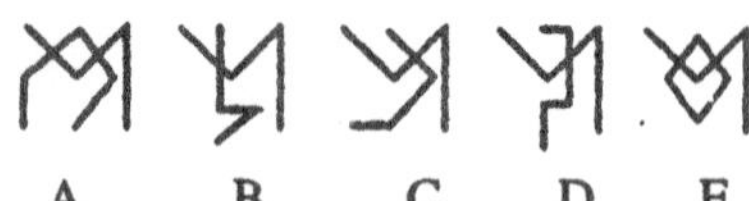

A B C D E

Explanatory Answer (E): In all other figures, except E, the design which

intersects the curve has open ends while in E, the design intersecting the curve is a closed design.

Example 5: In the question that follows, find out the number which does not belong to the group for lack of common property.

A. 35 B. 14
C. 49 D. 28
E. 43

Explanatory Answer (E): Except E, all others are multiple of 7.

Example 6: Find the odd man out:

A. Lawyer B. Gentleman
C. Doctor D. Clergyman
E. Professor

Explanatory Answer (B): Except B, all others are associated with profession.

EXERCISE - 1

Direction (Qs. 1 to 20): *In each of the questions, four of the given five words are alike in a certain way and hence form a group. You have to identify the word which does not belong to the group.*

1. A. Tomato
B. Cabbage
C. Cauliflower
D. Brinjal
E. Cucumber

2. A. Foot B. Finger
C. Tongue D. Eye
E. Ear

3. A. Wall B. Sand
C. Stone D. Cement
E. Lime

4. A. Lizard B. Cobra
C. Snake D. Earthworm
E. Fox

5. A. Professor B. Principal
C. Student D. Teacher
E. Lecturer

6. A. Volleyball B. Hockey
C. Football D. Cricket
E. Polo

7. A. Bird B. Mynah
C. Duck D. Crow
E. Parrot

8. A. Jujube B. Turnip
C. Banana D. Pomegranate
E. Mango

9. A. Tiger
B. Jaguar
C. Wild buffalo
D. Fox
E. Leopard

10. A. Sanders B. Champa
C. Rose D. Marigold
E. Jasmine

11. A. Asia B. Arabia
C. America D. Australia
E. Africa

12. A. Television B. Drama
C. Cinema D. Play
E. Radio

13. A. Polite B. Gentle
C. Religious D. Humble
E. Good

14. A. Cow B. Panther
C. Ox D. Crocodile
E. Lion

15. A. Oil B. Chimney
C. Wick D. Flame
E. Lamp

16. A. Earth B. Cloud
C. Horizon D. Sun
E. Moon

17. A. Bull B. Horse

C. Goat D. Buffalo
E. Cow

18. A. Brown B. Paint
C. White D. Yellow
E. Black

19. A. Eagle B. Parrot
C. Bird D. Pigeon
E. Hawk

20. A. Youngman B. Man
C. Woman D. Soldier
E. Girl

Directions (Qs. 21 to 30): *Three of the following four are alike in a certain way and so form a group. Find the odd one out.*

21. A. Petticoat B. Saree
C. Turban D. Blouse

22. A. Wolf B. Elephant
C. Deer D. Wild buffalo

23. A. Quarter B. Garage
C. Apartment D. Flat

24. A. Jupiter B. Pluto
C. Indra D. Neptune

25. A. Lorry B. Truck
C. Tractor D. Ski

26. A. Prince B. Hireling
C. Commander D. Governor

27. A. Principal B. Student
C. School D. Teacher

28. A. Direction
B. Advice
C. Consultation
D. Suggestion

29. A. London B. New Delhi
C. Sri Lanka D. Paris

30. A. Pencil B. Pen
C. Ball Point D. Paper

Directions (Qs. 31 to 42): *In each of the following questions find the odd man out.*

31. A. Windows B. Walls
C. Floor D. Room

32. A. England B. Colombia
C. Japan D. German
E. Europe

33. A. Tractor B. Khurpa
C. Farmer D. Spade
E. Plough

34. A. Copper B. Metal
C. Silver D. Gold
E. Iron

35. A. Malaria B. Typhoid
C. Terramycin D. Pneumonia

36. A. Mountaineer
B. Photographer
C. Hero
D. Director
E. Musician

37. A. Root B. Stem
C. Plant D. Mango
E. Tree

38. A. Chisel B. Tongs
C. Tool D. Saw
E. Knife

39. A. Friend B. Aunt
C. Brother D. Cousin
E. Nephew

40. A. Ghee B. Juice
C. Cream D. Butter
E. Milk

41. A. Parrot B. Pigeon
C. Bird D. Crow
E. Peacock

42. A. Piano B. Guitar
C. Harmonium D. Musician
E. Flute

Directions (Qs. 43 to 61): *In the following questions choose the word from among the given four alternatives which is different from other three.*

43. A. KSTU B. EMNO
C. DFGH D. LTXK

44. A. YZYZ B. PQPQ
C. BC BC D. AKAK

45. A. Bedstead B. Radio
C. Table D. Almirah

46. A. August B. February
C. October D. July

47. A. Wolf B. Peacock
C. Jackal D. Cat

48. A. Orange B. Onion
C. Potato D. Brinjal

49. A. Dog B. Lion
C. Panther D. Elephant

50. A. Radio B. Newspaper
C. Telephone D. Television

51. A. Almirah B. Curtain
C. Table D. Chair

52. A. Pedlar B. Trader
C. Tailor D. Seller

53. A. Mat B. Table
C. Chair D. Sofa

54. A. Yellow B. Colour
C. White D. Red

55. A. KNMO B. DSTU
C. FYXZ D. HKJL

56. A. TIMN B. KAVW
C. PDGH D. MEND

57. A. July B. November
C. April D. September

58. A. Cells B. Spinal column
C. Veins D. Arteries

59. A. Banana B. Barfi
C. Rubber D. Juice

60. A. Small B. Fan
C. Table D. Curtain

61. A. Silk B. Cloth
C. Cotton D. Jute

EXERCISE - 2

Directions (Qs. 1 to 12): *In each of the following questions three of the given four pairs are alike in a certain way and so form a group. Find the odd one out.*

1. A. Criminal and Prison
B. Bird and Nest
C. Student and Teacher
D. Fish and River

2. A. Cow and Calf
B. Sheep and Lambkin
C. Ox and Buffalo
D. Bitch and Puppy

3. A. Ear-Nose
B. Head-Hair
C. Mouth-Teeth
D. Face-Mouth

4. A. Large and Small
B. Rigid and Heavy
C. Easy and Difficult
D. Light and Heavy

5. A. Lion and Roar
B. Tambourine and Pat
C. Bird and Trumpet
D. Ass and Bray

6. A. Accurate and Correct
B. Pain and Anguish
C. Happy and Glad
D. Trouble and Relief

7. A. Red Sea and Black Sea
B. Krishna and Kaveri
C. Surdas and Tulsidas
D. Hema Malini and Maithili Sharan Gupta

8. A. Disease-Death
B. Pleasure-Delight
C. Distress-War
D. Peace-Pleasure

9. A. Aeroplane-Sky
B. Peace-Pleasure
C. Pleasure-Delight
D. Railway track-Train

10. A. Grateful-Ungrateful
B. Cloth-Textile
C. Poison-Nectar
D. Life-Death
11. A. Table-Chair
B. Black-Yellow
C. Man-Child
D. Great Millet-Pearl Millet
12. A. Tiger-Forest
B. Bird-Nest
C. Man-House
D. Horse-stable

EXERCISE - 3

Directions (Qs. 1 to 46): *In each of the following questions find the odd man out.*

1. A. Hawker B. Retailer C. Vendor D. Peddler E. Buyer
2. A. Chicken B. Kitten C. Cup D. Calf E. Pup
3. A. Fox B. Whale C. Lion D. Panthers E. Crocodile
4. A. Lake B. Tank C. Pool D. Brook E. Pond
5. A. VQLGB B. XSNKG C. UPKFA D. ZUPKF E. YTOJE
6. A. RKGAB B. CNOUG C. NMASF D. ZTIEN E. EDOAK
7. A. IKOQR B. NPRTU C. ACEGH D. EGIKL
8. A. SRPMI B. EMQOT C. ZYWTP D. UTROK
9. A. NPRQO B. SUWVT C. DFGHE D. ACEDB
10. A. LOS B. VYC C. KNR D. UXZ
11. A. EOY B. CMW C. BLV D. AKU E. DPR
12. A. AFKP B. DINS C. CHMR D. EAJO
13. A. HDEFG B. NIJKL C. UPQRS D. RMNOP
14. A. FEDC B. XWUV C. SRQP D. ONML
15. A. ABCD B. TUVW C. NMLO D. IJKL
16. A. TRNG B. MNOP C. RSTU D. UVWX
17. A. BFJN B. IMQJ C. CGKO D. JNRV
18. A. Cup B. Vase C. Spoon D. Bowl
19. A. Pigeon B. Kite C. Crow D. Bird
20. A. Spine B. Navel C. Eye D. Elbow
21. A. Calf B. Hireling C. Cub D. Porker
22. A. Kathak B. Kathkali C. Karnatic D. Manipuri
23. A. Trough B. Basin C. Bowl D. Barrel
24. A. KSL B. ZAY C. XCW D. TUP
25. A. Mansion B. Hut C. Workshop D. Flat
26. A. Magazine B. Almirah C. Book D. Novel
27. A. Heavy B. Sizeable C. Light D. Large

28. A. VUT B. YXV
C. TSR D. ZYX

29. A. SUT B. MIN
C. XAZ D. BOC

30. A. EGI B. GIL
C. MOQ D. ACE

31. A. MNO B. GIJ
C. ACD D. PRS

32. A. SPM B. FCA
C. LIF D. ZWT

33. A. E B. B
C. O D. A

34. A. ACF B. KMO
C. EFG D. GIK

35. A. CBD B. VUW
C. NMO D. XYZ

36. A. TOP B. BYC
C. XCW D. KCL

37. A. CEAR B. BEAR
C. FEAR D. WEAR

38. A. igmO B. ropZ
C. Adel D. itsk

39. A. GMRGS B. WJWYO
C. ACAZV D. MONJK

40. A. YHGCY B. NDWVS
C. QCWRO D. JSXYM

41. A. JSAFE B. ZGPKU
C. FRGSP D. LANCP

42. A. Walk B. Run
C. Listen D. Slip

43. A. Swarm B. Flock
C. Union D. Team

44. A. Pail B. Bowl
C. Jumbler D. Vessel

45. A. 13 B. 11
C. 9 D. 7
E. 5

46. A. February B. June
C. April D. August
E. October

Directions (Qs. 47 to 55): *Three of the following four words given in each question are alike in a certain way and so form a group. You are to spot the one that does not belong to that group.*

47. A. Pen B. Pencil
C. Stationary D. Eraser

48. A. Tobacco B. Cigar
C. Pipe D. Bidi

49. A. Poster B. Photograph
C. Picture D. Painting

50. A. Intimacy B. Attachment
C. Enmity D. Friendship

51. A. Pitiful B. Merciful
C. Cruel D. Kind

52. A. Tent B. Canopy
C. Courtyard D. Verandah

53. A. General
B. Unusual
C. Customary
D. Commonplace

54. A. Innocent B. Guilty
C. Faultless D. Harmless

55. A. Cap B. Uniform
C. Pant D. Shirt

EXERCISE - 4

Directions (Qs. 1 to 10): *In each of the following questions a few numbers have been given of which all excepting one are alike in a certain way and hence form a group. You have to find out the one number which does not belong to the group.*

1. A. 1347 B. 4210
C. 2683 D. 1472

2. A. 7314 B. 3115
C. 2709 D. 7029

3. A. 8244 B. 9238
C. 6311 D. 5188

4. A. 144 B. 196

C. 181 D. 121

5. A. 8791 B. 7819
C. 8971 D. 7619

6. A. 3269 B. 4249
C. 1745 D. 7586

7. A. 23 B. 46
C. 59 D. 67

8. A. 12 B. 48
C. 42 D. 36

9. A. 9865 B. 4756
C. 6572 D. 2074
E. 4677

10. A. 28 B. 126
C. 217 D. 64

EXERCISE - 5

Directions: *Each of the following questions is based on figures marked as A, B, C, D and E. Out of these five figures four figures are alike in some way and one is different from others. You are to find out the different one.*

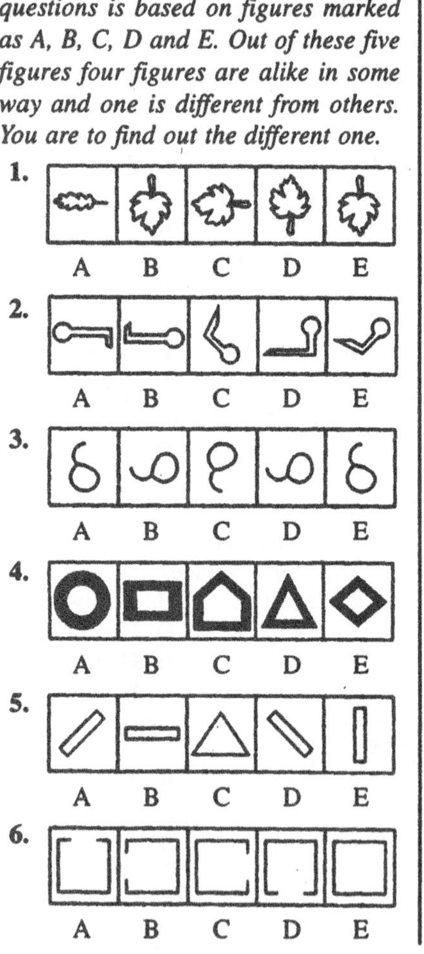

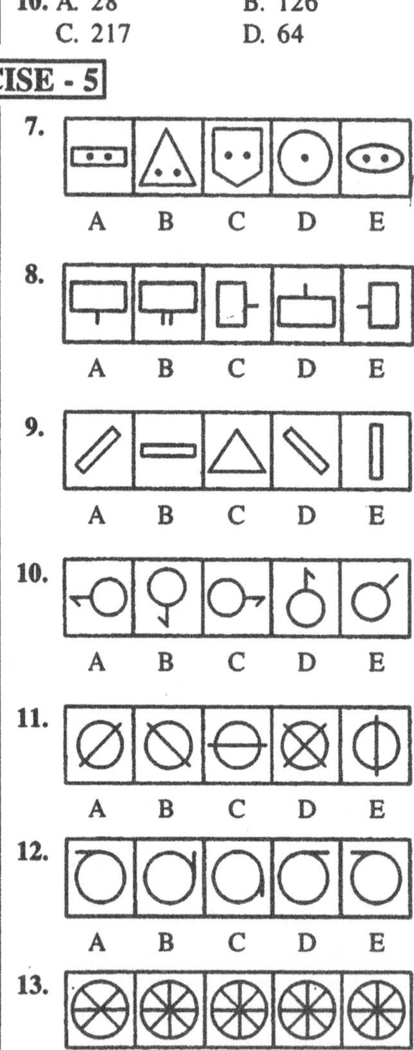

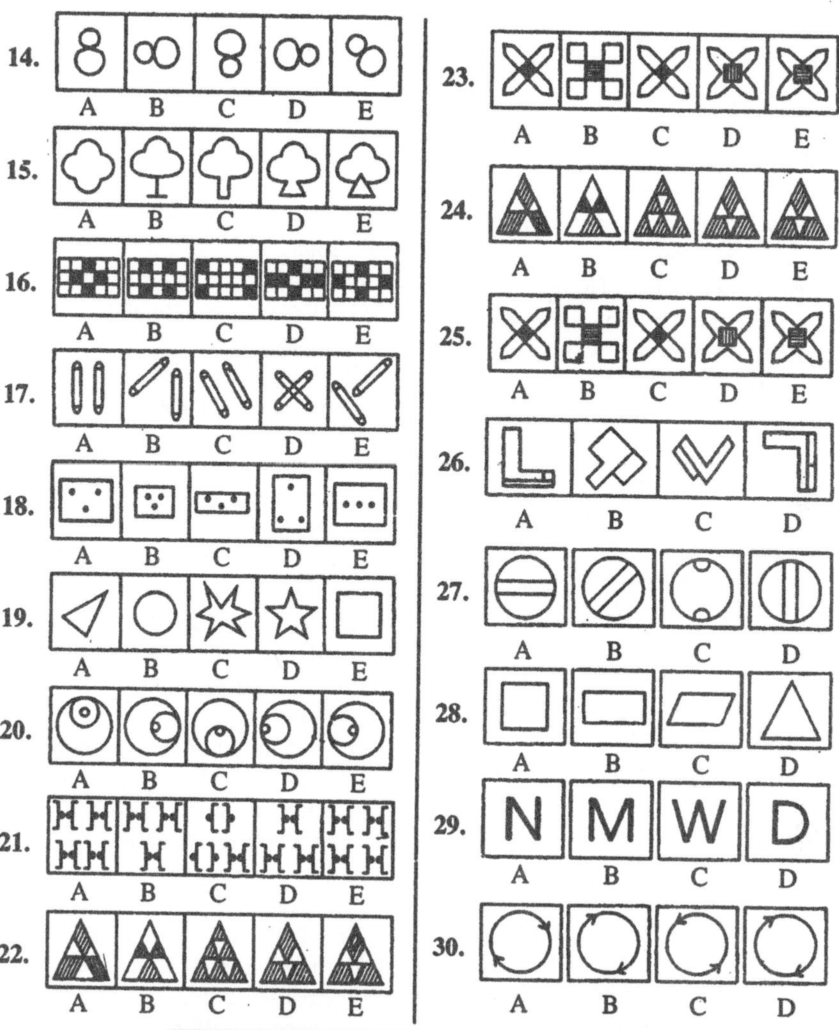

EXPLANATORY ANSWERS

EXERCISE - 1

1. A: All others are Juiceless Vegetables.

2. C: All others are external organs while tongue is the organ present in the inside of our mouth.

3. A: All others are used for building houses.

4. E: All others are Creepers.

5. C: All others are educators.

6. E: Only Polo is played riding on the back of a horse.

7. C: Only Duck swims in water.

8. B: All others are names of fruits

9. C: All others are carnivorous.

10. A: All others are flowers while Sanders is wood.

11. B: Arabia is name of a country while all others are continents.

12. E: All others are watched while Radio is heard.

13. C: All others are synonymous to each other.

14. D: Crocodile can live both on earth and in water while others live only on earth.

15. D: Lamp is lightened to produce flame. All others are contributory factors.

16. B: All others are related to astronomy.

17. E: All others are masculine.

18. B: All others are names of different colours.

19. C: All others are names of different kinds of birds.

20. D: The word 'Soldier' indicates a particular rank while others do not.

21. C: All others are names of dresses worn by ladies.

22. C: All others are carnivorous

23. B: All others are living places of man.

24. C: All others are names of planets.

25. D: All others have wheels.

26. B: All others are related to ruling class.

27. C: All others are human being.

28. A: Direction is related to order. Others are not.

29. C: All others are names of cities while Sri Lanka is a country.

30. D: All others are writing instruments.

31. C: All others are different parts of room.

32. E: All others are names of countries.

33. C: All others are agricultural instruments.

34. B: All others are names of metals.

35. C: All others are names of diseases.

36. A: All others are related to film production.

37. D: All others are tree and its different parts.

38. C: All others are different kinds of tools.

39. A: All others are members of family.

40. B: All others are milk made items.

41. C: All others are different kinds of birds.

42. D: Rest are musical instruments.

43. D: In all other alternatives last three letters are in natural order.

44. D: In all other alternatives a pair of two consecutive letters are being repeated.

45. B: All others are furnitures.

46. B: In all other months there are 31 days while the month of February consists of 28 days.

47. B: All others are animals

48. A: All others are names of different vegetables.

49. A: All others live in forest.

50. B: All others are electrical instruments.

51. B: All others are furnitures.

52. C: All others are hawkers.

53. A: All others are furnitures.

54. B: All others are names of different colours.

55. B: In all others, the third, second and fourth letters are in natural order.

56. C: Each of the remaining words contains one vowel.

57. A: All other months consist of 30 days.

58. B: All others are blood vessels.

59. C: All others are eatables.

60. A: Excepting A, all others are nouns while A is an adjective

61. B: All others are raw materials.

EXERCISE - 2

1. C: In all other pairs second is abode of the first.

2. C: In all other alternatives names of the animal and its kids are given. While in 'C' names of two different species have been given.

3. A: In all other alternatives second is part of the first.

4. B: In all other alternatives second is antonym of the first.

5. C: In all other alternatives second word is the sound produced by animals and birds.

6. D: In all other alternatives synonymous words have been given while in 'D' the words given are antonymous to each other.

7. D: All other pairs are of similar nature.

8. C: In all other alternatives first word is reason and the second word is result thereof.

9. C: In all other alternatives second is in the first.

10. B: In all other pairs, words are antonymous to each other.

11. C: In all other alternatives, names of things of the same nature are given.

12. A: In all other alternatives, second is the name of abode of the first while in 'A', Tiger lives in Den which is the abode of tiger. But the word tiger has been paired with forest. Therefore, alternative 'A' contains the odd pair.

EXERCISE - 3

1. E: All others are sellers.

2. C: All others are young ones of animals.

3. E: All others give birth to their young ones.

4. D: All others are full of water.

5. B: In all other groups four letters in natural order have ben omitted in between two given letters.

6. D: In all other groups any two letters of the group are given in natural order of alphabet.

7. A: In all other groups any two letters of the group are given in natural order of alphabet.

8. B: In all other groups first and second letters of the group are in natural order. Second letter is two steps ahead of the third letter. Third letter is three steps ahead of the fourth letter and fourth letter is four steps ahead of the fifth letter.

9. C: In all other groups first, fifth, second, fourth and third letters are in the natural order.

10. D: In all other groups, two letters have been dropped in between the first and the second letters of the group and three letters have been dropped in between the second and the third letters of the group.

11. E: Except E, in between any two letters of all other groups nine letters in alphabetical order have been dropped.

12. D: Except D, in all other letter series four letters in alphabetical order have been dropped in between any two letters of the series.

13. A: Except A, in each of the other groups of letters first letter of the group is five steps ahead of the second letter of the group and second, third, fourth and fifth letters are in alphabetical order.

14. B: Except B, in each of the other groups letters are in reverse order.

15. C: Except C, in each of the other groups letters are in alphabetic order.

16. A: Except A, in each of the other groups letters are in alphabetic order.

17. B: Except B, in each of the other groups 3 letters in alphabetic order have been dropped in between any two letters of the group.

18. C: Except spoon, in all other utensils something is poured or kept while we eat or take something with a spoon.

19. D: All others are names of birds.

20. A: All others are names of different parts of our body.

21. B: Except B, all others are names of kids of animals.

22. C: Except C, all others are names of different types of dances.

23. D: All others are made of glass and soil while 'Barrel' is made of wood.

24. D: Except D, in each of the other groups, end letters are in elphabetic order.

25. C: All others are places of residence while workshop is place of working.

26. B: We read Magazines, Books and Novels but not Almirah.

27. C: Light is different from other three as the three words at A, B and D are, to a greater extent, synonymous to each other.

28. B: Except B, in each of the other groups letter are in reverse order.

29. C: In each of the other groups first and third letters are in alphabetic order.

30. B: Except B, one letter between two consecutive letters in each set has been dropped.

31. A: Except A, in each of the other groups second letter is two steps ahead of the first letter.

32. B: Except B, in each of the other groups two letters have been dropped in between two consecutive letters.

33. B: Except B, others are vowels.

34. C: Except C, in all other groups one letter has been dropped is between first and second letters and in between second and third letters.

35. D: In other groups second, first and third letters are in alphabetic order.

36. A: In other groups end letters are in alphabetic order.

37. A: Except A, all other sets of letters are the set of meaningful words.

38. D: Except D, in all other sets one of the letters is capital letter.

39. D: Except D, in all other sets one letter has come twice.

40. A: Except A, in all other sets one letter has come twice.

41. C: Except C, in all other sets at least one vowel is given.

42. C: Except C, all others are actions related to foot.

43. D: Number of persons in a team is fixed.

44. D: Others are the names of different types of vessels.

45. C: Except C, all others are prime numbers.

46. A: All other months have a fixed number of days while February consists either 28 or 29 days.

47. C: Others are the names of different kinds of stationery.

48. A: In all others tobacco is used.

49. B: All others are made with hand while 'Photograph' is prepared by using a Camera.

50. C: All others are synonymous to each other.

51. C: All others are synonymous to each other.

52. C: All others are covered.

53. B:

54. B:

55. B:

EXERCISE - 4

1. C: Digit of 4 appears in all other alternatives.

2. A: In all other numbers, the sum of the digits placed at tens, hundreds and thousands places respectively is equal to the digit placed at ones place.

3. B: In all other numbers the two digits placed at ones and tens places are alike.

4. C: All other numbers are perfect square numbers.

5. D: All other numbers consist of the digits 1, 7, 8 and 9.

6. B: Digit of 4 has not been used twice in any of the numbers except B.

7. B: Except B, all others are prime numbers.

8. C: Except C, in all other numbers digit placed at ones place is double the digit placed at tens place.

9. E: Digit of 7 has no been used twice in any of the numbers except 'E'.

10. D: All other numbers are in the form of $3^3 + 1$, $5^3 + 1$, $6^3 + 1$

EXERCISE - 5

1. C: Other flowers given in the figures have five petals.

2. B: In all other figures, one line at the tip of the figure is a little bigger than the other.

3. C: In all other figures, the tip of the nail is curved clockwise.

4. A: All other figures are made with the combination of simple lines.

5. C: All other figures have four sides.

6. E: All other figures are opened figures while E is closed.

7. D: All other figures have two dots inside while in 'D' there is only one dot.

8. B: All other figures have only one dash attached with the rectangle while in B two dashes are attached with the rectangle.

9. C: All other figures are rectangles while C is a triangle.

10. E: In all other figures curved line attached to the circle is either vertical or horizontal.

11. D: In all other figures one line is drawn across the figure while in D two lines crossing each other have been drawn inside the figure.

12. C: In all other figures the dash attached to the circle is little bigger than the dash attached to the circle in figure 'C'.

13. A: In all other figures four lines cross each other inside the figure while in A there are only three lines.

14. E: All other figures are either vertical or horizontal.

15. A: All other figures are attached with some structure from bottom.

16. D: In all other figures four small blocks are shaded.

17. D: Only in D the two structures are intersecting each other.

18. D: Except D, in all other figures the bigger side of the figure is horizontally drawn.

19. B: All figures are drawn of simple lines.

20. A: In all other figures the small cicle drawn in the inside of the figure is touching the middle circle.

21. C: In all other figures the pair of brackets are drawn in the opposite direction to each other while in C they have been drawn facing each other.

22. B: The upper corner in B is blank.

23. E:

24. C: Except C, all other figures are divided in six parts.

25. B:

26. C: In all other figures any of the two sides of the figure is inclined at 90°.

27. C: In all other figures two simple lines have been drawn inside the circle.

28. D: All other figures have four sides.

29. D: All other figures have simple lines.

30. C: The direction of arrowhead is clockwise in all other figures while in 'C' it is anticlockwise.

3

SERIES

Each of the questions in this section contains a series or sequence of either numbers or of alphabets. Elements of the series are called terms of the series which follow a certain pattern throughout the series in both the orders, *i.e.*, from left to right and from right to left. Each of the questions asked contains one or more blank spaces or question marks (?) which are to be replaced from amongst the alternatives given below each question. The candidates are required to recognise the specific pattern being followed in each question and then have to complete the series with most suitable alternative.

Example 1: What should come in place of blank space in the following number series?

1, 5, 10, 16, 23, 31, ...

A. 39 B. 40
C. 50 D. 45
E. 48

Explanatory Answer (B): Each time difference between the two consecutive numbers of the series increases by 1. These are in the order of 4, 5, 6, 7 and 8. Therefore, correct answer in place of blank space should be 31 + 9 = 40.

Example 2: Find out the missing letter of the series from amongst the alternatives given below:

Z, A, Y, B, X, C, ...

A. W B. P
C. V D. F
E. D

Explanatory Answer (A): The first, third and fifth letters of the series are in reverse order. Therefore seventh letter of the series will be 'W'.

Example 3: In the question given below find out the figure from amongst the alternatives 'A', 'B', 'C', 'D' and 'E' which should come after the question figures if the sequence were continued.

Questions Figures:

Answer Figures:

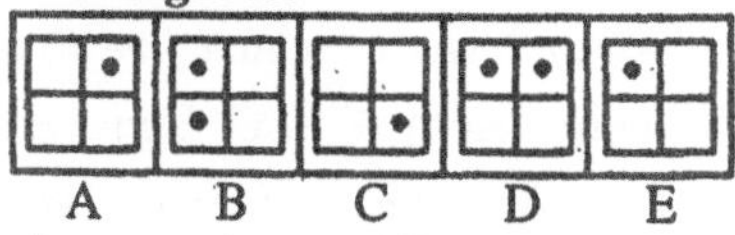

A B C D E

Explanatory Answer (E): In each of the figures given in the question, a big square is divided into four small squares out of which one small square positioned at left top consists of a dot which rotates anticlockwise in subsequent figures. As such answer figure 'E' will be the fifth figure of the given series.

Example 4: In the following question, one term in the given number series is wrong. Find out the wrong term.

2, 3, 5, 8, 15, 21, 34, 55

A. 8 B. 21
C. 15 D. 3
E. 5

In the given series, every third number is sum of the preceding two numbers. This rule does not hold in number 15. Therefore the number 15 is wrong in the series and it should be replaced by 13.

Example 5: Which one set of letters when placed sequentially at the gaps shall complete the following series?

a b ..... abb ..... ab ..... a

A. b b a a B. a a b b
C. a b b a D. b a a b
E. a b a b

Explanatory Answer (D): When the letters given in 'D' is placed sequentially in the given blank spaces, we get the following letter series: abba/abba/abba

We don't find any letter series with the other set of letters. Therefore 'D' is the correct alternative.

Example 6: Find out the correct alternative to replace the question mark in the given letter series.

$D_4, F_5, H_6, J_7, (?)$

A. P_9 B. N_5
C. M_8 D. L_8
E. K_8

Explanatory Answer (D): In each of the groups of the given series, we find one letter and one number. Each letter of the series is two steps ahead of the preceding letter while the numbers are in natural order. Therefore L_8 will replace the question mark.

EXERCISE - 1

Direction (Qs. 1 to 5): *In each of the following questions a set of six figures has been given of which five figures are indicated by A, B, C, D and E and figure on the extreme left is unnumbered. A series is established if the position of the figure at extreme left is kept unchanged and positions of any two of the five numbered figures are interchanged. The number given to the first of these two figures is your answer. If beginning from extreme left the series is established without interchanging positions of any two of the given five figures indicated by A, B, C, D and E, then your answer will be 'E'.*

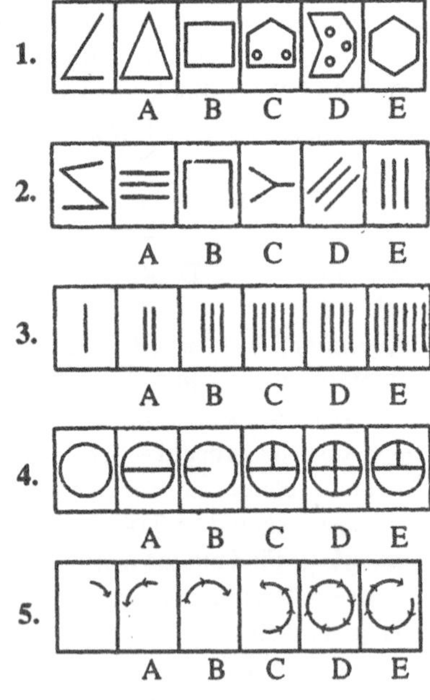

Directions (Qs. 6 to 40): *In each of the following questions there are two sets of figures. The figures on the left are Problem Figures which consist of four figures*

and one question marked space while the figures on the right are Answer Figures which are indicated by A, B, C, D and E. Find out a figure from amongst the answer figures which should be placed at question marked space so that all the four problem figures and one answer figure placed at question marked space form a series.

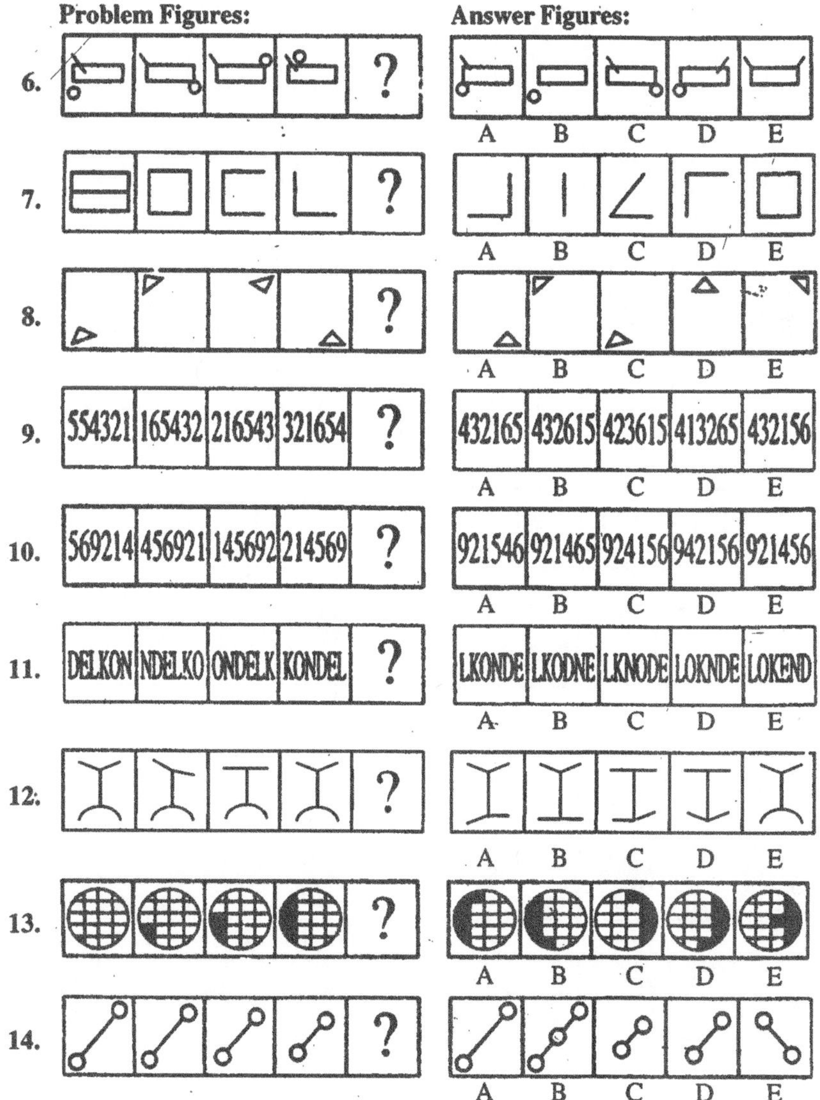

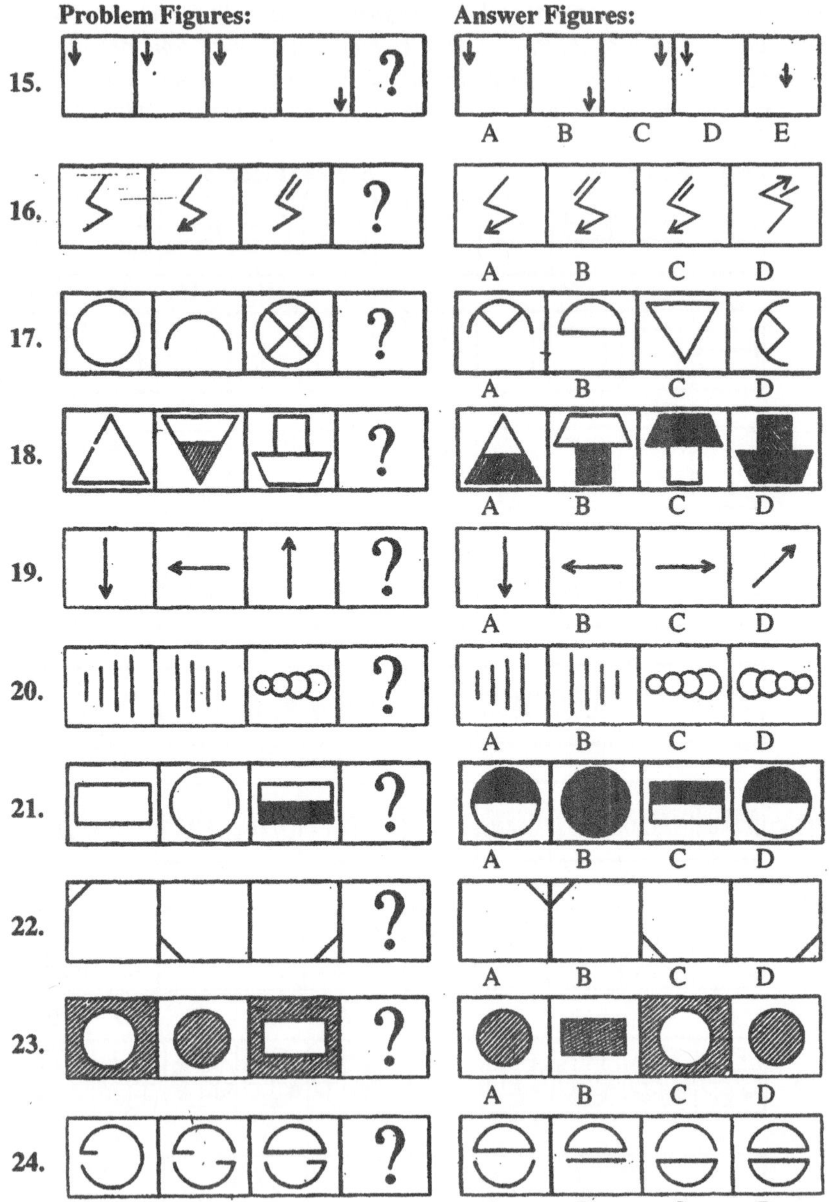

Problem Figures:
Answer Figures:
15.
A B C D E
16.
A B C D
17.
A B C D
18.
A B C D
19.
A B C D
20.
A B C D
21.
A B C D
22.
A B C D
23.
A B C D
24.
A B C D

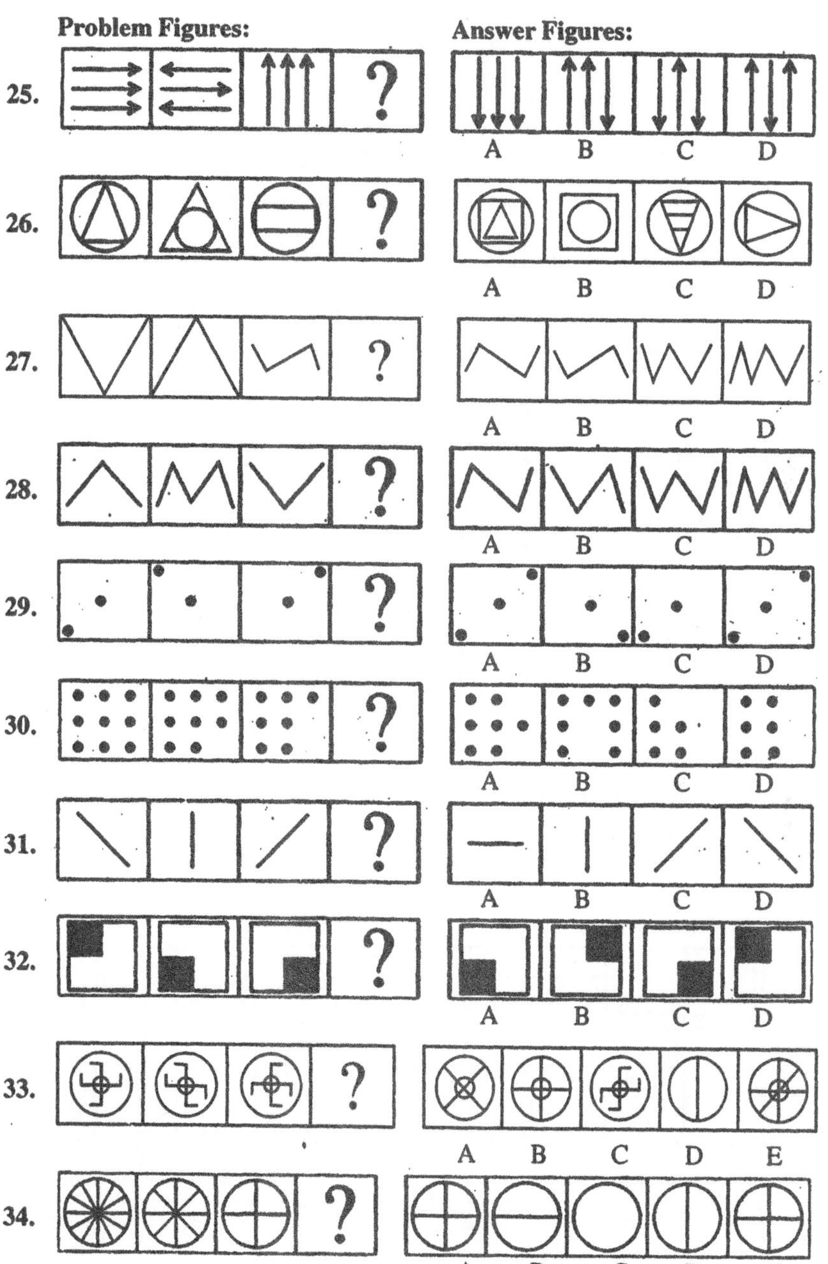
Problem Figures:
Answer Figures:
25.
26.
27.
28.
29.
30.
31.
32.
33.
34.
A B C D
A B C D E

Problem Figures: **Answer Figures:**

35. 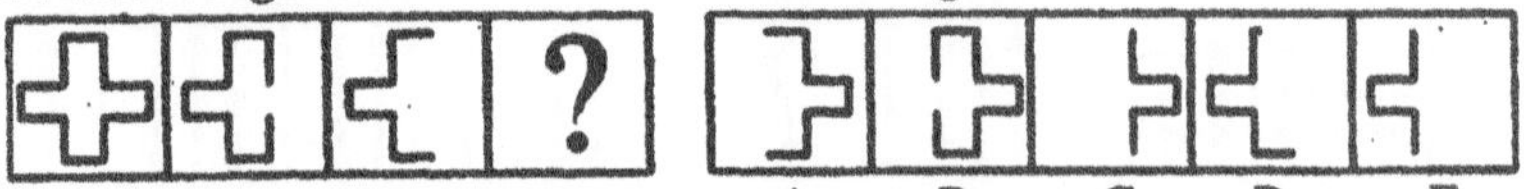 ? A B C D E

36. 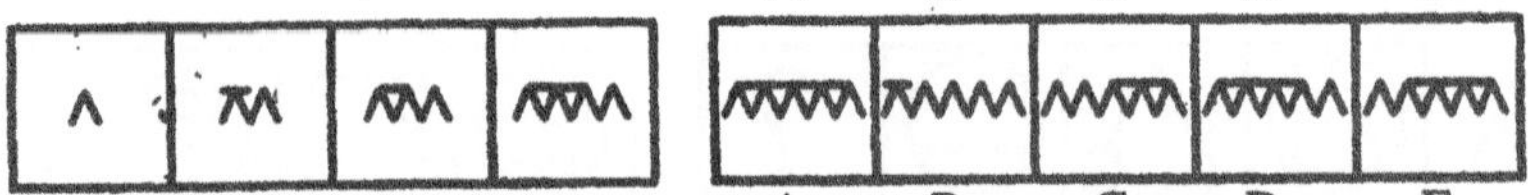 A B C D E

37. 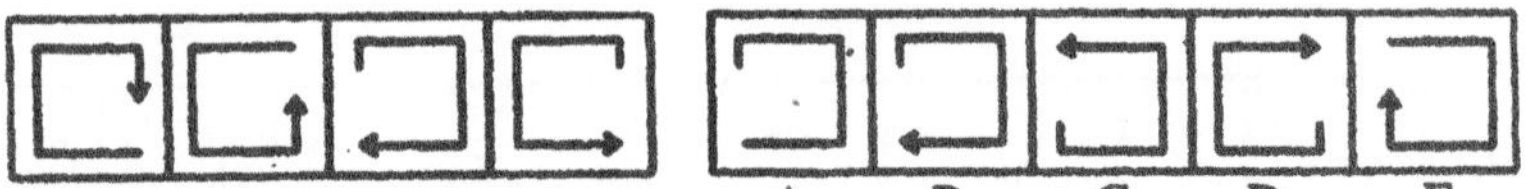 A B C D E

38. 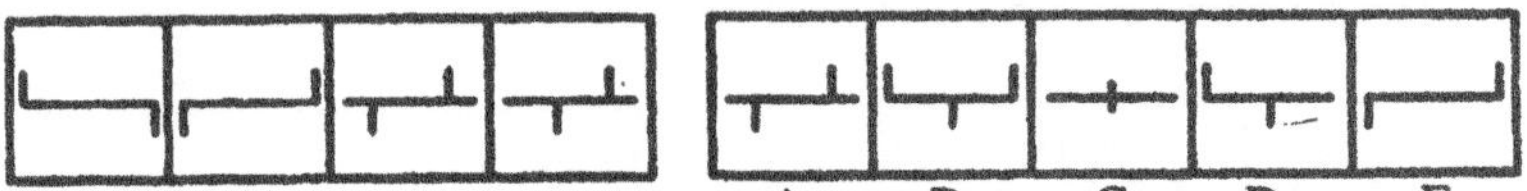 A B C D E

39. 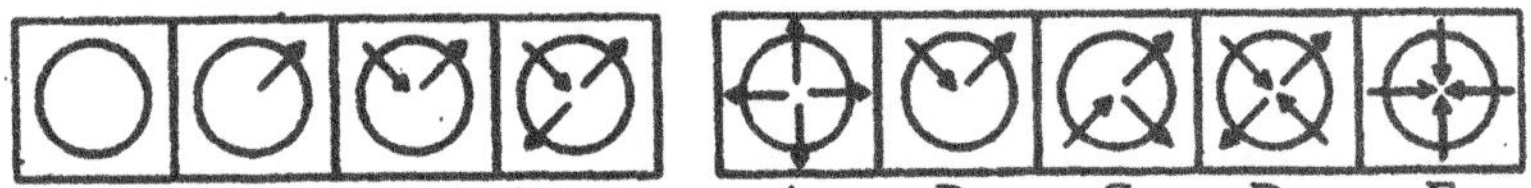 A B C D E

40. 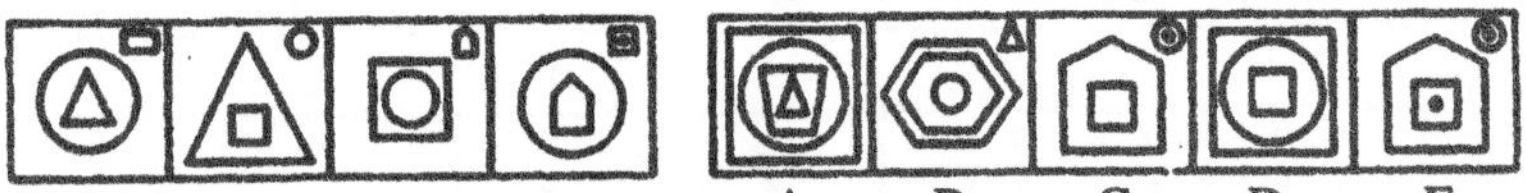 A B C D E

Directions (Qs. 41 to 72): *In each of the following questions there are two sets of figures. The figures on the left are Problem Figures while the figures on the right are Answer Figures. Problem Figures form a series, i.e., they change from left to right according to some rule. You have to select one figure from amongst the Answer Figures which will continue the same series as is given in Problem Figures.*

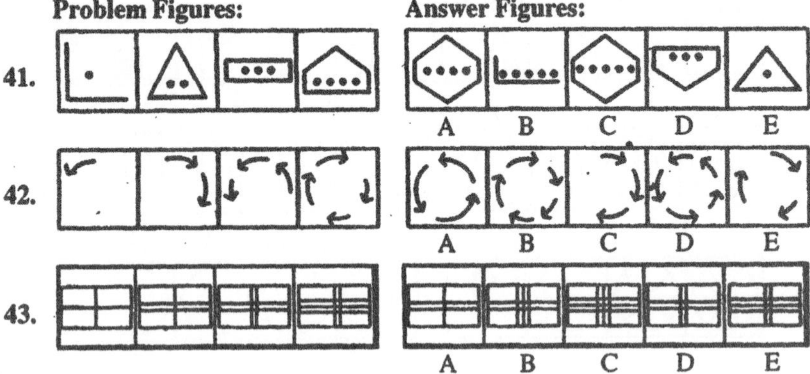

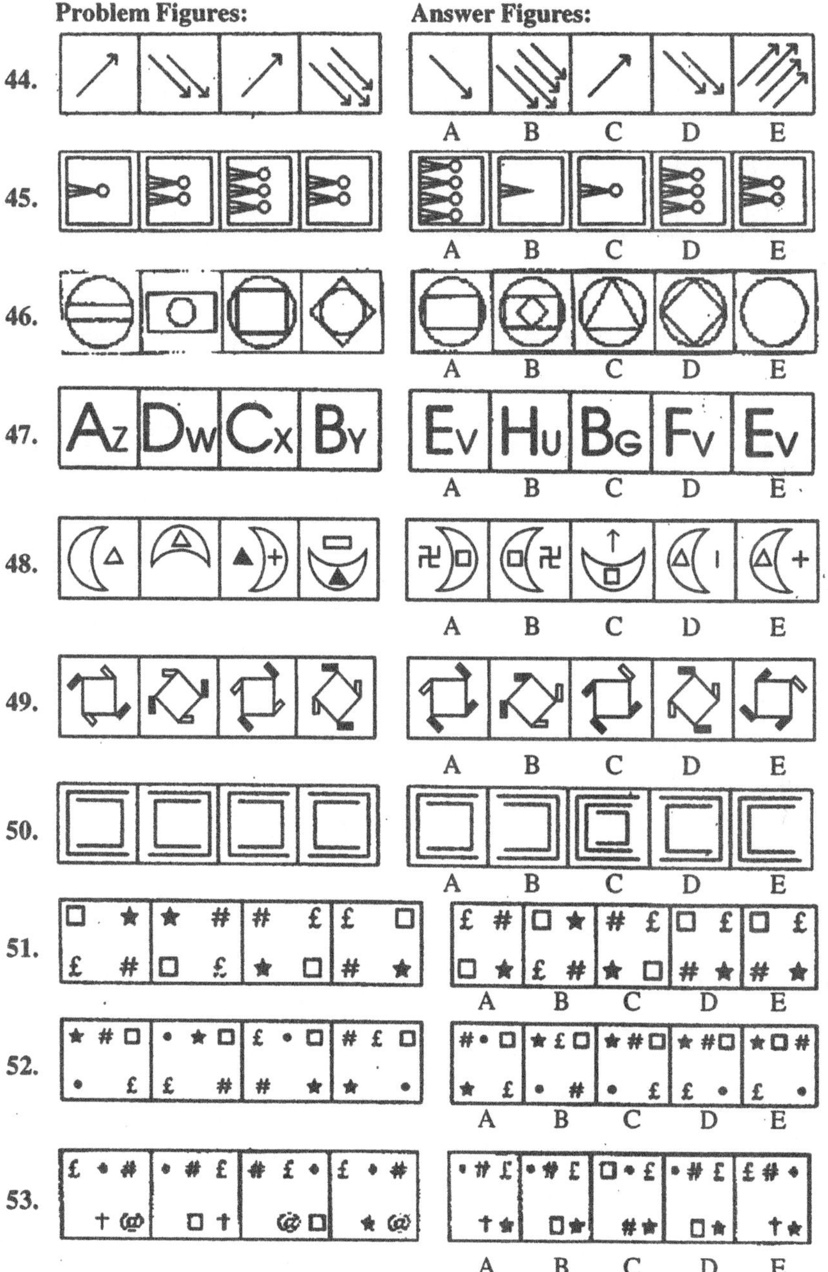
Problem Figures:
Answer Figures:
44.
45.
46.
47.
48.
49.
50.
51.
52.
53.
A B C D E

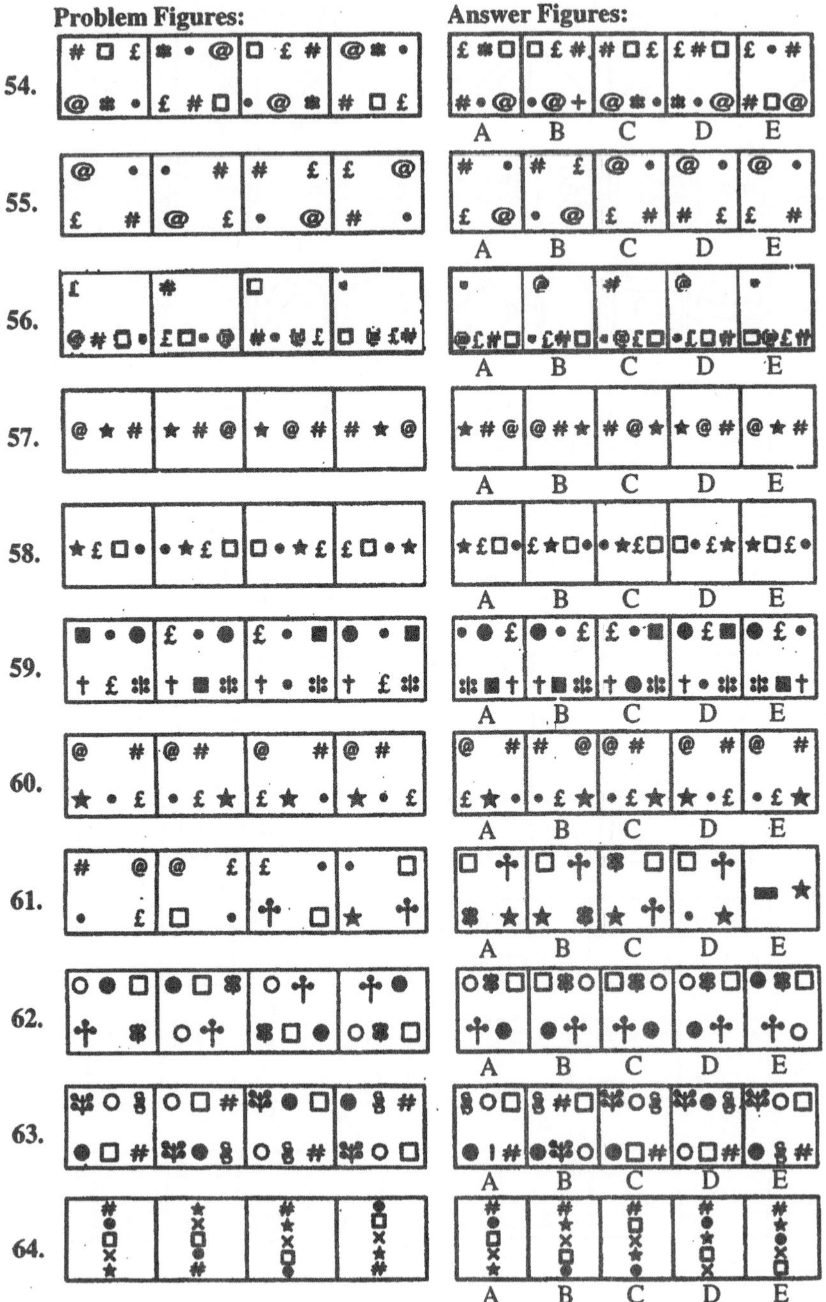

Problem Figures:
Answer Figures:
54.
55.
56.
57.
58.
59.
60.
61.
62.
63.
64.
A B C D E

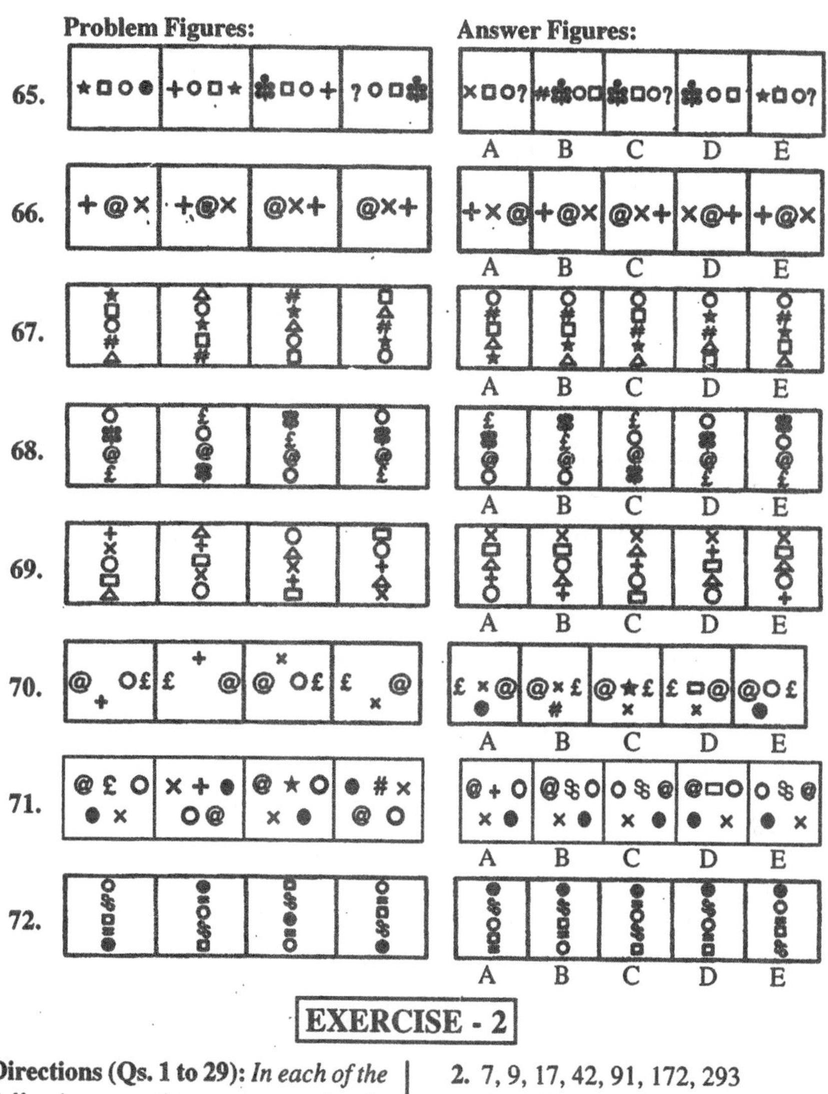

EXERCISE - 2

Directions (Qs. 1 to 29): *In each of the following questions one term in the given number series is wrong. Find out the wrong term and mark your answer.*

1. 112, 114, 120, 124, 132, 142, 154

A. 114 B. 120

C. 124 D. 132

E. 142

2. 7, 9, 17, 42, 91, 172, 293

A. 42 B. 172

C. 17 D. 91

E. 9

3. 380, 188, 92, 48, 20, 8, 2

A. 188 B. 92

C. 48 D. 20

E. 8

4. 3, 4, 5, 9, 22.5, 67.5, 270, 945
A. 270 B. 4.5
C. 22.5 D. 9
E. 67.5

5. 5, 11, 23, 47, 96, 191, 383
A. 11 B. 96
C. 191 D. 23
E. 47

6. 16, 17, 21, 30, 45, 71, 107
A. 21 B. 107
C. 16 D. 45
E. 71

7. 3, 4, 10, 32, 136, 685, 4116
A. 136 B. 10
C. 4116 D. 685
E. 32

8. 54, 43, 34, 26, 22, 19, 18
A. 34 B. 26
C. 43 D. 18
E. 22

9. 325, 259, 202, 160, 127, 105, 94
A. 127 B. 259
C. 94 D. 202
E. 105

10. 8, 14, 26, 48, 98, 194, 386
A. 194 B. 98
C. 14 D. 386
E. 48

11. 15, 45, 90, 360, 1080, 2160, 6480
A. 90 B. 360
C. 6480 D. 1080
E. 2160

12. 105, 85, 60, 30, 0, –45, –90
A. 0 B. 30
C. 85 D. –45
E. –90

13. 36, 49, 100, 144, 196, 256, 324
A. 100 B. 49
C. 256 D. 144
E. 36

14. 7, 14, 56, 168, 336, 1344, 2688, 8064
A. 1344 B. 56
C. 2688 D. 8064
E. None of these

15. 12, 18, 27, 90, 270, 945, 3780
A. 20 B. 18
C. 945 D. 27
E. 270

16. 8, 13, 21, 32, 47, 63, 83
A. 21 B. 13
C. 32 D. 83
E. 47

17. 582, 605, 588, 611, 634, 617, 600
A. 634 B. 617
C. 611 D. 600
E. 588

18. 46080, 3840, 384, 48, 24, 2, 1
A. 3840 B. 384
C. 48 D. 24
E. 2

19. 22, 33, 66, 99, 121, 297, 594
A. 297 B. 121
C. 99 D. 66
E. 33

20. 169, 218, 254, 269, 295, 304, 308
A. 304 B. 254
C. 269 D. 218
E. 275

21. 36, 54, 18, 27, 22.5, 13.5, 4.5
A. 13.5 B. 18
C. 22.5 D. 27
E. 54

22. 17, 19, 23, 29, 33, 37, 41
A. 23 B. 33
C. 17 D. 19
E. 29

23. 2, 5, 10, 18, 33, 37, 50
A. 2 B. 5
C. 18 D. 37
E. 50

24. 7, 28, 63, 124, 215, 342, 511
A. 7 B. 124
C. 342 D. 28
E. 215

25. 3, 18, 38, 78, 123, 178, 243
A. 123 B. 18
C. 178 D. 38
E. 3

26. 1, 4, 7, 11, 16, 22, 29
A. 4 B. 22
C. 1 D. 29
E. 11

27. 0, 1, 3, 6, 10, 15, 21, 28, 37, 45
A. 0 B. 10
C. 45 D. 37

28. 1, 6, 16, 26, 76, 156, 316
A. 1 B. 316
C. 236 D. 76
E. 26

29. 1, 1, 3, 3, 5, 7, 7, 9
A. 3 B. 7
C. 9 D. 1
E. 5

EXERCISE - 3

Directions (Qs. 1 to 34): *Find out the correct alternative to replace the question mark/blank space in the given letter series.*

1. G, ?, I, X, K, V, M, T
A. H B. Y
C. Z D. J
E. None of the above

2. ICV, 5FU, 9IT, ?, 17OR
A. 14JS B. 15JS
C. 11LS D. 13LS
E. None of the above

3. ACD, GIJ, ...
A. MOP B. MNO
C. NOPQ D. NOP
E. MNOP

4. B, E, I, ?, P
A. S B. L
C. Y D. X
E. Z

5. HKN, QTW, ZCF, ?
A. KMN B. BDG
C. ILO D. HKM
E. PSR

6. BEH, KNQ, TWZ, ?
A. CFI B. DGH
C. PRS D. FIJ
E. CFH

7. DJG, MSP, VBY, ?
A. PSM B. EKH
C. YBX D. GHD
E. EKJ

8. AAZ, BBY, CC ?
A. Y B. D
C. Z D. X
E. C

9. ABZ, BCY, CDX, DEW, ?
A. EFW B. EGH
C. FHG D. EVF
E. EFV

10. XYZ, CBA, UVW, FED, ?
A. GHI B. HIJ
C. STU D. RST
E. PQR

11. MOQ, SUW, YAC, ?
A. FIL B. XAD
C. DHS D. EGI
E. DGI

12. YCL, MQZ, AEN, ?
A. OSB B. PUE
C. MPX D. OTC
E. KLG

13. AZY, BYX, CXW, DWV, ?
A. EVT B. FUT
C. EVU D. GHS
E. UFT

14. Q, L, ... E, C, ...
A. B, A B. I, G
C. A, G D. G, B
E. H, B

15. A Z X B V T C R .....
A. P, D B. E, O
C. Q, E D. O, Q
E. Q, O

16. C-3, E-5, G-7, I-9, ...
A. X-24, M-21
B. K-14, M-18
C. O-15, X-24
D. M-18, K-14
E. K-10, Z-5

17. A/2, B/4, C/6, D/8, ..., ...
A. E/16, F/32 B. F/32, I/4
C. F/12, E/16 D. E/10, F/12
E. G/10, I/4

18. C, e, G, i, K ....., ...
A. O, K B. M, O
C. K, S D. M, K
E. P, N

19. Z X V T R .....
A. O, K B. N, M
C. K, S D. M, N
E. P, N

20. B C Y X E F V U ....., ...
A. H, I B. R, R
C. I, J D. S, T
E. J, I

21. a - a - bbaa - bbba - a
A. aabb B. abaa
C. abab D. aaab

22. DCXW, FEVU, HGTS, ...
A. LKPO B. JIRQ
C. ABYZ D. LMRS

23. BA, YZ, DC, WX, ...
A. DE B. EF
C. FE D. FG

24. X, U, R, O, L, ...
A. M B. J
C. K D. I

25. B, A, Z, D, C, Y, F, E, ...
A. W B. X
C. U D. G

26. BG, GC, HN, N .....
A. X B. J
C. I D. H

27. B, F, K, Q, ...
A. X B. R
C. T D. Y

28. MAN, KZP, IBR, GYT, ...
A. ECV B. EXV
C. OCL D. ODU
E. LXO

29. N, P, R, T, ...
A. K B. E
C. V D. W
E. M

30. A B D ..... K
A. G B. U
C. X D. H
E. T

31. A D C G E .....
A. L B. J
C. N D. K
E. T

32. N L J ..... F
A. K B. P
C. H D. J
E. M

33. B E I ..... T
A. M B. L
C. O D. N
E. Q

34. a - b - c - a - b
A. aabc B. cbcb
C. acba D. cabc
E. abcb

EXERCISE - 4

Directions (Qs. 1 to 43): *In each of the following questions one or two terms in the given number series are missing. Find out the correct alternative to fill in the blanks.*

1. 4, 6, 12, 14, 28, 30, ...
A. 32, 50 B. 64, 70
C. 62, 85 D. 60, 62

2. 5, 16. 51, 158, ..., ...
A. 481, 1452 B. 483, 1658
C. 1452, 1650 D. 1454, 1581

3. 13576, 17365, 75361, 63517 ....., ...
A. 13576, 73381
B. 75381, 57632
C. 56713, 16537
D. 16537, 35482
E. 57632, 16537

4. 1357, 2068, 1591, 5425, ..., ...
A. 8800, 4444
B. 0000, 2564
C. 6954, 2564
D. 4444, 8888
E. 2564, 6954

5. 34, 61, 16, 52, ..., ...
A. 70, 114 B. 92, 114
C. 43, 70 D. 27, 144
E. 81, 114

6. 1, 9, 25, 49, ..., ...
A. 81, 121 B. 225, 296
C. 55, 112 D. 100, 194
E. 121, 204

7. 0, 7, 26, 63, ..., ...
A. 126, 215 B. 217, 124
C. 124, 215 D. 64, 216
E. 215, 298

8. 98, 87, 74, ..., 46, 35, ...
A. 58, 25 B. 57, 20
C. 59, 22 D. 69, 32

9. 2, 6, 12, 20, 30, 42, ...
A. 48 B. 60
C. 64 D. 56

10. 1 + 1 + 2 + 3 + 5 + 8 + 13 + ...
A. 22 B. 28
C. 34 D. 21

11. 2, 7, 14, 23, ..., 47
A. 38 B. 34
C. 28 D. 31

12. 4, 196, 16, 144, 36, 100, 64, ...
A. 64 B. 48
C. 125 D. 256

13. 22, 22, 24, 19, 27, 16, 31, ...
A. 21 B. 13
C. 34 D. 17

14. 12, 24, 37, 51, 66, 82, ...
A. 97 B. 89
C. 99 D. 109

15. 24, 35, 48, 63, ...
A. 75 B. 68
C. 97 D. 80

16. 27, 25, 25, 22, 23, 19, ...
A. 20 B. 21
C. 16 D. 17

17. 4, 12, 36, 108, ...
A. 216 B. 324
C. 432 D. 3888

18. 240, ..., 120, 40, 10, 2
A. 216 B. 220
C. 432 D. 120

19. 0.5, 2, 5, ... 15.5
A. 5.5 B. 9
C. 12.5 D. 9.5

20. 3, 6, 9, 12, 15, ...
A. 16 B. 18
C. 21 D. 24

21. 35, 34, 31, 22, ...
A. 5 B. 2
C. –5 D. 18

22. 6, 5, 24, 25, ...
A. 144, 210 B. 96. 120

C. 100, 125 D. 120, 175
E. 144, 175

23. 3, 13, 53, 213, ...
A. 553 B. 853
C. 653 D. 753

24. 7, 14, 21, 28, ...
A. 47 B. 49
C. 35 D. 56

25. 2, 4, 8, 16, 32, ...
A. 64 B. –64
C. 128 D. –128

26. 71, 65, 60, 56, 53, ...
A. 48 B. 51
C. 49 D. 50

27. 35, 44, 49, 58, 63, ...
A. 77 B. 67
C. 72 D. 81

28. 144, 72, 24, 12, 4, ...
A. 2 B. 3
C. 4 D. 1

29. 6, 13, 27, 55, 111, ...
A. 221 B. 223
C. 225 D. 227

30. 45, 47, 49, 52, 56, 59, ...
A. 64 B. 63
C. 61 D. 62

31. 4, 16, 36, 64, 100, ...
A. 142 B. 81
C. 136 D. 144

32. 89, 83½, 80, 74½, 71, ...
A. 62 B. 65½
C. 65 D. 61½

33. 0, 7, 26, 63, ...
A. 125 B. 124
C. 215 D. 98
E. 135

34. 8, 27, 64, ...
A. 100 B. 316
C. 216 D. 125
E. 121

35. 3, 6, 8, 16, 18, ...
A. 32 B. 42
C. 36 D. 38
E. 26

36. 3, 5, 9, 17, ...
A. 26 B. 33
C. 65 D. 42
E. 46

37. 4, 9, 16, 25, ...
A. 32 B. 55
C. 49 D. 36
E. 42

38. 7, 13, 21, 31, ...
A. 43 B. 41
C. 37 D. 40
E. 39

39. 3, 5, 9, 17, ...
A. 42 B. 26
C. 46 D. 42
E. 33

40. 5, 7, 21, 23, ..., 71
A. 69 B. 37
C. 29 D. 31
E. 43

41. 2, 6, 24, 120, 720, ...
A. 2440 B. 5040
C. 4080 D. 6400
E. 8200

42. 3, 10, 29, 66, 127, ...
A. 164 B. 215
C. 218 D. 187
E. 252

43. 2, 5, 7, 11, 14, 19, 23, 29, ..., 41, 47
A. 30 B. 36
C. 38 D. 35
E. 34

Directions (Qs. 44 to 58): *In each of the following questions find out the* *correct alternative to replace the quesion mark (?) in the given number series.*

44. 0.75, 1.5, 3, (?)
A. 6 B. 3/1
C. 1 D. 9

45. 2, 5, 11, 20, (?)
A. 25 B. 32
C. 38 D. 42

46. 1, 7, 19, 43, (?)
A. 89 B. 91
C. 62 D. 86

47. 1, 5, 3, 7, 5, (?)
A. 3 B. 10
C. 9 D. 7

48. 23, 30, 38, 47, (?)
A. 56 B. 60
C. 57 D. 67

49. 2, 5, 3, 6, (?)
A. 8 B. 4
C. 7 D. 9

50. 8, 4, 2, 1, 1/2, (?)
A. 1/8 B. 1/4
C. 1 D. 1/3

51. 7, 12, 15, 16, (?), 12, 7
A. 11 B. 13
C. 15 D. 17

52. 5, 9, 15, 23, 33, 45, (?)
A. 55 B. 57
C. 59 D. 61

53. 16, 30, 32, 60, (?), 120
A. 64 B. 72
C. 90 D. 112

54. 1, 4, 5, 10, (?)
A. 16 B. 18
C. 20 D. 24

55. 7, 8, 6, 9, 5, 10, 4, (?)
A. 8 B. 9
C. 11 D. 12

56. 1, 4, 9, 16, (?)
A. 24 B. 25
C. 26 D. 27

57. 2, 2, 4, 12, (?), 240
A. 32 B. 48
C. 64 D. 120

58. 2, 4, 12, 48, (?)
A. 240 B. 120
C. 90 D. 60

EXPLANATORY ANSWERS

EXERCISE - 1

1. D: In each subsequent figure the number of line segment is increased by one and in each alternate figure the number of dot is increased by one. Thus fourth and fifth numbered figures should interchange positions to form the series.

2. C: In each subsequent step the elements of the design disjoin which were joint in the previous step. Thus third and fourth figures should interchange positions to establish the series.

3. C: In each subsequent figure the number of line segment is increased by one. Therefore third and fourth numbered figures should interchange positions to establish the series.

4. A: In each subsequent figure from A to D, one radius is increased inside the circle. From E, the number of radius inside the circle starts diminishing. Therefore A and B should interchange positions to form the series.

5. D: In each subsequent figure number of arrow heads is increased by one and direction is reversed. Therefore D and E should interchange positions to establish the series.

6. D: In subsequent figures the small circle is rotating anticlockwise from one corner to another corner of the design.

7. B: One line segment of the design is decreasing in each subsequent figure.

8. C: In each subsequent figure the small triangle inside the rectangle rotates clockwise from one corner to another corner.

9. A: In each subsequent figure the last digit of the number given in the inside of previous figure becomes first digit of the number.

10. E: In each subsequent figure last digit of previous design comes in the beginning.

11. A: In each subsequent figure last letter given in the previous design comes in the beginning.

12. E: In the first step one of the two bent lines at the upper edge becomes horizontal and in the second step the other bent line becomes horizontal. Again in the third step one of the two segments bends upward. Therefore in the fourth step the other segment will bend upward.

13. A: In the first step first two lower blocks get shaded. In the second step one block gets shaded and in the third step one another block gets shaded. Therefore in the fourth step two upper blocks will become shaded.

14. C: In each subsequent figure s the given design is being diminished.

15. B: In each subsequent step the arrow is moved towards left and towards bottom of the design.

16. C: In the second figure one arrowhead is attached to the design given in the first figure. Therefore 'C' is the correct answer in which one arrow head is attached with the figure given in third position.

17. A: On removing the lower half portion of the design given in the first figure, we get the design given in the second figure. Therefore for getting the design of fourth figure we remove the lower half portion of the third fiure. Thus we find A as the correct answer.

18. B: In the second figure design of the first figure is reversed and lower portion of the figure is shaded. Similarly in the fourth figure design of the third figure will be reversed and its lower portion will be shaded.

19. C: The arrow rotates 90° clockwise in the subsequent figures.

20. D: From first figure to second figure, there is lateral reversal. Therefore 'D' will be the correct answer.

21. D: Rectangle of the first figure becomes circle in the second figure.

22. B: A straight line segment rotates anticlockwise from one corner to the other corner of the given design.

23. B: From the first figure to the second figure shaded portion of the design becomes unshaded and unshaded portion becomes shaded in the second figure.

24. D: In the first step a line segment is added to the lower semicircle and in the second step another line segment is added to the upper semicircle and the same pattern continues.

25. C: From first to second figure the direction of the arrow positioned in the middle does not change while direction of arrows positioned at the two sides gets reversed. Using the same pattern in the third and fourth figures, we find that 'C' is the correct answer.

26. B: In the first figure a triangle is drawn inside the circle while in the second figure circle comes inside the triangle. Similarly the rectangle drawn inside the circle in the third figure will come outside and circle will be in the inside of figure in the fourth place.

27. A: The first figure is reversed to form the second figure. Similarly the third figure will be reversed to form the fourth figure.

28. C: Design at second place is double the design at first place. Therefore design placed at 'C' in the answer figures will be the correct answer as it is the design which is double the design given at third problem figure.

29. C: In each of the subsequent figures one dot positioned at the corner of the design moves clockwise from one corner to another corner while the dot positioned at the centre of the rectangle remains stationary. Thus we find that the correct answer figure is 'B' which will replace the question mark of problem figure.

30. D: In the first step one dot from beneath of the third column disappears. In the second step one more dot from beneath of the same column disappears. Therefore in the third step the remaining dot of the third column will disappear and 'D' will be correct answer figure to replace question mark.

31. A: In the subsequent figures the line is rotating 45° clockwise.

32. B: The small shaded square positioned at one corner of the big square rotates anticlockwise from one corner to another adjacent corner of the big square.

33. C: From first to third figure direction of small dashes at the end points of vertical and horizontal lines gets reversed. Therefore the same rule holds for the figures from second to fourth. Thus the correct answer figure is 'C' which will replace the question mark given in the problem figure.

34. C: In each step of the problem figures two diameters of the circle disappear. Therefore 'C' will be the correct answer figure in which the remaining two diameters of the third problem figure disappeares and this is the figure to replace question mark.

35. D: In the first step three dashes attached to the first figure disappeares. In the second step two dashes attached to the second figure disappeares. Therefore in the third step one dash attached to the third figure should disappear to form the figure in place of question mark. Thus 'D' is the correct answer figure.

36. D: In each of the subsequent figures the design of the first figure, (*i.e.*, reverse symbol of 'V') is increasing by one and in each subsequent figure a dash is drawn above the symbol carried from the previous figure. Therefore 'D' will be correct answer figure to continue the series.

37. E: From first figure to third, the design rotates 90° clockwise. Therefore in the fifth figure the design will rotate further 90°. 'E' is the correct answer.

38. C: In the first step dashes attached to the horizontal line change their direction. In the second step they cover a little distance towards the mid point of the horizontal line. In the third step dashes come close to the mid point of the horizontal line. Therefore in the fourth step, *i.e.*, in the fifth figure, these dashes will touch each other at the mid point of the horizontal line. Thus we find that answer figure 'C' is the correct answer.

39. D: In each subsequent step one arrow is added to the design and each time the arrow joining the design is opposite in direction to that of the arrow which joins in the step prior to the existing one.

40. E: The inner design becomes the outer design after being enlarged in each subsequent figure and a new inner structure is introduced from above the right top corner of the previous design.

41. C: In each subsequent figure one line and one dot is increasing. Thus fifth design will have five dots and six lines. Therefore answer figure 'C' is the correct answer.

42. D: In each subsequent figure number of curved arrow is increasing by one and direction of rotation is changing from anticlockwise to clockwise and again from clockwise to anticlockwise.

43. C: In the first figure there are one horizontal and one vertical line segment within the rectangular block. In the second figure one horizontal line is increased and in the third figure one vertical line segment is increased. Similar pattern is followed by rest of the figures.

44. C: First and third figures are alike. So fifth figure will be same as first and third figures are.

45. C: In the design of first figure there is a triangle which joins a small circle. One triangle joined with one small circle is added to this design in each subsequent figure upto third figure wherefrom one triangle joined with one small circle is disappearing in each subsequent figure. Therefore 'C' is the correct figure at fifth position.

46. C: The inner design becomes the outer design after being enlarged in each subsequent figure. In the first figure there is rectangle inside the circle which comes outside in the second figure and circle comes inside. In the third figure square is inside the circle which in the fourth figure becomes outer and circle comes inside. Therefore in the fifth figure a new structure will come inside the circle.

47. A: In each subsequent figure capital letters follow a specific pattern in alphabetic order. The same pattern is followed by the small letters in reverse order.

48. B: The half moon is rotating 90° clockwise in each subsequent figure and the structure present outside the half-moon is coming inside the half-moon and some new structure is coming forth outside the half-moon. This pattern continues.

49. C: The design is rotating 45° anticlockwise in each subsequent figure.

50. A: The design rotates 180° clockwise in each subsequent figure.

51. B: In each subsequent step entire design rotates 90° anticlockwise.

52. C: In each subsequent step entire design, excepting the small square, rotates 90° clockwise.

53. D: In each subsequent figure lower left symbol comes in the lower right portion and in place of lower left symbol a new symbol comes. In upper portion of the design middle symbol comes in the first and first symbol comes in the last in each step.

54. D: From first to second figure, the upper designs from the previous figure come to the bottom line following a pattern in which last design becomes first and the first design comes in between. Again in the next figure, the designs at the bottom of the previous figure follow the same pattern and come to the upper line. Following this pattern we find that answer figure 'D' is the correct answer figure.

55. E: In each subsequent figure entire design rotates 90° anticlockwise. Therefore answer figure 'E' is the correct answer figure.

56. B: From first to second figure, the symbol positioned at the second place from left in lower line reaches at the upper portion of the design and symbol positioned at the upper portion reaches at the first place from left in the lower line. In addition to this the symbol positioned first in the lower line in the design of the first figure reaches at the last place (*i.e.*, first from right) in the lower line of second figure. The same sequence is being followed by rest of the figures.

57. E: First two designs given in first and third figures interchange positions. Similarly, first two designs in second and third figures interchange positions. Therefore the correct answer will be answer figure 'E'.

58. A: From first to second figure the symbol positioned at last place from right in the first figure comes at first place from left in the second figure and the second symbol from left in the first figure comes at the third position in the second figure. The same sequence is followed by other figures of the series. Therefore 'A' is the correct answer figure.

59. B: From first to second figure, the symbol placed at first position from left in the upper line of symbols in first figure and the symbol positioned at second place from left in the lower line in first figure interchange positions to form the second figure. Again the symbol positioned at third place from left in the upper line of the second figure and the symbol positiond at second place in the lower line of the second figure interchange positions to form the third figure. The same pattern is followed in rest of the figures of the given series. Therefore 'B' is the correct answer figure.

60. E: Symbol positioned at third column in the upper line change position from third to second column and again from second to third column in subsequent figures. Furthermore, symbols of the second line change their positions clockwise in each subsequent figure.

61. A: In each subsequent figure the entire design rotates 90° anti-clockwise but the design which comes after rotation in each subsequent figure at lower left corner, gets changed into a new one.

62. D: From first figure to second figure, the designs inside the first figure is rotated one place anti-clockwise. From second to third figure designs at the lower line in the second figure come in the upper line in the third figure but the designs at the upper line in second figure come in reverse order in the lower line of third figure. The whole pattern starts repeating from third to fourth figure onwards.

63. C: From first to second figure, designs of third column in first figure is reversed in third column of second figure and remaining four designs of the first figure get their respective places in second figure after rotating one place anticlockwise. From second to third figure, designs of first column in second figure is reversed in first column of third figure and remaining four designs of the second figure get their respective places in third figure after rotating one place clockwise. The whole pattern starts repeating from third to fourth figure onwards.

64. A: From first to second figure the uppermost and the lowermost designs interchange their positions and remaining three strucures of the first figure is rotated 180° anticlockwise. From second to third figure one and only one design positioned at lowermost place rotates 180° anticlockwise and remaining structures remain unchanged. The whole pattern is repeating from third to fourth figure onwards.

65. A: From first to second figure the three structures at the end of the first figure comes in reverse order in second figure and a new design appears in place of first design. The same patern is followed by other figures of the series. Therefore 'A' is the correct answer.

66. E: Designs in first and second figures are alike but in third figure first design of the second figure is rotated 180° clockwise. This pattern is followed by remaining figures. Therefore 'E' is the correct answer figure.

67. A: In each subsequent figure all the designs of previous figure occupy a new place.

68. C: Places occupied by designs in first, second and third figures are different from each other. Places occupied by designs in fourth figure are same as first figure. Therefore fifth figure will follow the pattern of second figure. Thus 'C' is the correct answer figure.

69. E: In each subsequent figure all the designs of previous figure occupy a new place.

70. E: We find all the designs in the first line of first figure in the second line of third figure. Therefore all these designs should occur in the first line of fifth figure. The lower and upper portions of first and second figures bear sign of plus (+) respectively and the upper and lower portions of third and fourth figures bear sign of multiplication (×) respectively. So the lower portion of fifth figure should bear a new sign. We find all these characteristics in answer figure 'E'. Therefore it is the correct answer figure.

71. D: We find first and third symbol present in first line of first figure in the first and third place in first line of third figure. Therefore first and third place in the first line of fifth figure should bear these two symbols respectively. The symbol present in between the first and third symbol of first line is different in all the figures. In each alternate figure the two symbols at the lower portion of the figures interchange positions.

72. D: In each subsequent figure only the first two designs from bottom are rotated 180° clockwise. Remaining designs change their places accordingly in subsequent figures.

EXERCISE - 2

1. B: There is a gradual difference of 2, 4, 6, 8, 10 and 12 between two consecutive numbers of the given series. Therefore the number 120 is wrong in the series and it should be replaced by 118.

2. E: Order of difference between two consecutive numbers is as follows:
$(1)^2, (3)^2, (5)^2, (7)^2, (9)^2\ (11)^2$.
Thus, the number 9 is wrong in the series and it should be replaced by 8.

3. C: Difference between two consecutive numbers is in the order of 192, 96, 48, 24, 12 and 6. Therefore number 48 is wrong in this series and it should be replaced by 44.

4. A: 270 is wrong in this series and it should be replaced by 236.25 so that ratio of two consecutive numbers may become 1.5, 2, 2.5, 3, 3.5 and 4 respectively.

5. B: 96 is wrong in this series and it should be replaced by 95 so that series may get rearranged in the following order:

5	11	23
↓	↓	↓
5	$5 \times 2 + 1$	$11 \times 2 + 1$
47	95	191
↓	↓	↓
$23 \times 2 + 1$	$47 \times 2 + 1$	$95 \times 2 + 1$
383		
↓		
$191 \times 2 + 1$		

6. D: 45 is wrong in this series and it should be replaced by 46 so that series may get rearranged in the following order:

16	17	21
↓	↓	↓
16	$16+(1)^2$	$17+(2)^2$
30	46	71
↓	↓	↓
$21+(3)^2$	$30+(4)^2$	$46+(5)^2$
107		
↓		
$71+(6)^2$		

7. E: Second term= (First term + 1) × 1
$= (3 + 1) \times 1 = 4$
Third term = (Second term + 1) × 2
$= (4 + 1) \times 2 = 10$
Fourth term = (Third term + 1) × 3
$= (10 + 1) \times 3 = 33$
Therefore 32 is wrong in this series and it should be replaced by 33.

8. B: 26 is wrong in this series and it should be replaced by 27 so that difference between two consecutive terms may become in the order of 11, 9, 7, 5, 3, and 1.

107
↓
$71 + (6)^2$

9. D:

325	259	202
↓	↓	↓
325	325–(11 × 6)	259–(11 × 5)
160	127	105
↓	↓	↓
204–(11 × 4)	160–(11 × 3)	127–(11 × 2)
94		
↓		
105 – (11 × 1)		

Therefore, the number 202 is wrong in this series and it should be replaced by 204.

10. E: Each subsequent number is obtained by first multiplying the preceding number by 2 and then subtracting 2 from the product so obtained. Therefore 48 is wrong in this seris and it should be replaced by 50.

11. C: Second number is three times the first number, third number is two times the second number and fourth number is four times the third number. The same sequence is being followed by the remaining numbers of the given number series. Therefore 6480 is wrong in this series and it should be replaced by 8640.

12. A: O (Zero) should be replaced by –5 so that difference between two consecutive numbers may become 20, 25, 30, 35, 40 and 45 respectively.

13. B: Because given terms are in the order of 6^2, 8^2, 10^2, 12^2, 14^2, 16^2, 18^2.

14. C: Second number is two times the first number, third number is 4 times the second number and fourth number is three times the third number. The same sequence is being repeated in the remaining numbers of the given number series. Therefore 2688 is wrong in this series and it should be replaced by 4032.

15. D: Second number is 3/2 of the first number, third number 2 times the second number, fourth number is 2½ times the third number and fifth number is 3 times the fourth number. Therefore 27 is wrong in this number series and it should be replaced by 36.

16. E: Difference between two consecutive numbers is in the order of 5, 8, 11, 14, 17 and 20 respectively. Therefore 47 is wrong in this number series and it should be replaced by 46.

17. A: Second number is 23 more than the first number and third number is 17 less than the second number. The same sequence is being followed by the remaining numbers of the given series. Therefore 634 is wrong in this series and it should be replaced by 594.

18. D: Second number is $\frac{1}{12}$ of the first number, third number is $\frac{1}{10}$ of the second number, fourth number is $\frac{1}{8}$ of the third number, fifth number is $\frac{1}{6}$ of the fourth number, sixth number is $\frac{1}{4}$ of the fifth number and seventh number is $\frac{1}{2}$ of the sixth number. Therefore 24 is wrong in this series and it should be replaced by 8.

19. B: Second number is $1\frac{1}{2}$ times the first number and third number is double the second number. The same sequence is being followed by the remaining numbers of the given series. Therefore 121 is wrong in the series and it should be replaced by 198.

20. C: Numbers obtained by subtracting two consecutive numbers are perfect square numbers. Therefore 269 is wrong in this series and it should be replaced by 279.

21. C: Second number is 3/2 times the first and third number is 1/3 of the second number. This specific sequence is being maintained by the remaining numbers of the given number series. Therefore 22.5 is wrong in this series and it should be replaced by 9.

22. B: All other numbers except 33 are prime numbers.

23.C: Numbers given in this series are in the order of 1^2+1, 2^2+1, 3^2+1, ..., therefore 18 is wrong in this series and it should be replaced by 17.

24. D: Numbers given in this number series are in the order of (2^3-1), (3^3-1), (4^3-1) ..... . Therefore 28 is wrong in this series and it should be replaced by 26.

25. E: Except 3, all other numbers of the given series are composite numbers whereas 3 is a prime number.

26. C: Difference between two consecutive numbers is in the order of 2, 3, 4, 5, 6 and 7 respectively. Therefore 1 is wrong in this number series and it should be replaced by 2.

27. D: Difference between two consecutive numbers are in the order of 1, 2, 3, 4, 5, 6, 7, 8 and 9 respectively. Therefore 37 is wrong in this series and it should be replaced by 36.

28. E: Each subsequent number is equal to double the preceding number of the series plus 4. Therefore 26 is wrong in this series and it should be replaced by 36.

29. C: The series consists of two sequences viz 1, 3, 5, 7 ..... and 1, 3, 7, ..., *i.e.*, 1, (1+2), (3+2), (5+2) ..... and 1, (1+2), (3+4), ... Therefore 9 should be replaced by 13.

EXERCISE - 3

1. C: Letters at odd numbered places are moved two steps forward and letters at even numbered places are moved two steps backward.

2. D: Number in each subsequent group is increasing by 4. Letter positioned next to the number is moving three steps forward in each subsequent group and letter positioned last is in the reverse order of alphabet in each subsequent group.

3. A: Second positioned letter in each group is two steps ahead of its preceding letter and two letters skip in between each group of letters.

4. B: Two letters skip in between B and E and three letters skip in between E and I. As 6 letters skip in between I and P, so two letters should skip in between I and the letter in place of question mark and three letters should skip in between P and the letter in place of question mark. Therefore alternative 'B' is the correct answer and 'L' should come in place of question mark.

5. C: In each group the second positioned letter is three steps ahead of the first positioned letter and the third positioned letter is also three steps ahead of the letter positioned second. In addition to this, two letters in alphabetic order skip in between the last and the first letters of two consecutive groups. Therefore 'C' is the correct alternative to replace question mark.

6. A: In each group the second positioned letter is three steps ahead of the first positioned letter and the third positioned letter is also three steps ahead of the letter positioned second. In addition to this, two letters in alphabetic order skip in between the last and the first letters of two consecutive groups. Therefore 'A' is the correct alternative to replace the question mark.

7. B: In each group two letters skip in between first and third letters and in between second and third letters. In addition to this, two letters also skip in between second letter of the first group and first letter of second group.

8. D: In the given series there are groups of three letters in which second positioned letter is repetition of the first and the third letter of the group is the letter having same place in alphabetic series when numbered from the last as has the first and second letters of the group in alphabetic series when numbered from the beginning.

9. E: In the given groups, first and second letters are in the alphabetic order while third letters are in the reverse order.

10. D: All the three letters of the first group are in alphabetic order while all the three letters, in the second group are in reverse order. The same sequence is continued. In addition to this, first letter of the first group comes immediately after the third letter of the third group in alphabetic order. This sequence is continued in other groups also.

11. D: First and second letters of the given groups are two letters ahead of their preceding letters in alphabetic order. In addition to this, one letter skip in between third letter of a group and first letter of the next succeeding group in alphabetic order.

12. A: In each of the groups three letters in alphabetic order skip in between first and second letters. Similarly, eight letters in alphabetic order skip in between second and third letters. In addition to this, the last letter of a group comes immediately before the first letter of the next succeeding group in alphabetic order.

13. C: In each subsequent group the first letter of the group is moved one step forward while second and third letters are moved one step backward.

14. E: The given letter series is in the reverse alphabetic order and from the last end of the series, letters in the order of 0, 1, 2, 3, 4 respectively skip in between the consecutive letters arranged in reverse order.

15. A: First, fourth and seventh positioned letters are in consecutive order but the two letters positioned next to these letters are in reverse alphabetic order and one letter skips in between them.

16. C: If we give a number from 1 to 26 to the letter of alphabet from A to Z, then each letter will represent a specific number as shown below:

A, B, C, D, ... W, X, Y, Z
1, 2, 3, 4, ... 23, 24, 25, 26

17. D: Letters are in alphabetic order while numbers are in the order of 2, 4, 6, 8, ...

18. B: Letters of the given series are in alphabetic order but they skip one letter in between. Also, letters are alternately capital and small.

19. E: Letters are in reverse alphabetic order and one letter skip in between them.

20. A: Firstly two letters are in alphabetic order and then two letters are in reverse alphabetic order. In addition to this, fifth positioned letter is two steps ahead of the letter positioned second in the given letter series.

21. B: When the letters given in 'B' is placed sequentially in the given blank spaces, we get the following letter series.

aaa/bbb/aaa/bbb/aaa

We don't find any letter series with the other set of letters. Therefore 'B' is the correct alternative.

22. B: In all the three given sets (from first to third) second and first positioned letters, when arranged together, form a natural order of alphabet. Similarly in the sets (from third to first) fourth and third positioned letters together form a natural alphabetic order.

23. C: Both the letters of given groups

of the series are two consecutive letters of the alphabet. But in the alternate groups letters are in reverse order and in natural order of alphabet.

24. D: Letters of the series are in reverse order and two letters skip in between two consecutive letters.

25. B: The third, sixth and ninth letters of the series are in reverse order of alphabet.

26. C: First letter of the first group and second letter of the second group are in the natural order. Similarly, first letter of the third group and second letter of the fourth group will be in natural order.

27. A: The difference between the letters is increasing by 1.

B ↓ F ↓ K ↓ Q ↓ ↓ ×

+4 step +5 step +6 step +7 step

28. A: First letters of all the four groups of this letter series are in reverse order and skip one letter in between. Similarly third letters of all the four groups skip one letter in between but they are in natural order of alphabet. Letter present in between the first and third letter of first group is the letter positioned first in the alphabet while that between first and third letter of second group is the last letter of the alphabet. The same sequence is being followed by remaining groups of the series.

29. C: Letters of the series are in natural order and skip one letter in between.

30. A: The difference between the letters is increasing by 1.

A ↓ B ↓ D ↓ [G] ↓ K ↓

+1 step +2 step +3 step +4 step

31. B: There are two alternate letter series: AC and DG. Two letters skip in between D and G. Therefore two letters will also skip in between G and the letter at the blank space. Hence J should replace the blank space.

32. C: Letters of the series are in the reverse order and skip one letter in between.

33. C: The difference between the letters is increasing by 1.

B ↓ E ↓ I ↓ [N] ↓ T ↓

+3 steps +4 steps +5 steps +6 steps

34. D: When the letters given in D are placed sequentially in the blank spaces, we find the following letter series:

acb/acb/acb

We don't find any letter series with the other set of letters. Therefore 'D' is the correct alternative.

EXERCISE - 4

1. D: Here we find two alternate series, *i.e.*,

4, 12, 28, 60, ... and

6, 14, 30, 62, ...

2. A: $16 = 5 \times 3 + 1$, $51 = 16 \times 3 + 3$, $158 = 51 \times 3 + 5$

$\therefore$ Next term $= 158 \times 3 + 7 = 481$

3. C: Each of the given numbers contains similar digits but places of these digits are different in each subsequent number.

4. A: In each of the given numbers, sum of digits is 16.

5. C: In each of the given numbers, sum of digits is 7.

6. A: Given numbers are perfect squares of odd numbers.

7. C: The sequence is as under:
$1^3 - 1, 2^3 - 1, 3^3 - 1, ...$

8. C: Each subsequent number of the series is decreasing in the order of 11, 13, 15, 13, 11.

9. D: Difference between two consecutive numbers of the series is in the order of 4, 6, 8, 10, 12, 14, ...

10. D: Eighth number = 13 + 8 = 21.

11. B: Difference between two consecutive numbers is in the order of 5, 7, 9, 11 and 13 respectively.

12. A: This is a mixed series which consits of following two alternate series:
4, 16, 36, 64 ..... and
196, 144, 100, ...

13. B: Series consists of following two alternate series:
22, 24, 27, 31 ..... and
22, 19, 16, 13 .....

14. C: Difference between two consecutive numbers is in the order of 12, 13, 14, 15, 16 and 17 respectively.

15. D: Difference between two consecutive numbers is in the order of 11, 13, 15, and 17 respectively.

16. B: Series consits of following two alternate series:
27, 25, 23 ..... and
25, 22, 19 .....

17. B: Ratio of any two consecutive numbers is 3.

18. C: Ratio of two consecutive numbers is in the order of 1, $\frac{1}{2}$, $\frac{1}{3}$, $\frac{1}{4}$, $\frac{1}{5}$.

19. D: Difference between two consecuive numbers is in the order of 1.5, 3, 4.5 and 6 respectively.

20. B: There is a difference of 3 in between any two consecutive numbers.

21. C: Each subsequent number is decreasing in the order of 1, 3, 9, 27 .....

22. E: Third number is four times the first number and fourth number is five times the second number. Therefore, fifth number should be six times the third and sixth number should be seven times the fourth.

23. B: Each subsequent number is equal to four times the preceding number plus one.

24. C: Numbers are in the order of $7 \times 1, 7 \times 2, 7 \times 3, 7 \times 4, 7 \times 5$ .....

25. C: Each subsequent number is equal to double the preceding number.

26. B: Subsequent numbers are decreasing in the order of 6, 5, 4 and 3 respectively.

27. C: Second number is 9 more than the first number and third number is 5 more than the second number. The same sequence continues.

28. A: Second number is half of the first and third number is one-third of the second. The same sequence continues.

29. B: Each subsequent number is equal to double the preceding number plus 1.

30. C: Second number is 2 more than the first, third number is 2 more than the second and fourth number is 3 more than the third. The same sequence is being followed by the other numbers of the series.

31. D: Numbers are squares of 2, 4, 6, 8 and 10 respectively.

32. B: Second number is $5\frac{1}{2}$ less than the first number and third number is $3\frac{1}{2}$ less than the second number. Other numbers of the series follow this very sequence.

33. B: Numbers of the series are in the order of $1^3 - 1$. $2^3 - 1$, $3^3 - 1$ and $4^3 - 1$ respectively.

34. D: Numbers of the series are perfect cubes of consecutive numbers.

35. C: Second number is double the first number and third number is 2 more than the second number.

36. B: Sequence is as under:
Second number (5) = $3 \times 2 - 1$
Third number (9) = $5 \times 2 - 1$.

37. D: Numbers of the series are perfect squares of consecutive numbers.

38. A: Difference between two consecutive numbers is in the order of 6, 8, 12, 14 respectively.

39. E: Difference between two consecutive numbers is in the order of 2, 4, 8, 16 respectively.

40. A: 2 is added to the first number to get the second number and 3 is multiplied with the second number to get the third number. The same sequence is being followed by remaining numbers of the given series.

41. B: The series is:

2	2×3	6 × 4	24 × 5	120 × 6
↓	↓	↓	↓	↓
2	6	24	120	720

720 × 7
↓
5040

42. C: The series is:

1^3+2	2^3+2	3^3+2	4^3+2	5^3+2
↓	↓	↓	↓	↓
3	10	29	66	127

6^3+2
↓
218

43. E: There are two alternate series:
2, 7, 14, 23, ?, 47, and
5, 11, 19, 29, 41.
Difference between two consecutive numbers in 1st series is in the order of 5, 7, 9, 11, 13, respectively while difference between two consecutive numbers in 2nd series is in the order of 6, 8, 10, 12 respectively.

44. A: Each subsequent number is equal to double the preceding number.

45. B: Difference between two consecutive numbers of the given series is in the order of 3, 6, 9, 12, ... respectively.

46. B: Difference between two consecutive numbers of the given series is in the order of 6, 12 24, 48 ..... respectively.

47. C: Number positioned third is 2 more than the number positioned first and the number poitioned fifth is 2 more than the number positioned second. Therefore sixth positioned number should be 2 more than the number positioned fourth.

48. C: Difference between two consecutive numbers is in the order of 7, 8, 9, 10 ..... respectively.

49. B: Number positioned third is one more than the number positioned first. Similarly number positioned fourth is also one more than the number positioned second. Therefore fifth positioned number should be one more than the third positioned number.

50. B: Each subsequent number is half of the preceding number.

51. C: First and seventh positioned letters are alike, second and sixth positioned letters are alike. Therefore third and fifth letters will be alike.

52. C: The series is:

5	9	15	23	33	45	?
↓	↓	↓	↓	↓	↓	↓
5	5+4	9+6	15+8	23+10	33+12	45+14 = 59

Therefore 'C' is the correct answer.

53. A: Fourth term is two times the second and sixth term is two times the fourth. Similarly third term is two times the first. So fifth term will be two times the third term.

54. C: Third term is sum of the first and second terms. Fourth term is sum of the first, second and third terms. Therefore fifth term will be sum of the first, second, third and the fourth terms.

55. C: There are two alternate series:
7, 6, 5, 4, ... and
8, 9, 10, ?
Therefore 11 will replace the question mark.

56. B: The series is:

1	4	9	16	?
↓	↓	↓	↓	↓
1^2	2^2	3^2	4^2	$5^2 = 25$

Therefore 25 will replace the question mark.

57. B: $2 = 2 \times 1, 4 = 2 \times 2, 12 = 4 \times 3$
$\therefore ? = 12 \times 4 = 48$

58. A: $4 = 2 \times 2, 12 = 4 \times 3, 48 = 12 \times 4$
Therefore $? = 48 \times 5 = 240$

4

DISTANCE AND DIRECTION TEST

This test is meant to judge the candidate's ability to trace, follow and perceive correctly the distance covered and direction obtained by a body in course of movement. While attempting such questions candidates must have an accurate sense of direction and ability to understand the changes in the distances an directions based on the information provided in the question.

Example: A man starts walking from a place and goes 3 kms towards East. Then he turns to his left and covers another 3 kms. Once again he turns to his left and travels further 3 kms. In which direction is he from his starting point ? Find out the correct answer from amongst the five options given below:

A. North

B. West

C. South

D. East

E. None of the above

Explanatory Answer: He starts moving from A and reaches at B after covering a distance of 3 kms. Here he turns to his left and travels another 3 kms to reach at 'C'. Again at point 'C' he turns to his left and covers another 3 kms to reach his destination, *i.e.*, at point 'D'. We find this point 'D' exactly in the north of initial point 'A', therefore out of the given options. A is the correct answer.

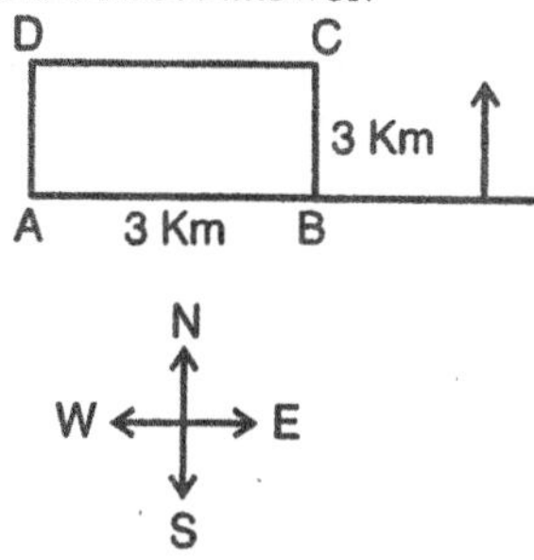

Example 2: Two friends 'A' and 'B' start walking from a place. 'A' walks towards North and after moving a disance of 3 kms, he turns to his right and walks another 4 kms. 'B' walks towards West and after moving 5 kms, he turns to his right and goes another 3 kms. How far is he from his friend'A'? Find out the correct alternative from amongst the given below:

A. 8 kms B. 9 kms

C. 1 kms D. 4 kms

E. 5 kms.

Explanatory Answer: As shown in the diagram given below, final destination of 'A' is 'K' and that of 'B' is M. We find distance between K and M as 4+5 = 9. Therefore alternative 'B' is the correct answer.

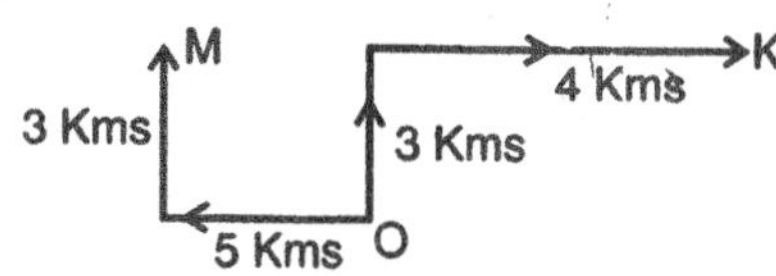

Example 3: Rampur is situated to the west of Chandpur. Bharatpur is to the East of Rampur. Lakhanpur is to the west of Chandpur. Bharatpur is to the East of Chandpur. If Lakhanpur is situated to the west of Rampur, then in which direction is Lakhanpur situated with reference to Bharatpur?

A. North-East B. West
C. South D. East
E. North

Explanatory Answer: The situation of various towns is given as under: Lakhanpur, Rampur, Chandpur, Bharapur

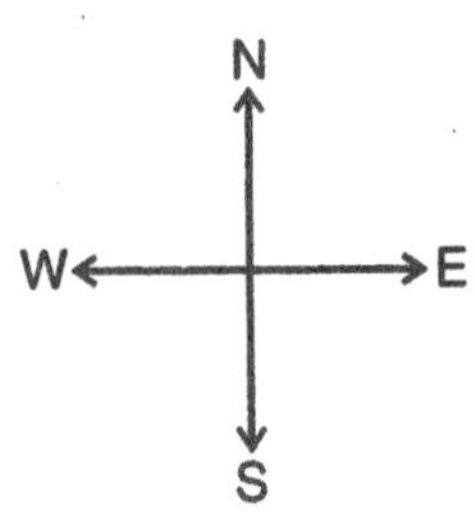

EXERCISE - 1

Direction (Qs. 1 to 3): *Read the following statement carefully and answer the questions (1-2) asked below:*

"A, B, C, D, E and F are six villages of which village 'C' is situated to the south of village 'A', village 'D' is situated to the North of village 'E' and to the west of village 'A', village 'B' is situated to the south-west of village 'C', village F is situated to the west of village 'B' and village C is situated to the east of village 'E'.

1. Which of the following two villages are farthest from each other?
   A. A and B B. A and E
   C. D and C D. A and F
2. Which of the following three villages are in a straight line?
   A. AEB B. DEB
   C. FBC D. DEF
3. Five friends are standing in a circle. Amar is between Ram and John. Sunil is to the left of Bali. Ram is to the left of Sunil. Who is standing to the right of Amar?
   A. John B. Bali
   C. Sunil D. Ram
   E. Either of Sunil and Bali

Directions (Qs. 4 to 8): *A circular park is divided into 16 plots. This park is surrounded by a band of 4 policemen A, B, C and D. Four thieves P, Q, R and S are hidden in this park. Policemen move around to catch these thieves and thieve are trying to escape.*

Now based on the above statement try to answer the questions given below:

4. Each policeman moves four plots ahead in anticlockwise direction and each thief moves two plots ahead in north direction, the policeman who catches the thief is:
   A. A, P B. D, S
   C. B, Q D. C, R
5. A, B, C and D move two plots ahead in clockwise direction and P, Q, R and S move two plots ahead in north direction. The policeman who catches the thief is:
   A. A, R B. B, Q
   C. C, P D. D, S

6. P, Q, R, S and A, B, C, D both groups move three plots ahead in clockwise direction. Who of the two groups will be in north-east and south-west direction respectively?
   A. A and P B. B and Q
   C. C and P D. D and Q
7. P, Q, R and S move six plots ahead in anticlockwise direction and A, B, C and D move four plots ahead in clockwise direction. The two mentioned in which of the following groups will be in north and south direction respectively?
   A. P and A B. R and D
   C. Q and B D. P and C
8. Which of the following two are in the north-west and south-east directions?
   A. S and D B. Q and C
   C. A and P D. B and R
9. 6 friends are playing a card game. Sunil and Ram are facing each-other. Ram is to the left of Aman and to the right of Pranav. Aman is to the left of Dheeraj. If Yogesh and Dheeraj interchange their places and so do Pranav and Ram then who will be sitting to the left of Dheeraj?
   A. Ram B. Sunil
   C. Pranav D. Yogesh
   E. Aman
10. Six children A, B, C, D, E and F are standing in a row. B is in between F and D and E is in between A and C. A is not standing next to F or D. C is not standing next to D. F is standing in between which of the following pairs of children?
   A. B and D B. B and E
   C. B and C D. B and A
   E. C and A
11. Ketaki is in between Manas and Sagar. Raju is to the left of Sagar and Sonal is to the right of Manas. If all these friends are sitting facing south, then who is on their exreme right?
   A. Manas B. Sagar
   C. Raju D. Sonal
12. Gate of my house is towards east. Close to the rear wall of my house, there is Mansi's house whose gate is just in the opposite direction of my house but it is situated at the main road. The house situated at the opposite side of road will have gate in which direction?
   A. Towards East
   B. Towards Noth
   C. Towards West
   D. Towards South
13. One evening before the Sunset at a central market place in Badodara Samaksha and Manas were standing in front of each other facing opposite directions. If shadow of Manas was lying to his right, in which direction Samaksha was facing?
   A. North B. South
   C. East D. West
14. Five friends are standing in a row facing South. Aman is standing to the right of Deva, Chandan is in between Deva and Ekal. Bobby is standing exreme right. Who is standing exactly in the middle?
   A. Aman B. Chandan
   C. Deva D. Ekal

15. Post Office is situated to the east of the school but my home is to the south of the school. The market place is situated to the north of Post office at a distance equal to the distance of my home from the school. In which direction the market is situated from my home?

A. East B. West-South
C. North D. North-East

16. I am standing on a riverside with my back to the river. Something floating freely in the river is going from my left to right. If flow of the river is from west to east, then towards which direction am I facing?

A. South B. East
C. North D. West

17. Five books A, B, C, D and E are kept one above the other in such a way that E is above A, C is below D and A is above D and B is below C. Which on of the books is kept at the lowermost position?

A. C B. D
C. B D. A

18. Rakesh, Mohit, Diwakar, Sawan and Twinkle and sitting in a row. Twinkle is not sitting next to Diwakar and Sawan is not sitting next to Rakesh. Mohit is sitting next to Rakesh and Twinkle is not sitting next to Sawan. Their sitting sequence may be given as under:

A. Rakesh, Mohit, Diwakar, Sawan, Twinkle
B. Mohit, Twinkle, Diwakar, Sawan, Rakesh
C. Sawan, Mohit, Rakesh, Twinkle, Diwakar
D. Twinkle, Rakesh, Mohit, Diwakar, Sawan

19. Five sticks have been fixed up in a row. B is to the left of C and D is to the right of E. E is to the right of C. If A is to the left of 'B' then which of the following sticks is in the middle?

A. E B. D
C. C D. B

20. Gauri, Isha, Frany and Henry are sitting on a bench. Next to Henry and to his left Frany is sitting. Isha is sitting in between Frany and Gauri. Who is sitting on the extreme right?

A. Gauri B. Isha
C. Frany D. Henry

21. Six families A, B, C, D, E and F live in flats built in a row. F and D are next door neighbours of B. A and C are next-door neighbours of E. Family A is not a next-door neighbour of F or D. C is also not the neighbour of D. Which of the families given below are next-door neighbours of F.

A. B and A B. B and E
C. B and C D. B and D

22. Four friends A, B, C and D are climbing up on a ladder. A is at comparatively more height with respect to B and B is in the middle of A and C. If D is positioned at more height than A then who of the following is at third position from beneath?

A. C B. B
C. A D. D

23. Six children Ashu, Bhanu, Chandu, Devu, Yogesh and Pranav are standing in a row. Bhanu is in the middle of Pranav and Devu. Yogesh is in the middle of Ashu and Chandu. Pranav is not standing next to Devu or Yogesh. If Chandu is not standing next to Devu then which of the following pairs of children is on the either side of Pranav?
A. Bhanu and Yogesh
B. Bhanu and Chandu
C. Bhanu and Devu
D. Chandu and Ashu

24. Six persons are sitting around the campfire. Sagar is in front of Bantu, Bantu is to the left of Kashi and to the right of Rashi. Kashi is to the left of Dheeraj and Yogesh is in between Rashi and Sagar. If the places of Dheeraj and Yogesh are interchanged and so also of Rashi and Bantu, then who will be sitting to the left of Dheeraj?
A. Rashi B. Kashi
C. Sagar D. Bantu

25. Four girl friends are sitting around a square table. Meera is to the right of Parasi and Venu is to the left of Kritika. If Kritika is sitting to the left of Parasi, then which of the following pairs of girl friends is sitting in front of each-other?
A. Venu, Meera
B. Meera, Parasi
C. Kritika, Venu
D. Meera, Kritika

26. Four things X, Y, Z and W are kept on a table. X is kept 10 cm away to the east of Y. W is kept 10 cm away to the east of Z and 15 cm away to the south of X. If Z is also 15 cm apart from Y then in which direction Z is kept from Y?
A. North B. West
C. South D. East

27. Six children are sitting in a circle facing towards the centre of the circle. Pranav is to the left of Sawan. Yogi is in between Aman and Vizu. If Harish is sitting in between Pranava and Aman, then who is sitting to the left of Vizu?
A. Aman B. Pranav
C. Harish D. Sawan

28. All the six faces of a solid cube have been painted in different colours. Bottom of this cube has been painted in red colour while the top face of this cube has been painted in white colour. Remaining four faces of the cube have been painted in green, yellow, blue and violet colours respectively in clockwise direction. If yellow painted face of the cube is kept at the bottom, then which colour will be at the top of the cube?
A. White B. Violet
C. Red D. Green

29. Five girls are sitting on stairs. Sarala is sitting a few steps above Chitra but a few steps below Dezy. Vimmy is in between Sarala and Chitra on the stairs while Dezy is sitting in between Anu and Sarla. Who is sitting at the top?
A. Anu B. Dezy
C. Vimmy D. Chitra

30. In a row of six persons, E is sitting in between D and E. B is sitting immdiately next to A. A is sitting at the fourth place from F. Who of the following are sitting at the two ends of the row?

A. F-B B. F-C
C. B-D D. C-A

31. Five persons are sitting in a row and all of them are facing west. D is sitting to the left of C. B is sitting to the right of E. A is sitting to the right of C and B is sitting to the left of D. If E is sitting at one end of the row, then who is at the middle in the row

A. B B. C
C. A D. D

32. In the above question who is sitting at the other end of the row?

A. A B. D
C. C D. B

EXERCISE - 2

1. Akshaya starts walking from an initial point 'P' towards South. He covers a distance of 10 m and turns towards West in which direction he covers another 20 m. Again he turns towards South and walks 10 m. Here he once again turns towards East and walks 20 m and then turns towards North and goes 5 m. Thus he reaches at the final destination of Q. What is the shortest distance in metres between his initial position 'P' and final destination 'Q'?

A. 5 B. 10
C. 15 D. Zero

2. A man walks 10 kms towards north from a place. Then he turns towards South and covers a further distance of 20 kms where he turns Northward and covers an another distance of 20 kms. Then he once again turns towards South and moves further 20 kms and there he turns towards East and goes 10 kms. How far is he from his initial position?

A. 30 kms
B. 25 kms
C. 20 kms
D. None of the above

3. Neha started walking from her home for the temple which was situated to the North of her home. When the temple was at a distance of 90 m, she turned to her left and reached Vicky's house. Vicky's house was 50 m away from the place where she had turned to the left. She gathered some information from Vicky's house and walked 100 m towards West and then turned to her right and walked 90 m. At that point how far was she from the temple?

A. 90 m B. 50 m
C. 0 m D. 1500 m

Directions (Qs. 4-5): *A child has strayed from his path while coming home from the school. He first goes 3 kms towards South and then turns to his right and then goes 2 kms on the road towards west. He again turns to his right and then reaches to his home.*

Now based on the above statement give

answers of the questions given below:

4. In which direction is the home of this child situated from his school?
   A. East B. North-East
   C. South D. West
5. How far is the home of this child situated from his school?
   A. 8 kms B. 4 kms
   C. 7 kms D. 6 km
6. A pole on a crossing is indicating North, South, East and West directions respectively. Due to an accident that had taken place sometime in the past, this pole was rotated by some angle and then the part of the pole which was earlier indicating Eastward correctly, now indicates Southward. If a traveller starts his travel on the road which is being indicated in the West direction by this rotated pole (which is erroneous indication), then in fact in which direction he started his travel?
   A. North-East B. South
   C. West D. North
7. I walked 10 m towards North of my home, turned to my left and walked 20 m. There once again I turned to my left and walked another 20 m. I again turned to my left and covered a further distance of 10 m and then turned left. Therefrom I walked 10 m further. At that point in which direction was I from my home?
   A. South B. North
   C. West D. East
8. Raju walks 16 m towards South, turns to his left and walks 5 m. Then he turns towards North and walks another 7 m. He once again turns to his right and walks another 12 m. He again turns to his left and walks 9 m more. How far is he from his initial position?
   A. 19 m B. 17 m
   C. 18 m D. 16 m
9. Sarita says to Saurabh that she is going Northward. But she goes 2 kms towards East, then 3 kms towards South and again 2 kms towards West and then she goes 2 kms towards the initial point from where she had started. In which direction is she from her initial position?
   A. East B. South
   C. North D. West
10. Bhanu and Rinku start together from one point. Bhanu goes towards west and covers a distance of 4 kms, turns to his right and covers a further distance of 3 kms. Rinku goes towards north and covers a distance of 3 kms, turns to his right and covers a further distance of 5 kms. How far are Bhanu and Rinku from each other?
    A. 7 kms B. 1 km
    C. 9 kms D. 3 kms
11. I travel in South direction and then turn left. After travelling for some time I turn left again and then right. Later in the journey I once again turn to my right. What is the direction I am facing?
    A. North B. East
    C. South D. West

12. If all the directions are rotated and due to this South-East direction is changed to North, then what will come in place of West?

A. South-East B. South
C. North-East D. North-West

13. A person is walking in the North direction. In a little while he turns to his right and then after walking some distance he again turns to his left. He covers a distance of 1 km in this direction and then once again turns to his left. In which direction is he walking now.

A. East B. North
C. South D. West

14. I was standing at a certain place where I turned to my left and covered a distance of 10 m towards East. From there I turned once again to my left and covered another distance of 10 m. Then at that print I turned 45° right and walking straight in that direction I covered a distance of 25 m. In which direction am I from the starting point?

A. North-West B. South-East
C. North-East D. South-West

15. If South-East is changed to North and North-East to West and so on, then what will come in place of West?

A. North-East B. East
C. North D. South-East

16. Bheeku and Bhaully start walking at some speed from a point in opposite directions to each other. After covering an equal distance they turn towards each other. Now if Bhaully is facing North, then in which direction Bheeku started walking from his initial point?

A. West B. East
C. South D. North-East
E. North

17. A man leaves his home and walks 3 kms towards North. Then he turns to his left and walks another 2 kms. He again turns to his right and walks further 1 km. Here he once again turns to his right and walks 5 kms. How far is he from his home?

A. 6 kms B. 4 kms
C. 3 kms D. 5 kms

18. Rakhi and her friend started together from a point. They walked 5 kms towards West and then they turned to their left and walked 3 kms. There Rakhi left her friend and turned to her right and walked 1 km in that direction. After that she walked 3 kms towards North. At that point how far was she from the point she had started in the beginning?

A. 6 kms B. 3 kms
C. 4 kms D. 10 kms

19. A man goes for a walk daily in the evening with his pet dog. He goes 500 m in the West and then another 500 m in the South. From this point in which direction he walks to come back to his home?

A. South-East B. North-East
C. North-West D. North

20. A person started walking towards West. After walking for some time he turned to his right. Later in the journey he once again turned to his right and then to his left. In which direction was he facing then?

A. North B. West
C. North-East D. East

21. Starting from my home, I went 2kms straight and then turned to my right and covered a distance of 1 km. I once again turned to my right and covered a further distance of 1 km. If I was to the North-West of my home, then in which direction had I started from my home?

A. East B. North-West
C. West D. North

22. Beenu goes 45 kms towards East, turns South and goes 4 kms. He again turns towards North-West and covers another 4 kms. In which direction is he from his starting point?

A. East
B. Initial position
C. South-East
D. North-East

EXPLANATORY ANSWERS

EXERCISE - 1

Explanation for question number 1-2:

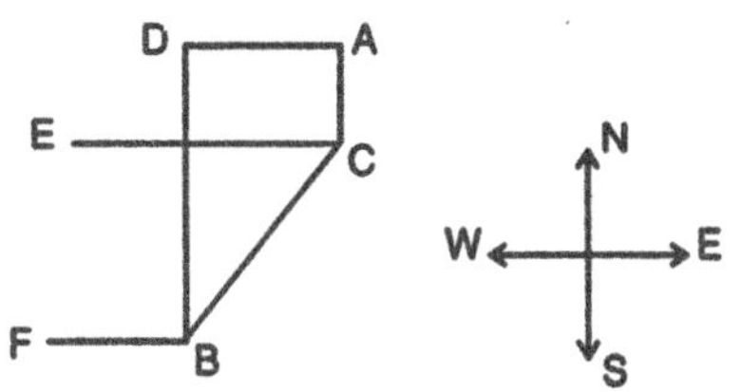

1. D:

2. B:

3. D: The pattern of standing is:

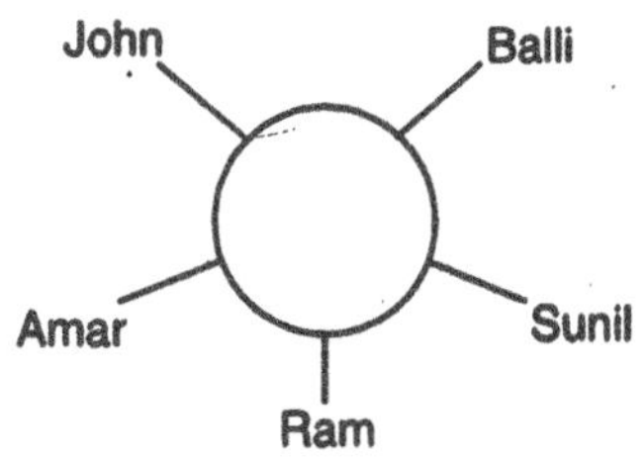

4. B: On moving ahead, their positions will be as under:

5. C:

6. A: On moving ahead, their positions will be as under:

7. A: The new positions will be:

8. C:

9. B: The sitting position was:

Sunil ⊗

Yogesh ⊗ Dheeraj ⊗

Pranav ⊗ Aman ⊗

Ram ⊗

After interchanging places, their positions will be:

Sunil ⊗

Dheeraj ⊗ Yogesh ⊗

Ram ⊗ Aman ⊗

Pranav ⊗

10. C: The pattern of standing is:

⊗	⊗	⊗	⊗	⊗	⊗
A	E	C	F	B	D

11. D: Their sitting pattern is:

⊗	⊗	⊗	⊗	⊗
Sonal	Manas	Ketaki	Sagar	Raju

12. A: The gate of Mansi's house is facing West and therefore gate of the house situated in the opposite side of the road will be facing East.

13. B: In the evening the sun will be in the West. Therefore shadow of Manas will be towards his East. As the shadow is to the right of Manas, so Manas is facing North. But Samaksha and Manas are facing each other, therefore Samaksha is facing towards South.

14. C: The order in which they are standing is: Bobby, Aman, Deva, Chandan, Ekal.

15. D:

Market

School

Post Office

Home

N

W E

S

16. C:

17. C: Books are placed in the following order:

E ⊗

A ⊗

D ⊗

C ⊗

B ⊗

18. D:

19. C: The order of laying sticks is:

D, E, C, B, A

20. A: Their pattern of sitting is:

Gauri, Isha, Frany, Henery

21. C: They are living in the following order:

A, E, C, F, B, D

22. C: On the stairs their ascending order is:

D ⊗

A ⊗

B ⊗

C ⊗

23. B: Children are sitting in the following order:

⊗	⊗	⊗
Ashu,	Yogesh,	Chandu,
⊗	⊗	⊗
Pranava	Bhanu,	Devu

24. C: In the begining their sitting pattern was:

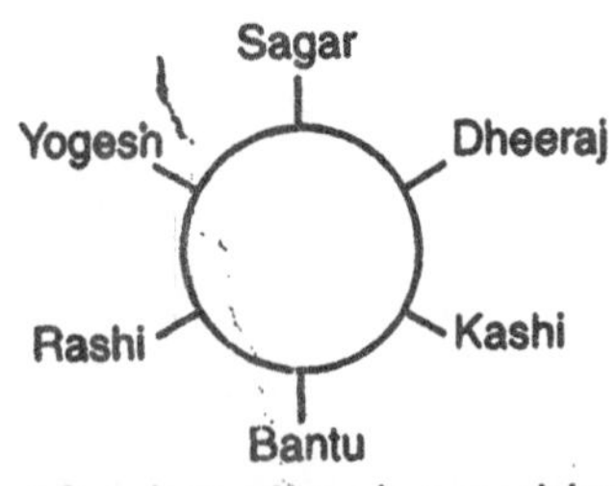

After interchanging positions the order will be:

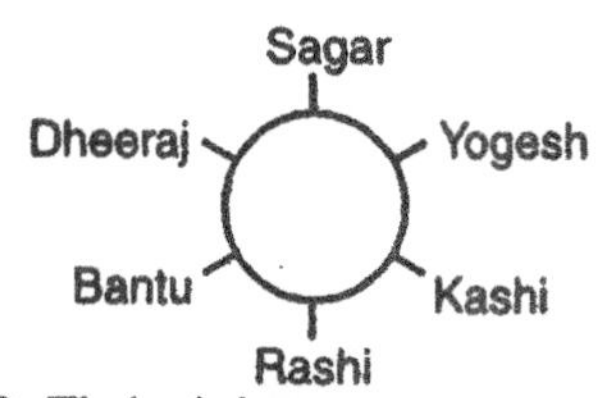

25. D: Their sitting pattern was:

⊗ Meera

Venu ⊗ ⊗ Parasi

⊗ Kritika

26. C: Positions of X, Y, Z and W are:

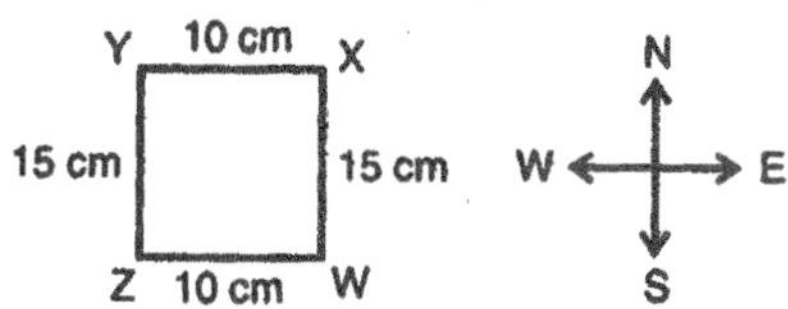

27. D: Their sitting pattern is:

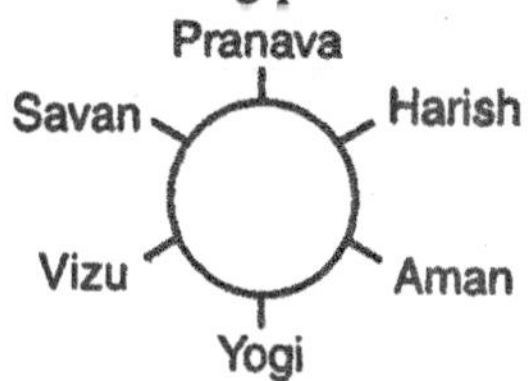

28. B: Just opposite to red coloured face is white coloured face, opposite to green coloured face is blue coloured face and to the opposite of yellow coloured face is the face which has been painted in violet colour.

29. A: ⊗ Anu

⊗ Dezy

⊗ Sarala

⊗ Vimmy

⊗ Chitra

30. A: Their sitting pattern is:

⊗	⊗	⊗	⊗	⊗	⊗
B	A	D	E	C	F

31. D: They are sitting in the following order:

⊗	⊗	⊗	⊗	⊗
A	C	D	B	E

32. A:

EXERCISE - 2

1. C: The direction of his movement is:

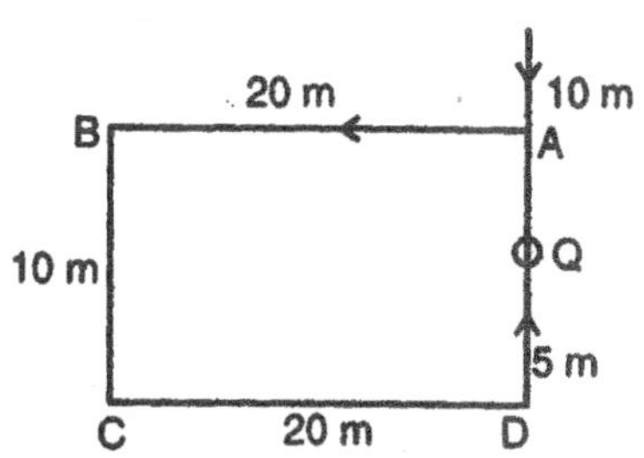

$AQ = 10 - 5 = 5$ m

$\therefore$ $PQ = 10 + 5 = 15$ m

2. D: Route adopted by that man is:

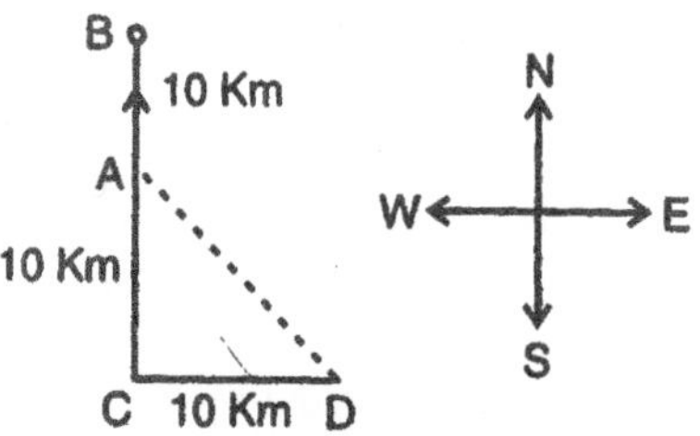

A is his initial position and D is his final position

$\therefore$ Distance between A to D

$= \sqrt{10^2 + 10^2} = 10\sqrt{2}$

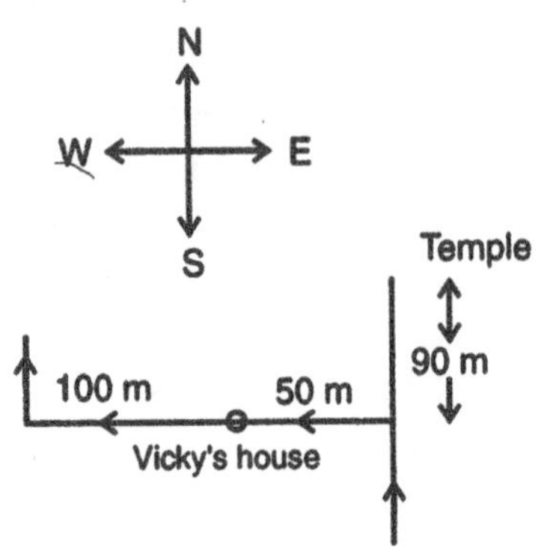

4. C:

5. D:

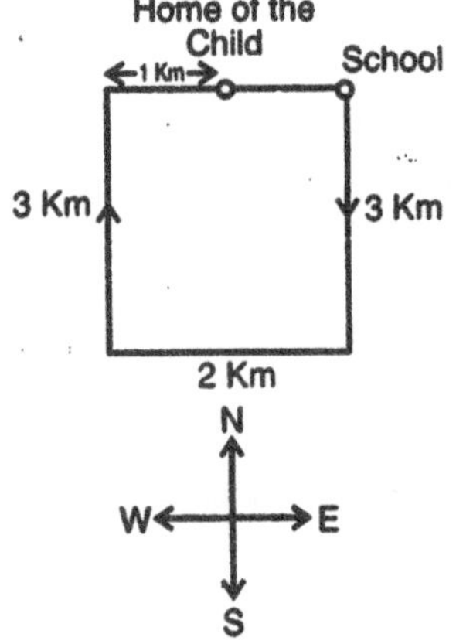

6. D: The part of the pole which was earlier indicating Eastward correctly, now indicates Southward (pole has rotated by 90° clockwise). Therefore the part of the pole which was earlier indicating West direction, now indicates North.

7. C: Direction of movement is:

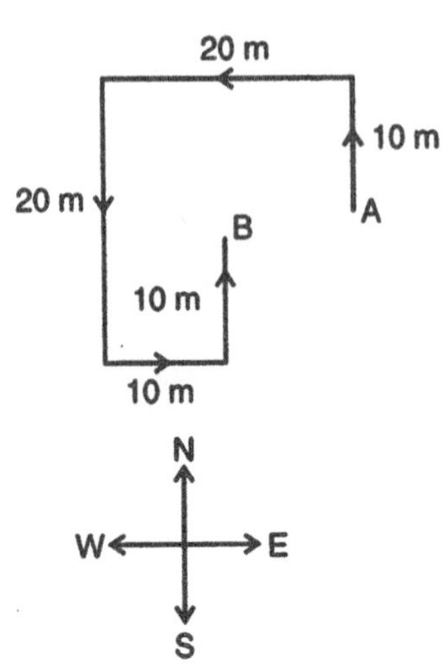

8. B: Distance Covered

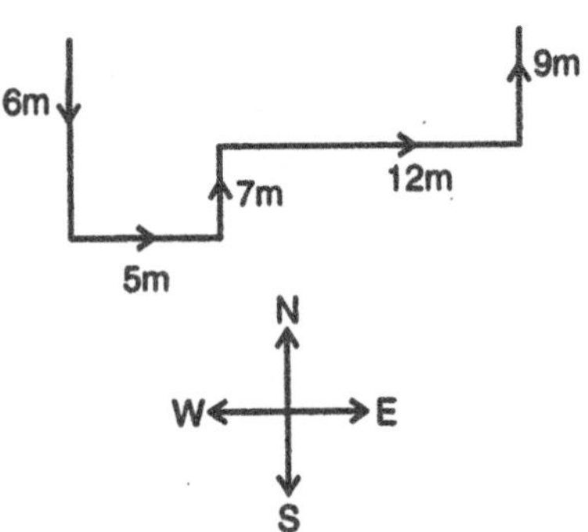

9. B: Distance and direction of her movement:

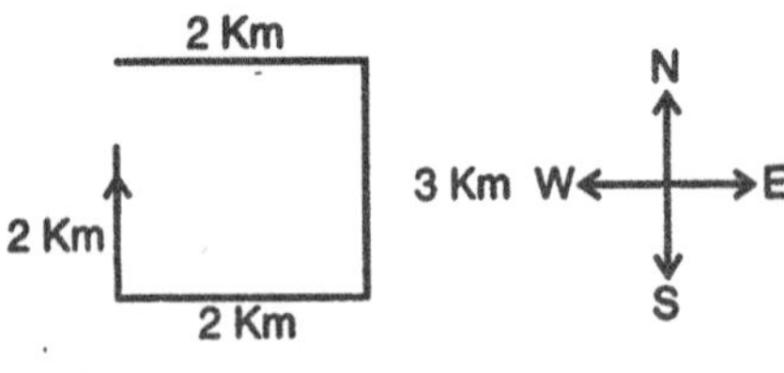

10. C:

10. C:

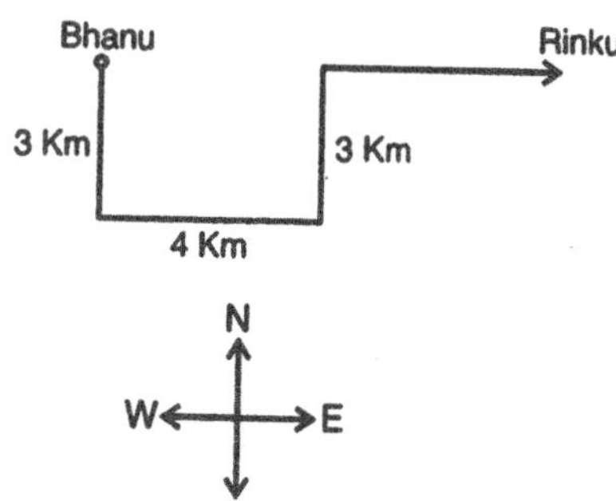

11. C:

12. A: Original Directions

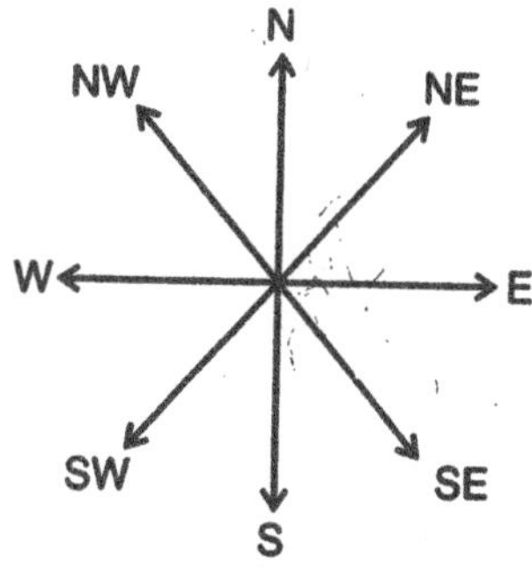

Changed Directions

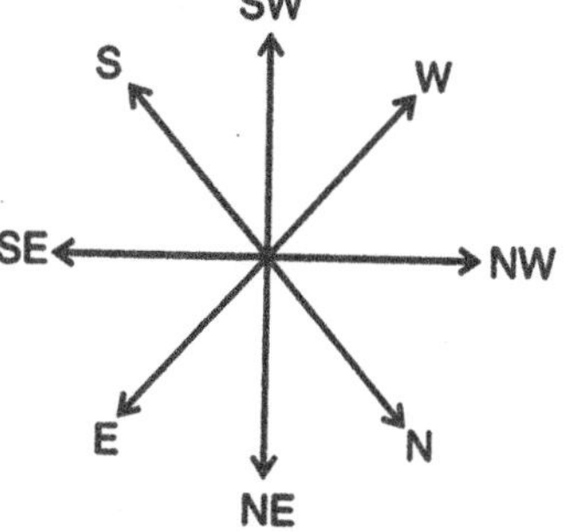

13. D: The direction of his movement is:

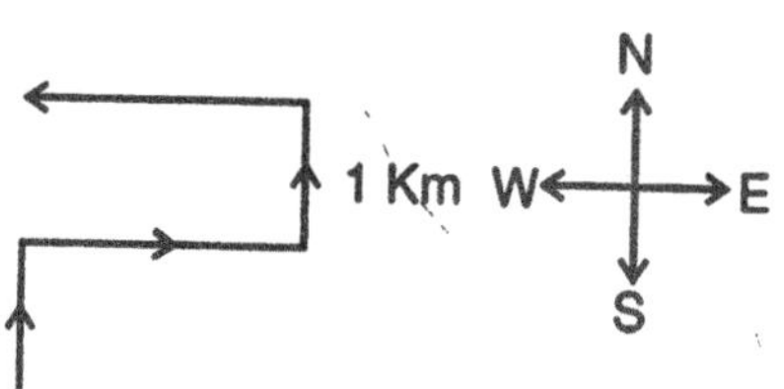

14. C: Assuming 'A' is the starting point, direction of movement is:

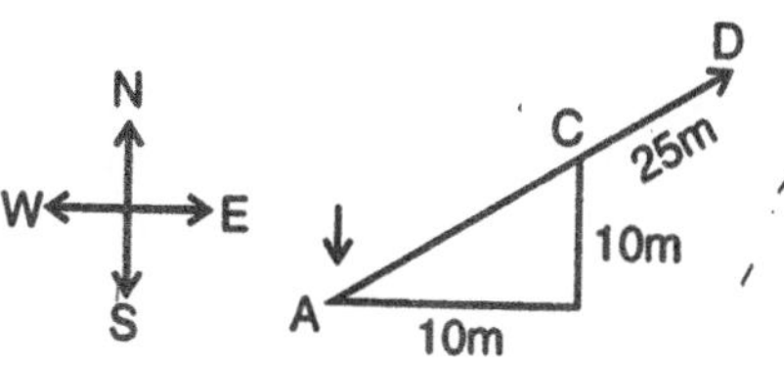

15. D: Original Direction

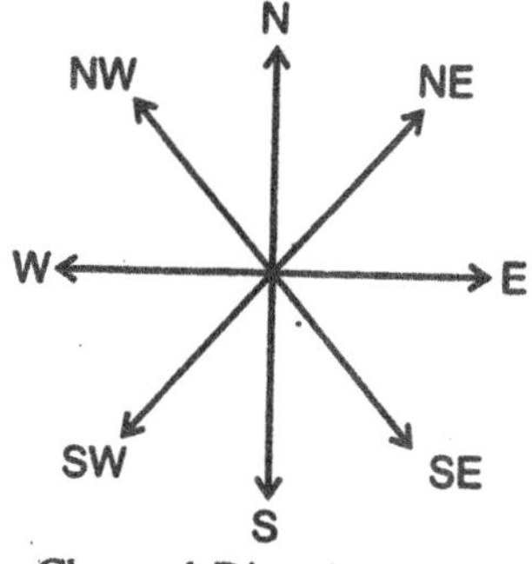

Changed Direction

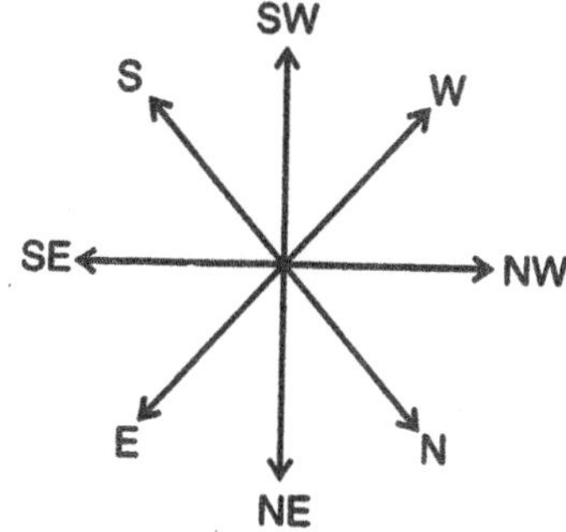

16. E: Routes of movement of Bheeku and Bhaully are:

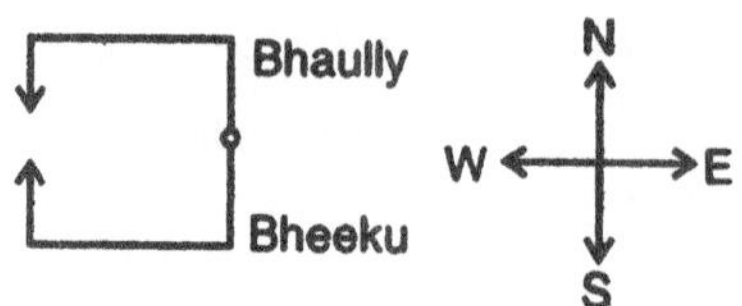

17. D: Movement of this man is expressed as follows:

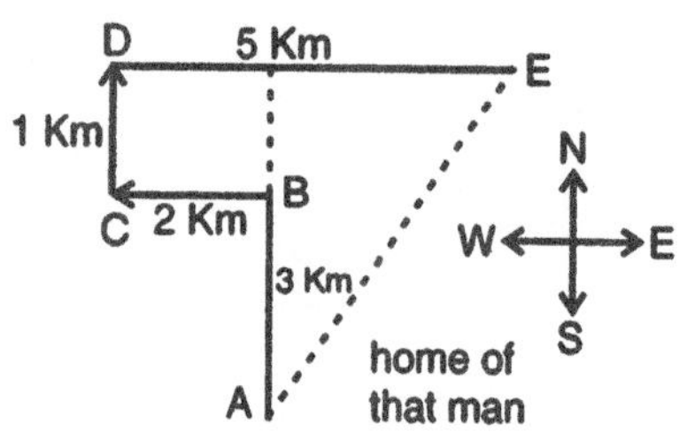

$EF = 5 - 2 = 3$ km
$AF = 3 + 1 = 4$ km

$\therefore \; AE = \sqrt{(3)^2 + (4)^2}$
$= 5$ km

18. A: Diagram of their journey is given as under:

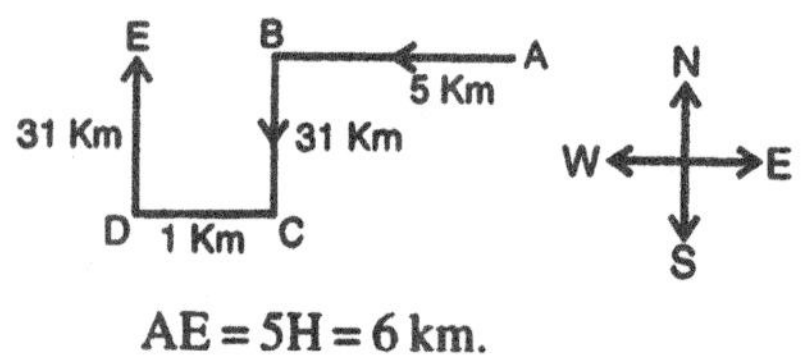

AE = 5H = 6 km.

19. B: The man starts walking from A

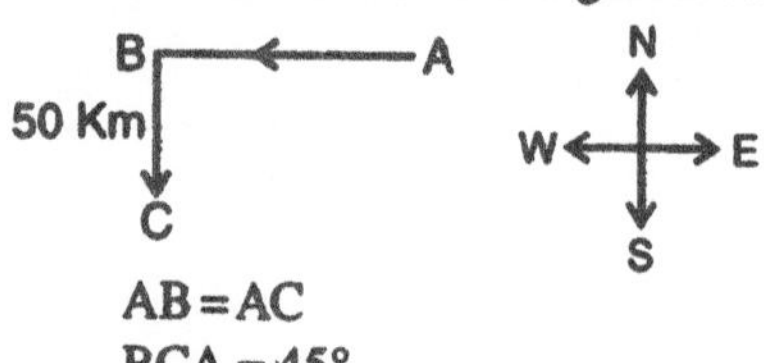

AB = AC
BCA = 45°

20. A: The direction of journey is:

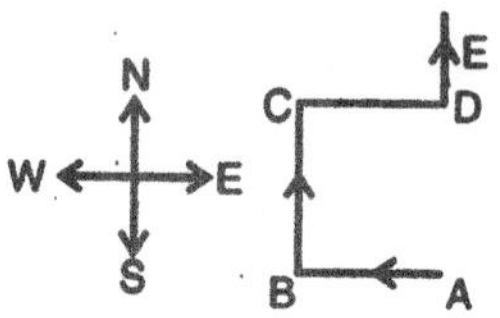

21. C: Direction and distance covered during my journey is:

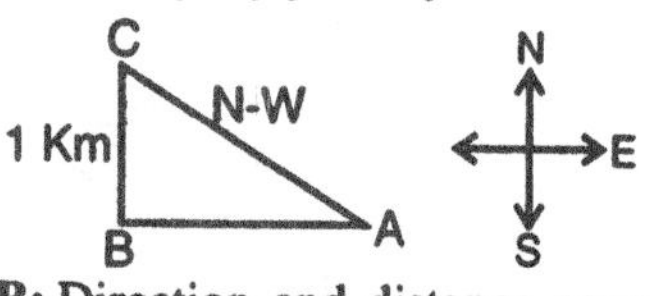

22. B: Direction and distance covered during Beenu's journey is:

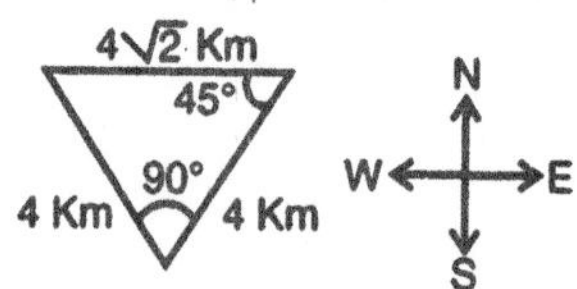

Here $\angle C = 90°$. This is because $4^2 + 4^2 = (4\sqrt{2})^2$. Therefore he reaches to his initial position.

5

CODING-DECODING TEST

A code is a system of words, letters, or symbols which represent sentences or other words to ensure economy or secrecy in transmission. It is a system of rules and regulations which is understandable by the sender and the receiver only and to which any third person cannot understand or comprehend. The coded message can be deciphered or decoded by the receiver as he/she only knows the rules and regulations or methods which were applied in encoding the message. The coding-decoding test is given to judge the candidates ability to read or transliterate or interpret from secret, unknown, or difficult writing. Each question is based on a specific rule of coding. Candidates are required to find out the implied rule of coding and break the code to reveal the messsage. They are also required to imply the same specific rule of coding to encode another word of the given question.

Example 1: In a certain code language FIRE is written as DGPC. How will SHOT be written in that code language? Given below are five alternatives which suggest the last letter of the word written for SHOT in that code language. Select the write choice as your answer:

A. P B. S
C. R D. Q
E. None of these

Explanatory Answer (C): The word is coded by moving the alphabet two steps backward, *i.e.*,

D Comes for F
G Comes for I
P Comes for R
C Comes for E

Similarly,

Q Will come for S
F Will come for H
M Will come for O
R Will come for T

Therefore in that code language SHOT will be written as QFMR. Since R is its last letter, alternative (C) is the correct answer.

Example 2: If GUN is coded as HVO, then in the same manner IBU will be diciphered as:

A. CAP B. NOT
C. RAP D. HEN
E. HAT

Explanatory Answer (E): The word is coded by moving the letters one step forward, *i.e.*,

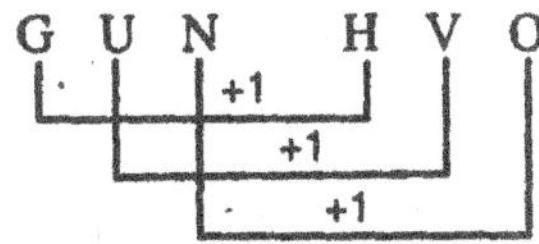

Similarly, IBU will be deciphered by moving the letters one step backward.

i.e.,

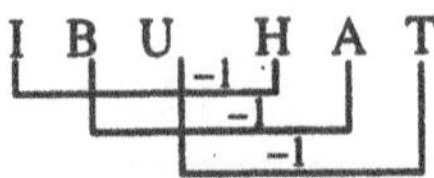

Therefore HAT is the correct word for IBU. Alternative (E) is the correct answer.

Example 3: In a certain code language TOUR is written as 1 2 3 4, CLEAR is written as 5 6 7 8 4 and SPARE is written as 9 0 8 4 7. What will be the fifth digit of the code ciphered for SCULPTURE in the same code language?

A. 6 B. 4
C. 0 D. 3

Explanatory Answer (C): Thorough examination of given words and digits reveals that: T = 1, O = 2, U = 3, R = 4, C = 5, L = 6, E = 7, A = 8, S = 9 and P = 0. In SCULPTURE, P is the fifth letter and 0 stands for P in that code language. Therefore alternative (C) is the correct answer.

Example 4: In a certain code language DINESH KU is written as 82517493. How will SHKNUDI be coded?

A. 7945382 B. 7495238
C. 7453298 D. 7393582
E. 7495382

Explanatory Answer (E): In this code 7 stands for S, 4 stands for H, 9 stands for K, 5 stands for N, 3 stands for U, 8 stands for D and 2 stands for 1. Therefore SHKNUDI will be written as 7495382 in this code language.

Example 5: In a certain code language, (1) 'Rill Ba' stands for 'yellow pen'; (2) 'Pic Ba Sa' stands for 'Flower and Pen'; (3) 'Ul Tam Rill' stands for 'Lovely Yellow Mango', and (4) 'Sa Ul' stands for 'Lovely Flower'. Which of the following words in the above code language stands for 'Mango'?

A. Sa B. Tam
C. Ril D. Ba

Explanatory Answer(B):

Code	Message
1. Rill Ba	Yellow Pen
2. Pic Ba Sa	Flower and Pen
3. Ul Tam Rill	Lovely Yellow Mango
4. Sa Ul	Lovely Flower

From 1 and 2 we find that 'Ba' stands for 'Pen' and 'Rill' stands for 'Yellow'. Similarly we find from 2 and 4 that 'Sa' stands for 'Flower', 3 and 4 reveal that 'Ul' stands for 'Lovely'.

Thus we find that code word 'Tam' stands for 'Mango'. Therefore alternative (B) is the correct answer.

EXERCISE - 1

Directions (Qs. 1 to 6): *Certain letter codes have been assigned to certain numbers. Based on the pattern below, answer the questions given.*

Numbers:	7	2	1	5	3	9	8	6	4
Letter Codes:	V	L	M	S	I	N	D	J	B

1. 1 2 3 4 5 6 will be coded as:
A. M L I D B J
B. M L I B S J
C. I L M B J S
D. M L I J S B

2. 6 4 9 2 8 will be coded as:
A. J B N L D
B. B J N L D
C. J B L N D
D. D B N L S

3. 83175 will be coded as:
A. D I M V S

B. J I L S V
C. D L I M V
D. J S M V I

4. 39674 will be coded as:
A. D N V J B
B. S N J V D
C. I N J V B
D. I N J B V

5. 184632 will be coded as:
A. M J D V L I
B. V D J B V L
C. M D J B S L
D. M D J B I L
E. None of the above

6. 5 2 3 7 9 will be coded as:
A. M L S V I
B. S L I V N
C. S L I N J
D. S L N V I
E. None of the above

Directions (Qs. 7 to 14): *Certain letter codes are assigned to certain numbers. Based on the pattern below, answer the questions.*

Numbers:	7	2	1	5	3	9	8	6	4
Letter Codes:	W	L	M	S	I	N	D	J	B

7. 1 2 3 4 5 6 will be coded as:
A. M L I D B J
B. M L I B S J
C. M L I J S N
D. I L M B J S
E. None of the above

8. 1 8 4 6 3 2 will be coded as:
A. M D B J I
B. B D J B W L
C. M D J B I L
D. M D J B S L
E. None of the above

9. 83175 will be coded as:
A. J S M W I
B. B D J B W L
C. M D J B I L
D. M D J B S L
E. None of the above

10. 69413 will be coded as:
A. J N B I M
B. J N B W I
C. J N B M I
D. J N B W D

11. 52379 will be coded as:
A. M L S W I
B. S L I W N
C. S L I N J
D. S L N W I

12. 879 341 will be coded as:
A. N D W B I M
B. D W N B I M
C. D W N I B M
D. D W N I M B

13. 64928 will be coded as:
A. JB NLD
B. BJNLD
C. JBLND
D. DBNLS

14. 39674 will be coded as:
A. DNWJB
B. SNJWD
C. INJWB
D. INJBW

Directions (Qs. 15 to 24): *Below in column I are given some words and in column II are given their equivalent small letter codes. The letters in column II are jumbled up. Moreover, the codes in Column II do not appear in the same order as in column I. Decode the language and select the correct code for the words/letters given in each question.*

Column I	Column II
BID	nnrw
BAT	emps

BAD	lwz
CHEAP	aejmng
HILL	kms
PORK	emrux
QUOTE	ehgr
ROSE	iotx
VEX	acceenoww
WAVE	elv
NAMELY	befms
FAMILIAR	moty
HAZY	elz
VAGUE	afmtu

15. Which of the following letters stands for B in the given code language?
A. z B. u
C. l D. e

16. Which of the following letters stands for C in the given code language?
A. p B. u
C. e D. z

17. Which of the following letters stands for D in the given code language?
A. z B. u
C. e D. k

18. Which of the following letters stands for F in the given code language?
A. f B. r
C. c D. w

19. Which of the following letters stands for G in the given code language?
A. a B. b
C. c D. j

20. Which of the following letters stands for H in the given Code language?
A. b B. c
C. a D. r

21. Which of the following letters stands for A in the given code language?
A. t B. s
C. e D. r

22. Which of the following letters has been used for K in the given code language?
A. R B. i
C. j D. k

23. Which of the following letters has been used for M in the given code language?
A. b B. c
C. d D. a

24. Which of the following letters stands for z in the given code language?
A. f B. g
C. h D. i

Directions (Qs. 25 to 32): *Certain codes are assigned to certain numbers. Based on the pattern below encode the given numbers in each of the questions and mark your answer from amongst the alternatives suggested in each question.*

Numbers :	3	6	2	7	1	9	4	8	5
Letter Codes:	B	M	P	R	D	H	K	F	S

25. 918765
A. HDRFMS
B. HPFRMS
C. HDFMRS
D. HDFRMS

26. 12845
A. DFPKS B. DPFKS
C. DPFSK D. DPBKS
E. None of the above

27. 213549
A. PDBSHK B. PDSHKB

C. PDBSKH D. PDBSKH
E. None of the above

28. 624839
A. MPKFBM B. MPKFBH
C. MPKFHB D. MPFKBH

29. 73786
A. RVRFS B. RVRFM
C. RRBFM D. RBRFM

30. 73571
A. RBSRD B. RSBDR
C. RBSDR D. HBSRD

31. 58147
A. SFKDR B. SFKRD
C. SFDKR D. SFDRK

32. 12345
A. DPSBK B. BPDKS
C. DPBSK D. DPBKS
E. None of the above

Directions (Qs. 33 to 40): *Below in column I are given some words and in column II are given their equivalent small letter codes. The letters in column II are jumbled up. Moreover, the codes in column II do not appear in the same order as in column I. Decode the language and select the correct code for the words/letters given in each question.*

Column I	Column II
SOUND	abi
ADDRESS	cjmv
CRUX	ikmop
NET	ijktv
CRONY	jkgotv
CROWDY	bloopp

33. Which of the following small letter codes stands for T?
A. a B. b
C. e D. None of these

34. Which of the following small letter codes stands for T?
A. k B. p
C. v D. None of these

35. Which of the following small letter codes signifies R ?
A. o B. p
C. v D. None of these

36. Which of the following small letter codes signifies O?
A. i B. j
C. k D. None of these

37. Which of the following small letters stands for N in the given code langauge?
A. a B. e
C. g D. None of these

38. Which of the following small letters stands for D in the given code language?
A. k B. l
C. m D. None of these

39. Which of the following small letters of the given code language stands for C?
A. j B. k
C. l D. None of these

40. Which of the following letter codes stands for A?
A. b B. l
C. v D. None of these

Directions (Qs. 41 to 50): *Below in column I are given some words and in column II are given their equivalent number codes which are jumbled up. Decode the language and select the correct code for the words given in each question.*

Column I	Column II
ABLMS	24538
QRLBA	93526

PTQAB	52601
LRNPQ	93716
ATRNP	29071
MSPTQ	84106
QPNAR	16729
RABLS	29583
TSLBA	80325
PLQST	31860

41. Which of the following Number Codes stands for P ?
A. 3 B. 8
C. 0 D. 1
E. 6

42. Which of the following Number Codes stands for S?
A. 5 B. 0
C. 2 D. 3
E. 8

43. Which of the following Number Codes signifies the capital letter A?
A. 3 B. 8
C. 2 D. 5
E. 9

44. Which of the following Numbers stands for N?
A. 1 B. 2
C. 9 D. 7
E. 6

45. Which of the following Numbers stands for M?
A. 6 B. 1
C. 8 D. 0
E. 4

46. Which of the following Number Codes signifies T?
A. 9 B. 2
C. 0 D. 1
E. 7

47. Which of the following Number Codes stands for the Letter R?
A. 9 B. 1
C. 6 D. 7
E. 3

48. Which of the following Number Codes stands for the Letter Q?
A. 2 B. 7
C. 6 D. 5
E. 1

49. Which of the following Number Codes stands for the Letter 'L'?
A. 2 B. 5
C. 3 D. 9
E. 6

50. Which of the following Number Codes stands for the Letter B?
A. 3 B. 8
C. 2 D. 5
E. 4

Directions (Qs. 51 to 55): *In a secret map of a defence establishment following codes were being used to indicate heights and distances of military posts in metres.*

0	1	2	3	4	5	6	7	8	9
D	A	N	G	R	Y	C	H	I	L

Due to suspicion of exposure of secrecy of the codes, these codes have been changed. Now certain new codes have been assigned to metric measurements of these posts as under:

0	1	2	3	4	5	6	7	8	9
H	G	L	A	N	D	Y	R	I	C

Based on the above informations, suggest the answer of the questions (51 to 55) from amongst the alternatives given under each question.

51. During war a new post 'Leopard' was established between the 'Tiger' and 'Zebra' posts.

According to the new codes, the distance between 'Leopard' and 'Zebra' is DCA meters. If according to the old codes distance between 'Tiger' and 'Zebra' is ADLC meter then what is the distance in metres between 'Tiger' and 'Leopard' according to the new codes?

A. DCA B. DAH
C. HAD D. DHA
E. DAC

52. Chief of an army battalion read the distance between two posts 'Fox' and 'Lion' as LRGY. This distance was actually encoded in the old code. But the officer translated this distance according to the new code. Due to this eroneous interpretation the distance got in meters will be less than the actual distance between the two posts by:

A. 6719 meters
B. 6971 meters
C. 6179 meters
D. 6791 meters
E. 7619 meters

53. According to the old code 'Zebra' post was RHY meters far from 'Tiger' post. Keeping in view a strategy, the distance between the two posts has been reduced by 50 meters. Now according to the new code distance between the two posts in meters will be:

A. IND B. NLD
C. DLP D. DNL
E. NLL

54. According to the old code, 'Tiger' post is at the height of DGIAH meters from the sea level. This height in the new Code will be:

A. AHIRG meters
B. RIGHA meters
C. HAIGR meters
D. HARIG meters
E. HARHI meters

55. According to the old code, distance between 'Fox' and 'Lion' posts is RDNH meters. According to the new code, this distance in meters will be:

A. DRNH B. YLHN
C. NHDR D. NRHR
E. NHLR

Directions (Qs. 56 to 60): *Certain codes have been assigned to certain letters. Based on the pattern below, answer the questions that follow:*

Letters:	W	L	M	S	I	N	J	B	D
Number Codes:	7	2	1	5	3	9	6	4	8

56. JBNLDM

A. 313276 B. 691824
C. 642189 D. 469218
E. 649281

57. LDINS

A. 28753 B. 24375
C. 28395 D. 13496
E. 28397

58. JNBMI

A. 31697 B. 12694
C. 69412 D. 64139
E. 69413

59. NDBJIL

A. 984632 B. 173621
C. 432184 D. 184362
E. 621394

60. SLIWN

A. 21689 B. 52937
C. 52397 D. 52379
E. 23764

EXERCISE - 2

1. In a certain code language, (1) 'Tim Nac' stands for 'Blue Shirt'; (2) 'Pit Mit Tim' stands for 'Shirt and Pant'; and (3) 'Nac Pit' stands for 'Blue Pant'. Which of the following words will be written for 'and' in that code language?

A. Nac B. Pit
C. Tim D. Mit
E. None of the above

2. In a certain code language, (1) 678 stands for 'How are you'; (2) 347 stands for 'How is life' and (3) 569 stands for 'You are wonderful'. Which of the following numbers indicates 'you' in that code language?

A. 9 B. 6
C. 5 D. 7
E. None of the above

3. In a certain code language, (1) 'Au Cil' stands for 'Big Ship'; (2) 'Sin Lit Au' stands for 'Ship and Boat'; (3) 'Mere Gaw Cil' stands for 'Big Sea River' and (4) 'Sin gow' stands for 'Sea Boat'. From amongst the following alternatives suggest the word for 'River' in that code language.

A. Sin B. Lit
C. Mere D. Gaw

4. In a certain code language '1 2 3' signifies 'Hot filtered coffee'; (2) '3 5 6' signifies 'very hot day' and (3) '5 8 9' signifies 'day and night'. Which of the following digits indicates 'very' in that code language?

A. 2 B. 5
C. 8 D. 6
E. 9

5. In a certain code language, (1) 'Kew Xas Kuna deke' stands for 'She is eating apples'; (2) 'Kew tepo qua' stands for 'She sells toys' and (3) 'Sut Lim deke' stands for 'I like apples'. In this code Language which of the following words will be written for 'She' and 'apples'?

A. 'Kew' and 'Xas'
B. 'Xas' and 'Kew'
C. 'Xas' and 'deke'
D. 'deke' and 'tepo'
E. 'Kew' and 'deke'

6. In a certain code language, (1) 'Lim tok pur' stands for 'sour red apple'; (2) 'tok tuk pa' stands for 'apple is sweet' and (3) 'top tok pa mob' stands for 'Ram is eating apple'. In this code language which of the following words stands for 'sweet'?

A. top B. pa
C. tuk D. tok
E. lim

7. In a certain code language (1) 'Pe sa de ni' stands for 'yes well no mean' and (2) 'Pa ni sa de' stands for 'sell mean well no'. What is the code for word 'Yes' in the said code language?

A. de B. Pe
C. ni D. Sa

8. In a certain code language, (1) '247' stands for 'Beautiful white Rose', (2) '652' stands for 'Beautiful green bottle' and (3) '423' stands for 'Beautiful Yellow Rose'. Which of the following digits stands for the word 'Yellow' in the above code language?

A. 4 B. 7
C. 5 D. 3
E. 2

9. If '1+2+3' is written for 'some are brave', '2+3+4' is written for 'some are cowards' and '3+4+5+6' is written for 'some cowards have come', then which of the following digits could be written for 'are'?

A. 4 B. 3
C. 2 D. 1

10. In a certain code language, (1) 'tom kun sud' stands for 'Dogs are barking'; (2) 'Kun jo mop' stands for 'Dogs and Horses' and (3) 'mut tom ko' stands for 'They are mad'. Which of the following words stands for 'barking' in the above code language?

A. sud B. jo
C. kun D. tom

11. In a certain code language, (1) 'RILL PA' stands for 'My Dog'; (2) 'PA SEM TA' stands for 'Dog is Black'; (3) 'RILL HAK KOP' stands for 'My Dear Friend' and (4) 'TA KOP' stands for 'Black Friend'. Which of the following words signifies 'Dear' in the above code language?

A. SEM B. PA
C. HAK D. KOP
E. RILL

12. In a certain code language, (A) '1 2 3' stands for 'tall clever man'; (B) '3 4 5' stands for 'clever naughty boy' and (C) '2 4 6' stands for 'boy is tall'. Which of the following digits stands for 'naughty' in the above code language?

A. 6 B. 4
C. 3 D. 5
E. Above information is incomplete

13. In a certain code language, (1) 'yob yera se' stands for 'child is unknown'; (2) 'Pes la yera' stands for 'unknown and tall' and (3) 'neg la se' stands for 'man is tall'. Which of the following word stands for 'and' in the above code language?

A. yera B. yob
C. la D. neg
E. Pes

14. In a certain code language 'BRAIN' is encoded as '1 2 3 4 5'; 'DRAIN' is encoded as '0 2 3 4 5', 'GRADE' is encoded as '72308' and 'STATE' is encoded as '78388'. Which of the following digits could be written for 'D' in the above code language?

A. 9 B. 2
C. 0 D. 1

15. In a certain code language, (1) 'Lim po Kin he' stands for 'Puroshottam is drinking milk'; (2) 'Het La po kin' stands for 'Sunil is drinking maza' (3) 'Ket lip hot kin' stands for 'They are drinking tea' and (4) 'Ret lim la' stands for 'Milk and maza. What is the code for word 'Sunil' in the above code language?

A. Po B. Het
C. La D. Pot
E. He

16. In a certain code language, (1) 'cinto badi tsi nzro' means 'Her village is Sarurpur'; (2) 'mhri cinto kepi tsi oind' means 'Literature is her first love' and (3) 'Oind geit tsi cinto kepi' means 'Literature reading is her hobby. Which of the following words stands for 'Literature' in the above code language?

A. geit B. kepi
C. oind D. cinto
E. mhri

Directions (Qs. 17 to 21): *Given below are a few sentences which have been translated into a certain code language. Based on the pattern, answer the questions that follow:*

1. Home of Hari is located near the School - 'Kivi doom sim saman si loodo'
2. Rama goes to home - 'waei auro doom si'
3. Your name has been struck off from the school - 'saman tressa si heither teep auri.
4. What is your name - 'tressa heither si van.
5. Ram is a friend of Hari - 'Kivi si waei jim'.
6. What is your name - 'van heither tressa si'.

17. Which of the following means 'friend' in the given code language?

A. heither B. waei
C. see D. kivi
E. jim

18. Which of the following is the code for 'struck off'?

A. Saman
B. teep
C. auri
D. Can not be determined
E. None of the above

19. In the given code language 'van' has been written for which of the following words?

A. What B. School
C. friend D. name
E. Hari

20. Which of the following codes stands for word 'is'?

A. jim B. waei
C. auro D. tressa
E. si

21. Which of the following codes stands for word 'home' in the above code language?

A. Loodo B. Kup
C. doom D. Saman
E. Kivi

22. In a certain code language, (1) 'sau pe te' means 'Doctor Vimal Kumar'; (2) 'ting pau sau' means 'Rajesh is Doctor' and (3) 'ping pong ting' means 'Rajesh and Rajendra'. Which of the following codes stands for word 'is' in this code language?

A. pe B. pau
C. te D. ting
E. sau

Directions (Qs. 23-24): *In a certain code language, (1) 'D I L' means 'Dogs are mad'; (2) 'C L D' means 'Remove* *mad dogs' and (3) 'C K D' means 'Remove bad dogs'. Based on this code language, answer thre questions asked below:*

23. Which of the following codes stands for word 'are' in the above code language?

A. L B. D
C. I D. C
E. K

24. Which of the following are the codes for 'Mad dogs are bad'?

A. LIKD B. LDKI
C. LCDK D. LDIK
E. LIDK

EXERCISE - 3

1. If in a certain code language CARPENTER is written as B A Q P D N S E Q then in that code language first letter of the word written for SANJIV will be:

A. C B. V
C. R D. N
E. T

2. If MOHAN is coded as NAHOM, then in the same manner the last two letters of the code word written for KARIM will be:

A. AM B. MK
C. KA D. RI
E. AK

3. In a certain code language 'GREEN' is written as FSDFM. Which of the following will be last letter of the code word written for BLUE in the above code langauge?

A. R B. F
C. U D. S
E. P

4. In a certain code language LINE CLEAR is written as OKQGFN HCU. Which of the following will be the first and the last letter of the word written as ZKUGSCU VXTH in this code language?

A. WK B. YG
C. WE D. ZH
E. ZF

5. In a certain code language SON is written as TUPQOP. In this code language the first and the last letters of the word written for FATHER will be:

A. PQ B. GT
C. PS D. GH
E. DE

6. If in a certain code language BEDGE is written as AFCHD, then in that code language last letter of the word written for HQISQ will be:

A. P B. R
C. Q D. S
E. T

7. If in a certain language ACNP is written as NPJL, then in that code language last letter of the word written for CINPQSRTG will be:

A. C B. F
C. D D. E
E. None of the above

8. In a certain code language BOX is written as CDPQYZ. In this code language the last two letters of the word written for HERO will be:

A. Q, P B. M, N
C. P, Q D. N, M
E. None of these

9. In a certain code language SEND-MONEY is written as QCLB-KLCW. In this code language the first and the last letters of the word written for MOST-SECRET will be:

A. V, U B. K, R
C. R, K D. Q, V
E. None of these

10. If in a certain code language 'SCRIPT' is written as TCQIQT, then which of the following will be the first and the last letters of the word written for DIGEST in that code language?

A. C, E B. E, F
C. C, T D. E, T

11. In a clock 1-12 numbers have been indicated by alphabets starting from T in reverse order. Which of the following letters has been used for 9 in this clock?

A. K B. M
C. J D. L
E. None of these

EXERCISE - 4

1. In a certain code language SENT is written as '+ ÷ × –' and ANT is written as '* × –', then in the same code language TEN will be written as:

A. × – × B. × ÷ –
C. – ÷ × D. ÷ × –
E. * – ×

2. In a certain code language TEN is coded as WBZ, Run as XUZ and LATE as YDWB. In the same way ZDWUXDY will be deciplined as:

A. TARANUL B. NARUTAL
C. RANUTAL D. NATUALR
E. NATURAL

3. If in a certain code language MAT is coded as ZCW, OUT as XYW and NIB as VQS, then MOUNTAIN will be coded in the same code as:

A. XYZWQVWV
B. ZXYVWCQV
C. WYXZCQVV
D. ZXYWVVQC
E. ZXYVQWVC

4. If 'DUST' is called 'AIR', 'AIR' is called 'FIRE', 'FIRE' is called 'WATER', 'WATER' is called 'COLOUR', 'COLOUR' is called 'RAIN' and 'RAIN' is called 'DUST', then where do fishes swim?

A. COLOUR B. RAIN
C. WATER D. FIRE
E. DUST

5. In a certain code language YZW denotes BAD and HZRW denotes SAID, then in the same code LOVE will be denoted by:

A. MIUD B. RNTX
C. KOAF D. OLEV

6. If in an infantry SYSTEM is denoted by SYSMET and NEARER by AENRER then in the same manner FRACTION is denoted by:

A. FRACNOIT

B. CARFNOIT
C. ARFCNOIT
D. RECAITNO

Directions (Qs. 7 to 12): *Suggest the appropriate answer from amongst the alternatives to fill in the blanks in each of the questions given below.*

7. G 39 33 J
C 47 41 F
R – – Y
A. 4, 12 B. 1, 15
C. 15, 1 D. 3, 17
E. 17, 3

8. S 16 10 V
L 28 20 P
F – – J
A. 35, 41 B. 40, 32
C. 18, 30 D. 30, 28
E. 35, 45

9. P 34 32 Q
V 44 40 X
G – – I
A. 14, 18 B. 12, 14
C. 14, 12 D. 18, 14
E. None of the above

10. K 21 15 H
O 29 39 T
D – – B
A. 5, 3 B. 5, 7
C. 7, 5 D. 3, 5
E. 7, 3

11. B 6 8 D
J 14 17 M
N – – S
A. 15, 20 B. 14, 19
C. 18, 23 D. 16, 21
E. 17, 22

12. If in a certain code REST is written as 0987 and BEAST is written as 29187, then in the same code BREAST will be coded as:
A. 209187 B. 211987
C. 201987 D. 219187
E. 229187

13. If in a certain code language BILL is coded as 2466, DIG as 345 and NUT as 798, then BUILDING will be coded as:
A. 29467435 B. 29463475
C. 92463475 D. 92643475
E. 27493465

14. If TOM means 48 and DILK means 27 then HARRY stands for:
A. 67 B. 50
C. 60 D. 70
E. 46

15. Find the value of J – B + D from amongst the numeric values given below:
A. 15 B. 12
C. 16 D. 9
E. 23

16. H + B + F stands for:
A. 11 B. 15
C. 16 D. 17
E. 20

EXERCISE - 5

1. If in a certain code language KTIZ is coded as HPEX, then LIFE will be coded as:
A. ECIB B. IEBC
C. BICE D. IBEC
E. IECB

2. In a code language CROWD is written as DQPVE. How will HOUSE be written in the same code?
A. RIVNF B. VIRFN
C. INVRF D. IVRNF
E. INVER

3. If in a certain code language THEN is coded as RLBS, then in the same code language code word AEPJ will be deciphered as:
A. CAES B. EASC
C. CASE D. CSAE
E. SACE

4. If in a code language ILPB is desciplined as GONE then in the same code language EOKY will be deciphered as:
A. CRIB B. IBCR
C. CIRB D. RIBC
E. CRBI

5. If in a code language DIVISION is written as DVISIOIN, then how will STATES be written in the same manner?
A. TSTASE B. SATEST
C. SAETTS D. STTASE
E. SATETS

6. If ACNPXZ denotes BOY, then RTNPMO will denote:
A. RAT B. DOG
C. SON D. PEN
E. COT

7. If LOVE is denoted by MNPQWXFG, then the set of letters IJBCUVFG will denote:
A. WIFE B. HATE
C. KITE D. HOME

8. In a certain code language GBOQX code is deciphered as HAPPY. In the same way CROSS will be coded as:
A. BSPRT B. BNSTR
C. BSNTR D. BSPTR
E. BSNRT

9. If in a certain code language MPKHG denotes KNIFE then in the same manner code DTGCF will denote:
A. BRDAE B. BRAED
C. BRADE D. BARED
E. BREAD

10. If in a certain code language SKEW is written as POCY, then in the same language code JYQV will be written for?
A. SUTM B. MSUT
C. SUMT D. MUST
E. MUTS

EXERCISE - 6

1. If in a certain code language AWAKE is written as ZVZJD, then in the same manner FRIEND will be written as:
A. EQHDMF B. EQHDEM
C. EQHDMC D. UQHDME

2. If BOND is coded as DRRI, then code for JAMES will be:
A. LDQJY B. LDQJX
C. LDQKX D. LDQIY

3. In a certain code language TREASURE BURIED HERE is written as QOBXPROB YROFBA EBOB. What is the code for HERE in the above code language?
A. BEUC B. EBAB
C. EBOB D. PROR

4. If in a certain code language SHIRT is written as 'RGHQS'. How will PANTS be written in the same manner?
A. OZNST B. QZNSR
C. OZMST D. OZMSR

5. If in a certain code language 'STABILISE' is written as 'UVCDKNKUG', then in the same

code language 'CRICKET' will be written as:
A. ESLEMGV
B. ETKFMGV
C. ETKEMGV
D. ETKATCR

6. If YZW stands for 'Bad', then in the same manner ZXY will stand for:
A. Age B. Bag
C. Eye D. Ace

7. If in a certain code language LOJGF stands for 'knife', then in the same code language USBJO will stand for:
A. Strain B. Train
C. Tails D. Trail

8. If in a certain code language EXCELLENT is written as DWBDKKDMS, then in the same manner ENEMY will be written as:
A. DMDMZ B. DMCMZ
C. EDPMW D. DMDLX

9. If in a certain code language GREAT is coded as ITGCV, then in the same manner FRIEND will be coded as:
A. HTKGRP B. DPGCLB
C. HTGKPF D. HSKGPF

10. If AFTER is written as CHVGT then in the same manner BEFORE will be written as:
A. EFGHDH B. DFGTQS
C. DGHQTG D. GHTQDG

11. If PINK is written as NGLI, then in the same manner IRON will be written as:
A. PGLM B. GPML
C. MIGP D. GPLM

12. In a certain code ENGLAND is written as 1234526 and FRANCE as 785291. How will GREECE be written in that code?
A. 985545 B. 831171
C. 832252 D. 381191

13. In a certain code language COURAGE is coded as UOCREGA. How will JOURNAL be coded?
A. JOUNRLA B. UOJRANL
C. UOJRLAN D. UOJARANL

14. In a certain code language BRIDE is written as EULGH. How will FRUIT be written in that code?
A. IUXIS B. IUXLV
C. IUVLS D. IUXLW

15. In a certain code language RATIONAL is written as RTANIOLA. How will TRIBAL be written in that code?
A. TIRABL B. TIRLBA
C. TIRALB D. TIRBLA

16. INSTITUTE is coded in a certain code language as ZLXQZQEQF. How will NUT be coded in the same language?
A. QZL B. LWQ
C. XZQ D. LFQ

17. If HAPPY is coded as 51223. How will PAHPY be coded?
A. 52123 B. 21235
C. 21523 D. 21253

18. If in a certain code language WEAKNESS is code as 15342566, then in the same code language ANESWESK will be coded as:
A. 32561564 B. 32651654
C. 32651564 D. 32651645

19. If HONESTY is coded as

2304516, then in the same manner NEHSOYT will be coded as:

A. 0452631 B. 0425631
C. 0423561 D. 0425361

20. If in a certain code language YESTERDAY is written as 537634205 then in the same code STARYEDYE will be written as:

A. 760453253
B. 760432535
C. 760452353
D. 760453235

21. If in a certain code language MARRIAGE is written as 53220341 then in the same manner code for AGRAMEGIR will be:

A. 342531402
B. 342351402
C. 342351402
D. 342351402

22. If 5213647 denotes POINTED, then in the same code language TIPONDE will be denoted by:

A. 6152374
B. 6135274
C. 6153274
D. 6135724

23. If PUNCTUALITY is written as 23546371860 in a certain code language then in the same manner TULIPUNCTAY will be written as:

A. 63182334760
B. 63182534630
C. 63182354670
D. 63182357460

24. If REGULARITY is coded as 2357982460 then code for TRLGREUAIY will be:

A. 6295237840
B. 629273840
C. 6292537840
D. 6292573980

25. DAUGHTER is coded as 51426378 in a certain code language. How will GRAUDEHT be coded in the same code language?

A. 28146573
B. 28147563
C. 281447653
D. 28145763

26. ENGLISH is coded in a certain code language as 2357964. How will ISHNGEL be coded in the same language?

A. 9435276 B. 9643527
C. 9643257 D. 9435276

27. If LIPTON is coded in a certain code language as IFMQLK, then in the same language MUKESH will be coded as:

A. JRBHPE B. JRHBOE
C. JRHAOE D. JRHBPE

28. If in a certain code language UMESH is written as FNVHS, then in the same language POT will be written as:

A. KLS B. KLG
C. LKG D. ILG

29. If in a certain code THGUAN stands for NAUGHT, then which of the following will stand for LABOUR?

A. RUOLAB B. ROUBLA
C. RUOBAL D. BALROU

30. If in a certain code language MATTER is written as TAMRET, then in the same language

BEYOND will be written as:
A. YEBDON B. YEDNOB
C. DNOYEB D. YEBDNO

31. If in a certain code language GOLDEN is written as ODNGLE, then in the same language SENIOR will be written as:
A. EIRSON B. IORSEN
C. EIRSNO D. NOSEIR

32. If BEFORE is written as FEBERO in a certain code language, then in the same manner JUNGLE will be written as:
A. NUELJE B. NUJLEG
C. NUJELG D. NEJLG

33. If NUMBER is coded as UNBMRE, then GHOST will be coded as:
A. HGOTS B. HGTOS
C. HGDST D. HGSOT

34. If in a certain code language BEAT is coded as YVZG, then in the same language MILD will be coded as:
A. ONWR B. ONRW
C. WORN D. NORW
E. NROW

35. If BACK in a certain code language is written as YZXP, then in the same language SAND will be written as:
A. WMZH B. KPER
C. HZMW D. PLGD

36. If HAND is coded as SZMW, then MILK will be coded as:
A. NROP B. ROPN
C. PNRO D. ORPN

37. If in a certain code language GAME is written as TZNV, then in the same manner BOSS will be written as:
A. LYHH B. YLHH
C. HHYL D. LUYH

38. If in a certain code language REPEAT is written as SDQDBS, then in the same language SOURCE will be written as:
A. TPVSDF B. TRPBSF
C. RPTSBF D. RTPBSF
E. TNVQDD

39. LOKESH in a certain code language is coded as GRDJNK. How will SUDHIR be coded in this code language?
A. RTCQHG B. QCTHGR
C. QHGCTR D. RTCGHQ

40. In a certain code language GAMA is coded as 3253. Here digits used as codes for the letters do not follow the same order as is the order of letters in the word of the original language. How should ARM be written in this code language?
A. 573 B. 317
C. 325 D. 367

41. In a certain code language CGZ is written as XTA. How should DFP be written in the same code?
A. YTO B. WSM
C. WSK D. WUK

42. In a certain code TEACHING is written as CHEATING. How will GRADIENT be written in the same code?
A. RADIGENT
B. RDIEGNT
C. DIERATNG
D. DIARGENT
E. DIRAGENT

43. In a certain code BANGALORE

is coded as CZOFBKPQF. How will CHANDIGARH be coded in the same manner?

A. HHRAAJDGPS
B. CTRVQTABKL
C. DGBMEHHZSG
D. DXTURUASPK
E. DGBNEHHZSG

44. If code for DELHI is EFMIJ, then which of the following should be the code for BOMBAY?

A. AMJWUR B. MJXVSU
C. AIJMJX D. CPNCBZ
E. CPNCDZ

45. If in a certain code language 'PARENTS' is coded as 'RCTGPVU', them in the same code language CHILDREN will be coded as:

A. EJKNEGTP
B. EJKNFHTP
C. EJKNFGTO
D. EJKNFITP
E. EJKNFTGP

46. If in a certain code language PRACTICE is written as PICCTRAE, them in the same code language FLAMES will be written as:

A. FMEALS B. FALMES
C. FMELAS D. FALEMS
E. FEMALS

EXPLANATORY ANSWERS

EXERCISE - 1

1. B:
2. A:
3. A:
4. C:
5. E: Correct answer is MDBJIL.
6. B:
7. B:
8. E: The correct answer is MDBJIL.
9. E: The correct answer is DIMWS.
10. C:
11. B:
12. C:
13. A:
14. C:

(Explanation for 15 to 24): On writing correct code against the words in column I, we find the following order of words and the codes in which the codes in column II appear in the same order as in column I.

15. C: BID	lwz
16. B: BAT	lev
17. A: BAD	lez
18. C: VEX	smk
19. B: HILL	rmnn
20. D: PORK	xtoi
21. C: ROSE	otym
22. B: WAVE	Pesm
23. D: HAZY	rehg
24. C: CHEAP	urmex
25. D: QUOTE	dftvm
26. E: VAGUE	Sedfm
27. E: NAMELY	jeamng
28. B: FAMILLIAR	ceawnweo

29. B:
30. A:
31. C:
32. E:

(Explanation for 33 to 40): On writing correct code against the words in

Column I, we find the following order of words and the codes in which the codes in column II appear in the same order as in column I

Column I	Column II
SOUND	ikmop
ADDRSS	bloopp
CRUX	cjmv
NET	abi
CRONY	ijktv
CROWDY	jkgotv

33. A:

34. B:

35. C:

36. C:

37. D:

38. D:

39. A:

40. B:

41. D:

42. E:

43. C:

44. D:

45. E:

46. C:

47. A:

48. B:

49. C:

50. D:

51. D: According to the new code, value of DCA = 593 meters and value of ADLC as per the old code = 1096 meters. Therefore distance between Leopard and zebra posts = 593 meters and distance between the Tiger and Zebra posts = 1096 meters.

∴ Distance between Tiger and Leopard posts = 1096 – 593 = 503 meters. Now on converting 503 into new codes, we find this distance as DHA

52. A:

53. B:

54. C: On converting DGIAH meters into numerical values according to the old code, height of the Tiger post from the sea level = 03817 meters. New code for 03817 is HAIGR. Therefore alternative C is the correct answer.

55. E: According to the old code distance between 'Fox' and 'Lion' Posts = RDNH meters = 4027 m. New Code for 4027 = NHLR. Therefore 'E' is the correct answer.

56. E:

57. C:

58. E:

59. A:

60. D:

EXERCISE - 2

1. D: In 1st and 2nd codes 'Tim' stands for shirt. In 2nd and 3rd code 'Pit' stands for Pant. Therefore, it is clear that 'mit' stands for 'And'.

2. B: In 1st and 3rd codes, 6 stands for 'you'.

3. C: From (3) and (4) it is clear that "gaw" starts for 'Sea' and from (1) and (3) it is clear that 'Cil' stands for 'Big'. Therefore it is clear that 'mere' stands for 'River' in the given code language.

4. A: On comparing first and second sentences we find that 3 = hot. Comparison of second and third sentences reveals that 5 = day.

and comparison of first and third sentences reveals that 6 = very.

5. E:

1. Kew Xas Kuna deke
↓
She is eating apples
2. kew tepo qua
↓
she sells toys
3. Sut Lim deke
↓
I like apples

From 1st and 2nd it is clear that 'kew' stands for 'she' and from 1st and 3rd sentences it is clear that 'deke' stands for apples.

6. C:

1. Lim tok pur
↓
sour red apple
2. tok tuk pa
↓
apple is sweet
3. top tok pa mob
↓
Ram is eating apple

Comparison of above 1 and 2 reveals that in the code language 'tok' is used for 'apple' and that of 2 and 3 suggests that 'pa' of the code language is used for 'is'. Therefore 'tuk' stands for 'sweet'. So alternative 'C' is the correct answer.

7. B:

1. Pe sa de ni
↓
Yes well no mean
2. Pa ni sa de
↓
sell mean well no

In both the sentences we find 'well no mean' and the codes 'Sa de ni'. Therefore in the 1st sentence 'pe' stands for yes.
So alternative (B) is the correct answer.

8. D:

1. 247
↓
Beautiful white Rose
2. 652
↓
Beautiful green bottle
3. 423
↓
Beautiful yellow Rose.

From 1 and 2 above, it is clear that 2 stands for 'Beautiful' and from 1 and 3 above it is clear that 3 stands for 'yellow'. Therefore 'D'is the correct alternative.

9. C: From 1st and 2nd statements
Some are = 2 + 3 ... (i)
From 1st, 2nd and 3rd statements,
Some = 3 ... (ii)
From (I) and (II) above,
are = 2
Therefore 'C' is the correct answer.

10. A: From 1st and 2nd statements it becomes obvious that 'kun' stands for 'Dogs'. From 1st and 3rd statements it is clear that 'tom' stands for 'are'. Therefore 'sud' of the code language stands for barking
Alternative (A) is the correct answer.

11. C: RILL PA = My Dog
PA SE M TA = Dog is Black
PA = Dog

RILL HAK KOP = My Dear Friend
∴ RILL = My
∵ TA KOP = Black friend
KOP = Friend
Therefore,
HAK = Dear
Here alternative (C) is the correct answer.

12. D:
(A) 1 2 3 → tall clever man
(B) 3 4 5 → clever naughty boy
(C) 2 4 6 → boy is tall
From (A) and (B), it is clear that "3" stands for "clever". Comparison of (A) and (C) reveals that "2" stands for "tall" and comparison of (B) and (C) reveals that 4 is the code for boy.
Therefore '5' is the digit in the code language which stands for 'naughty'. Alternative 'D' is the correct answer.

13. E: On comparison of (1) and (2) we find that 'yera' is the code word for 'unknown'. Similarly, comparison of (2) and (3) reveals that code word for 'tall' is 'la'.
Therefore 'pes' is the code word for 'and'.

14. C: Comparison of DRAIN and GRADE and their number codes reveals that 0 is the number code for D.

15. B: 1st and 2nd statements reveal that 'po kin' means 'is drinking'. Comparison of 1st and 3rd statements reveals that 'Kin' stands for 'drinking'.
∴ 'po' means 'is'
From 1st and 4th statement, it is clear that 'lim' stands for 'milk'. From 2nd and 4th statements, it is clear that 'la' means 'maza'.
∴ 'het' stants for 'Sunil'.

16. C: In all the three given sentences 'Her' and 'is' are common. Similarly in the sentences of the Code language 'Cinto' and 'tsi' are common. Therefore, it is clear that 'Cinto' and 'tsi' have been used for 'Her' and 'is'. In the second and third sentences 'Literature' is common for which a common code 'Oind' has been used.
Therefore, alternative 'C' is the correct answer.

(Explanation for 17 to 21): For the sentences given from 1-6.

Code	Expression
Hari	Kivi
Home	doom
School	saman
Ram	waei
goes	auro
is	si
your	tressa
name	heither
what	van
friend	jim

17. E:
18. D:
19. A:
20. E:
21. C:

22. B: From first and second sentences:
Sau → Doctor
From second and third sentences:
ting → Rajesh
Therefore in the second sentences, 'pau' of the code language has been used to indicate 'is'.

Alternative 'B' is the correct answer

23. C:-

24. D: Comparison of (1) and (3) reveals that in the code language 'D' has been used to indicate Dogs.

Similarly comparison of (1) and (2) shows that 'L' has been used for Mad. Therefore I has been used for 'are', C has been used for 'Remove' and 'K' has been used for bad.

EXERCISE - 3

1. C: The word is coded by moving the letters at the odd positions one step backward. In the same manner code for SANJIV will be RAMJHV. Here first letter of the code is R. Therefore alternative 'C' is the correct answer.

2. E: The letters of the word is written backward to form the code word
MOHAN → NAHAM
KARIM → MIRAK
Therefore AK will be last two letters of the code for KARIM.
E is the correct answer.

3. B: The code is formed by moving the letters one step backward and one step forward alternately.

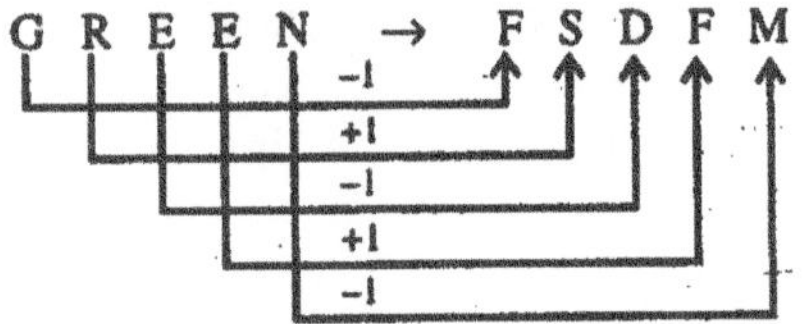

Similarly,

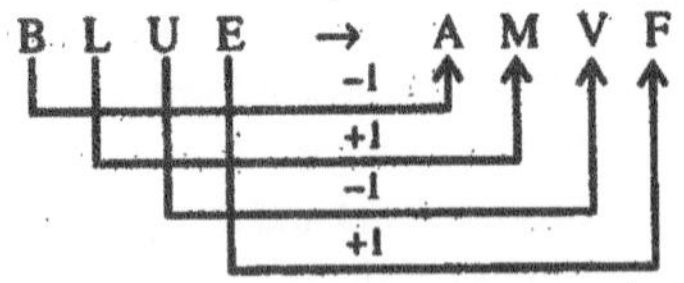

Code word for BLUE is AMVF. Its last letter is F. Therefore alternative 'B' is the correct answer.

4. C: First and the last letters of the given word are three steps behind the corresponding letters the word in code language.

5. B: First letter of the given word comes exactly before the first two letters of the code word and last letter of the given word comes exactly before the last two letters of the code word.

6. A: The code is formed by moving the letters one step backward and one step forward alternatly.

7. A: The last letter of the word written for ACNP, *i.e.*, L is four steps behind the corresponding letter in the given word. Therefore last letter of the word written for CINPQSRTG will be four steps behind G. *i.e.*, the answer will be C. Therefore alternative 'A' is the correct answer.

8. C: Last two letters of the code word come next to the last letter of the given word. (*i.e.*, YZ of the code word follow X of the given word BOX).

9. B: The word is coded by moving the letters two steps backward.

10. D: The word is coded by moving only the letters at odd positions

one step forward and one step backward alternately.

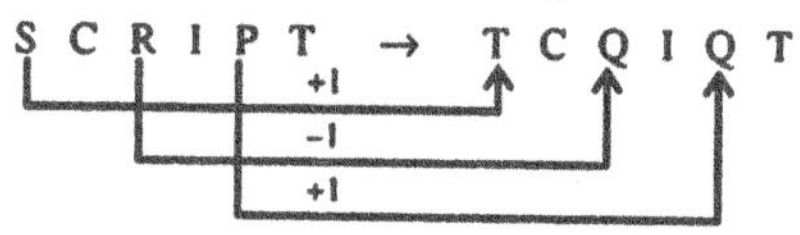

Similarly,

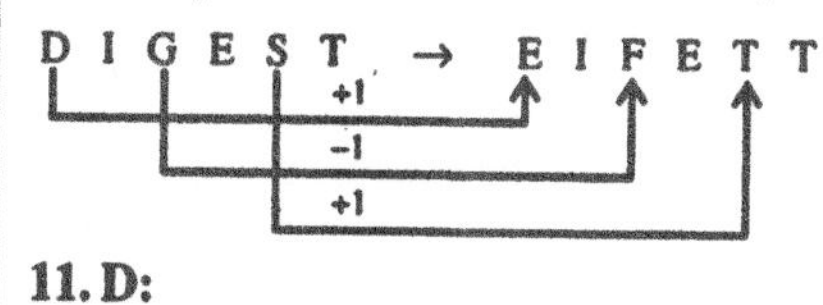

11. D:

EXERCISE - 4

1. C: SENT = + ÷ × −
and ANT = * × −
∴ S = +
E = ÷
N = ×
and T = −
∴ TEN = − ÷ ×

2. E: 1. W → T, B → E, Z → N
2. X → R, U → U, Z → N
3. Y → L, D → A, W → T, B → E
∴ ZDWUXDY → NATURAL

3. B: 1. M → Z, A → C, T → W
2. O → X, U → Y, T → W
3. N → V, I → Q, B → S
∴ MOUNTAIN → ZXYVWCQV

4. A: Fishes swim in 'water' and 'water' is called 'colour'.

5. D: The letters of the word are coded by their represented letters in the reverse series.

6. B: The word is divided into two equal parts and then the letters of each part are written backwards.

7. E: Three letters are missing in between G and C and there is a difference of 8 between their representative numbers (*i.e.*, 39 and 47).
Hence 8 = 2n+2 (where n = number of letters missing)
Since 14 letters are missing in between C and R, so difference of digits 2n+2 = 2×14+2 = 30
Therefore 17 will come at the place of first blank space.
Similarly on substituting the difference between F and Y *i.e.*, 18.
2n + 2 = 2 × 18 + 2 = 38
Now 41 − 38 = 3. Therefore 3 will be substituted at the second blank space.
17, 3 is the answer.
Therefore alternative E is the correct answer.

8. C: Six letters are missing in between S and L whereas difference of 12 exists in between the numbers. Since there is a difference of 5 between L and F, so diference of 10 exists between 28 and the number at the blank space. Therefore 18 should come at the first blank space.
In the next column five letters are missing in between P and V and difference of numbers is 10. Again five letters are missing in between P and J and difference of numbers should again be 10. Therefore 30 should be placed in place of second blank space. Hence, alternative C is the correct answer.

9. D: No letter is missing in between P and Q but difference of numbers is 2. One letter is missing in between V and X and difference of numbers is 4. Similarly one letter is missing in between G and 1. Therefore there should be a difference of 4 in between the numbers at blank spaces. We find the first number greater than the second number is previous two lines, therefore 18, 14 is the correct answer.

10. E: In the alphabetic series, H is at the 8th position. The number beside H bears the relationship of 2n–1 where n is the number of place of H in the alphabetic series. Therefore 3 will be placed at the blank space beside 'B'. Similarly 7 will be placed at the blank space beside D.

11. C: One letter has been dropped in between B and D and one number has been dropped in between 6 and 8. Two letters have been dropped in between J and M and in between 14 and 17 two number have been dropped. Now 7 letters have been dropped in between B and J and 7 numbers have been dropped in between 6 and 14. As 3 letters have been dropped in between J and N, so 3 numbers will be dropped in between 14 and the number at the place of blank space. Therefore 18 should come at the place of 1st blank space. As 4 letters have been dropped in between N and S, so 4 numbers should also be dropped in between 18 and the number at the second blank space. Therefore number at the second blank space should 23.
Hence, answer is 18, 23.

12. A: From the given words and the codes we find that:
B = 2, R = 0, E = 9, A = 1, S = 8 and T = 7.
∴ BREAST will be written as 209187 in the said code language.

13. B: I is common in BILL and DIG
∴ Number Code for I = 4
L is being repeated in BILL so is 6 being repeated in the number code for BILL
Therefore L = 6
∴ B = 2
Apart from this, number codes have been arranged in the same order as that of the words. Therefore,
U = 9
N = 7
D = 3
G = 5
BUILDING → 29463475

14. D: T is the 20th letter in the alphabet.
∴ TOM = 20 + 15 + 13 = 48
and DICK = 4 + 9 + 3 + 11 = 27
∴ HARRY = 8+1+18+18+25=70

15. B:

16. C: B is the 2nd, F is the 6th and H is the 8th letter in the alphabet.
If we assume that,
B = 2, then F = 6 and H = 8
∴ H + B + F = 8 + 2 + 6 = 16

EXERCISE - 5

1. B: The word is coded by moving the letters 3, 4, 4 and 2 steps backward respectively. Therefore the word LIFE will be coded as IEBC. Alternative 'B' is the correct answer.

2. C: The word is coded by moving the letters one step forward and one step backward alternately.

3. C: The word is coded by moving the letters –2, +4, –3 and +5 steps repsectively.

4. A: The coded word is deciphered by moving the letters two steps backward and three steps forward alternately.

5. E: While encoding, positions of the first and last letters of the given word are kept unchanged but on the contrary rest of the letters are divided into sections of two letters and then the places of the letters in the each section are interchanged.

6. C: The word is divided into three sections containing two letters each and then the letters present in between each section are picked up to form the word in the given code language.

7. B: The word is coded by writing two letter in consecutive order after each of the four letters present in the given word.

L O V E — Given word
MN PQ WX FG — Coded word

Similarly,

IJ BC UV FG will denote:
H A T E

Therefore alternative 'B' is the correct answer.

8. C: The letters of the coded word are deciphered by moving one step forward and one step backward alternately.

9. E: Letters of the code word MPKHG are moved two steps backward to represent KNIFE. Similarly letters of the code DTGCF are moved two steps backward:

CODE	:	M P K H G
Deciphered letters	:	K N I F E
Similarly, CODE	:	D T G C F
and deciphered letters	:	B R E A D

Therefore alternative E is the correct answer.

10. D: In the given code language POCY in the code for SKEW.

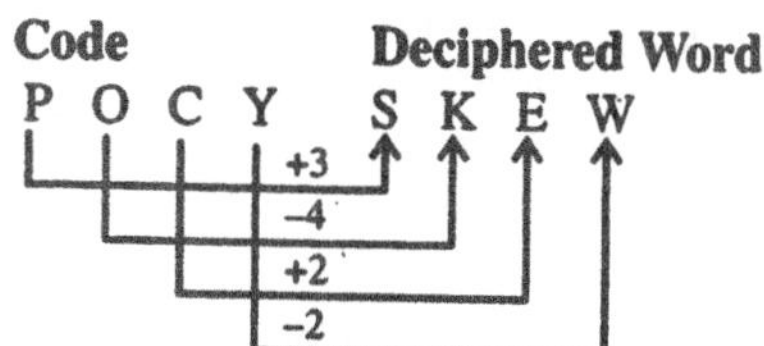

Similarly,

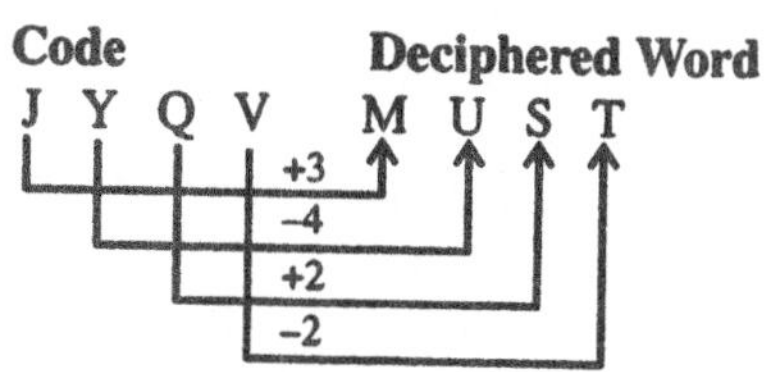

Therefore, alternative D is the correct answer.

EXERCISE - 6

1. C: The letters of the word are coded by moving the letters one step backward.

2. A: While encoding, letters of the given word are moved forward by increasing steps starting from two.

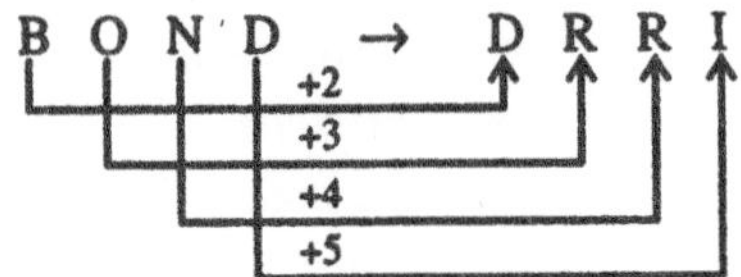

Similarly,

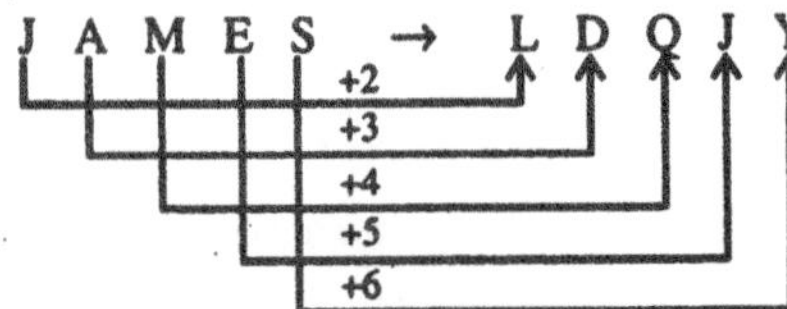

3. C: Each letter of the coded words are three steps behind the corresponding letter in the words of the original language.

4. D: The letters of the word are coded by moving the letters one step backward.

5. C: The letters of the word are coded by moving the letters two steps forward.

6. D: The letters of the code YZW are deciphered by their represented letters in the reverse alphabetic order.

letters of the code word	Y	Z	B
Letters of the deciphered word	B ↓	a ↓	d ↓
Position of the letters in natural and in reverse alphabetic order	2nd	1st	4th

Similarly,

		Position of the letters in natural and in reverse alphabetic order
Z →	A →	1st
X →	c →	3rd
V →	e →	5th

7. B: The word is decoded by moving the letters one step backward.

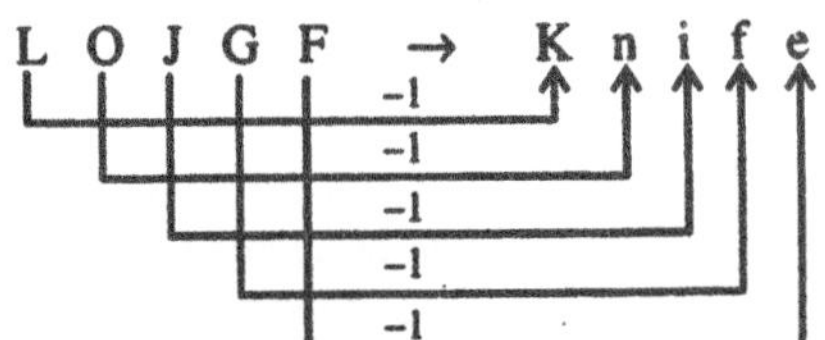

Similarly,

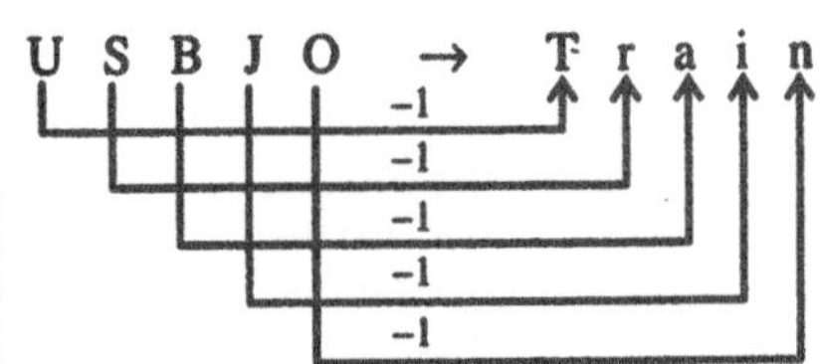

8. D:

9. A:

10. C:

11. B: Word in the code language is framed by moving the letters two steps backward.

12. D: The words are coded as:

ENGLAND FRANCE
1 2 3 4 5 2 6 7 8 5 2 9 1

It is clear that code for G is 3, for R is 8, for E is 1 and for C is 9.

Therefore, code for GREECE is 381191. So alternative D is the correct answer.

13. C: The word is divided into two sections containing three letters each. In these sections the first group contains the group of letters COU and the second group contains the group of letters A G E. The middle positioned letter R is left ungrouped. Then letters at odd numbered positions in each group interchange their places. Once again the middle positioned R in the word COURAGE is left unaltered. Thus in the given code language, we find the alternative 'C' as the correct answer.

14. D: The letters of the code word of 'BRIDE', *i.e.*, EULGH is written by moving the letters of the word BRIDE three steps forward

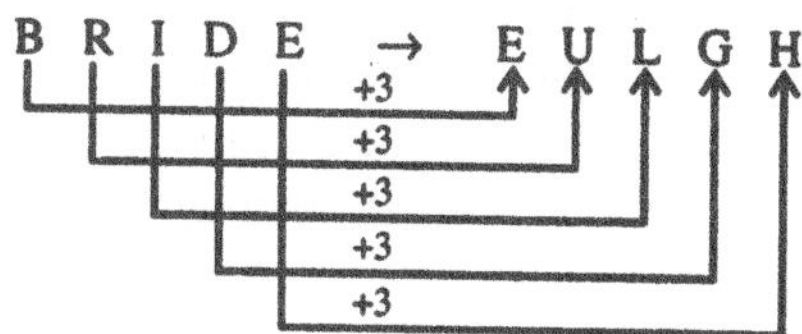

Similarly,

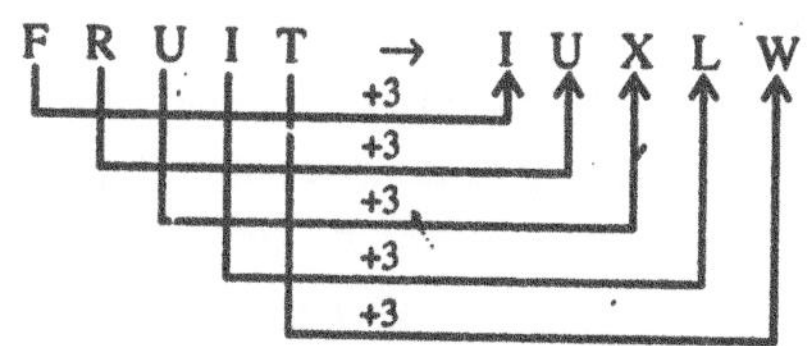

15. B:

16. B: From the given word and its code, we find that

N → L

U → W

T → Q

Therefore NUT will be coded as LWQ.

17. C: Letters → H A P P Y

Number codes → 5 1 2 2 3

Here code for P = 2

Code for A = 1

Code for H = 5

Code for Y = 3

Therefore PAHPY will be coded as 2 1 5 2 3.

18. A: Letters → W E A K N E S S

Number Codes → 1 5 3 4 2 5 6 6

Therefore, A N E S W E S K will be coded as 3 2 5 6 1 5 6 4.

19. D: Code for H is 2

Code for O is 3

Code for N is 0

Code for E is 4

Code for S is 5

Code for T is 1

Code for Y is 6

Therefore, code for NEHSOYT will be 0425361.

20. A: Letters: Y E S T E R D A Y

Number code: 5 3 7 6 3 4 2 0 5

Therefore, number code for STARYEDYE will be : 7 6 0 4 5 3 2 5 3

21. : Letters: M A R R I A G E

Number code: 5 3 2 2 0 3 4 1

Therefore, number code for AGRAM EGIR will be : 3 4 2 3 5 1 4 0 2

22. A: Letters: P O I N T E D

Number code: 5 2 1 3 6 4 7

Therefore, number code for T I P O N D E will be : 6 1 5 2 3 7 4.

23. C: Letters: PUNCTUALITY
Codes: 2354637186 0
Therefore number code for TULIPUNCTAY will be: 6318235467 0

24. A: Letters: REGULARITY
Codes: 2357982460
Therefore number code for TRLGREUAIY will be : 6295237840

25. D: Letters: DAUGHTER
Codes: 5 1 4 2 6 3 7 8
Therefore number code for GRAUDEHT will be : 28145763

26. B: Letters: ENGLISH
Number Codes: 2 3 5 7 9 6 4
Therefore number code for ISHNGEL will be : 9643527

27. D: The letters of the word are coded by moving the letters three steps backward

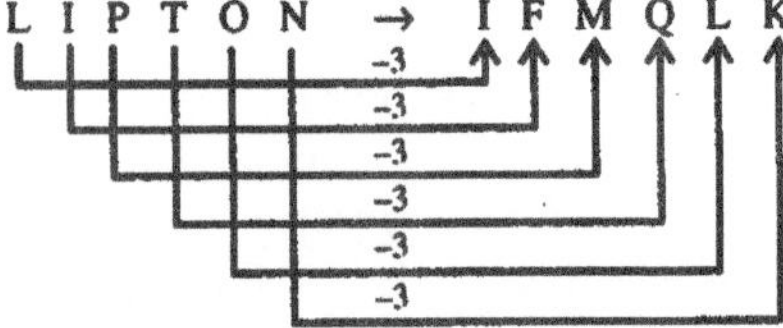

Similarly,

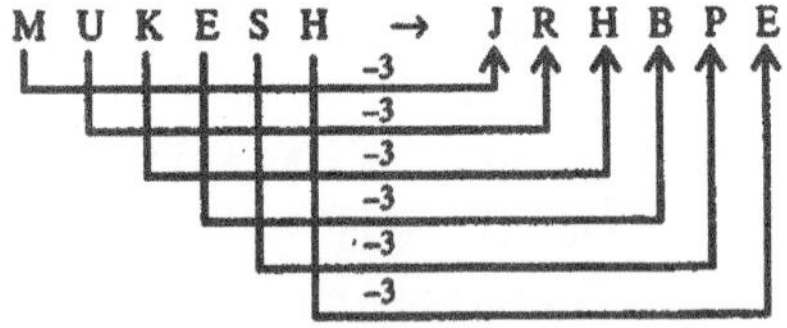

28. B: The letters of the word are coded by their represented letters in the natural alphabetic order.
Letters of the word UMESH when positioned in reverse alphabetic order:

U → 6th position
M → 14th position
E → 22nd position
S → 8th position
H → 19th position

In natural alphabetic order letter codes according to the above positions:

6th positioned letter → F
14th positioned letter → N
22nd positioned letter → V
8th positioned letter → H
19th positioned letter → S

Similarly, letters of the word POT when positioned in reverse alphabetic order:

P → 11th position
O → 12th position
T → 7th position

In natural alphabetic order letter codes according to the above positions will be:

11th positioned letter : K
12th positioned letter : L
7th positioned letter : G

Therefore alternative 'B' is the correct answer.

29. C: In the code word, letters of the original word have been written in reverse order.

30. D: The word is divided into two equal sections containing three letters each and then the letters in each section are written backward.

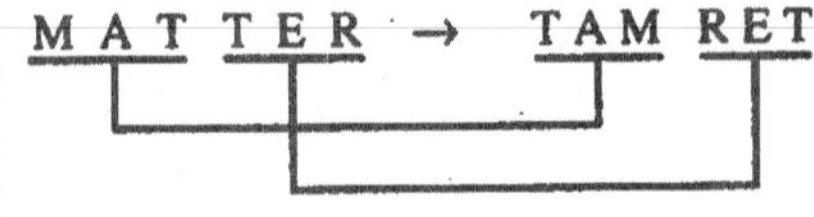

Similarly,

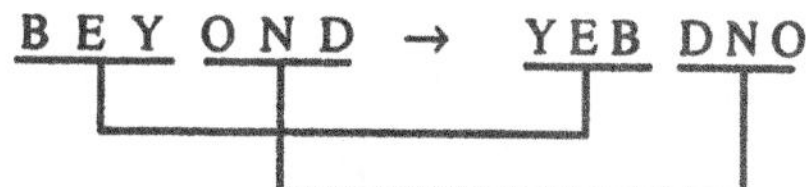

31. C: The code for the given word GOLDEN is formed by writing only the even positioned letters in consecutive order first and then the odd positioned letters again in consecutive order.

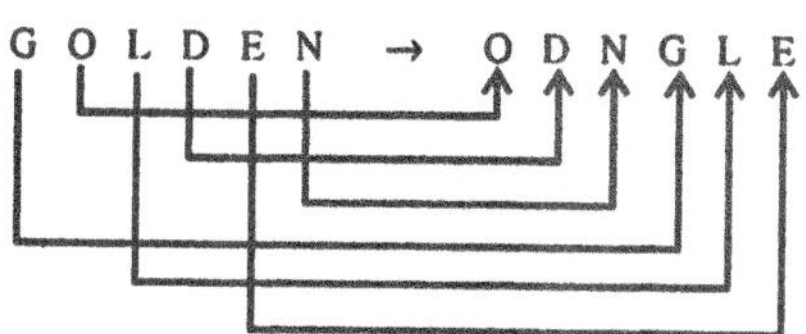

Similarly,

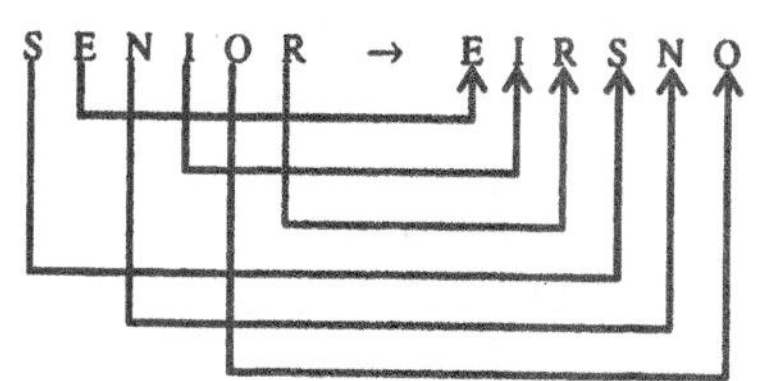

32. C: The word is divided into two equal sections containing three letters each and then the letters in each section are written backwards.

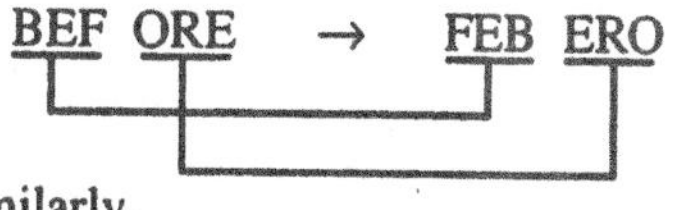

Similarly,

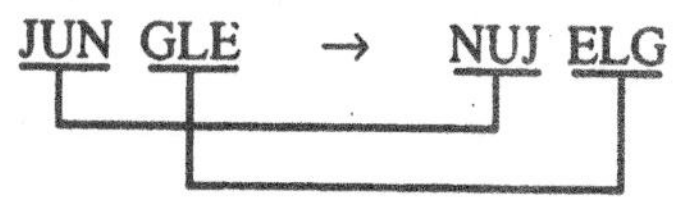

33. D: The word is divided into sections containing two letters each and then the letters in each section are written backward.

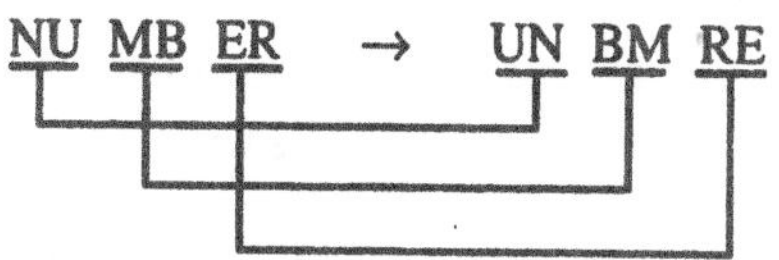

Similarly,

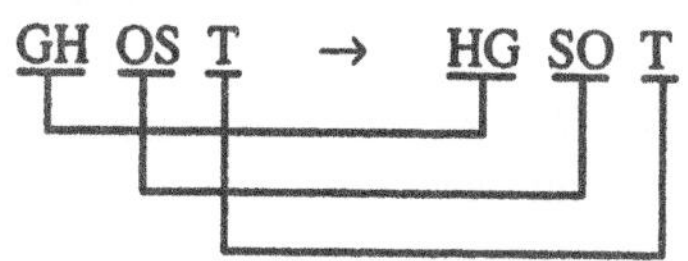

34. E: The letters of the given word B E A T are coded by their represented letters in the reverse alphabetic order.

B E A T → Letters in natural order
Y V Z G → Letters in reverse order
↓ ↓ ↓ ↓
2nd 5th 1st 7th

Similarly,

M I L D → Letters in natural order
13th 9th 12th 4th
N R O W → Letters in reverse order

35. C: The letters of the given word BACK are coded by their represented letters in the reverse alphabetic order.

B A C K → Letters in natural order
Y Z X P → Letters in reverse order
↓ ↓ ↓ ↓
2nd 1st 3rd 11th

Similarly,

S A N D → Letters in natural order
19th 1st 14th 4th
H Z M W → Letters in reverse order

Therefore, alternative 'C' is the correct answer.

36. A: The letters of the given word HAND are coded by their represented letters in the reverse alphabetic order.

H A N D → Letters in natural order

S Z M W → Letters in reverse order

↓ ↓ ↓ ↓

8th 1st 14th 4th

Similarly,

M I L K → Letters in natural order

13th 9th 12th 11th

N R O P → Letters in reverse order

37. B: The letters of the given word G A M E are coded by their represented letters in the reverse alphabetic order.

G A M E → Letters in natural order

T Z N V → Letters in reverse order

↓ ↓ ↓ ↓

7th 1st 13th 5th

Similarly,

B O S S → Letters in natural order

2nd 15th 19th 19th

Y L H H → Letters in reverse order

Therefore alternative 'B' is the correct answer.

38. E: The word is coded by moving the letters one step forwad and one step backward alternately.

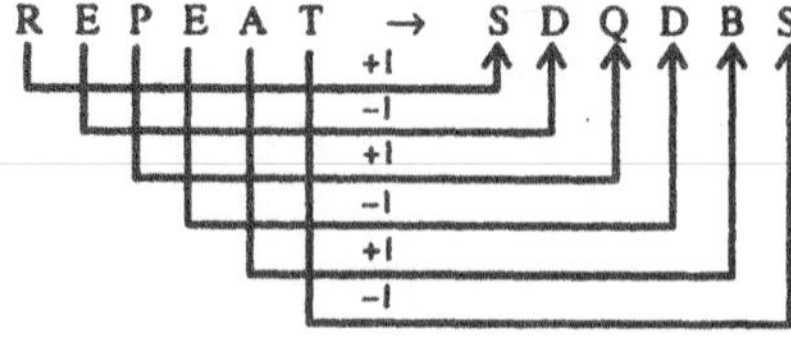

Similarly,

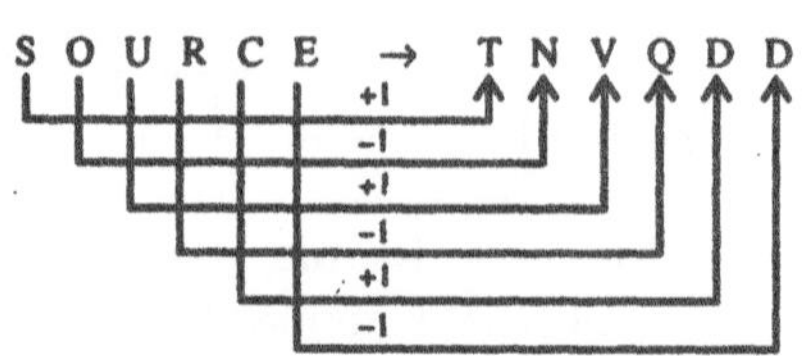

39.C: The first letter of the code GRDJNK, *i.e.*, G is one step behind the last letter of the given word LOKESH. This pattern is followed while encoding the word, *i.e.*, every consecutive letter of the code word is one step behind its corresponding letter of the given word in reverse order. Therefore alternative C is the correct answer.

40. A: In the given word G A M A the repeated letter is A and so code for A is 3. It means either 2 or 5 has been used for G or for M. Therefore in the number code of ARM 3 and either of the 2 and 5 and a third new number should be used. Only 573 is such a code. Therefore alternative 'A' is the correct answer.

41. D: The letters of the word CGZ are coded by their represented letters in reverse alphabetic order.

C G Z → Letters in natural order

X T A → Letters in reverse order

↓ ↓ ↓

3rd 7th 1st

Similarly,

D F P → Letters in natural order

4th 6th 16th

W U K → Letters in reverse order

Therefore 'D' is the correct alternative.

42. E: The word is coded by putting 1st, 2nd, 3rd, 4th and 5th letters of the given word TEACHING at the 5th, 3rd, 4th, 1st and 2nd positions respectively in the code word CHEATING. Positions of the remaining letters of the given word TEACHING remaining unchanged.

43. C: The word is coded by moving the letters one step forward and backward alternately.

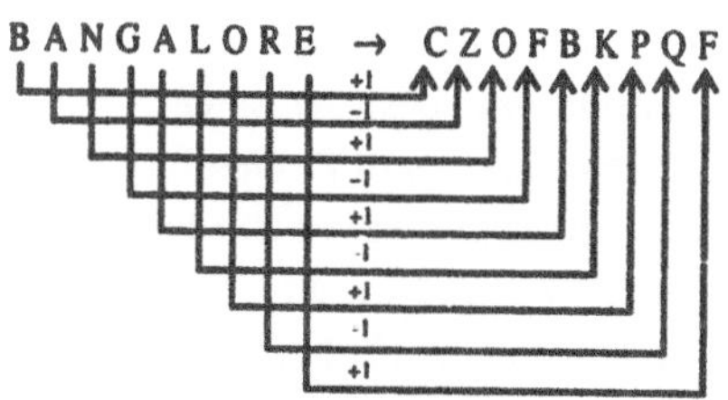

Similarly,

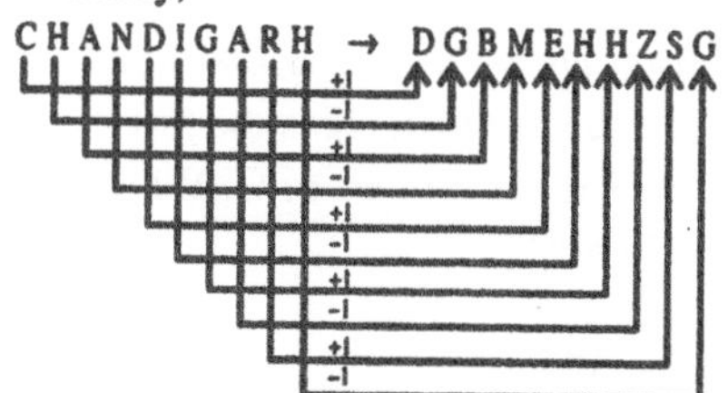

44. D: The word is coded by moving the letters one step forward.

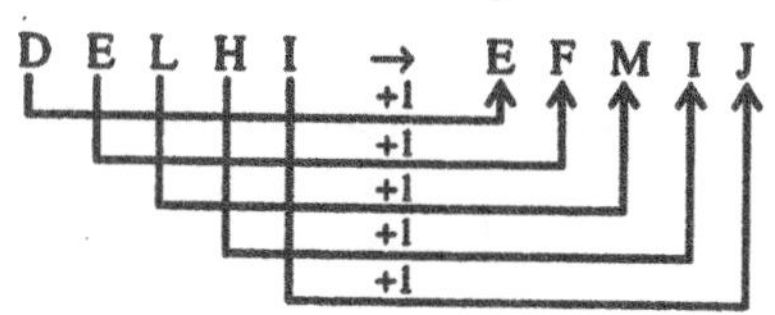

Similarly,

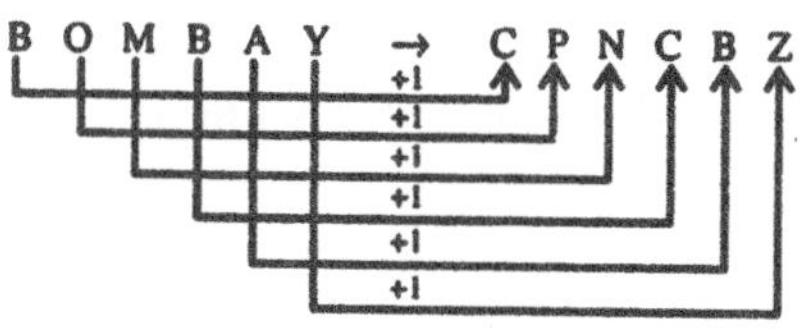

45. E: The letters of the word is coded by moving the letters two steps forward.

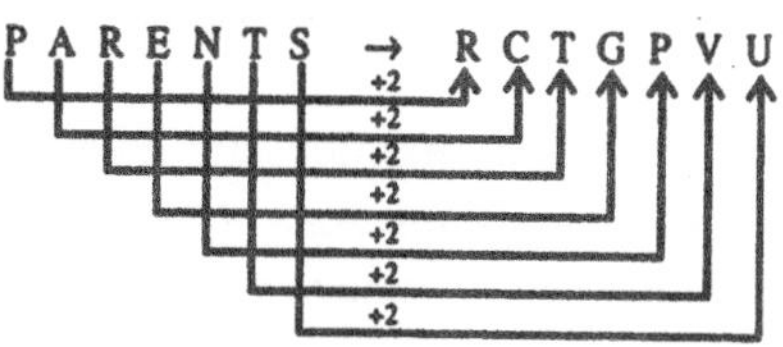

Similarly,

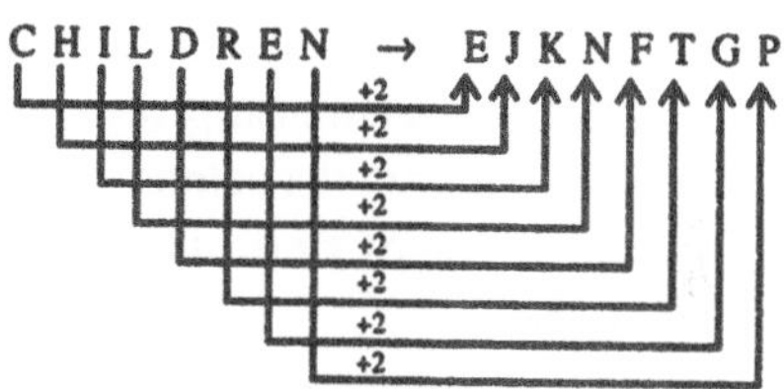

Therefore alternative E is the correct answer.

46. C: In the code word positions of first and last letters of the given word are kept unaltered while the remaining intermediate letters of the given word are divided into sections containing two letters each and then the sections are written in reverse order.

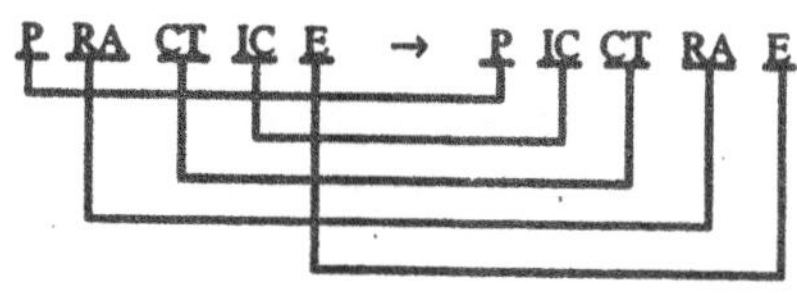

Similarly,

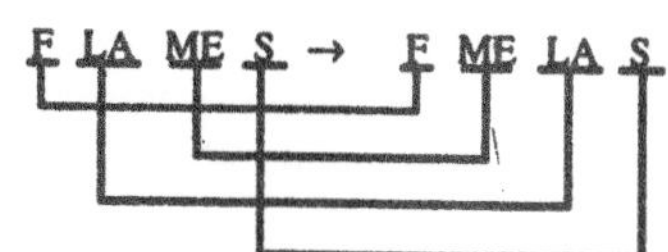

Therefore alternative 'C' is the correct answer.

6

TEST ON BLOOD RELATIONSHIP

In this section, questions are asked on blood relationships. As a person living in family and in society, we are related with our kiths and kins through a chain of relationships. This test aims at testing the candidate's ability to comprehend or establish the relationship between the two persons with the help of rather complicated set of definitions and explanations.

Example 1: A is the son of C. C is the sister of Q. Z is the mother of Q. If P is the son of Z, then which of the following statements is correct?

A. P is the cousin brother of A
B. P is the maternal uncle of A.
C. Q is the grandfather of A.
D. Z is the brother of C.
E. C is the sister of P.

Explanatory Answer (B): C is the sister of Q and A is the son of C. Therefore C is the mother of A and Q is the maternal aunt of A. Now Z is the mother of Q. Therefore Z is the maternal grandmother of A.

Since P is the son of Z, therefore P is the maternal uncle of A. Hence, from amongst the alternative given above (B) is the correct statement.

Example 2: X and Y both are children of Z. If Z is the father of X but Y is not the son of Z, then what is the relationship between Y and Z.

A. Daughter — Father
B. Sister — Brother
C. Niece — Maternal Uncle
D. Uncl — Niece
E. None of the above

Explanatory Answer: Since X and Y both are children of Z, therefore X and Y are either sons or son and daughter or daughters of Z. Now it is given that Y is not the son of Z, hence she is the daughter of Z. Therefore alternative A is the correct answer.

Example 3: F is the brother of A, C is the daughter of A, K is the sister of F and G is the brother of C. Who is the uncle of G?

A. K
B. C
C. A
D. F
E. None of the above

Explanatory Answer: G is the brother of C and C is the daughter of A, so G is the son of A. F is the brother of A, so F is either the uncle or the maternal uncle of G. Since we have to establish the relationship of uncle - nephew, therefore it is clear that F is the uncle of G.

EXERCISE

1. If A * B means 'A' is the mother of 'B' and A × B means 'A' is the husband of 'B', then which of the following would mean 'P' is the father of 'Q'?

A. Q * P B. QM × P
C. P * Q D. P × M * Q

2. If son of that old man is the uncle of my son, then how is that old man related to me?

A. Father-in-law
B. Father
C. Brother
D. Grandfather
E. Brother-in-law

3. Three persons are going somewhere. If two of them are fathers and two are sons, then how is the eldest related with the youngest?

A. Grandson
B. Grandfather
C. Father
D. Son

4. A is the brother of B and C. D is the mother of C. E is the father of A. Which of the following is not certainly correct?

A. B is the son of E
B. A is the son of D
C. E is the husband of D
D. None of the above

5. A man said to a lady, "The only sister of your brother is my mother". How is the lady related to the maternal grandmother of that man?

A. Mother-in-law
B. Sister
C. Husband's Sister
D. Mother
E. Daughter

Directions (Qs. 6 to 8): *Read the following statements and answer the questions given below:*

In a family 6 members *viz.*, A, B, C, D, E and F are living together. B is the son of C but C is not the mother of B. A and C are married couple. E is the brother of C. D is the daughter of A and F is the brother of B.

6. How is E related to D?

A. Brother B. Son
C. Uncle D. Father

7. Who is the wife of E?

A. C B. D
C. A D. B
E. None of the above

8. Who is the mother of B?

A. E B. F
C. C D. D
E. A

9. Leela, who is the daughter of Sohan, said to Latika, "Your mother Alka is the younger sister of my father and my father is the third child of Gagan". How is Gagan related to Latika?

A. Maternal grandfather
B. Father-in-law
C. Brother
D. Uncle

Directions (Qs. 10 to 14): *Read the following statement carefully and answer the questions given below.*

There are five men and women sitting on a bench. The dark blue eyed lady sitting at the middle is my mother. The white haired gentleman sitting at left end is my maternal uncle and the lady sitting at the other end has a mole on her nose. This lady is the wife of the gentleman having long sharp nose who is sitting in between the dark blue eyed lady and white haired gentleman. Another lady having scars of small pox on her face, is the younger sister of the lady having dark blue eyes. She is sitting on fifth place. The gentleman having long sharp nose is the son of dark blue eyed lady.

10. How is the lady having mole on her nose related to me?
A. Mother's sister
B. Father's sister
C. Maternal aunt
D. Brother's wife
E. Aunt

11. How is the white haired gentleman sitting at the left end related to the lady having scars of small pox on face?
A. Son-in-law
B. Nephew
C. Husband
D. Son
E. Brother

12. How is the dark blue eyed lady related to the lady having mole on her nose?
A. Mother
B. Aunt
C. Mother-in-law
D. Sister
E. Daughter

13. How is the lady having scars of small pox on face related to the white haired gentleman?
A. Sister
B. Sister-in-law
C. Daughter
D. Daughter-in-law
E. Sister's daughter

14. How is the gentleman having long sharp nose related to the white haired gentleman?
A. Nephew
B. Maternal uncle
C. Father
D. Uncle
E. Brother

15. How is the daughter of the son of the husband of the mother of my mother related to my mother?
A. Grand daughter
B. Sister's daughter
C. Brother's daughter
D. Sister
E. None of these

16. A is the brother of B and C. D is the mother of B. E is the father of A. Which of the following is certainly not correct?
A. B is the brother of C
B. E is the father of C
C. A is the son of E
D. A is the son of D
E. D is the wife of E

17. P+K means P is the sister of K and P × K means P is the brother of K. If P-K means P is the father of K, then which of the following means A is the sister of B's father?
A. $A+P-B$ B. $A+P\times B$
C. $A-P+B$ D. $B-P+A$

18. Pointing to a photograph, Dinesh said, "His father is the only son of my mother". Who is the person in the photograph?

A. Uncle of Dinesh
B. Father of Dinesh
C. Son of Dinesh
D. Brother of Dinesh
E. Dinesh himself

19. K and L are brothers, O and P is a married couple, N is the daughter of K, L is the husband of Q and father of P. If relationship between M and K is that of the mother and the son and O is the son-in-law of L, then what is the relationship between P and M?

A. Grand daughter and Grand-mother
B. Grand son and Grand-mother
C. Grand daughter and Grand-father
D. Daughter-in-law and father-in-law
E. Son and mother

20. Introducing a woman, a man said, "Her mother is the only daughter of my mother-in-law". How is the man related to the woman?

A. Uncle   B. Father
C. Brother   D. Son

21. How is father's sister of the son of my maternal uncle related to me?

A. Aunt
B. Mother's sister
C. Father's sister
D. Sister

22. If the uncle of Mary's father is the grandson of Edward's father and Edward is the only child of his father, then how is Edward related to Mary?

A. Father's elder brother
B. Uncle
C. Great grandfather
D. Grandfather

23. A is the son of X, X and Y are sisters and Z is the mother of Y. If P is the son of Z, then which of the following statements is correct?

A. A is the grand daughter of Z
B. X is the daughter of A and Y is the daughter of Z
C. P is the maternal uncle of A
D. X and Y are cousin sisters

24. Six persons A, B, C, D, E and F are living in a family. C is the wife of D. A is the brother of E's husband B. D is the father and F is the grandfather of A. In this family two are fathers, two are brothers and one is mother. What is the relationship between E and D?

A. Mother –Daughter
B. Wife – Husband
C. Mother – Son
D. Daughter-in-law – Father-in-law
E. None of the above

25. A is the father of B, E is the brother of A and D is the father of A. If C is the sister of B, then how is E related to C?

A. Sister's husband
B. Brother's daughter
C. Nephew
D. Uncle

26. A man said to a lady, "Your only brother's son is my wife's brother". How is this lady related to the man's wife?

A. Mother
B. Sister-in-law

C. Paternal aunt
D. Sister

27. A lady was going somewhere with a boy. On the way they met a man who said to the lady, "What relationship do you have with this boy?" In her reply the lady said, "My maternal uncle is the brother of this boy's maternal uncle's maternal uncle".
How was the lady related to the boy?
A. Elder brother's wife
B. Aunt
C. Mother
D. Wife

28. Pointing to Pooja, Vikram said, "Her father is the son of my maternal aunt". How is Pooja related to Vikram?
A. Cousin brother's daughter
B. Grandmother
C. Cousin sister
D. Sister's daughter

29. Pointing to a lady who had then worn a red coloured saree, another lady dressed in blue coloured saree said, "Her uncle's sister is my son's aunty". How is the lady dressed in blue saree related to the lady who had worn red coloured saree?
A. Mother
B. Maternal grandmother
C. Sister
D. Paternal aunt

30. L is the mother of K and the sister of N. K is the sister of O. If P is the husband of O and N is the husband of M then how is O related to N?
A. Elder brother's wife
B. Maternal uncle's wife
C. Mother's Sister
D. Sister's daughter (Niece)

EXPLANATORY ANSWERS

1. D: P × M means P is husband of M and M * Q means M is the mother of Q. Therefore P × M * Q means P is the father of Q.

2. B: Since son of the old man is uncle of my son, therefore he is my brother. Hence, the old man is my father.

3. B:

4. A: Only this statement is not certainly correct because B is either son or daughter of E.

5. E: Only sister of the lady's brother is the lady herelf. Therefore that man is son of this lady. So this lady is daughter of the maternal grandmother of that man.

6. C: D is the daughter of A and A and C are married couple, so D is daughter of C. Now E is the brother of C, therefore E is the uncle of D.

7. E: C is the father of B, A is the mother of B and D E is the brother of C. F is the brother of B and D is the daughter of A. Therefore none of this family members is wife of E.

8. E: C is the father of B and A is the wife of C. Therefore A is the mother of B.

9. A: Alka is the sister of Sohan and Sohan is the son of Gagan.

Therefore Alka is the daughter of Gagan. Since Latika is the daughter of Alka, therefore Gagan is the maternal grand father of Latika.

Chart for the answer of Qs. 10 to 14

White haired gentleman	Gentleman having long sharp nose	Dark blue eyed lady
↓	↓	↓
Maternal uncle	Brother	Mother
Lady having scars of small pox on her face	Lady with a mole on her nose	
↓	↓	
Mother's Sister	Elder Brother's Wife	

10. D:

11. E:

12. C:

13. A:

14. B:

15. C: My mother's mother is my maternal grand mother. Son of the husband of my mother's mother is my maternal uncle. My maternal uncle's daughter is my mother's brother's daughter.

16. A: All other statements except 'A' are absolutely correct. There is a possibility of being not certainly correct is only about the statement 'A'. Therefore alternative 'A' is the correct choice.

17. A: A + P – B means A is the sister of P and P is the father of B. Therefore only this alternative means that A is the sister of B's father.

18. C: Since mother of Dinesh has only one son, therefore he is that son. Thus the person in photograph is son of Dinesh.

19. A: Relationship is explained in the following diagram:

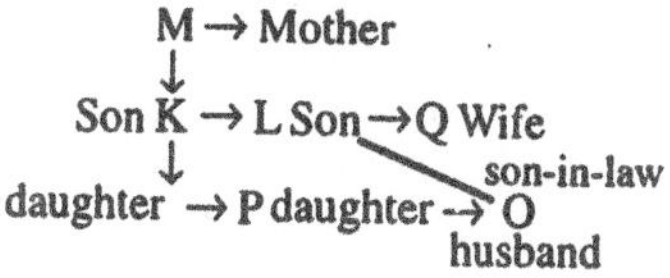

M → Mother
↓
Son K → L Son → Q Wife
↓
daughter → P daughter → O (son-in-law, husband)

20. B: Mother of the woman is the only daughter of that man's mother-in-law. Therefore mother of the woman is that man's wife and that man is the father of the woman.

21. B: Father's sister of the son of maternal uncle is the sister of my maternal uncle. Therefore she is my mother's sister.

22. C: Mary's Grand father is the son of Edward. Therefore Edward is the great grandfather of Mary.

23. C: X is the mother of A
Y is the mother's sister of A and Z is the maternal grandmother of A but P is the son of Z.
Therefore P is the maternal uncle of A.

24. D: In this family A and B are brothers. B is the husband of E. D is the father of B and F is the father of D. Therefore E is the daughter-in-law of D.

25. D: C is the sister of B and A is the father of B. Therefore A is the father of C. E is the brother of A, therefore E is the uncle of C.

26. C: The son of the only brother of

this lady is the brother of the man's wife. Therefore the man's wife is the daughter of this lady's brother and this lady is the paternal aunt of the man's wife.

27. C: As the boy's maternal uncle's maternal uncle is the maternal uncle of this lady, therefore the maternal uncle of the boy is the brother of this lady and this lady is the mother of the boy.

28. A: Pooja's father is the son of Vikram's maternal aunt. Therefore Pooja is Vikram's cousin brother's daughter.

29. D: Uncle's sister of the lady dressed in red coloured saree is the wife of the younger brother of the husband of the lady dressed in blue coloured saree. Therefore the lady dressed in blue coloured saree is the paternal aunt of the lady dressed in red coloured saree.

30. D: L is the mother of K and the sister of N. Therefore N is either the maternal uncle or the maternal aunt of K. But N is the husband of M, therefore it is clear that N is the maternal uncle of K. K is the sister of O and O is the wife of P, therefore N is also the maternal uncle of O. Thus O is the Sister's daughter (Niece) of N.

7
TEST ON ALPHABET

This type of test is based on English alphabet. This test is meant to check the candidate's ability to arrange the jumbled letters in the alphabetic order as is used in a dictionary. So it is necessary to keep in mind the alphabetic series in natural as well as in reverse order.

Example 1: Letters of certain word have been jumbled as SARBS. On rearranging in right order it is the name of a metal. Find that word and choose the first letter of this correct word.

A. S B. R
C. A D. B
E. None of these

Explanatory Answer: On arranging in right order we find the name of a metal, *i.e.*, BRASS. Its first letter is B. Therefore alternative D is the correct answer.

Example 2: If letters of alphabet in reverse order are assigned numerical values beginning from 1 then third letter to the right of sixteenth letter from left will be:

A. J B. H
C. I D. F
E. E

Explanatory Answer (B): In reverse alphabetic order the sixteenth letter from left is K and third letter to the right of K is H. Therefore alternative B is the correct answer.

Example 3: In the following letter series how many letters of M are not preceded by H but followed by R?

H P M X T M R H M R C K M H P T L M R N U S

A. 1 B. 3
C. 4 D. 2
E. None of these

Explanatory Answer (D): Letters of M not preceded by H but followed by R are:

H P M X <u>T M R</u> H M R C K M H P T <u>L M</u> <u>R</u> N U S

There are such two letters of M. Therefore alternative (D) is the correct answer.

Example 4: You have to find out a few names given below in Telephone Directory. Which of them will be in the middle?

A. Shashidharan
B. Sasidharan
C. Shasidharna
D. Shashidaran
E. Shasidaran

Explanatory Answer: Names in the Telephone Directory are given in following order:

A. Sasidharan
B. Shashidaran
C. Shashidharan
D. Shashidaran
E. Shasidharan

In the Telephone Directory name at the middle will be 'Shashidharan'

Therefore alternative 'A' is the correct answer.

Example 5: If there are two such letters in the word DOUBLE which have as many letters between them in the word as in the alphabet, then of them which of the following is the last letter in alphabetic series?

A. D B. E
C. L D. B
E. O

Explanatory Answer: In the word DOUBLE, there are two letters U and B in between O and L. In the alphabetic series M and N are two letters in between O and L. Therefore O and L are the required letters of which O is the last letter in the series.

EXERCISE

1. In the natural order of alphabet the positions of A and B are interchanged. Similarly the positions of C and D are interchanged and so on. Which letter will be 21st from the right end after rearrangement?
   A. D B. V
   C. G D. F
   E. None of these
2. In the alphabetic series which letter is exactly midway between 7th letter from the left end and 8th letter from the right end?
   A. N B. G
   C. M D. L
3. In the following list of letters, how many letters of R are immediately followed by P but not immediately preceded by S?
   SRPRQRSPRPRPORPSTPRO
   A. 1 B. 3
   C. 2 D. 4
4. Which of the following words will be enlisted last in the Dictionary?
   A. Rhythm B. Rollic King
   C. Rumour D. Recite

Directions (Qs. 5 to 14): *In each of the following questions a word followed by four alternatives have been given. You have to find out the word from amongst the alternatives which can not be made by using the letters of the given word as many times as you wish.*

5. ELEMENTRY
   A. MEANLY B. LAMENT
   C. LUMEN D. TERMER
6. FALLACIOUS
   A. FALLS B. FILLS
   C. FAILS D. FILES
7. ARTICULATES
   A. LATER
   B. COURTS
   C. ELECTRIC
   D. ARTICLE
8. UNDERTAKING
   A. DENTER B. DRINKER
   C. TRICKER D. TANKER
9. RAVENOUS
   A. VENER B. NEVER
   C. ROVER D. RIVER
10. EVOLUTION
    A. LOOT B. VALE
    C. VOLT D. TOOL
11. DUTIFUL
    A. TILL B. FLIT
    C. DUTY D. LIFT

12. JERUSALEM

A. MAIL B. SALE

C. EASE D. RULE

13. INTERCORRELATE

A. ENTICE B. ENTRY

C. ENTIRE D. ENTER

14. PRINCIPAL

A. CRAP B. PLAIN

C. PRICE D. PAIL

15. Which of the following words will find place at the middle in Telephone Directory?

A. Peremjibhai

B. Preaajeebhai

C. Premjibhai

D. Premajibhai

16. If there are two such letters in the word TROUBLE which have as many letters between them in the word as in the alphabet, then of them, which of the following letters has been placed first in alphabetic series?

A. U B. R

C. O D. T

E. L

17. If letters of English alphabet are written in reverse order, then which of the following letters will be the 13th to the right of the third letter from the left end?

A. O B. N

C. K D. Q

18. If letters of the alphabet are written in reverse order then which of the following letters will be tenth from the left end?

A. Q B. P

C. J D. R

19. In the following letter series how many letters of y are followed by i but not preceded by x?

y i x y i y x y i i y x i i y i x y i y x y i y i x

A. 8 B. 5

C. 4 D. 7

20. If there are two such letters in the word DPHTLSKC which have as many letters between them in the word as in the alphabet, then of them, which of the following letters is placed first in alphabetic series?

A. T B. K

C. L D. D

Directions: *In each of the questions from 21 to 23, a group of letters has been given. The given group of letters is followed by four alternatives A, B, C and D. Select the one from amongst the alternatives which bears certain relationship with the group of letters given in the question.*

21. MNOR

A. STAB B. KJKL

C. CDFG D. HIJM

22. PRTV

A. KMNO B. RSTV

C. RTVX D. VXYZ

23. JKMN

A. STUN B. EFGH

C. EFHI D. ABCD

24. If small letters of English alphabet are written in reverse order, then which of the following letters will be the fourth letter to the left of fifteenth letter from the right end?

A. d B. r

C. t D. s

25. Which of the following words is

placed at the last in Dictionary?

A. Hair B. Here
C. Heir D. Hare

26. Which of the following words will find place in Dictionary at the last?

A. Opine B. Opium
C. Outer D. Odour

27. If the positions of the first and second letters of the word CONFIGURATION are interchanged; similarly the positions of the third and fourth letters are interchanged and so on, then which of the following letters will be 12th from the left end after rearrangement?

A. I B. C
C. F D. N

28. In the following list of letters, how many letters of y are followed by l, but the letters of l are not followed by x?

y l y x f z y l x z l y l l x f z x y l f y l x l z y l z

A. 7 B. 4
C. 5 D. 6

29. In the following list of letters find the letter which is exactly midway between the tenth letter from right end and the seventh letter from the left end

ABCDEFGHIJKLMNOP QRSTUVWXYZ

A. M B. L
C. N D. K

30. Which of the following is the 18th consonant begining from 2nd consonant in reverse order of English alphabet?

A. C B. K
C. B D. D

31. There are two such letters in the word ROUBLE which have as many letters between them in the word as in the alphabet which of these two letters comes first in the alphabet?

A. O B. R
C. L D. E

32. Given below are names of a few persons. Which of them will find place first in the Dictionary? Shyam Lal, Sohan Lal, Shomesh Lal, Sulochan Lal, Shamim

A. Shyam Lal
B. Sohan Lal
C. Shomesh Lal
D. Shamim

33. There are two such letters in the word DREAM which have as many letters between them in the word as in the alphabet. Which of these two letters comes first in the alphabet?

A. D B. R
C. A D. E

34. If the positions of the first and second letters of the word CORRESPONDENCE are interchanged; similarly the positions of the third and fourth letters are interchanged and so on, then which of the following letters will be 9th from the right end after rearrangement?

A. R B. S
C. O D. E

35. If you are given liberty to use the letters of the word UNDERTAKING as many times as you wish, then how many of the following list of words can you make?

RAKER, INK LING, REDUCE, RATER, KANTER, DRINKER, REDUNT, KINGLE, TAKEN, UNAIMED

A. 7 B. 5
C. 6 D. 4

Directions (Qs. 36 to 46): *In each of the questions from 36 to 46 letters of certain word has been rearranged and jumbled. You are required to arrange them in right order to make a meaningful word.*

36. If rearranged in right order, EABCLRT gives the name of an ornament. First letter of the name of this ornament is:

A. C B. L
C. A D. B

37. If rearranged in right order, we get a meaningful word from jumbled word TRUIEV which is opposite of VICE. What is the last letter of the word formed so?

A. I B. E
C. T D. R

38. On rearranging the letters of word BHENCA in right order, we get the name of a river. Which of the following letters is the third from left end of that river's name?

A. N B. C
C. E D. H

39. On writing the letters of jumbled word TAQUO in right order we find the word which is synonymous to 'SHARE' which of the following is second from left end of that meaninful word so obtained?

A. U B. T
C. Q D. O

40. If letters of PEARESH are rearranged in right order, we find a meaningful word which is synonymous to RECAST. Which of the following will be the letter at the middle in that meaningful word?

A. S B. H
C. E D. A

41. If letters of MVAINSTHA HAPPAK are rearranged in right order, we find the name of a port. Which of the following will be the fourth letter from the right end of that word?

A. A B. H
C. T D. S

42. On rearranging the letters of CHOCCAKOR in right order, we find the name of certain insect. Which of the following will be the fourth letter from left end of that word?

A. O B. A
C. H D. K

43. On rearranging in right order the letters of RVLISE, we find the name of certain metal. Which of the following letters is the second from the last letter of that metal's name?

A. V B. I
C. S D. R
E. E

44. If letters of KHRIRANASDNAH are rearranged in right order, we find the name of a philosopher. Which of the following is the third letter from the left end of that word?

A. S B. I
C. D D. P

45. On rearranging the letters of ATRAASUIL in right order we get the name of a continent. Which of the following is the last letter of that continent's name?

A. S B. I
C. T D. A

46. On rearranging the letters of ENOCNCT we find a word which means 'to joint'. Which of the following letters is the last letter of that word?

A. N B. C
C. E D. O
E. T

Directions: *Select the right option from amongst the alternatives given in each of the following questions.*

47. If the first three letters of the word INTRODUCTION are written in reverse order; similarly next three letters are also written in reverse order and so on, then which of the following will be the ninth letter from the left end of the word so formed?

A. T B. D
C. U D. R

48. If it is possible to make a meaningful word with the third, the fifth, the sixth, the seventh and the eighth letters of the word FOUNDATION, then which of the following will be the first letter of that meaningful meaningful word? If no such word can be made, then give X as the answer.

A. F B. T
C. A D. U

49. If the letters of English alphabet are written in reverse order and then from the left end every second letter of this reverse alphabetic series is removed then which of the following letters will be thrid to the right of eighth letter from the left end?

A. J B. F
C. H D. P
E. L

50. On rearranging the jumbled spelling of the words CIGNELI and OOFR, we get the words which are synonymous to each other. Which of the following pairs of letters suggests the last letters of the two new words so obtained?

A. C, G B. N, F
C. G, F D. R, G

51. In the alphabetic series which letter is the fourth to the right of that letter which is fourteenth from the left end?

A. Q B. S
C. L D. R

52. What will be the 7th letter to the right of 12th letter from the left, if the alphabet series is written in reverse order?

A. J B. G
C. S D. F
E. H

53. If a certain letter is removed from the word FRIEND, then the new word formed is just opposite in meaning to the given word

FRIEND. That letter is:

A. E B. J

C. R D. N

E. F

54. How many such pairs of letters are there in the word PROPORTION that are as many letters apart as they are in the alphabetic series?

A. 1

B. 2

C. 3

D. More than three

E. 0

55. If K denotes 'know', then which of the following will be denoted by H?

A. Hut B. Hour

C. House D. Help

56. If the letters of English alphabet are written in the reverse order, which letter will be 13th from the right end?

A. L B. O

C. M D. N

57. Words in the sentence given below are in the jumbled order. If words of this sentence are re-arranged to convey a meaningful sentence, then which of the words given in alternatives A, B, C and D will come in last?

"Fought all the bravely soldiers battle field in the."

A. Field B. Battle

C. Bravely D. The

58. Four words have been given in the alternatives A, B, C and D. Spelling of these words are not in proper order. If letters of these words are rearranged in correct order, one of them will convey the name of a famous queen of mediaeval India. Which one of the given alternatives suggests that name?

A. JPHANTERO

B. OROJHANAN

C. KORJHENTS

D. ORJHANORE

59. Which of the following is the 8th letter to the left of fourth vowel in the alphabetic series?

A. M B. N

C. G D. H

60. Which of the following letters is the fourth letter to the right of tenth letter of the alphabet starting from the last letter Z.

A. O B. M

C. S D. T

61. If the alphabetic series is written in reverse order, what will be the 8th letter to the right of N?

A. G B. U

C. E D. V

E. F

62. In alphabetic series which of the following is the sixth letter to the right of eleventh letter from C?

A. R B. K

C. T D. S

63. In which of the following groups of letters, the positions of 1st and last letters of the group are identical in natural and reverse alphabetical order respectively and similarly the positions of 2nd letter from the beginning and 2nd letter from the last are also identical?

A. BCWY B. EVOM

C. BCXW D. EMNV

64. In which of the following words, the letters are vowels and consonants alternately?

A. Circular B. Alenot

C. Emulsion D. Violence

65. Which of the following alternatives suggests the correct order of words as is followed in dictionaries?

1. SIGN 2. SOLID
3. SIMPLE 4. SCENE
5. SCIENCE

A. 51432 B. 54132

C. 41532 D. 45132

E. 14532

EXPLANATORY ANSWERS

1. E: After rearrangement we find the following alphabetic series:
B A D C F E H G J I L K N M P O R Q T S V U X W Z Y.
Here 21st letter from the right end is E.

2. C: In the alphabetic series 8th letter from the right end is S and 7th letter from the left end is G. Between G and S there are 11 letters. Therefore sixth letter to the right of G, *i.e.*, M is exactly midway between G and S.

3. B: There are three such letters of R in the given set of letters which indicated below by dark letters:
S R P R Q R S P R P R P O R P S T P R O

4. C:

5. C: In the word ELEMENTRY given in the question, U is not present.

6. D: E is not included in the given word FALLACIOUS.

7. B: O's letter is not included in the given word ARTICULATES.

8. C: C is not present in the given word UNDERTAKING

9. D: In the given word RAVENOUS, I's letter is not present.

10. B: In the given word EVOLUTION, A's letter is not included.

11. C: In the given word DUTIFUL, Y's letter is not included.

12. A: I's letter is not included in the word JERUSALEM.

13. B: Y's letter is not included in the word INTERCORRELATE.

14. C: In the given word PRINCIPAL, E's letter is not included.

15. D:

16. E: The two letters are O and L. There are U and B between O and L in the word and there are M and N between O and L in the alphabetic series. Since L comes before O in the alphabetic series, therefore alternative E is the correct answer.

17. C: In reverse order of the alphabetic series third letter from the left end is X and 13th letter to the right of X is K.

18. A:

19. C:

20. B: Such two letters in the word DPHTLSKC are P and K. There are H, T, L and S four letters in between P and K in the word and alphabet series also, there are four letters L, M, N and O in between P and K. Of these two letters P and K, K is placed first in the alphabetic series.

21. D: First three letters are in consecutive order and two letters have been left in between the third and fourth letters.

22. C:

23. C: One letter is missing in between second and third letters.

24. D: In reverse order series from the right end 15th letter is o and 4th letter to the left of o is s. Therefore alternative 'D' is the correct answer.

25. B:

26. C:

27. B: The positions of letters after interchanging the places of letters in the word CONFIGURATION will be: OCFNGIRUTAOIN. In this 12th letter from the right end is C.

28. C:

29. B: In the alphabetic series, 10th letter from the right end is Q and 7th letter from the left end is G. There are 9 letters in between Q and G in the centre of which is L.

30. A: 2nd consonant in reverse order of alphabet is Y and from Y 18th consonant leaving 4 vowels in route is C.

31. C: Two such letters in the word ROUBLE are O and L between which there are two letters U and B in the word and there are M and N letters between O and L in the alphabetic series. Out of O and L, L comes before O in the alphabetic series.

32. D:

33. C: In the given word DREAM, A and D have R E in the word and BC in the alphabetic series. A comes prior to D in alphabet.

34. D: After making the required changes we get the word OCRRSEOPDNNEEC.

35. C: Raker, Rater, Kanter, Drinker, Redunt and Taken words will be formed.

36. D: Word formed is BRACELET.

37. B: Word formed is VIRTUE.

38. C: Word formed is CHENAB

39. A: Word formed is QUOTA

40. B: Word formed is RESHAPE

41. C: Word formed is VISHAKHAPATNAM.

42. D: Word formed is COCKROACH.

43. E: Word formed is SILVER.

44. C: Word formed is RADHA KRISHNAN

45. D: Word formed is AUSTRALIA

46. E: Word formed is CONNECT.

47. C: Word formed is TNIDORT-CUNOT

48. C: Word formed is AUDIT

49. B:

50. C: The words formed are CEILING and ROOF which are synonymous to each other. The last letters of these two words are G and F respectively.

51. D: In alphabetic series from the left end the 14th letter is N and the 4th letter to the right of N is R.

52. E: In reverse alphabetic order 12th letter from the left end is O and 7th letter to the right of O is H.

53. C: On removing R from the given word FRIEND, we get the word

FIEND. which means an EVIL PERSON. This is opposite in meaning to the given word FRIEND.

54. D: OP, ON, RO, PR are such pairs.

55. B: K is silent in know and H is silent in Hour.

56. C:

57. A: The right sentence is:
"All the soldiers fought bravely in the battle field.

58. B: Name of that queen is NOORJAHAN.

59. C: In the English alphabet vowels are a, e, i, o and u, the fourth voel is O and 8th letter to the left of O is G.

60. D: In alphabetic series, the tenth letter from Z is P and 4th letter to the right of P is T.

61. E:

62. C: Eleventh letter from C is N and sixth letter to the right of N is T.

63. D: E is the 5th from the begining and V is 5th from the last. Similarly M is 13th letter in natural alphabetic series and N is 13th letter in reverse alphabetic series.

64. B: 'Alenot' is the only word in the given alternatives which starts from a vowel and then consonants and vowels follow alternately.

65. D: In dictionaries sequence of words is given as under:

1.	SCENE	(4)
2.	SCIENCE	(5)
3.	SIGN	(1)
4.	SIMPLE	(1)
5.	SOLID	(2)

8

TEST ON ORDER ARRANGEMENT

In this type of questions, a set of information relating to persons, objects or some other entities along with qualities which can be compared is provided. Candidates are required to arrange the given set of information in either ascending or descending order depending upon the relative quality. The questions asked are related either to naturally arranged qualities/attributes or to the size, age or characteristics of the given enumeration. For better understanding of the nature of questions a few examples are given below:

Example 1: Arrange the following words in a logical order:

"Look, Go, Stop"

A. Look, Stop, Go
B. Stop, Go, Look
C. Stop, Look, Go
D. Go, Look, Stop
E. Look, Go, Stop

Explanatory Answer(C): While going across a road, we first stop and then look whether any vehicle is coming towards or not so that no accident could be envisaged. After that we go forward. Therefore the arranged order is Stop, Look, Go.

Example 2: John, Mack, Ganesh, Sunder and Radhey are five boys. John is taller than Sunder and Sunder is taller than Mack. Radhey is taller than John but shorter than Ganesh. Whose height is next to the tallest boy of the group?

A. Sunder B. John
C. Mack D. Ganesh
E. Radhey

Explanatory Answer (E): In the ascending order of their heights, boys can be grouped as: "Mack, Sunder, John, Radhey and Ganesh." Therefore excepting Ganesh, who is tallest, Radhey is tallest amongst the remaining four boys.

EXERCISE

1. Five bus stops A, B, C, D and E are located at equal distances. C is not the bus stop in the middle, A and E are not the bus stop located at one or the other end. While travelling upward number of bus stops between A and B is half the number of bus stops between D and C. If D is the last bus stop in downward journey, then which of the following orders of Bus stops falls in upwards journey?

   A. DEACB B. DACEB
   C. DAECB D. DCBAE

2. If the words given below are arranged according to their order of occurrence then which of the

words given in alternatives will be fourth in the order of occurrence?

Doctor, Game, Recovery, Dressing, Injury, Collide

A. Recovery B. Collide

C. Game D. Doctor

3. Which of the following are the correct order of ranks?

A. Captain, Lieutenant, Major, Lt Colonel, Colonel

B. Lieutenant, Captain, Major, Colonel, Lt. Colonel

C. Lieutenant, Captain, Major, Lt. Colonel, Colonel

D. Lieutenant, Major, Captain, Colonel, Lt. Colonel

E. Lieutenant, Major, Captain, Lt. Colonel, Colonel

4. Which of the following is the correct natural order of the given words?

A. Childhood, Infancy, Adolescence, Pubery, Adulthood

B. Childhood, Infancy, Puberty, Adolescence, Adulthood

C. Childhood, Infancy, Adolescence, Adulthood, Puberty

D. Infancy, Childhood, Adolescence, Puberty, Adulthood

5. From amongst the alternatives given below, select the correct arrangement of words:

A. Believe, Work, Think, Hear

B. Think, Believe, Hear, Work

C. Believe, Think, Hear, Work

D. Beliee, Hear, Think, Work

E. Hear, Think, Believe, Work

6. Which of the following alternatives is the correct order of arrangement?

A. Digest, Cook, chew

B. Cook, Digest, Chew

C. Cook, Chew, Digest

D. Digest, Chew, Cook

7. A, B, C, D and E are five rivers. A is shorter than B but longer than E, C is the longest river. If D is a little bit shorter than B but somewhat longer than A, then which of the following is shorter river?

A. D B. A

C. B D. E

8. Five boys appeared in a competitive examination. Ayush got more marks than Sooraj, Sooraj got more marks than Prateek, Ayush got less marks than Nimesh, Kartik got number in between Ayush and Sooraj. Who among them got maximum marks?

A. Ayush B. Kartik

C. Sooraj D. Prateek

E. Nimesh

9. Out of five villages Phoolpur is smaller in size than Dhanpur. Ambapur is larger in size than Kelapur and Sonapur is largen in size than Dhanpur but it is not equal in size to Kelapur. Which of the following is the smallest village?

A. Kelapur B. Sonapur

C. Phoolpur D. Dhanpur

10. Jim is tall and thin and has white complexion, Anny is short and thin and she also has white complexion. Ramesh is short and fat and he has dark complexion while Nanoo is tall and fat and

has white complexion. Which of the following two boys do not possess any of the two similar characteristics?

A. Ramesh, Nanoo
B. Jim, Ramesh
C. Jim, Anny
D. Jim, Nanoo

11. Of the five girl friends two are younger and two are elder than Deepa. Kajal is youngest, Uma is elder than Nisha and Nisha is younger than Annu and Deepa. Who is the eldest girl?

A. Uma B. Annu
C. Kajal D. Nisha
E. The given information is not sufficient

12. Of the five villages Badgaon is smaller in size than Haldibari, Bhimbari is larger in size than Mohitpur and Ranjanpur is larger in size than Haldibari but it is not as big as Mohitpur. Which of the following is largest in size?

A. Mohitpur B. Ranjanpur
C. Badgaon D. Haldibari
E. Bhimbari

13. Which of the following words comes first if arranged in order?
"College, Home, University, School"

A. School B. University
C. Home D. School

14. Which of the following is the correct order of the words?
"Doctor, Sickness, Medicine, Recovery"

A. Medicine, Recovery, Sickness, Doctor
B. Doctor, Sickness, Medicine, Recovery
C. Recovery, Sickness, Doctor, Medicine
D. Sickness, Doctor, Medicine, Recovery

15. Population of Lucknow is more than Meerut and of Meerut is more than Khurja. But population of Delhi is more than Lucknow. If Vadodara is less populated than Varanasi then which of the following is the least populated?

A. Delhi B. Khurja
C. Lucknow D. Meerut

16. In an examination Swati secured marks equal to Kajal. Meeta secured more marks than Gessu but her marks were less than Swati. Who of the following secured the least marks?

A. Meeta B. Swati
C. Gessu D. Kajal

17. Height of Papaya's plant is less than Jujube plant but more than mango tree. Trees of Mango and custard apple are of same height but heights of these two trees are less than rose-apple tree. Which of the following is the shortest in height?

A. Rose-Apple
B. Jujube
C. Papaya
D. Custard apple

Directions: *Annu is elder to Sanjana, Bhanu is elder to Annu but younger to Deepa. Deepa is elder to Sanjana. Sanjana is younger to Bhanu and Gessu is the eldest of them. Based on this information give answer of the* *questions from 18-19 below.*

18. Who is the youngest of them?

A. Deepa B. Sanjana
C. Bhanu D. Annu

19. If all these children are standing in a row in ascending order of their ages, then who of them will be in the middle?

A. Annu B. Deepa
C. Bhanu D. Sanjana

20. In human body quantity of water is more than fat, plasma is more than protein, water is more than plasma and fat is less than plasma. Quantity of which of the following substances is maximum in human body?

A. Plasma B. Water
C. Fat D. Protein

21. Aman is taller than Somu. Shahid is not as tall as Aman but he is taller than Ashu. Somu also is not as tall as Shahid but he is taller than Ashu. Who is the tallest of them?

A. Aman B. Shahid
C. Somu D. Ashu

22. Of the five districts, Ambegaon is smaller in size than Falpur, Dhanbad is larger in size than Palem and Baulpur is larger than Falpur, but it is not as large as Palem. Which of the following is the largest district?

A. Palem B. Baulpur
C. Falpur D. Dhanbad

23. Arrange the following words in a meaningful order:

1. Sea 2. Stream
3. Ocean 4. River
5. Glacier

A. 54321 B. 54132
C. 54231 D. 53214
E. 52413

24. Shalu is elder than Renu. Prateek's age is equal to Annu's age. Ranee is younger to Somu and Somu's age is equal to Annu's age. Renu is elder than Praveen. Which of the following is the eldest?

A. Ranee B. Annu
C. Shalu D. Prateek
E. Renu

25. Arrange the following five words in a meaningful order:

1. Snake 2. Grass
3. Eagle 4. Frog
5. Insect

A. 32145 B. 52143
C. 25413 D. 24531
E. 24513

26. Gopi is elder than Monu but younger than Raj. Monu is elder than Sonu but younger than Raj. Who of them is the eldest?

A. Monu B. Sonu
C. Raj D. Gopi

27. Arrange the following words in ascending order:

1. State 2. Individual
3. Town 4. District
5. House

A. 1, 2, 3, 4, 5
B. 3, 1, 4, 5, 2
C. 2, 3, 5, 1, 4
D. 1, 5, 3, 4, 2
E. 2, 5, 3, 4, 1

EXPLANATORY ANSWERS

1. A: In upward journey, bus stops fall in the following sequence:

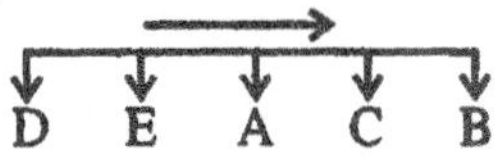

2. D: In the order of occurrence, words may be arranged in the following sequence:
Game, Collide, Injury, Doctor, Dressing, Recovery

3. C:

4. D:

5. E:

6. C:

7. D: The arrangement of rivers according to their length in ascending order is:
E, A, D, B, C

8. E: Name of the candidates in ascending order of marks obtained by them is:
Prateek, Sooraj, Kartik, Ayush, Nimesh.
Therefore Nimesh got maximum marks.

9. C: The arrangement of the villages according to their size in ascending order is as under:
Phoolpur, Dhanpur, Sonapur, Kelapur, Ambapur.

10. B:

	White Complexion	Tall	Thin	Black Complexion	Short	Fat
Jim	✓	✓	✓	×	×	×
Anny	✓	×	✓	×	✓	×
Ramesh	×	×	×	✓	✓	✓
Nanoo	✓	✓	×	×	×	✓

11. E: Given information is not sufficient to arrive at the conclusion.

12. A: The arrangement of the villages according to their size in ascending order is as under:
Badgaon, Haldibari, Ranjanpur, Mohitpur, Bhimbari.

13. C:

14. D:

15. B: Here information abut the population of Vadodara and Varanasi is irrelevant in the question. List of other towns according to their population in descending order is as under:
Delhi, Lucknow, Meerut, Khurja

16. C: The sequence of girls according to marks obtained by them in descending order is as under:
Kajal, Swati, Meeta, Gessu

17. D: Here Papaya's plant is shorter than Jujube's plant but taller than Mango tree. Trees of Mango and Custard apple are of same heights but these are shorter than Rose apple tree. Therefore shortest of these plant are those of Mango and Custard apple. But name of Mango tree is not mentioned in the given alternatives. Therefore Custard apple is correct alternative.

18. B: Sequence of children according to their age in descending order is as under:
Gessu, Deepa, Bhanu, Annu, Sanjana.

19. C:

20. B:

21. A: The sequence of boys according to their heights in descending order is as uner:
Aman > Shahid > Somu > Ashu

22. D: The sequence of districs accoding to their size in descending order is as under:
Dhanbad > Palem > Baulpur > Falpur > Ambegaon.

23. E:

24. C:

25. D:

26. C: The sequence of the children according to their age in ascending order is as under:
Sonu, Monu, Gopi, Raj

27. E:

9

CALENDAR AND/OR TIME TEST

This type of test is based on days of week and/or months of the year. Candidates are required to have a sound knowledge of months of year and days of months or weeks. They should also be prompt in certain types of computations for calculating time by a clock or calendar. At the first look, such questions appear to be quite easy but sometimes these are made a bit complicated by infusing intricacies. Candidates are supposed to be very cautious while attempting these questions. A few examples are given below to explain the intricacies involved.

Example 1: If third day from Sunday in a month is 8th, what will be the day on 17th of that month?

A. Thursday
B. Sunday
C. Wednesday
D. Friday
E. Tuesday

Explanatory Answer (D): Third day from Sunday is Wednesday and it is 8th of that month. Therefore next Wednesday in that month will fall on 15th. So on 17th the day will be Friday.

Example 2: Which of the following years is a "Leap Year"?

A. 1982 B. 1978
C. 1704 D. 1945
E. 1954

Explanatory Answer (C): Of the given years, 1704 is divisible by 4, therefore year 1704 is the leap year.

Some special features about clock:

1. Its long hand indicates minutes and short hand indicates hours.
2. In every hour, the minute hand moves 55 minutes more than hour hand.
3. In every hour, both hands of the clock point towards opposite directions to each other once.
4. In every hour the hands are at right angles twice.
5. When in opposite directions to each other, one hand of the clock remains 30 minutes apart from the other hand,
6. In every minute its long hand turns through an angle of 6° and short hand turns through an angle of 0.5°.
7. In every 12 hours both hands of the clock point 11 times and in every 24 hours 22 times towards the same direction.
8. In every 12 hours the hands are at right angles 22 times.
9. In every one hour both hands of the clock interchange their respective places if minute hand is ahead of the hour hand by 60/13 minutes or any multiple thereof.

Example 3: At what time between 5.00 A.M. and 6.00 A.M. will both hands of the clock point towards the same direction?

A. $5.33 \frac{3}{11}$ A.M.

B. 5.30 A.M.

C. $5.26 \frac{3}{11}$ A.M.

D. $5.27 \frac{3}{11}$ A.M.

E. $5.28 \frac{3}{11}$ A.M.

Explanatory Answer (D): At 5.00 A.M., minute hand is at a distance of 25 minutes from the hour hand.

∴ The minute hand gains 55 minutes in 1 hour, *i.e.*, in 60 minutes

∴ The minute hand will gain 25 minutes in $\frac{60}{55} \times 25 = \frac{300}{11}$

$= 27\frac{3}{11}$ minutes.

Therefore at $5.27 \frac{3}{11}$ A.M. both hands of the clock will point towards the same direction.

EXERCISE

1. On a pleasant day John saw the clock hanging on the wall in a mirror and said to Mary, "It is half past one now". What was the right time then?

   A. 2.30 P.M. B. 6.30 P.M.
   C. 4.30 P.M. D. 6.10 P.M.

2. There are two watches. One of the watches becomes 1 minute fast and another becomes 1 minute slow daily. Both these watches show similar time at sharp 12.00 O'clock at noon on 1st January, 2000. On which of the following day these watches will show similar time again?

   A. Sharp 12.00 O'clock at noon on 28th December, 2000.
   B. Sharp 12.00 O'clock at noon on 27th December, 2000.
   C. 12.00 O'clock at the midnight of 26th December 2000
   D 12.00 O'clock at noon on 25th December, 2000

3. Rahul went from his home for attending tutorial classes between 5.00 P.M. to 6 P.M. and he returned home between 6.00 P.M. to 7 P.M. When he returned home, he noticed that the positions of the minute and hour hands which he had seen at the time of going for attending the classes, had interchanged. At what time had Rahul gone for attending the tutorial classes?

   A. $5\text{-}32\frac{5}{13}$ P.M.

   B. $5\text{-}32 \frac{6}{13}$ P.M.

   C. $5\text{-}32 \frac{4}{13}$ P.M.

   D. $5\text{-}33 \frac{4}{13}$ P.M.

4. At what time between 9 A.M. and 10 A.M. both hands of the clock will be pointing towards opposite directions?

A. $9-17\frac{4}{11}$ A.M.

B. $9-14\frac{4}{11}$ A.M.

C. $9-16\frac{5}{11}$ A.M.

D. $9-16\frac{4}{11}$ A.M.

5. At what time between 6 O'clock and 7.O' clock in the morning both hands of the clock will be pointing towards the same direction?

A $42\frac{8}{11}$ minutes past 6 O'clock

B. $34\frac{8}{11}$ minutes past 6 O'clock

C. $30\frac{8}{11}$ minutes past 6 O'clock

D. $32\frac{5}{11}$ minutes past 6 O'clock

E. $32\frac{8}{11}$ minutes past 6 O'clock

6. What angle will be subtended by the minute hand of a clock in half an hour?
A. 90° B. 120°
C. 180° D. 60°
E. 75°

7. How many times between 4 P.M. to 10 P.M. the hands of a clock will be at right angles?
A. 10 B. 12
C. 9 D. 11
E. 6

8. What will be the measurement of angle between the two hands of a clock at 8.30 P.M.?
A. 70° B. 60°
C. 80° D. 85°
E. 75°

9. A century leap year is divisible by:
A. 100 B. 500
C. 400 D. 300
E. 200

10. John remembers that his brother's birthday will fall on someday between 7 February and 22 February. His brother says that his birthday is the day between 19 February and 24 February. Which of the following is John's brother's birthday?
A. 18 February
B. 22 February
C. 21 February
D. 20 February
E. 19 February

Directions (Qs. 11 to 16): *Read the following letter written by Raghava to his friend. Shubhang carefully and attempt the questions asked below.*

Delhi
4 Feb, 2000

Dear Shubhang,
I received your letter in the evening of 27th January. My heart was filled with joy when I knew that you have been declared fit for appointment by the UPSC. On that day itself I had thought

to write you day after next day on Saturday. But due to some unavoidable engagements, I could not write you. I beg your pardon for the delay. Actually since Wednesday of the last week I was engaged in writing an essay for which the publisher was reminding me time and again. The essay was to be incorporated in the ensuing issue of the magazine for which I write. I could complete the essay in the evening of Sunday, since then I remained engaged in some or other exhaustive work.

I am very happy to know that your uncle is coming to his homeland India with a plan to settle here for ever. He is leaving America on 24th February. You will also be glad to know that I was informed by the Writer's Guild two days before I received your letter that my name has been inclued in the list of the study team which is proposed to go for a study tour to European countries on 21st March. Convey my regards to uncle and aunty. My mummy had gone on a pilgrimage to Rameshwaram. She has returned home day before yesterday.

Yours Sincerely,
Raghava

11. On which date had Raghava started writing the essay?
    A. 24 January
    B. 25 January
    C. 28 January
    D. 27 January
    E. 26 January
12. On which date had Raghava's mother returned home from the pilgrimage to Rameshwaram?
    A. 1 February B. 3 February
    C. 2 February D. 29 January
    E. 30 January
13. On which day did Raghava come to know that his name has been enlisted for the study tour to Europian countries?
    A. Saturday B. Thursday
    C. Tuesday D. Wednesday
    E. Monday
14. On which day the study team is leaving India for a proposed study tour to European countries?
    A. Tuesday B. Friday
    C. Thursday D. Monday
    E. Wednesday
15. On which day is Shubhang's uncle leaving America with a plan to settle in India?
    A. Tuesday B. Thursday
    C. Wednesday D. Saturday
    E. Monday
16. On which day did Raghava receive Shubhang's letter?
    A. Friday B. Tuesday
    C. Thursday D. Monday
    E. Wednesday
17. If the day before yesterday was Friday, then what will be the day after tomorrow?
    A. Wednesday B. Sunday
    C. Tuesday D. Monday
18. Which of the under mentioned years is a Century Leap year?
    A. 1980 B. 1896
    C. 2000 D. 1904
19. Vakul was born on 3 March, 1998 and Rocky is 4 days older than him. That year's Independence Day was celebrated on Saturday.

What is the day of Rocky's birth?
A. Monday B. Tuesday
C. Friday D. Saturday

20. If in a month fourth day after 21st was Saturday, then what was the day on the 3rd of that month?
A. Tuesday B. Friday
C. Wednesday D. Monday
E. Sunday

21. Devanshu was born on 5 March, 1998 and Prayag is 25 days older to Devanshu. That year's Republic Day was celebrated on Monday. What is the day of Prayag's birth?
A. Saturday B. Wednesday
C. Sunday D. Friday
E. Monday

22. If it was Monday on 17 March, 1980 then what was the day on 12 July, 1980?
A. Tuesday B. Wednesday
C. Thursday D. Saturday
E. Monday

23. A Century leap year is divisible by
A. 4 B. 16
C. 40 D. 400
E. None of the above

24. Rinku was born on Sunday, 22 March 1968. On which day of the week his age will be 12 years, 2 months and 4 days?
A. Tuesday B. Sunday
C. Thursday D. Wednesday
E. Friday

25. My brother is 562 days older to me while my sister is 75 weeks older to him. If my sister was born on Tuesday, on which day was I born?
A. Tuesday B. Thursday
C. Monday D. Saturday
E. Sunday

26. If it was Friday on 3rd of a month, what will be the day falling on 4th day from 21st of that month?
A. Monday B. Wednesday
C. Saturday D. Thursday
E. Tuesday

27. If the fourth day from 6 January is Saturday, what was the day on 1st December of the last year?
A. Tuesday B. Wednesday
C. Thursday D. Monday
E. Saturday

EXPLANATORY ANSWERS

1. A:

2. B:

3. C:

4. D: At 9 O'clock in the morning minute hand is 15 minutes apart from the hour hand. We know that when in opposite directions to each other, one hand of the clock remains 30 minutes apart from the other hand. Therefore time spent in moving further 15 minutes $= \frac{60 \times 15}{55} = 16\frac{4}{11}$ minutes.

5. E: At 6.00 O'clock, minute hand is at a distance of 30 minutes from the hour hand. Therefore in order to point towards the same direction in which hour hand is pointing, the minute hand has to move further 30 minutes.

∴ The minute hand gains 55 minutes in 60 minutes.

∴ It will move 30 minutes in $\frac{60 \times 30}{55} = 32\frac{8}{11}$ minutes.
So both the hands will point towards the same direction at $32\frac{8}{11}$ minutes past 6 O'clock.

6. C:

7. D: We know that in every 12 hours the hands are at right angles 22 times.
∴ in 6 hours, hands of the clock will make right angles:
$\frac{22 \times 6}{12} = 11$ times

8. E: At 8.30 P.M. minute hand of the clock will be at 6 and hour hand will be in the middle of 8 and 9. At this position minute hand will be $5 + 5 + 2\frac{1}{2} = 12\frac{1}{2}$ minutes behind the hour hand. Now we know that in every minute, the minute hand turns through an angle of 6°. Therefore angle between minute hand and hour hand $= 12\frac{1}{2} \times 6 = \frac{25}{2} \times 6 = 75°$.

9. C:

10. D:

11. E:

12. C:

13. C:

14. A:

15. B:

16. C:

17. C:

18. C: A century leap year is divisible by 400.

19. C: Rocky was born 4 days before 3 March, 1998, *i.e.*, he was born on 27 Feb, 1998. Number of days from 27 February to 15 August $= 1 + 31 + 30 + 31 + 30 + 31 + 15 = 169$ days. Now on dividing 169 by 7 we get 1 as remainder. Therefore on 28 Feb, it was Saturday and on 27 February Friday.

20. B: Fourth day after 21st, *i.e.*, on 25th of the month it was Saturday. Dividing 25 by 7 we get 4 as remainder. Therefore on 4th of the month it was Saturday and on 3rd it was Friday.

21. C: Prayag was born 25 days before 5 March 1998, *i.e.*, on 8 February 1998. Number of days from the Republic Day (26 Jan) to 8 February = 5 + 8 = 13. Now on dividing 13 by 7 we get 6 as remainder. Therefore the required day will be 6 days after Monday, *i.e.*, Sunday.

22. D: Number of days from 17 March, 1980 to 12 July 1980 $= 14 + 30 + 31 + 30 + 12 = 117$. We get 5 as remainder on dividing 117 by 7. Therefore the required day will be 5 days after Monday, *i.e.*, Saturday.

23. D: A century leap year is divisible by 400.

24. D: There will be 3 leap years in 12years.
∴ 12 Years, 2 Months, 4 Day
$= 9 \times 365 + 3 \times 366 + 30 + 31 + 4$
$= 4448$ days
On dividing 4448 by 7 we get 3 as remainder and 3 days after Sunday will be Wednesday.

25. B: My sister is older to me by $75 \times 7 + 562 = 1087$ days
$1087 \div 2$ gives 2 as remainder
$\therefore$ 2 days after Tuesday will be Thursday.

26. C: 4th day from 21st is 25th. From 3rd of the month to 25th, there are 22 days
$22 \div 7$ gives 1 as remainder
$\therefore$ 1 day after Friday will be Saturday.

27. D: 4th day from 6th January is 10th January. From 1st December to 10th January, number of days $= 30 + 10 = 40$.
And $40 \div 7$ gives 5 as remainder. Hence, the required day will be 5 days before Saturday, *i.e.*, Monday.

10

TEST ON VENN DIAGRAMS AND CHARTS

In this type of questions, each of the questions asked contains a number of groups of entities. Candidates are required to choose from the given diagrams or charts, the diagram or element that best depicts the correct relationship among the given groups of entities or elements. A few examples are given below which will provide a clear insight into the nature of such type of questions. Candidates are expected to go through these examples and then attempt the exercises given thereafter.

Example 1: In the following diagram, rectangle represents illiterates, square represents employers, triangle represents farmers and circle represents people who are backward.

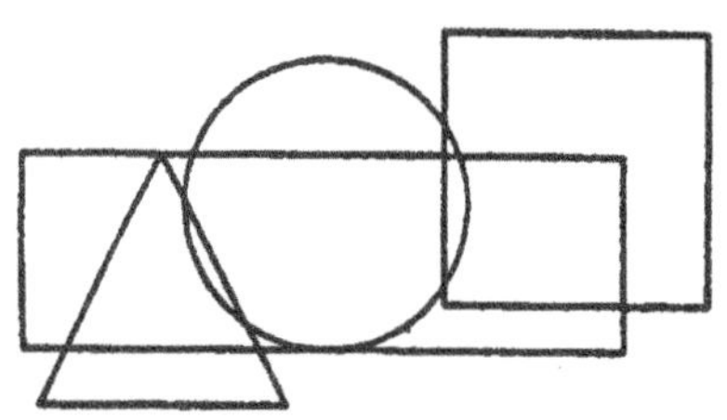

Which of the following statements is false?

A. A few farmers, who are employed, are either backward or illiterate or both.

B. A few people who are backward and illiterate, are neither farmers nor employed.

C. A few backward farmers who are employed, are not illiterate.

D. Those backward pe.sons who are not illiterate, are either farmers or employed or both.

E. A few unemployed farmers are backward and illiterate.

Explanatory Answer (C): There is a portion which is common to the circle, the triangle, the square and rectangle. Therefore backward employed farmers are illiterate. Thus 'C' is the false statement.

Example 2: In a group of five persons A, B, C, D and E, one is Tennis player, one is Chess player and one is Badminton player. A and D are unmarried girls and they do not play any of the above games. In this group, there is a married couple and E is the husband. None of the ladies plays either Chess or Badminton. B is the brother of C. He does not play either Tennis or Chess. Who of the given groups is a Badminton player?

A. E   B. D

C. A   D. B

E. C

Explanatory Answer: Based on the given information, following chart can be formed:

	Game			*Male*	*Female*	*Married*	*Unmarried*
	Badminton	*Tennis*	*Chess*				
A	✗	✗	✗	✗	✓	✗	✓
B	✓	✗	✗	✓	✗	–	–
C	✗	✓	✗	✗	✓	✓	✓
D	✗	✗	✗	✗	✓	✗	✓
E	✗	✗	✓	✓	✗	✓	✗

It is clear from the chart that the player of Badminton is B.

Example 3: Three circles are indicative of three different entities. The largest circle represents terrestrial animals. The smaller circle next to the largest one represents aquatic animals and the smallest circle represents amphibians. You are to choose from the following five venn diagrams, the diagram which best represents the animals of all these three types

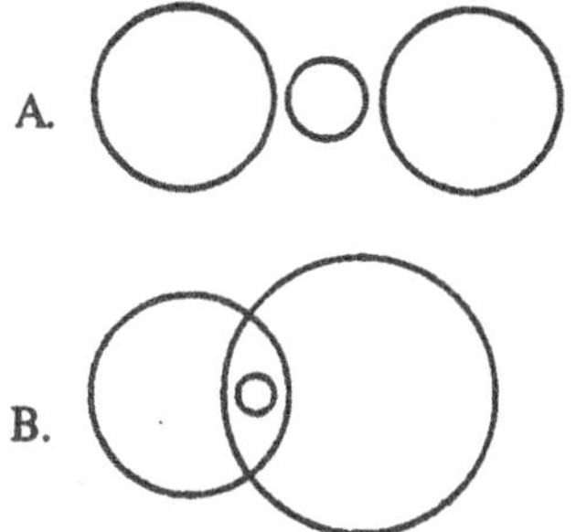

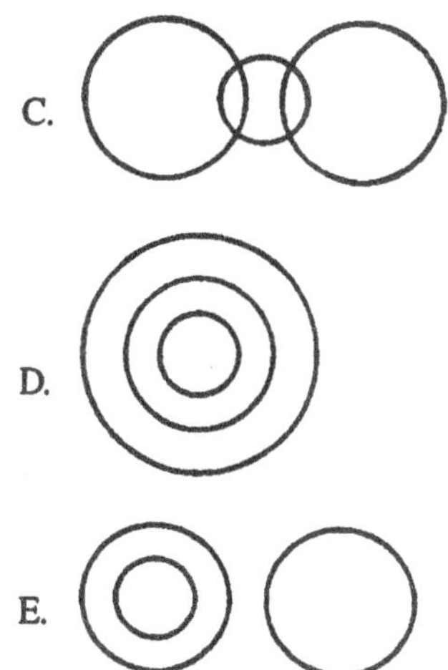

Explanatory Answer (B): The smallest circle represents the amphibians, therefore diagram 'B' is the correct answer.

EXERCISE - 1

Directions: *On the basis of the following statement answer questions 1 to 6.*

A, B, C, D and E were five different persons. Among them two were Authers, three were Poets, one was Playwright and one was Novelist. Two were the personalities of 17th Century, two were the personalities of 19th century and one was the personality of his respective field in 20th century. Among these five persons, two had authority on Marathi language, two on Tamil, two on Hindi and one had authority on English language. In 19th century 'B' and 'D' composed poems in Marathi language and D composed poems in Hindi also. 'A' wrote in Tamil and English languages, 'C' and 'D' composed poems in Marathi language but 'C' did not like the novels written by 'A'. 'E' was a famous playwright of 17th century but he departed for his heavenly abode in quite early age. C translated the poems originally written in Hindi by B into Marathi.

1. Playwrights had written their play in which of the following languages?
   A. Marathi
   B. English
   C. Tamil
   D. Information given in the statement is not sufficient to answer the question asked above
2. C had knowledge of how many languages?
   A. Four B. Two
   C. Three D. One
3. E composed his literary work in which of the following languages?
   A. English and Marathi
   B. Tamil and Marathi
   C. Tamil and English
   D. None of the above
4. Who of the following were eminent poets of Hindi language?
   A. B and D B. E and D
   C. D and C D. B and E
5. Who were the eminent personalities of 17th century?
   A. C and A
   B. E and A
   C. E and C
   D. None of the above
6. One among the following was the writer in Marathi language. He was an eminent personality of 20th century. Who was he?
   A. E B. C
   C. A D. None of these

Directions (Qs. 7 to 11): *Jonny, John, Jim and Jack were married to Jane, Julie, Maria and Mary. Here names of the wives are not given in the same order as the names of their husbands are given. Each couple has a son whose names are Roxy, Rocky, Rommy and Danny. But son's names are also not in the correct order. Rommy is the son of Jonny and Danny is the son of Jim. Jane is the wife of John and Mary is the mother of Roxy. Julie is not the wife of Jonny.*

7. Who of the following is the mother of Roxy?
   A. Jane B. Maria
   C. Mary D. Julie
8. Who is the husband of Maria?
   A. Jack B. Jim
   C. John D. Jonny
9. Who is the son of John?
   A. Rommy B. Rocky
   C. Roxy D. Danny
10. Who of the following is the wife of Jack?
    A. Mary B. Maria
    C. Julie D. Jane
11. Who of the following is the father of Roxy?
    A. Jack B. Jonny
    C. Jim D. John

Directions (Qs. 12 to 16): *Questions from 12 to 16 are based on the following statement:*

In an almirah 6 books A, B, C, D, E of F have been kept close to each other. Of these six books, three books C, B and E have blue coloured cover and two books A and D have red coloured cover. D and F are new books and others are old. A, C and D are books related to law and rest are the books of geography.

12. Which of the books names below is an old book, having blue coloured cover and related to law?

A. B B. C
C. D D. E

13. Which of the following books is an old book related to geography?

A. F B. E
C. D D. C

14. Which of the following books is a new book pertaining to law and having red coloured cover?

A. C B. A
C. F D. D

15. Which of the following books is an old book, having blue cover and relates to geography?

A. B and D B. A and E
C. B and C D. B and E

16. Which of the books is an old book containing red coloured cover and pertains to law?

A. C B. A
C. E D. B

Directions (Qs. 17 to 21): *The questions from 17 to 21 are based on following statements:*

1. A, B, C, D and E is a group of five persons.
2. Of these five persons, one is a horticulturist, one is a physicist, one is an editor, one is a businessman and one is a lawyer.
3. Of them three persons A, C and the lawyer prefer to take tea instead of coffee whereas B and the editor prefer coffee to tea.
4. The businessman, A and D are friends but two of them prefer cofee to tea.
5. The horticulturist is the brother of C.

17. Which of the above statements is quite irrelevant?

A. None B. Third
C. Second D. Fourth
E. Fifth

18. Who of the persons named below is a physicist?

A. C B. B
C. A D. E
E. D

19. Who is a businessman?

A. D B. B
C. A D. E
E. C

20. Which of the following is a group of persons who prefer tea and of the two in the group none is a lawyer?

A. A, C B. B, D
C. D, E D. B, C

21. Who is the horticulturist?

A. B B. E
C. C D. A
E. D

Directions (Qs. 22 to 26): *Answer the questions asked from 22 to 26 on the* *basis of following statements:*

"In a family six persons A, B, C, D, E and F are living together. C is the sister of F, A is the brother of E's husband, D is the father of A and grandfather of F. In this family two are fathers, three are brothers and one is mother."

22. Which of the following is a group of brothers?

A. ABC B. ABD

C. ABF D. BDF

E. BFC

23. Who is the husband of E?

A. B B. C

C. D D. F

24. How is F related to E?

A. Son

B. Daughter

C. Husband

D. Father-in-law

E. None of the above

25. How many males are there in the family?

A. 5 B. 4

C. 3 D. 2

E. 1

26. Who of the following is the mother?

A. A B. B

C. C D. D

E. None of the above

27. In a family Mr. & Mrs. Khosla live with their daughters Vimmy and Simmy and sons Rahul and Sahil. On one evening at 8.00 P.M. a thief entered into their house when Mr. Khosla had not returned back from his office and Sahil had gone to his friend's house with the consent of Rahul. Mrs. Khosla was also not in the house. She had gone to bring medicine from the chemist's shop. Vimmy had accompanied her mother. Simmy was feeling headache and she was asleep after taking a pain killer. Now tell who was in the house when the thief entered into?

A. Rahul

B. Simmy and Sahil

C. Simmy

D. Simmy and Rahul

Directions (Qs. 28 to 32): *Out of the five towns A, B, C, D and E, 3 are industrial towns, two are port towns and one is hill station, None of the industrial towns or port towns has population less than 30 lakhs, but population of hill station is less than 30 lakhs. Out of the 5 towns, University has been established in 3 towns. There is an university in the hill station but there is not a port. The industrial towns having university, do not have port. C and D are not the industrial towns. D is not the town having port. In the town having port, there is not any university and B is a port town. None of the industrial towns is a hill station. D is the hill station and E has an University.*

28. Which of the following is not a industrial town and has neither university nor hill station?

A. E B. A

C. C D. B

29. Which of the following groups of towns are industrial towns having universities but not port?

A. A, E B. C, D

C. A, B D. A, C

30. In which of the following industrial towns, there is not any university?

A. C B. B
C. D D. A

31. Which of the following are names of two port towns?

A. B, C B. A, E
C. B, D D. A, D

32. Which of the following towns is an indusrial town with port and does not have an university?

A. D B. B
C. A D. C

33. X, Y and Z are three ladies. They marry with the doctor, the lawyer and the engineer. A is the lawyer and Y's husband is not an engineer. If X is married to B who is a doctor then which of the following statements is correct?

A. Z is not the wife of engineer.
B. Husband of Z is a doctor
C. Husband of Y is not a lawyer
D. C and Z are Husband-wife

34. Every year a question is asked on any of the eight poets *viz.* A, B, C, D, E, F, G and H. Out of these poets first four are classical poets and last four are modern poets. There is a trend to ask one year a question on modern poets and then on succeeding year a question on classical poets. The teacher who likes H poet, also likes G poet and who likes F poet also likes E poet. On a certain year the teacher has liking for F poet but due to some reason he does not ask question on F poet. On the preceding year question was asked on classical poets. Guess which one of the following poets will probably be asked this year:

A. G B. E
C. F D. H

Directions (Qs. 35 to 39): *Questions from 35 to 39 are based on the following statement:*

"Annu, Sonu, Raju and Hari are four friends. Out of them one plays cricket and reads biology and chemistry. Annu and Sonu play football. Annu reads commerce. Both the players of football read mathematics. Hari is a boxer. Player of football reads physics also and the boxer reads mathematics and commerce.

35. The four friends play how many games and read how many subjects?

A. 3 game and 6 subjects
B. 4 games and 6 subjecs
C. 3 games and 5 subjects
D. 3 games and 7 subjects

36. Who of the following is a player of football and reads commerce?

A. Hari B. Sonu
C. Raju D. Annu

37. Who of the following reads physics?

A. Sonu B. Raju
C. Annu D. Hari

38. Who of the following does not read mathematics?

A. Hari B. Raju
C. Annu D. Sonu

39. Who of the following likes to play cricket?

A. Hari B. Annu
C. Raju D. Sonu

Directions (Qs. 40 to 44): *The questions from 40 to 44 are based on the following information:*

A, B, C, D, E and F, 6 persons are playing with cards. In this group, the father of A, his mother and his uncle are present. There are two ladies in the group. B is the mother of A. A's mother scored more marks than her husband, D scored marks more than E but less than F. Nephew of E scored less marks. A's father scored more marks than F but could not win the game.

40. Who won second position in the above game?

A. B B. A

C. E D. D

41. Except B, who is the second lady in the group?

A. A B. B

C. C D. D

42. Who is the husband of B

A. E B. D

C. F D. C

43. Who scored the least marks?

A. A B. C

C. B D. D

44. Who won the game?

A. F B. B

C. D D. A

Directions (Qs. 45 to 50): *The questions from 45-50 are based on the following statement:*

There are five towns A, B, C, D and E out of which two are Hill stations and three are located in the Plains. Out of the towns located in the Plains, two are Port towns. Out of these five towns, 4 are Capital towns and two are Industrial towns. Population of each of the two towns is less than 5 lakhs, population of one town is 20 lakhs and population of each of the remaining two towns is more than 50 lakhs. Two towns are situated at the same latitude and other two towns are situated at the same longitude. Latitude and longitude of both the Port towns are different and one of these Port towns is an Industrial town. Population of each of the two Industrial towns is more than 50 lakhs. Hill station and one Port town have the same longitude whereas the other Hill station and the other Port town are situated at different latitudes and longitudes. One Industrial town is neither Hill station nor Port town. None of the Hill stations is an Industrial town. The Hill station which longitude is equal to the longitude of Port, is a Capital town. B is a Hill station but longitude of E and D is equal and E is a Port. D and C are situated at the same latitude while population of D is 20 lakhs. All Port towns are the Industrial towns and also the Capital towns.

45. Which of the following is a Capial town with Port?

A. C B. B

C. E D. A

E. D

46. Which of the following is a Capital town situated on Hill Station?

A. D B. B

C. A D. E

E. C

47. Populations of which of the following towns are more than 50 lakhs?

A. C and D B. A and C

C. B and E D. C and E
E. A and D

48. Which of the following is a Port town, Capital town and an Industrial town?
A. D B. C
C. B D. A
E. F

49. Which of the following is not a Capital town?
A. E B. D
C. B D. A
E. C

50. Which of the following groups of two towns is a group of the towns with less than 5 lakhs population?
A. A and B B. B and C
C. A and C D. D and A
E. None of these

Directions (Qs. 51 to 56): *Read carefully the statement given below and based on the information provided, answer the questions from 51 to 56.*

A, B, C, D and E are five villages. Two of the villages are situated beside highways. There is a school in each of these two villages. Population of one of the villages is less than 3000. There is a school in another village also and its population is more than 3000. A village having population more than 3000 does not have school. There is a Post office in a village having school and population more than 3000. There is a Police Station in the village situated beside the highway and having population more than 3000. There is a school in the village A and its population is less than 3000. Village B neither has school nor is situated beside highway. Village C is situated beside highway and its population is more than 3000. Population of village D is less than 3000 and village E is not situated beside highway and there is no Post Office in this village.

51. Which of the following villages with population more than 3000 does not have school?
A. E B. A
C. C D. B
E. D

52. Which of the following villages has a Post Office?
A. B B. A
C. D D. E
E. C

53. In which of the following villages, there is a Police Station?
A. E B. D
C. C D. B
E. A

54. Which of the following villages situated beside highway does not have School?
A. E B. D
C. A D. C
E. B

55. Which of the following villages with population less than 3000 does not have School?
A. B B. D
C. C D. A
E. E

56. Except C, which of the following villages is situated beside Highway?
A. E B. D
C. A D. B
E. None of the above

Directions: *Questions from 57 to 60 are based on the following statement: Reema and Gessu are well versed in dance and music. Sonal and Gessu are well versed in music and painting whereas Reema and Neha are well versed in delivering speeches and dance. Neha and sonal are well versed in painting and delivering speeches.*

57. Who of the following girls is well versed in music, painting and delivering speeches?

A. Gessu B. Neha
C. Reema D. Sonal
E. None of these

58. The girl well versed in painting, dance and delivering speeches is:

A. Sonal B. Neha
C. Gessu D. Reema
E. None of the above

59. Who of the following girls is well versed in music, dance and painting?

A. Sonal B. Neha
C. Gessu D. Reema
E. None of the above

60. Who of the following girls is well versed in dance, music and delivering speeches?

A. Reema B. Sonal
C. Gessu D. Neha
E. None of the above

Directions (Qs. 61 to 65): *Questions from 61 to 65 are based on the information given below: There is a group of 6 persons A, B, C, D, E and F. In this group there are two couples of married persons. F is the sister of D. In this group one is a gardner whose son is E. C is the grand father of E. D is married to A. A is a Driver. Both ladies of the group are unemployed.*

61. Who is the father-in-law of F?

A. F B. A
C. B D. D
E. C

62. Who is the maternal aunt of E?

A. C B. F
C. D D. A
E. B

63. Which of the following is a married couple?

A. A, F B. C, D
C. A, B D. E, F
E. B, F

64. Who is the father of B?

A. E B. C
C. D D. F
E. E

65. Who of the following is a gardener in the group?

A. D B. E
C. B D. C
E. A

Directions (Qs. 66 to 68): *Answer the questions asked from 66 to 68 on the basis of statement given below: In a seminar P, E, V, D, M, R, Z and T expressed their views. One speaker spoke at one time. They did not speak in the order of their names given above. P spoke after R but he spoke before M and he took less time than E. V spoke before Z but he spoke after L and took less time than M. D spoke after T but he spoke before E and took less time than T but more time than M. T spoke after M and took less time than E.*

66. Who of the following spoke first?

A. R B. E

C. P D. D
E. T

67. Who spoke in the last?
A. D B. Z
C. V D. E
E. R

68. Who took maximum time?
A. E B. T
C. P D. D
E. M

Directions (Qs. 69 to 73): *Read the following statement carefully and answer the questions asked below:*

A group of five persons A, B, C, D and E are sitting in a round circle. In this group of five persons there is one doctor, one teacher and one businessman. The businessman is sitting in between the teacher and B. B is the wife of the teacher. A is the doctor and E is his wife. E is the sister of B. The teacher is sitting to the right of C and to the left of the doctor. Both ladies of the group are not employed.

69. The man whose wife is not sitting with him in the group is:
A. B B. C
C. A D. D
E. E

70. Who is sitting to the right of A?
A. Wife of C B. Wife of A
C. B D. Wife of B
E. C

71. How is A related to B?
A. Friend
B. Uncle
C. Brother-in-law (Sister's husband)
D. Brother-in-law (Wife's brother)
E. Brother

72. Who is the teacher in the group?
A. B B. D
C. E D. C
E. A

73. Who is unmarried in the group?
A. Teacher
B. Businessman
C. Professor
D. None of these
E. Information is not sufficient to answer this question

Directions (Qs. 74 to 78): *There is a group of five boys A, B, C, D and E. A and C are well versed in English and Mathematics. B and C are well versed in English and General Knowledge. E and D are well versed in Science and Painting. E is well versed in Painting, Mathematics and Science. B and D are well versed in Painting and General Knowledge.*

74. How many boys are well versed in two subjects?
A. 3 B. 4
C. 1 D. 2
E. None of these

75. Who of the following boys is well versed in Science and Mathematics?
A. A B. B
C. C D. E
E. D

76. Who of the following boys is well versed in General Knowledge but not so in English and Mathematics?
A. C B. E
C. A D. B
E. D

77. Who is weak in General Knowledge but well versed in English and Mathematics?

A. D B. C

C. A D. E

E. B

78. Who is well versed in English, Painting and General Knowledge?

A. D B. E

C. C D. B

E. A

Directions (Qs. 79 to 83): *Five persons A, B, C, D and E live in a family. E has two sons, one unmarried daughter and one daughter-in-law, 'D'. The daughter-in-law 'D' is a Bank Officer and earns more than her husband but less than her husband's younger brother who is a businessman. E's one son is an architect who earns least in the family. B's sister plays on sitar. She has learnt this art from B's wife. Income of A is less than that of E.*

79. How is A related to D?

A. Husband B. Brother

C. Wife D. Mother

E. Husband's younger brother

80. Who is the unmarried girl?

A. D B. B

C. C D. A

E. None of the above

81. Who of the following is the businessman?

A. A B. E

C. C D. A

E. None of the above

82. Who of the following is the B's wife?

A. A

B. D

C. C

D. cannot be guessed

E. None of the above

83. How is E related to B?

A. Father-in-law

B. Brother

C. Daughter

D. Mother or Father

E. None of the above

Directions (Qs. 84 to 88): *Questions from 84 to 88 are based on the following statement.*

There is a group of five persons A, B, C, D and E. In this group one is a teacher of Mathematics, one is a teacher of subjects related to agriculture and one is a teacher of commerce subjects. A and D are unmarried girls who do not know any of the subjects. One is a married couple in which E is the husband. B is the brother of C. He is not conversant with any of the subjects related to agriculture or commerce. None of the woman in the group is conversant with the subjects related to mathematics or commerce.

84. Who of the following is the teacher of Mathematics?

A. D B. A

C. C D. B

E. E

85. Which of the following is a group of women?

A. A, C, E B. A, B, C

C. A, B, D D. A, D, E

E. A, C, D

86. Married woman is the teacher of which of the following subjects?

A. Mathematics or Commerce

B. Mathematics

C. Agriculture

D. Commerce
E. None of the above

87. Who of the following is a married woman?

A. B B. A
C. D D. C
E. E

88. Who is the teacher of Commerce?

A. C B. D
C. A D. B
E. E

Directions (Qs. 89 to 93): *Questions from 89 to 93 are based on the following statement:*

There is a group of six persons A, B, C, D, E and F. In this group two are Doctors, two are Civil Engineers, One is Teacher and One is an Industrialist. D is the wife of B's friend and she is a Civil Engineer. Teacher in the group is the daughter of one of the Doctors. F is a Doctor but he is not the father of C. C is a Teacher. E has drawn the plan of B's factory. There are two ladies in this group.

89. Which of the following is a group of 2 Doctors and 1 Industrialist?

A. B, F, C B. A, D, F
C. A, B, F D. A, F, C
E. F, B, D

90. Which of the following is a group of ladies?

A. C and D B. C and B
C. C and F D. C and E
E. C and A

91. Who is the father of the Teacher?

A. D
B. A C. E
D. B E. F

92. If due to inclusion of one more member in this group, number of persons engaged in the profession adopted by F becomes equal to the number of persons engaged in the profession adopted by B, then the new member included in this group is:

A. Civil Engineer
B. Doctor or an Industrialist
C. Industrialist
D. Doctor
E. Teacher

93. Who is the Doctor other than F in this group?

A. C B. B
C. D D. A
E. E

Directions (Qs. 94 to 98): *Read carefully the statement given below and answer the questions from 94 to 98.*

Branches of five Nationalised Banks A, B, C, D and E are located in following main towns of India:

Name of Towns	**Name of Banks whose branches have been opened**
1. Meerut and Kanpur	A, B and C
2. Meerut and Goa	A, B and E
3. Rampur and Kanpur	B, C and D
4. Goa and Jaipur	A, E and D
5. Rampur and Jaipur	C, E and D

94. In which of the following towns branch of B bank is not located?

A. Kanpur B. Goa
C. Meerut D. Jaipur

95. The bank, branch of which is located in every town except

Goa, is:

A. B B. D

C. C D. A

96. The bank, branches of which are located in Rampur and Meerut but not in Kanpur, is:

A. D B. C

C. A D. E

97. Which of the following Banks does not have any branch in Meerut?

A. D B. B

C. E D. A

98. Which of the following banks have its branch in Meerut but not in Rampur?

A. B B. A

C. E D. C

EXERCISE-2

Directions (Qs. 1 to 5): *In each of the questions from 1 to 5, three words are given which are related in some way. This relationship is represented by one of the five Venn diagrams given below. You have to find out the diagram which best represents the relationships among the words in the question.*

A. 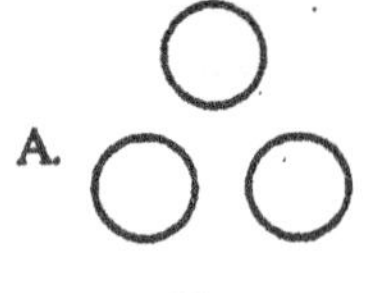

B. 

C. 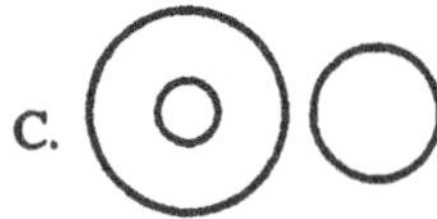

D. 

E. 

1. Tortoise, Crab, Cow

A. B B. E

C. A D. C

E. D

2. Fruit, Jam, Jelly

A. D B. B

C. A D. E

E. C

3. Rupee, Dollar, Paise

A. B B. C

C. D D. A

E. E

4. Russia, Volga, Moscow

A. C B. E

C. D D. A

E. B

5. Captain, Sea, Ship

A. D B. E

C. A D. B

E. C

Directiosn (Qs. 6 to 10): *The questions from 6 to 10 are based on the figure given below which represents a set of persons. The Triangle represents educated persons, the Quadrilateral represents policemen, the Small circle represents road tax payers and the Large circle represents shopkeepers.*

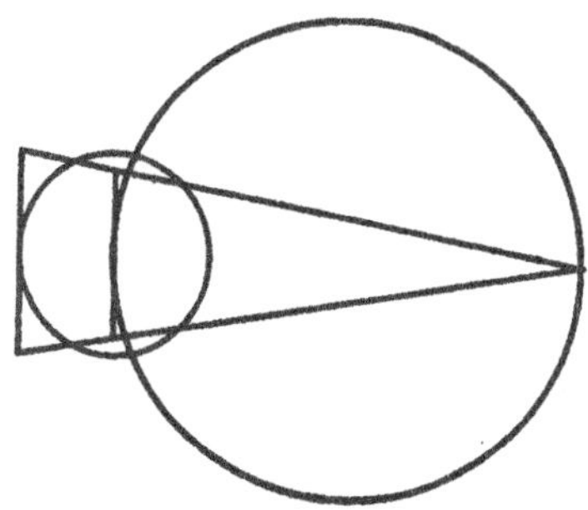

6. Looking at the above figure it can be concluded that:

A. Some persons who are neither shopkeepers not policemen, are educated.

B. Some persons who are either shopkeepers or policemen, pay road tax.

C. Some persons who are either shopkeepers or policemen, pay road tax and are also educated.

D. All the above statements are correct.

7. According to the figure we can say that:

A. Some of the road tax payers are shopkeepers and policemen too.

B. Educated shopkeepers pay road tax.

C. Some of the uneducated policemen pay road tax.

D. Some of the road tax payer policemen are shopkeepers too.

8. On perusal of the above figure we can conclude that:

A. Some of the shopkeepers are policemen.

B. None of the shopkeepers pays road tax.

C. All shopkeepers are educated.

D. None of the policemen pays road tax.

9. According to the figure we can say that:

A. None of the uneducated shopkeepers is a policeman though an uneducated policeman is a shopkeeper.

B. Some of the educated policemen who pay road tax are sharing profits with uneducated shopkeepers.

C. Some of the educated shopkeepers are road tax payers even though they discharge duties of a policeman.

D. None of the educated shopkeepers is policeman nor an educated policeman is a shopkeeper.

10. Looking carefully at the figure it can be concluded that:

A. All educated policemen pay road tax.

B. All road tax payer policemen are educated.

C. All road tax payer shopkeepers are educated.

D. All educated shopkeepers pay road tax.

Directions (Qs. 11 to 15): *In the Venn diaram given below, the triangle stands for Doctor, the rectangle stands for Artists and the circle stands for Players. Different regions in the diagram are numbered. Study the diagram and select the correct answer of each question from amongst the given alternatives.*

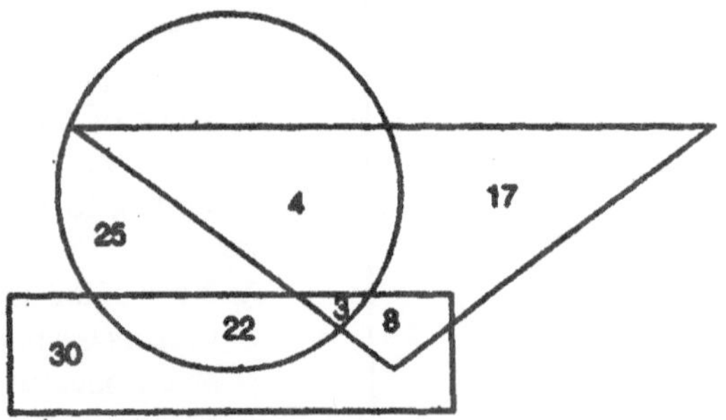

11. Number of persons who are 'players' but are neither 'doctors' nor 'artists' is:
    A. 3 B. 22
    C. 25 D. 4
    E. None of the above
12. Number of persons who are 'doctors' but are neither 'players' nor 'artists' is:
    A. 17 B. 25
    C. 8 D. 30
    E. None of the above
13. Number of persons who are 'artists' but are neither 'players' nor 'doctors' is:
    A. 8 B. 30
    C. 22 D. 29
    E. 25
14. Number of 'artists' who are 'players' is:
    A. 25 B. 17
    C. 22 D. 30
    E. 25
15. How many 'doctors' are 'artists' and 'players'?
    A. 4 B. 1
    C. 6 D. 3
    E. 8
16. Which one of the following four venn diagrams represents the persons who are "pickpockets, petty thieves as well as bad elements"?

A. 

B. 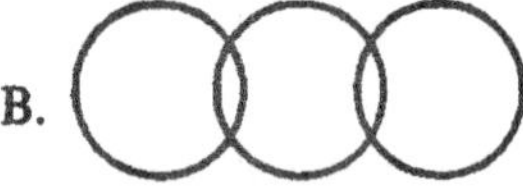

C. 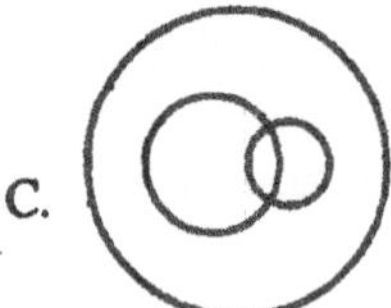

D. 

17. "Indians are mostly black. Some have long hairs and some have short hairs". Which one of the following venn diagrams best represents this statement?

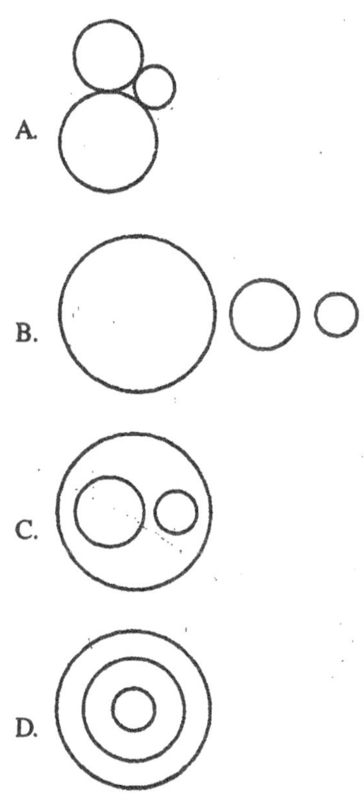

Directions (Qs. 18 to 23): *Questions from 18 to 23 are based on the following figure:*

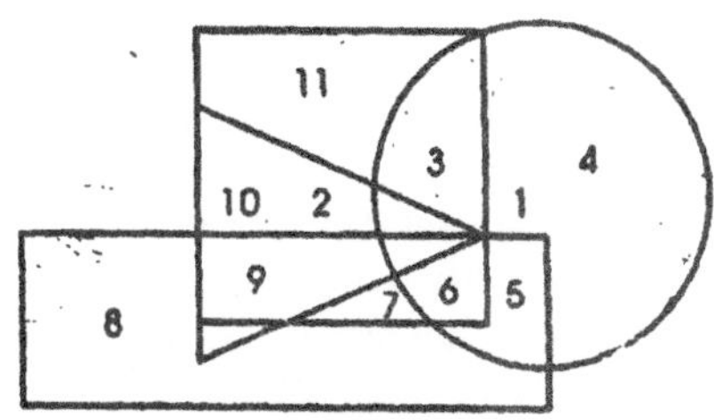

In the above figure the rectangle stands for men, the circle stands for the persons living in towns, the triangle stands for the civil servants and the square stands for educated persons. Look at the above figure carefully and answer the questions asked below:

18. Which area represents those females who live in towns but are neither educated nor civil servants?

A. 3 B. 11
C. 2 D. 4

19. Which area stands for those females who live in towns, are educated and civil servants?

A. 9 B. 5
C. 2 D. 1

20. Which region stands for those males who live in towns but are neither educated nor civil servants?

A. 9 B. 4
C. 5 D. 1

21. Which of the following regions stands for those females who live in rural areas, are educated and civil servants?

A. 10 B. 9
C. 8 D. 7

22. Which of the following regions stands for those males who live in rural areas, are educated but who are not civil servants?

A. 8 B. 7
C. 1 D. 6

23. Which of the following regions stands for those males who live in towns, are educated and civil servants?

A. 2 B. 8
C. 1 D. 3

24. In the figure given below the square represents 'tall persons', the circle represents 'mighty persons' and the triangle represents the 'army officers'. Which of the regions given in the alternatives represents those 'army officers' who are not mighty but tall?

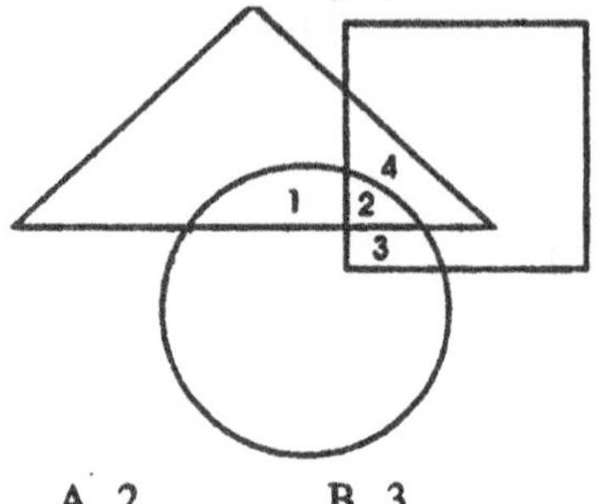

A. 2 B. 3
C. 1 D. 4

25. Which of the following figures best represents the relation between Europe, Russia and Asia?

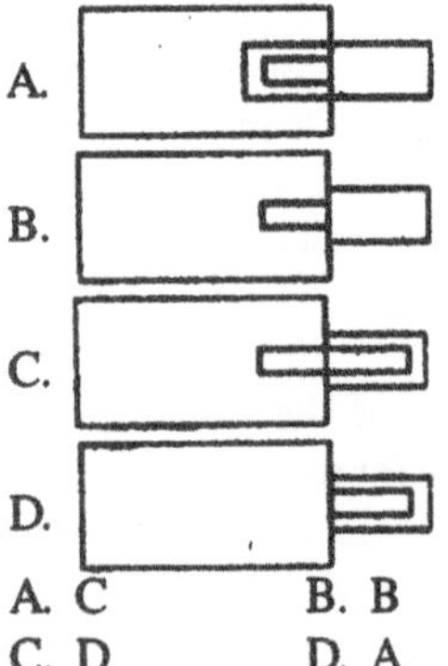

A. C B. B
C. D D. A

Directions (Qs. 26 to 29): *The following four diagrams depicts different relationships among three entities. You are to identify the correct relationship in each of the questions.*

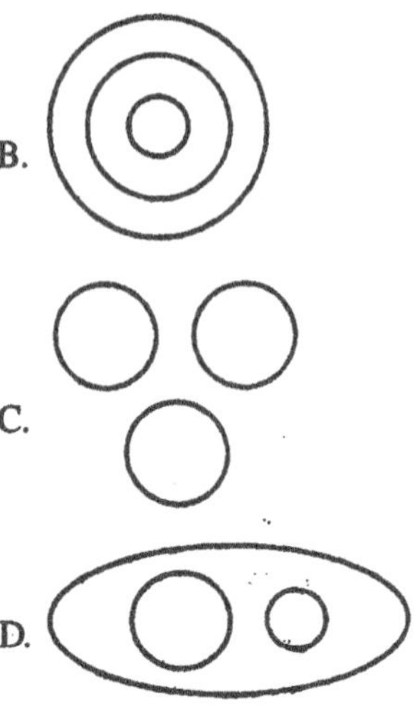

26. Cow, Snake, Dog
A. D B. A
C. C D. B

27. Mother, Father, Family
A. B B. C
C. A D. D

28. Author, Philosopher, Teacher
A. D B. A
C. B D. C

29. Sentence, Paragraph, Word
A. A B. C
C. B D. D

30. In the following four diagrams, each of the two large circles represents either the terrestrial animals or the aquatic animals and the small circle represents the amphibians. Select from the given alternatives the correct answer which depicts the relationship amongst these animals.

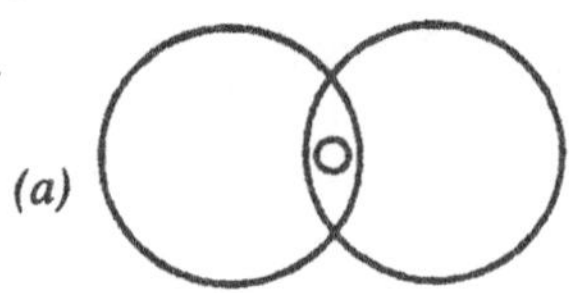

(b)

(c)

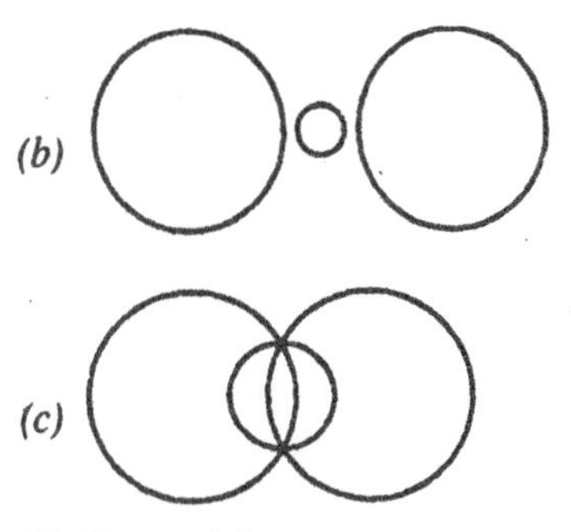

(d) None of these

A. (d) B. (c)

C. (a) D. (b)

31. In the animal kingdom a few animals live only in water and a few live only on earth. Which of the following figures best depicts the habitat of frog?

(a)

(b)

(c)

(d)

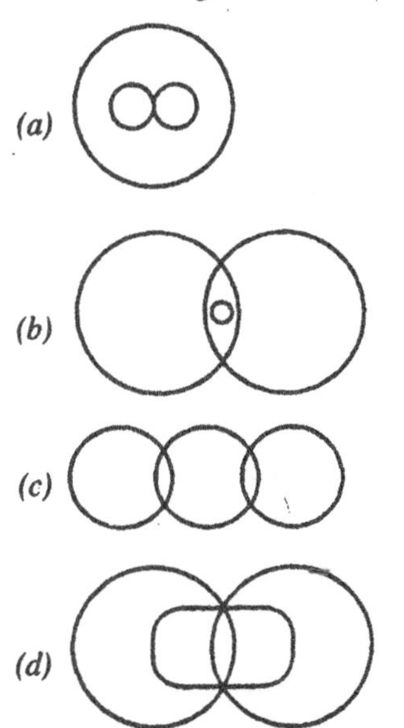

A. (c) B. (b)

C. (d) D. (a)

32. Which of the following figures represents the relationship among "Judge, Thief and Criminal"?

A. 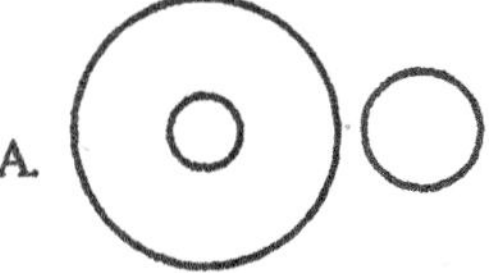

B. 

C. 

D. 

33. Which of the following diagrams best represents the relationship among "Elephant, Lion and Animal"?

(a) 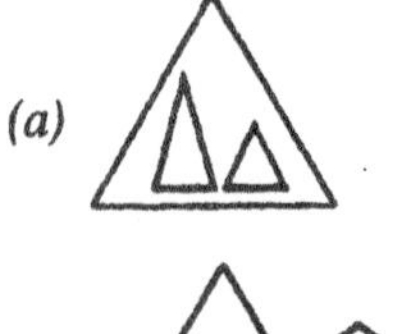

(b) 

(c) 

(d) 

(e) 

A. (a) B. (c)
C. (d) D. (e)
E. (b)

34. Which of the following figures best represents the relationship among "Women, Mothers and Doctors"?

(a) 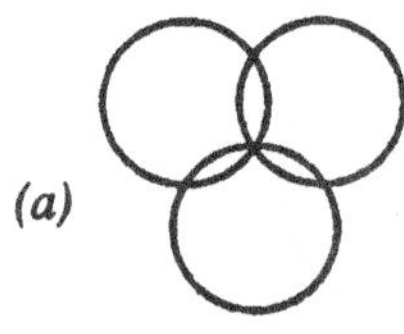

(b) 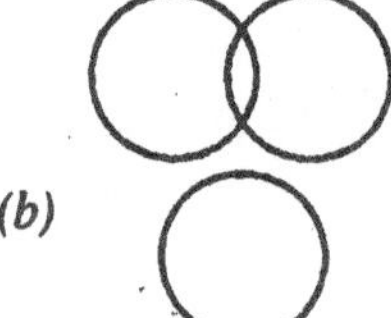

(c) 

(d) 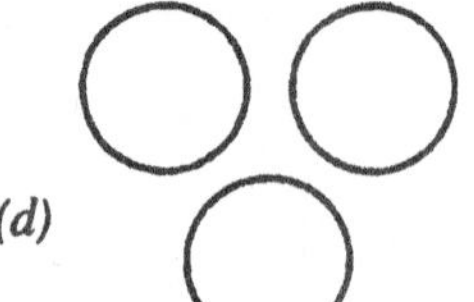

(e) 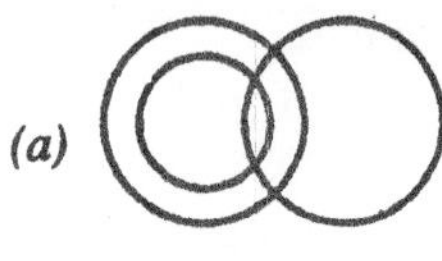

A. (c) B. (b)
C. (d) D. (a)
E. (e)

35. Which figure best represents the relationship among "Jalebi, Sweets and Eatables"?

(a) 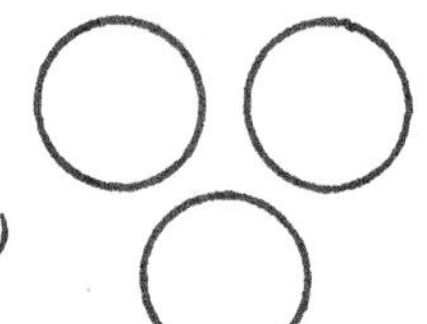

(b) 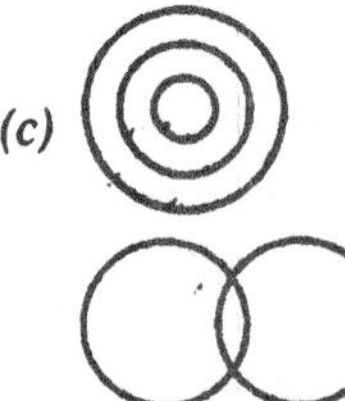

(c)

(d) 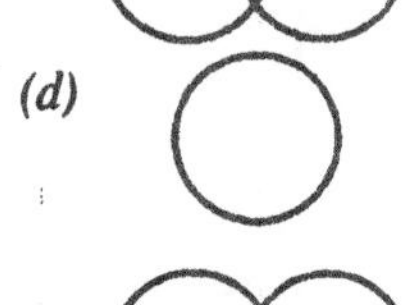

(e) 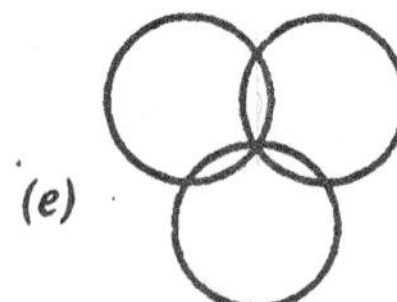

A. (d) B. (e)
C. (c) D. (a)
E. (b)

36. Which figure best represents the

mutual relationship among "Widowers, Men and Persons who smoke"?

(a)

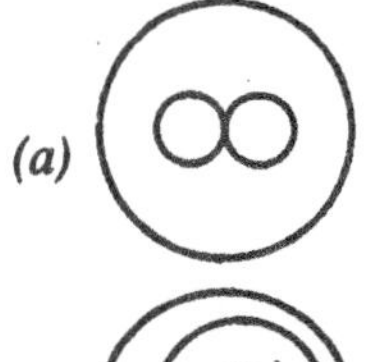

(b)

(c)

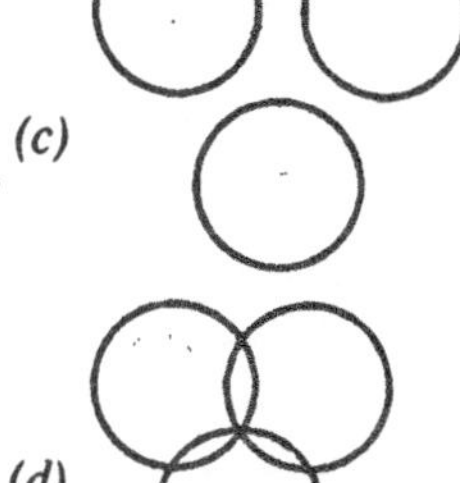

(d)

(e)

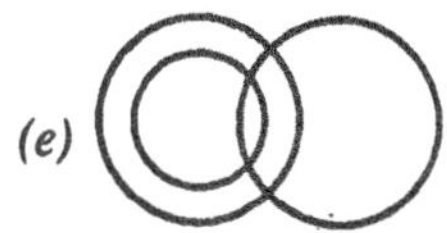

A. (d) B. (a)
C. (c) D. (b)
E. (e)

37. Which of the following five diagrams best depicts the relationship among "Mother, Father and Family"?

(a)

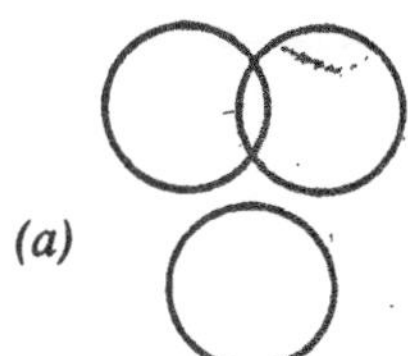

(b)

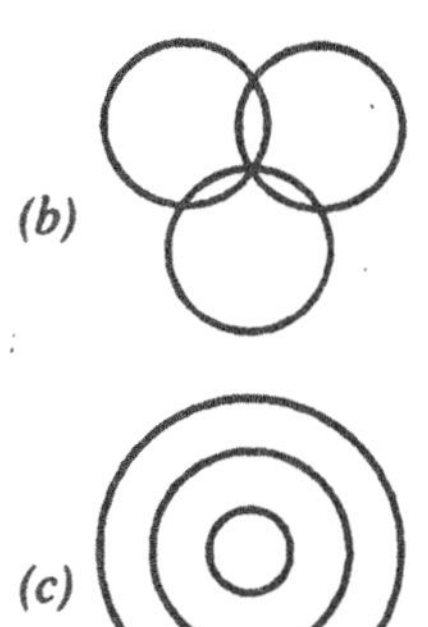

(c)

(d)

(e)

A. (a) B. (c)
C. (b) D. (d)
E. (e)

38. Which of the following five diagrams best depicts the relationship among "Language, Hindi and English"?

(a)

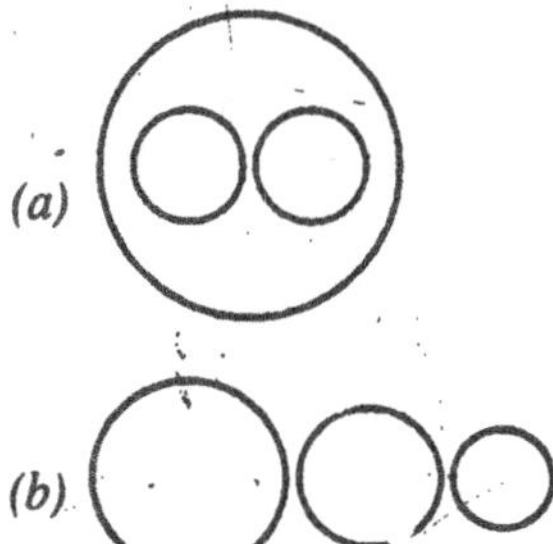

(b)

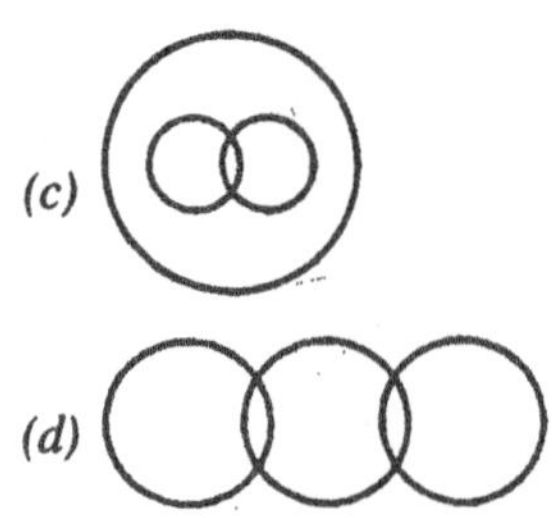

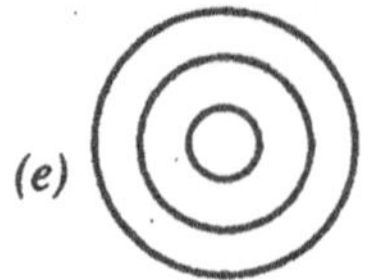

A. *(a)* B. *(d)*
C. *(b)* D. *(e)*
E. *(c)*

EXPLANATORY ANSWERS

EXERCISE-1

Chart for Qs. 1 to 6:

	Profession	Era	Language
A	Novelist	17th century	Tamil and English
B	Poet	19th Century	Marathi and Hindi
C	Poet, Author	20th Century	Marathi, Tamil and English
D	Poet, Author	19th Century	Marathi, Hindi
E	Playwright	17th Century	Marathi, Tamil

1. D:

2. C:

3. B:

4. A:

5. B:

6. B:

Chart for Qs. 7 to 11:

Father	Son	Mother
John	Rocky	Jane
Jonny	Rommy	Mary
Jim	Danny	Maria
Jack	Roxy	Julie

7. D:

8. B:

9. B:

10. C:

11. A:

Chat for Qs. 12 to 16:

	Red Covered	Blue Covered	Old	New	Pertaining to Geography	Pertaining to Law
A	✓	×	✓	×	×	✓
B	×	✓	✓	×	✓	×
C	×	✓	✓	×	×	✓
D	✓	×	×	✓	×	✓
E	×	✓	✓	×	✓	×
F	×	×	×	✓	✓	×

12. A:

13. B:

14. D:

15. D:

16. B:

Chart for Qs. 17 to 21:

	Persons who prefer tea	Specialist of the concerned subject	persons who prefer coffee
A	✓	Horticulturist	×
B	×	Businessman	✓
C	✓	Physicist	×
D	×	Editor	✓
E	✓	Lawyer	×

17. C:

18. A:

19. B:

20. A:

21. D:

Family Chart for Qs. 22 to 26:

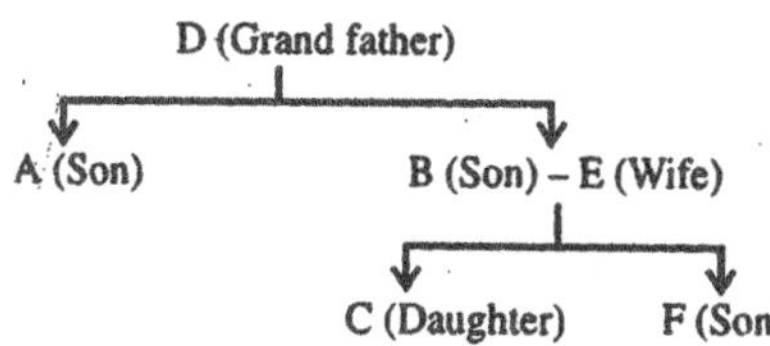

In this family, D is head of the family who has two sons A and B. E is the wife of B. C is the daughter and F is the son of B and E.

22. C:

23. A:

24. A:

25. B:

26. E:

27. D:

Chart for Qs. 28 to 32:

	Industrial town	Port town	Hill Station	Town with University
A	✓	×	×	✓
B	✓	✓	×	×
C	×	✓	×	×
D	×	×	✓	✓
E	✓	×	×	✓

28. C:

29. A:

30. B:

31. C:

32. B:

33. D: Observe the following relationship Chart.

Husband	A	B	C
	Lawyer	Doctor	Engineer
Wife	Y	X	Z

34. B: The teacher who has liking for F poet, also likes E poet. But he does not want to set question on F poet. So question will be asked on E poet.

Chart for Qs. 35 to 39:

	Cricket	Football	Boxing	Chemistry	Biology	Mathematics	Commerce	Physics
Annu		✓				✓	✓	
Sonu		✓				✓		✓
Raju	✓			✓	✓			
Hari			✓			✓	✓	

35. C:

36. D:

37. A:

38. B:

39. C:

Chart for Qs. 40 to 44:

A's father, his mother anu uncle are present in the group ..... (1)

A's mother B scored more than her husband ..... (2)

B is the mother of A. ..... (3)

D scored more than E ..... (4)

F scored more than F ..... (5)

Nephew of E scored less marks ..... (6)

Father of A who is the husband of B, has scored more than F ..... (7)

A's father could not win the game ..... (8)

It is clear that none of F, D, E and A is

the husband of B. .....(9)
From (6) it is also clear that A scored less .....(10)
It can also be concluded that D is the second lady in the group .....(11)
It can be concluded that C is at the second posiion and B won the game.

40. C:
41. D:
42. D:
43. A:
44. B:

Chart for Qs. 45 to 50:

Towns	Hill Stations	Port towns	Industrial Towns	Capital towns	Population less than 5 lakhs	Population 20 lakhs	Population more than 50 lakhs	Situated on same Latitude	Situated on same Longitude
A	✓	✗	✗	✓	✓	✗	✗	✗	✓
B	✓	✗	✗	✗	✓	✗	✗	✗	✗
C	✗	✗	✓	✓	✗	✗	✓	✓	✗
D	✗	✓	✗	✓	✗	✓	✗	✓	✗
E	✗	✓	✓	✓	✗	✗	✓	✗	✓

45. E:
46. C:
47. D:
48. E:
49. C:
50. A:

Chart for Qs. 51 to 56:

Village	Population less than 3000	Population more than 3000	School	Post Office	Police Station	Highway
A	✓	✗	✓	✗	✗	✓
B	✗	✓	✗	✗	✗	✗
C	✗	✓	✓	✓	✓	✓
D	✓	✗	✗	✗	✗	✗
E	✓	✓	✓	✗	✗	✗

51. D:
52. E:
53. C:
54. A:
55. B:
56. C:

Chart for Qs. 57 to 60:

	Dance	Music	Painting	Speech delivering
Reema	✓	✓	✗	✓
Sonal	✗	✓	✓	✓
Geesu	✓	✓	✓	✗
Neha	✓	✗	✓	✓

57. D:
58. B:
59. E:
60. A:

Family Chart for Qs. 61 to 65:

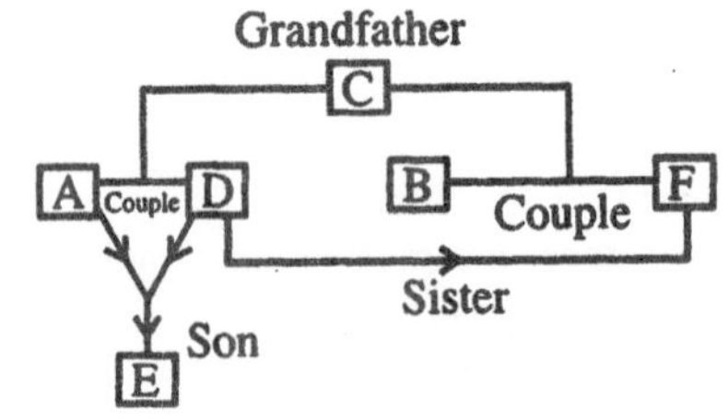

61. E:

62. C:

63. C:

64. B:

65. C:

Chart for Qs. 66 to 68:

Order of speaking:

R → P → M → D → E → T → V → Z

Series of persons according to the time taken in ascending order:

Z → V → M → T → E → D → P

66. A:

67. B:

68. C:

Chart for Qs. 69 to 73:

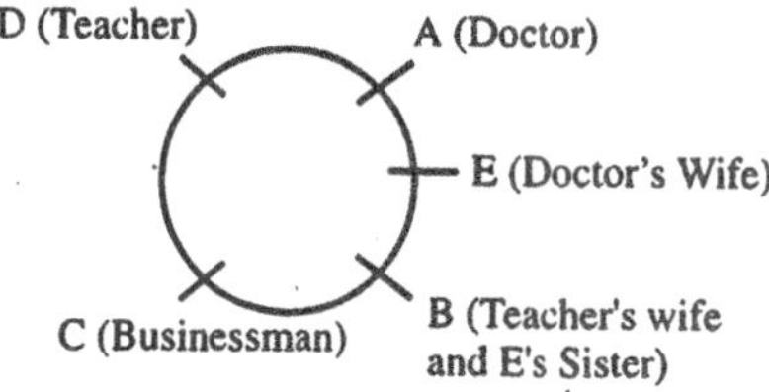

69. D: D is the teacher whose wife B is not sitting with him.

70. B: E is sitting to the right of A who is his wife.

71. C:

72. B: The Teacher is sitting to the right of Businessman and to the left of the Doctor (A). The Business-man is sitting in the middle of the Teacher and Teacher's wife (B). Therefore C is the Business-man and D is the Teacher.

73. B: B is the wife of the teacher and E is the wife of the doctor. Only businessman is the person in the group who is unmarried.

Chart for Qs. 74 to 78:

	English	Mathematics	General Knowledge	Painting	Science
A	✓	✓	×	×	×
B	✓	×	✓	✓	×
C	✓	✓	✓	×	×
D	×	×	✓	✓	✓
E	×	✓	×	✓	✓

74. C:

75. D:

76. E:

77. C:

78. D:

Chart for Qs. 79 to 83:

A = Businessman, earns more than D

B = Architect, lowest income

C = Unmarried daughter, plays on Sitar

D = B's wife, a bank officer and earns more than B

E = Mother or Father, income more than D

79. E:

80. C:

81. A:

82. B:

83. D: Either of the parents

Chart for Qs. 84 to 88:

A = unmarried girl

B = Teacher of Mathematics

C = Married lady and Teacher of subjects related to agriculture

D = Unmarried girl

E = Teacher of Commerce

84. D:

85. E:

86. C:

87. D:

88. E:

Chart for Qs. 89 to 93:

A = Doctor

B = Industrialist

C = Teacher and daughter of A

D = Civil Engineer and wife of B's friend

E = Civil Engineer

F = Doctor

89. C:

90. A:

91. B:

92. C:

93. D:

Chart for Qs. 94 to 98:

Meerut	A	B	C	X	E
Kanpur	A	B	C	D	X
Goa	A	B	X	D	E
Jaipur	A	X	C	D	E
Rampur	X	B	C	D	E

94. D:

95. C:

96. D:

97. A:

98. B:

EXERCISE - 2

1. C: Tortoise, Crab and Cow are three separate entities and don't bear any mutual relationship.

2. A: Jam and Jelly are different from each other but both are eatables and are made from fruit.

3. B: Paisa is a smaller denomination of rupee but dollar is different.

4. C: Volga is the name of a river and Moscow is name of a city. They are different from each other but both are included in Russia.

5. D: Captain lives in the ship and ship in the sea.

6. D:

7. B:

8. C:

9. D:

10. B:

11. C:

12. A:

13. B:

14. C:

15. D:

16. C:

17. C: Some Indians have long hairs and some Indians have short hairs. Both of them are different from each other in this particular way but both are after all Indians.

18. D:

19. C:

20. C:

21. A:

22. B:

23. C:

24. D: Region 4 is located inside the triangle and square but outside the circle. Therefore this region represents those 'army officers' who are not mighty but tall.

25. A: Russia is situated in Europe and Asia both continents.

26. C:

27. D:

28. B:

29. C:

30. A: Amphibians will be represented by the region common to the two large circles.

31. B: Frog can live in water and on earth.

32. C: 'Thief' belongs to the kingdom of 'Criminals' while 'Judge' is separate from these two.

33. A: Elephant and Lion are different species of animals but these two are included in 'animal' kingdom.

34. E: All mothers are women but some doctors may be mothers.

Some doctors may be such women who are not mothers.

There may be some doctors who are not women. They may be male doctors.

35. C: 'Jalebi' is included in the sweets and 'sweets' are included in 'eatables'.

36. E: All 'widowers' are 'men' but there may be such widowers 'who smoke'. There may be some men who smoke and who may be widowers. There may be some ladies also who smoke.

37. E: Mother and Father are two different entities but included in the family.

38. A: Hindi and English are two different languages but both are included in the term 'language'.

11

COMMON SENSE AND BEST REASON TEST

This test is meant to judge the candidate's practical acquaintance with day to day happenings and knowledge of various subjects. In this type of test, a statement is followed by four or more options. The candidate has to select from the options, the one that goes best with the given statement.

Example 1: The secret of success in life is:

A. One should be quite rich.
B. One should be honest and dutiful.
C. One should work hard regularly.
D. One should be in contact with influential and respectable persons.
E. One should be highly educated.

Explanatory Answer (C): Out of the alternatives given above "to work hard regularly" is the only alternative which brings fruit of success in one's life.

Example 2: What should a person do if he has hit a child while driving motor car and the child has been wounded?

A. He should go away on a pretext of child's fault
B. He should accompany the child to a clinic and thereby add to his treatment
C. He should get rid of the child by giving some money to him
D. He should run away from there as quick as possible
E. He should apologize for the accident.

Explanatory Answer (B): The wounded child needs clinical help as soon as possible. Therefore option 'B' is the correct answer.

EXERCISE

1. A man is your good friend if:

A. He helps you with money.
B. He helps you at the time of adversity.
C. He remains always with you.
D. He always admires you.

2. Walking is a good exercise because:

A. It takes less time.
B. It is done during the leisure period in the morning.
C. It is the least exhaustive of all the other exercises.
D. It provides opportunity to meet other persons who have come for a walk.

3. What will a person do if he finds himself standing near someone whose clothes are on fire?

A. He will make a noise and call for help.

B. He will go and call his family members quickly.

C. He will put out the fire by pouring water.

D. He will tear off that man's burning clothes and thus he will put out the fire.

4. Kamal wants to help the poor, because:

A. He will earn fame by doing so.

B. This is his holy duty.

C. This will help him in getting more votes in his favour for election to the post of M.L.A.

D. Such deed on his part will be admired by the poor.

5. A child collided against a bicycle which was coming from the wrong side. What should the child do?

A. He should let bicycle rider go away without creating any trouble for him.

B. He should lodge in police a complaint against the bicycle rider.

C. He should advise the bicycle rider to always keep his left while on road.

D. He should advise the bicycle rider to always keep his right while on road.

6. We should not sleep under a tree during night because:

A. Trees exhale carbondioxide during night.

B. Evil spirits take shelter on trees during night.

C. Trees might fall during night and persons sleeping under the tree could be crushed to death.

D. Dew drops fall from the leaves during night.

7. We can achieve success in our life only when:

A. We help others.

B. We remain healthy.

C. We work hard and have self-confidence.

D. We get recommendation from others.

8. Cables used for carrying electricity, are insulated with rubber. This is because:

A. Insulation makes the cable strong.

B. By providing insulation we can easily hold the cable.

C. Rubber is bad conductor of electricity.

D. Insulation saves cable from the effect of water.

9. If you happen to meet a handicapped person on the road, then:

A. You will not pay attention that side.

B. You will drag him to one side of the road.

C. You will be filled with anger to see him standing on the road and creating hindrance to traffic.

D. You will help him in reaching to his destination

10. A few persons don't like eating sugar, because:

A. They don't want to spend money on sugar.

B. They are diabetic patients.
C. They hate eating sugar.
D. They don't get sugar easily.

11. Ladies wear ornaments because:
A. They want to save their ornaments from thieves.
B. They want to hide their ugliness.
C. They want to look beautiful.
D. Wearing ornaments is a symbol of their wifehood.

12. During summer we wear light coloured clothes because:
A. Light coloured clothes are quite cheap.
B. Light coloured clothes absorb heat falling on the body from outside.
C. In light coloured clothes they appeare smart and good looking.
D. Light coloured clothes protect from atmospheric heat.

13. Persons having disease related to blood pressure, often go on hill stations because:
A. Cold climate is useful for them.
B. Doctors suggest them for doing so.
C. They go there with a view to change the climate.
D. Atmospheric pressure is low at the places located on high altitude.

14. Youths generally prefer to marry educated girls, because:
A. Educated wife is more trustworthy.
B. An educated wife can handle the household situations in a better way.
C. An educated wife can prove a earning hand if needed.
D. Educated wives are generally beautiful.

15. Policemen wear uniforms because:
A. Uniform keeps the criminal away.
B. Uniform is approved by the Government.
C. If keeps them smart.
D. Policemen in uniform can be identified easily.

16. These days youths prefer to wear high heel shoes because:
A. High heel shoes keep a better balance of their body.
B. This is the fashion these days.
C. It increases height of the person who has worn it.
D. This keep them safe.

17. If your friend borrows your scooter for some time and returns it back to you without giving thanks to you, what will you think about him?
A. No idea will come in mind.
B. It was a mistake to hand over scooter to such a person.
C. The friend does not possess good manners.
D. Exchange of thanks is not required among friends.

18. Fire engines are generally painted in red colour because:
A. Red colour is durable.
B. Red colour gives indication of danger.

C. Red colour makes fire engines different from other vehicles.
D. It is a colour prescribed by the Fire Service Department.

19. A younger brother brings a beautiful saree for his wife. Seeing that the elder brother's wife resists for the same saree. If financial position of the elder brother does not permit for that then what will he do?
A. He will bring the saree on credit.
B. He will create an understanding with his wife and express his inability.
C. He will scold his wife for being obstinate.
D. He will ask his younger brother's wife to give the saree to his wife on certain occasions.

20. Scientists and Research Associates wear apron because:
A. It keeps them Smart.
B. It is a symbol of learnedness.
C. It keeps their clothes safe.
D. It indicates that they are the members of Research Department.

21. A few persons wear spectacles because:
A. They want to protect their eyes.
B. They want to look graceful.
C. They want to hide their eyes.
D. They suffer from error of vision.

22. Deaf children generally become dumb also because:
A. They are deprived of this gift of God by birth.
B. Ear and throat are interconnected.
C. Others speak in front of children and hearing their voice, children learn to speak.
D. Deaf children do not try to speak.

23. A car running with high speed crushed a child and ran away from the place of accident with the same high speed. This all happened in front of a person who was passing by the place of accident. What should he do in such a case?
A. He should inform the police as soon as possible.
B. He should note the number of the car.
C. He should go accompanied with the child to a clinic and make arrangement for his treatment.

24. It is the midnight when a person is passing by an utterly deserted place. Just at that place a few armed persons appear who ask him to cast off his wrist watch and gold chain. What should he do in such a moment?
A. He should tell them that they are strangers for him and so he will not do so.
B. He should offer them his wrist watch and other valuables happily.
C. He should try to run away from scene.
D. He should instead scold them for such an immoral practice.

25. Every nation must maintain a strong army because:
A. This makes the people of the nation strong.
B. This helps in upliftment of the nation.
C. This is essential for the nation's defence.
D. This will contain the population of the country.

26. Mr. X and Mr. Y do not like each other because:
A. Mr. X is a dark-complexioned man.
B. Mr. X is a man of short stature.
C. Mr. X is not a gentleman.
D. Mr. X is not a poor man.

27. Ice floates on water because:
A. Its weight is less than the weight of the water of equal volume.
B. It is transparent.
C. It is spongy.
D. It melts quickly.

28. In summer, wet clothes dry earlier than in rainy days because:
A. We can not see the sun during rainy days.
B. During rainy days atmospheric air contains more humidity than during summer days.
C. During rainy days wet clothes absorb humidity from air.
D. During summer sharp wind blows.

29. Five persons have been produced as eye-witnesses to an accident but the person who has been charged with committing the accident says that he can produce fifty persons against these five persons who will say that they have not seen him committing the accident. The argument of the accused will not be accepted because:
A. We can not believe on an accused.
B. A witness is needed who can prove the careless driving of the accused.
C. Reality of the crime depends upon the authenticity of the witness not on the number of witnesses.
D. Respondents always produce false witnesses.

30. In a piece of land, there are snakes and vultures who eat rats. What will be instantanenous effect of coming wild dogs in this field?
A. Number of vultures will decrease.
B. Number of rats will decrease
C. Number of snakes will decrease.
D. Number of snakes will increase.

31. In the game of cards, the game depends upon the cards shown by the opponent player and cards held by him. Which of the following is essential to win in this game?
A. Memory
B. Chance
C. Paying attention on the pace of game
D. Foresight

32. In a certain year a cooperative milk society earned the net profit of Rs. 41,000. Next year its amount of profit increased to Rs. 59000. It was declared that year that 50% had been earned as profit. This profit was earned by:

A. Decreasing expenditure.
B. Maintaining the price of milk.
C. Containing the establishment expenditure of the society.
D. Maintaining the quality of milk.

33. We generally affix rubber sole on our shoes because:

A. It prevents noise.
B. Rubber is more perforated than leather.
C. Rubber fitted shoes look beautiful.
D. Affixing rubber is a fashion.

34. Platinum is costly than silver because:

A. It has more weight.
B. It is rarer than silver.
C. It is more white in colour.
D. It is harder than silver.

35. One should not smoke because:

A. Smoking is not a good habit.
B. Cigarette consists of tobacco.
C. Money spent on smoking goes waste.
D. Tobacco is injurious to health.

EXPLANATORY ANSWERS

1. B:	**2. C:**	**3. D:**	**4. B:**
5. C:	**6. A:**	**7. C:**	**8. C:**
9. D:	**10. B:**	**11. C:**	**12. D:**
13. B:	**14. C:**	**15. D:**	**16. B:**
17. C:	**18. B:**	**19. B:**	**20. C:**
21. D:	**22. C:**		

23. C: The child suffering from wounds needs urgent treatment.

24. B: There is safety in handing over wrist watch and ring.

25. C:

26. C:

27. A: Weight of ice is less than the weight of water of equal volume. Thus the buoyant force experienced by the piece of ice is more than the weight of ice, therefore the piece of ice floats on water.

28. B: During a rainy day air contains more humidity in comparison to a day in summer which reduces the rate of vapourisation. Therefore clothes during a rainy day take more time in drying.

29. C:

30. B: All of these three will eat more and more rats. Therefore number of rats will decrease.

31. A:

32. C: The members of the committee will be benefitted only when establishment expenditure is not increased. There is no any direct relationship between profit earned and the quality and price of milk sold.

33. B:

34. B: The rarer the substance, dearer is the price. Here platinum is a rare metal.

35. D:

12

TEST ON PAPER FOLDING, CUTTING AND UNFOLDING

This type of test is meant to judge the candidate's ability to trace, follow and perceive the pattern of folding and cutting a piece of paper. Given question consists of a set of three figures of which first is the figure showing a piece of paper. In the second figure the piece of paper is folded once and folded part of the paper is indicated by dotted line. In the third figure the folded paper of the second figure is shown as folded once again and a few holes are made by cutting it with scissors. Once again the folded part in the third figure is indicated by dotted line. The candidate has to select from the answer figures A, B, C, D and E, the figure which will appear on opening the paper of third figure.

Example 1: A paper is folded as shown in the given figure and two holes are made. When opened how will it appear? Choose from the given responses.

Question Figures: **Answer Figures:**

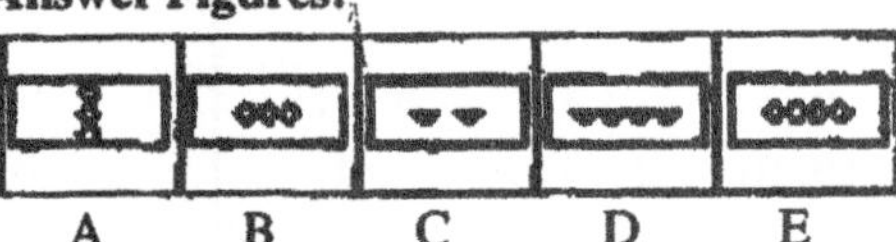

A B C D E

Explanatory Answer (E): If we unfold the first fold of the third figure, we get the figure as given below:

On unfolding the second fold of this figure we get the figure similar to answer figure E. Therefore alternative 'E' is the correct answer.

EXERCISE

Directions (Qs. 1 to 28): *In each of the following questions a paper is folded and cut with scissors as shown in the given question figures. You have to select from the given answer figures A, B, C, D and E, a figure which will appear on unfolding the paper shown in third question figure.*

Question Figures: **Answer Figures:**

1. 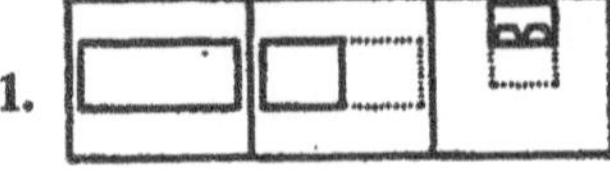 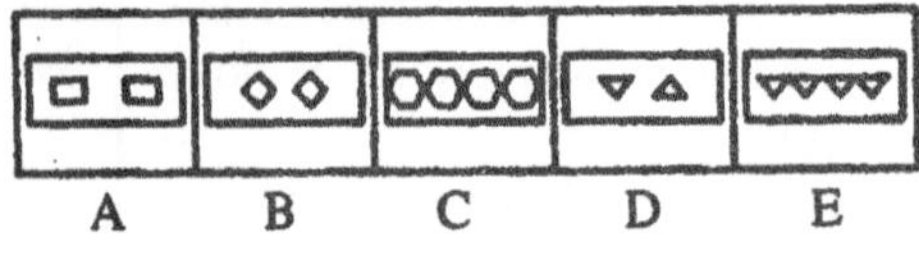

A B C D E

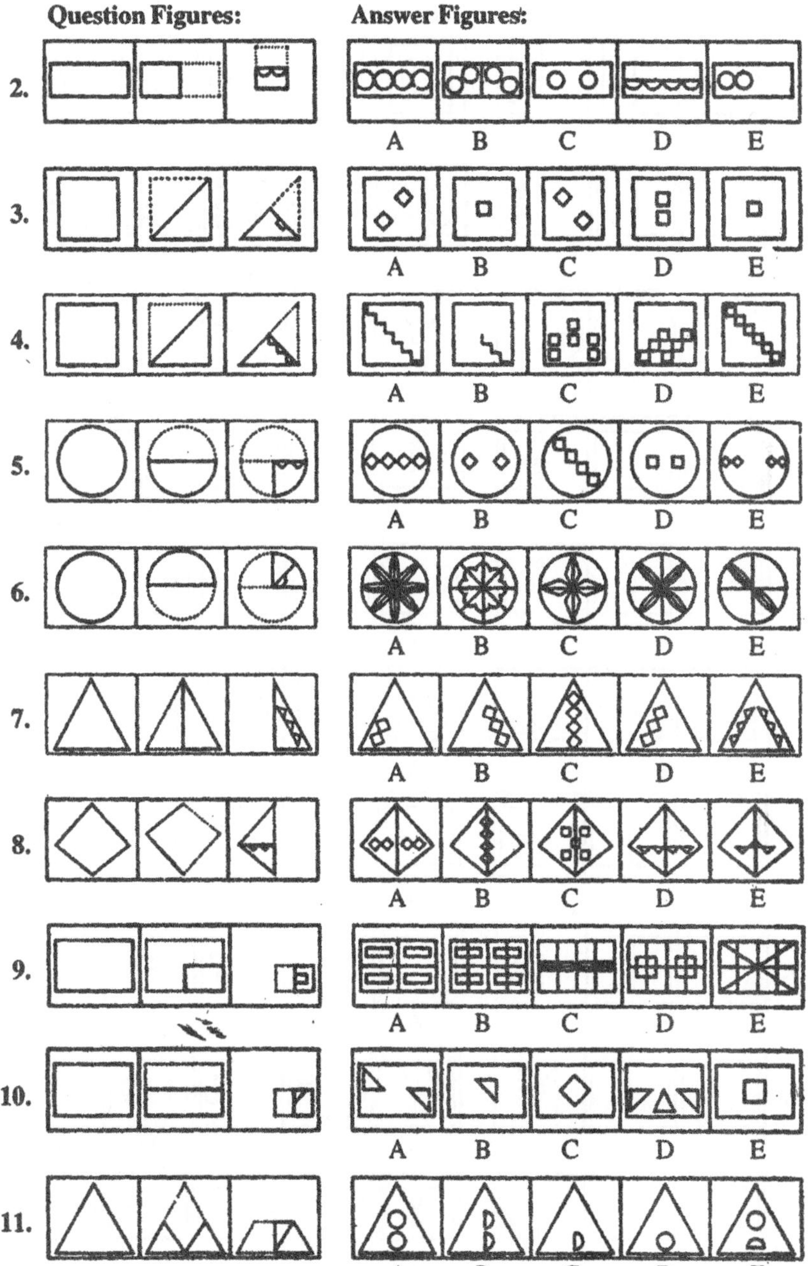
Question Figures:
Answer Figures:
2.
3.
4.
5.
6.
7.
8.
9.
10.
11.
A B C D E

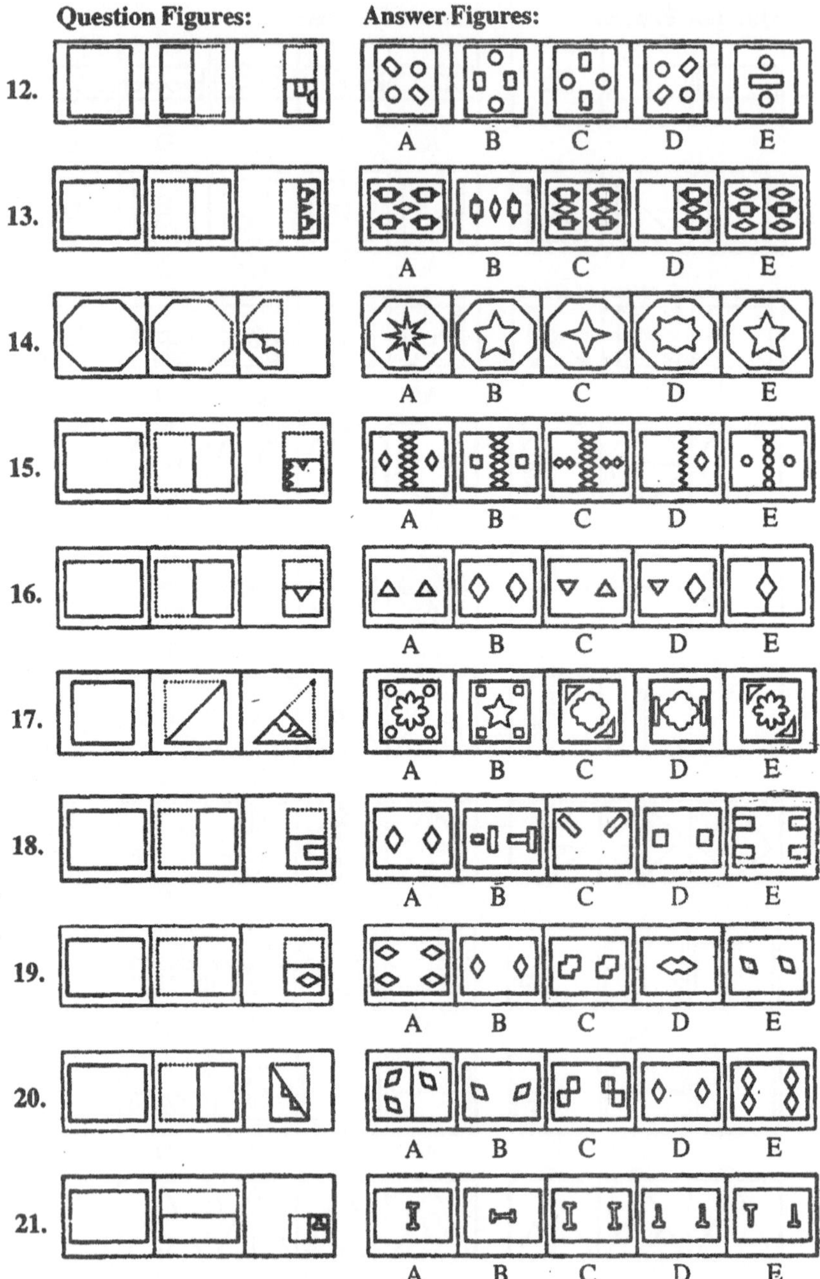
Question Figures:
Answer Figures:
12.
13.
14.
15.
16.
17.
18.
19.
20.
21.
A B C D E

Question Figures: **Answer Figures:**

22.

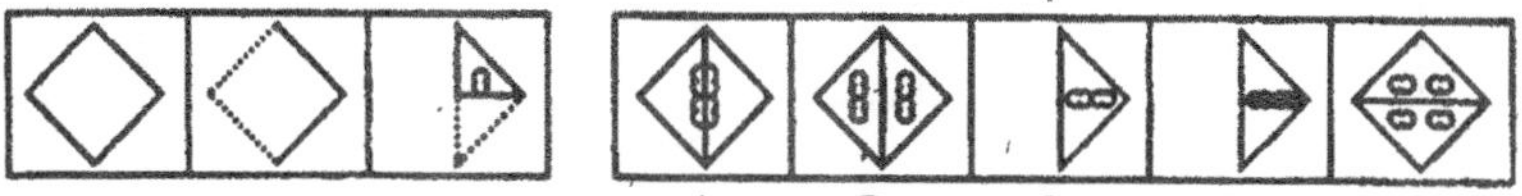

A B C D E

23.

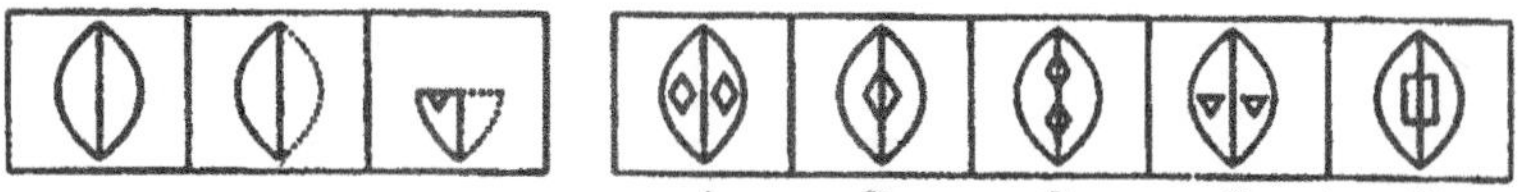

A B C D E

24.

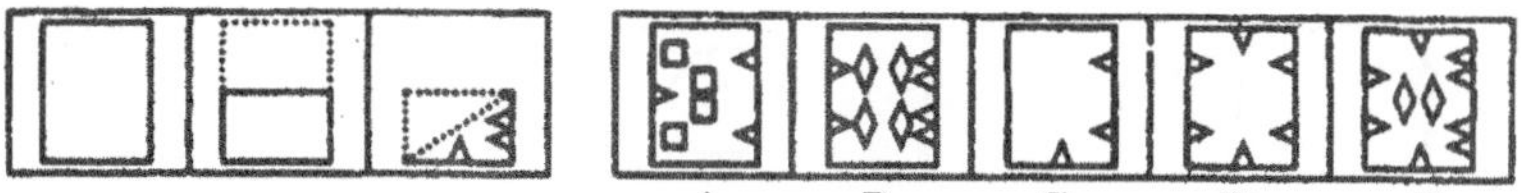

A B C D E

25.

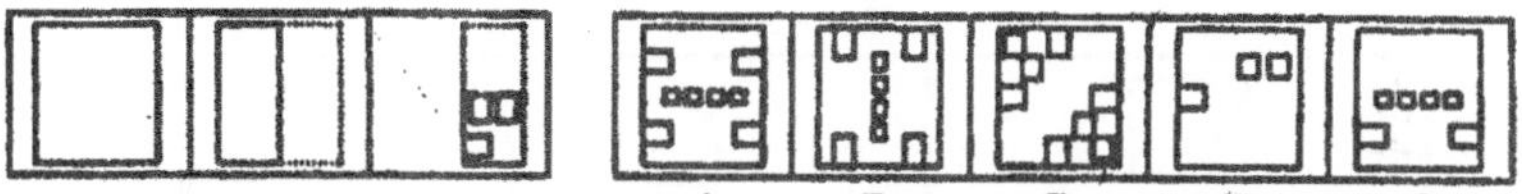

A B C D E

26.

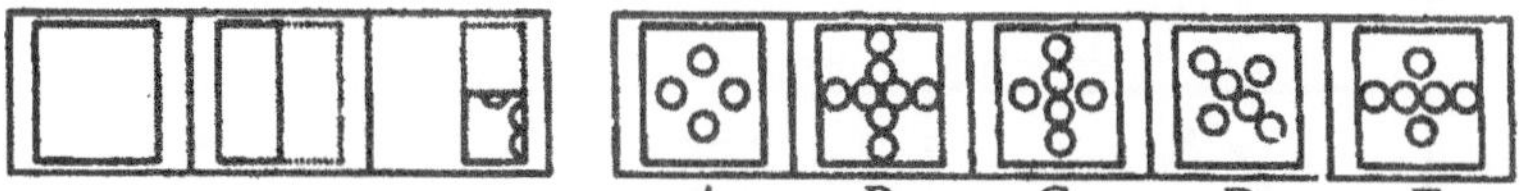

A B C D E

27.

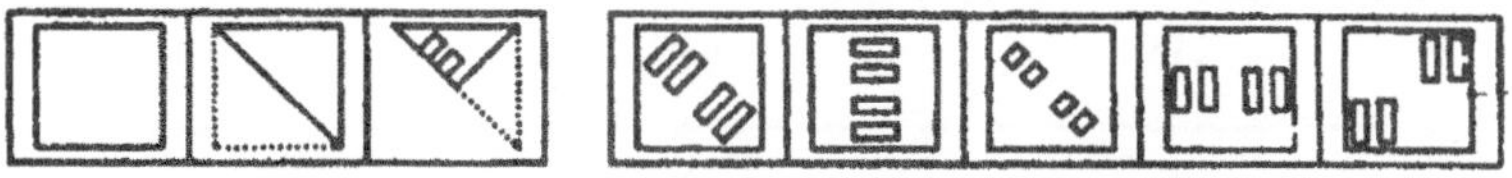

A B C D E

28.

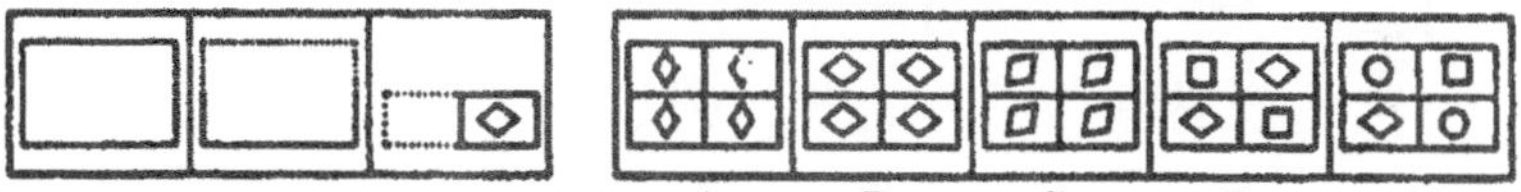

A B C D E

Directions (Qs. 29 to 38): *Given below are four answer figures A, B, C and D. In each of the questions from 29 to 38, there are three question figures numbered (1), (2) and (3). These figures are cut out pieces of one of the answer figures. You have to find out in each question, the answer figure which can be formed from the given three question figures.*

A B C D

29.

(1) (2) (3)

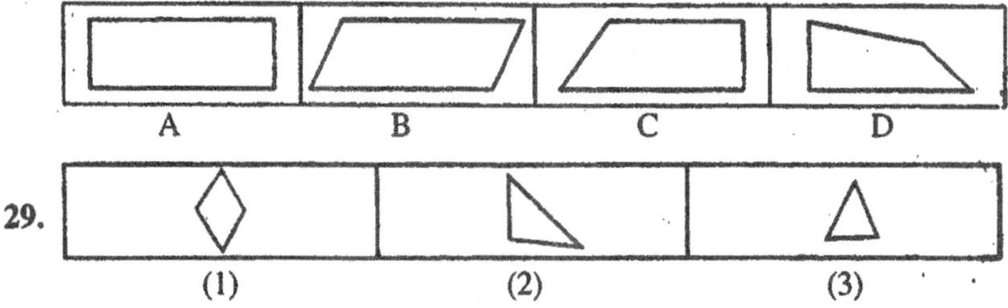

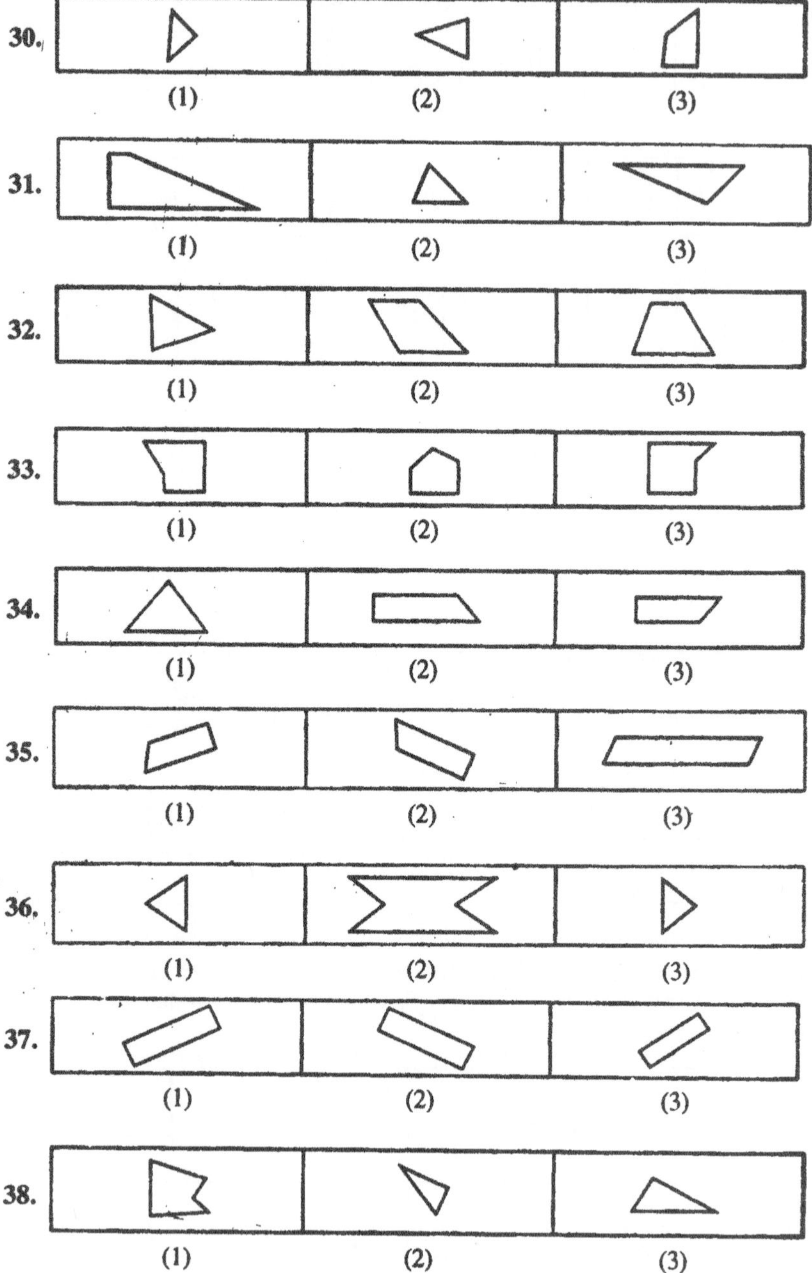
30.
(1)
(2)
(3)
31.
(1)
(2)
(3)
32.
(1)
(2)
(3)
33.
(1)
(2)
(3)
34.
(1)
(2)
(3)
35.
(1)
(2)
(3)
36.
(1)
(2)
(3)
37.
(1)
(2)
(3)
38.
(1)
(2)
(3)

ANSWERS

1. C:
2. A:
3. C:
4. E:
5. A:
6. B:
7. E:
8. A:
9. A:
10. C:
11. A:
12. B:
13. C:
14. D:
15. A:
16. B:
17. C:
18. E:
19. A:
20. C:
21. C:
22. B:
23. A:
24. E:
25. A:
26. C:
27. A:
28. B:
29. D: 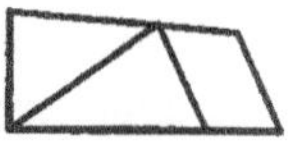
30. D: 
31. A: 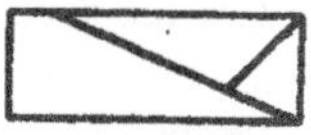
32. B: 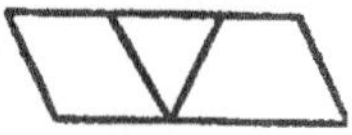
33. C: 
34. C: 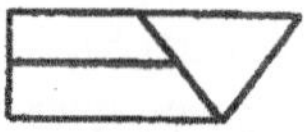
35. B: 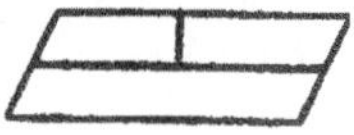
36. A: 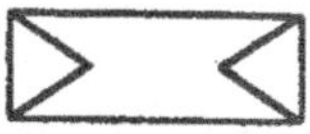
37. A: 
38. D:

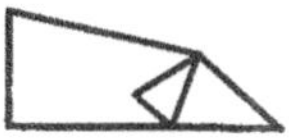

13

TEST ON EMBEDDED FIGURES

This test is meant to judge the candidate's ability to quickly find out a figure embedded in a somewhat complex figure. In this type of questions a question figure followed by four answer figures is given. The given question figure is placed in one of the answer figures containing a good number of lines thus making the answer figures somewhat complex. The candidates are asked to find out an answer figure from the given set of alternatives in which the question figure is found embedded.

Example 1: In which answer figure is the given question figure embedded?

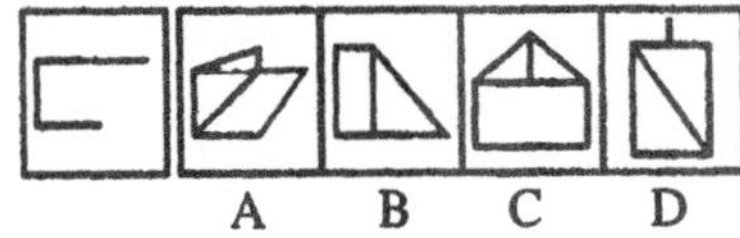

Explanatory Answer (A): A thorough examination of the above four answer figures reveals that the given question figure is placed in the first answer figure (A). Therefore answer figure 'A' is the correct answer.

EXERCISE

Directions: *In each of the questions given below one question figure followed by four answer figures has been given. The question figure is placed in one of the answer figures. You have to find out the answer figure in which the given question figure is embedded.*

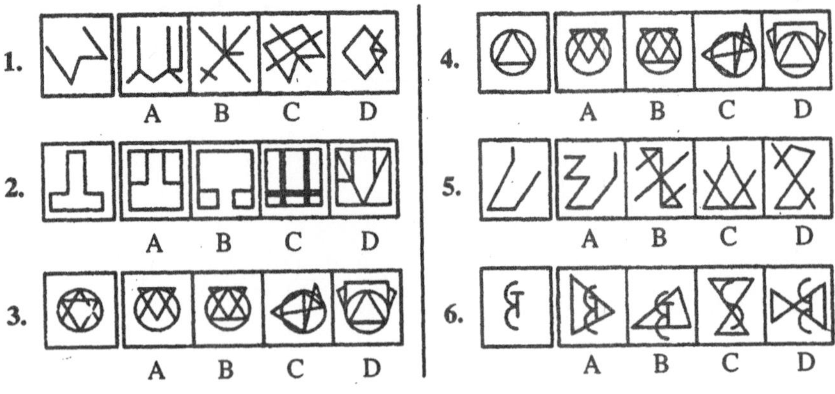

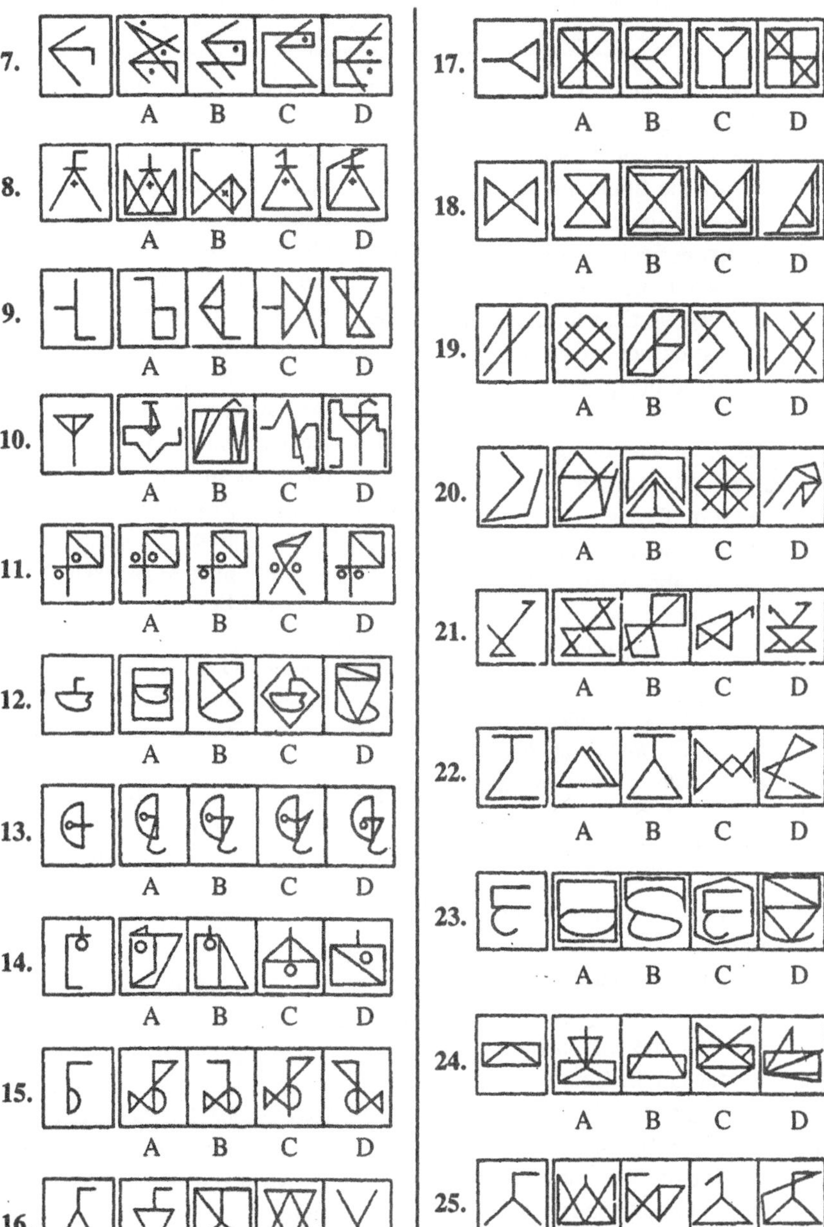
7. A B C D
8. A B C D
9. A B C D
10. A B C D
11. A B C D
12. A B C D
13. A B C D
14. A B C D
15. A B C D
16. A B C D
17. A B C D
18. A B C D
19. A B C D
20. A B C D
21. A B C D
22. A B C D
23. A B C D
24. A B C D
25. A B C D

EXPLANATORY ANSWERS

1. C: In answer figure 'C', on removing the cross lines and the upper line which encloses the figure, we get the figure similar to the question figure.

2. A: In answer figure 'A', on removing the two upper adjoining dashes and two vertical lines attached to these dashes, we get the figure similar to the question figure.

3. A: A little displacement in the design of answer figure 'A' will give the figure similar to question figure.

4. D: On removing the line drawing present above the circle we get the figure which is identical to the given question figure.

5. C: If we remove the obtuse angle forming lines from the answer figure 'C', we can get the figure as is given in question figure.

6. B: On removing the triangle from line-drawing given in answer figure 'B', we can get the figure similar to the given question figure.

7. B: If we remove one obliqe and one horizontal lines and the given dot from the answer figure 'B', we can get the figure as is given in the question figure.

8. D: In answer figure D, if we delete the lines drawn at the left and at the bottom, we can get the figure which is similar to that given in the question figure.

9. B: On removing left line drawings and base line from the answer figure 'B', we get the figure identical to the given question figure.

10. D: On removing the lateral line drawings and upper extension of the vertical line in the centre of the design in answer figure 'D', we get the figure as is given in the question figure.

11. B: Answer figure 'B' is similar to the question figure.

12. C: When lateral line drawings in answer figure 'C' is removed, we get the figure as is given in the question figure.

13. B:

14. B: On removing the enclosed figure of the right portion in answer figure 'B' we get the figure identical to question figure.

15. A: On removing the line drawings at lower left and upper left portion of the answer figure 'A', we get the figure similar to the given question figure.

16. B:

17. B: On removing the line drawings of the two horizontal lines drawn at the top and at the bottom of the design and one vertical and two oblique lines of the left from the answer figure 'B', we get the design as is given in the question figure.

18. B: On removing the horizontal lines present at the top and at the bottom of the design in answer figure 'B', we get the figure as is given in the question figure.

19. B:

20. A:

21. A:

22. B: On removing one oblique line at the right of the design in answer figure 'B', we get the design as is given in the question figure.

23. C: On removing the outer design of the answer figure 'C', we get the question figure.

24. C:

25. D: On removing the lower horizontal line, vertical line of the left and oblique line at the middle of the design in answer figure 'D', we get the design given in question figure.

14

VERIFYING THE FACT OF GIVEN STATEMENT

This type of test is based on certain incidents. In this type of questions a statement followed by four or more alternatives is given. One of these given alternatives proves or verifies the truth of given statement. The candidate has to check whether any incident or fact holds in all circumstances or they are restricted to certain conditions. These incidents are generally related to scientific, social, sports and geographical situations and also to the incidents which take place in our day to day life. Therefore candidates should be well aware about these situations. An example is given below to explain the pattern.

Example: A night-wanderer is going towards the north and he is being guided by the Polestar. He is seeing the Polestar on his right. Which of the following alternatives proves this fact?

A. Always B. Often
C. Sometimes D. Never

Explanatory Answers(D): It is stated that the man is seeing the Polestar on his right. The man is going towards the north and it is a fact that the Polestar is seen towards the north. Therefore the Polestar will be towards his face and never on his right. Here 'D' is the correct answer.

EXERCISE

Directions: *In each of the following questions a statement followed by four alternatives is given. One of these given alternatives proves or verifies the truth of given statement. Choose that alternative and mark your answer.*

1. Every vocal music essentially consists of:
   A. Accent
   B. Musician
   C. Harmonium
   D. Words
2. Restlessness is always associated with:
   A. Misfortune
   B. Unrest
   C. Severity
   D. Helplessness
3. Quarrel is essentially a result of:
   A. Injustice
   B. Hatred
   C. Disagreement
   D. Excitement
4. Disclosure is always related to:
   A. Mystery
   B. Representative
   C. Demonstration
   D. Accomplishment
5. Management is always associated with observance of:
   A. Encouragement
   B. Rules and Regulations

C. Advice
D. Inadequate pressure

6. Danger is always associated with:
A. Attack B. Enemy
C. Insecurity D. Help

7. Hills are always associated with:
A. Animals B. Trees
C. Water D. Height

8. A race is essentially associated with:
A. Success B. Contestant
C. Viewer D. Prize
E. Referee

9. Movement of Railway trains is essentially associated with:
A. Fans B. Passengers
C. Engine D. Driver

10. The most essential constituent of a hospital is:
A. Oxygen gas cylinder
B. Building
C. Telephone
D. Doctor
E. Nurse

11. A game is essentially associated with:
A. Victory B. Defeat
C. Referee D. Viewer
E. Player

12. Milk is always associated with:
A. Water
B. Oily matter
C. Whiteness
D. Cream
E. Curd

13. Every newspaper essentially consists of:
A. News
B. Date
C. Advertisement
D. Editor
E. Paper

14. In desert, there is always ample sufficiency of:
A. Heat B. Sand
C. Storm D. Camel
E. Water melon

15. Bedsteads essentially consists of:
A. Mattress
B. Bugs
C. Legs
D. Thick cotton tape
E. Tie

16. Human life is essentially dependant on:
A. Feet B. Eyes
C. Teeth D. Lungs
E. Hands

17. A state always consists of:
A. King B. Ships
C. Railways D. Army
E. Territory

18. Which of the following is always required for farming?
A. Labours B. Spade
C. Tractor D. Land
E. Cultivator

19. A school essentially consists of:
A. Black board
B. Register
C. Building
D. Teacher
E. Books

20. Following is essentially required for organizing a debate competition:
A. Stage B. Orator
C. Audience D. Typist
E. Building

21. Following is essentially required for holding an election:
A. Poster
B. Door-to-door campaign
C. Speech
D. Candidate

22. Fat person's life is always:
A. Healthy
B. Long
C. Full of joy
D. Short
E. None of the above

23. In comparison with their wives, husbands are always:
A. Older
B. Civilized
C. Younger
D. Handsome
E. None of the above

24. Sentence always consists of:
A. Composition
B. Terms
C. Terminology
D. Expression

25. Running of a factory essentially depends on:
A. Sellers B. Labours
C. Fluepipe D. Electricity

26. A river always consists of:
A. Fishes B. Weeds
C. Banks D. Boats

27. Passion is essentially a result of:
A. Indifference
B. Cruelty
C. Insight
D. Strong feeling

28. Acquittal is always related to:
A. Reprimand
B. Accusation
C. Prevention
D. Penalty

29. Astonishment is essentially associated with:
A. Rubbish
B. Wonder
C. Congestion
D. Rustic

30. Bravery is always related to:
A. Courage
B. Experience
C. Practical acquaintance
D. Effort towards the satisfaction of needs

31. Bargaining is always related to:
A. Meanness
B. Preciousness
C. Giving and taking
D. Generosity

32. A tree essentially consists of:
A. Fruit B. Leaves
C. Roots D. Flowers

33. Justice is always related to:
A. Greatness
B. Generosity
C. Righteous
D. Deceipt

34. A 10 year old girl might be taller than a 12 years old boy:
A. Always
B. Often
C. Sometimes
D. Never

35. Yesterday I saw an ice sheet which had melted into water due to heat of an oven placed nearby. This statement is correct:
A. Always B. Often
C. Sometimes D. Never

36. A woman in India can marry her deceased husband's brother while a man can not marry his deceased wife's sister. This statement is correct:

A. Sometimes B. Often
C. Always D. Never

37. A child is sitting on the rear seat in a car. The child will lean backward if the car moves ahead suddenly. This statement is correct:

A. Always B. Sometimes
C. Never D. Often

38. While going towards south in the morning we can see the sun rising on our left. This statement is correct:

A. Always B. Never
C. Sometimes D. Often

EXPLANATORY ANSWERS

1. D: Vocal music is recitation of words rhythmically. Therefore every vocal music essentially consists of words.

2. B: Restlessness always leads to mental tension which brings unrest.

3. C: Disagreement on some or other issue leads to quarrel.

4. A: Disclosure means to solve a mystery. Therefore it is clear that disclosure is related to mystery.

5. B: Management always aims at administrative reforms. Therefore the word 'Management' is always associated with observance of rules and regulations.

6. C: Insecurity may bring danger to one's life.

7. D: Hills are associated with height. They are at higher altitude than the plains.

8. B: A race is organized at least between two persons. Therefore association of a contestant is essential for a race.

9. C: Movement of rails is impossible in absence of engine.

10. D: In absence of doctors, a hospital can not serve its very purpose because in that case no patient will be given treatment.

11. E: Game can only be held if there are players.

12. C: Milk is always white.

13. A: Every newspaper essentially contains news.

14. B: Desert is a sandy plain covered with sand dunes. Therefore there is always ample sufficiency of sand in desert.

15. C: Bedsteads should essentially consist of four legs.

16. D: Human life can not sustain in absence of lungs. A man can survive in absence of any of the four organs mentioned in the other alternatives but not in the absence of lungs.

17. E: For concept of state a definite territory is inevitable.

18. D: Farming is done on land.

19. D: A school can not be run in absence of teacher.

20. B: Debate competition can not be organized in absence of orators.

21. D: Election means to elect a leader. Therefore contesting candidates are essentially required for holding an election.

22. D: Fat persons often suffer from diseases. Therefore their life span is short.

23. E:

24. B: Sentence is always a group of terms.

25. B: A factory can not be run without Labours.

26. C:

27. D: Strong feeling results into passion.

28. B: Acquittal is always related to accusation. In absence of accusation, there is no need of acquittal.

29. B: Astonishment and wonder are synonymous to each other.

30. A: Courage is the root of bravery.

31. C: Bargaining is posssible only when some thing is given and some other thing is taken.

32. C: Existence of tree is not possible in absence of roots.

33. C: Justice is always righteous.

34. B: Height of a man is not dependant only on his age.

35. D: Ice sheet when placed near an oven will be melted into water due to heat of the oven. Therefore it is not possible to see the ice sheet when it has melted into water.

36. A:

37. A: As per rule, the person sitting in the car will lean backwad on moving the car suddenly ahead.

38. A: Every morning the sun rises in the east. If a man goes towards south, he will be facing towards south and his left hand will be towards east. Therefore while going towards south, the sun will always rise towards the left hand.

15

MISCELLANEOUS

EXERCISE - 1

Directions: *In each of the questions from 1 to 10, the question figure is given on the extreme left. This question figure is followed by four answer figures indicated by A, B, C and D. You are required to find out the one and only one of the four answer figures which is nearest to the question figure given at the extreme left.*

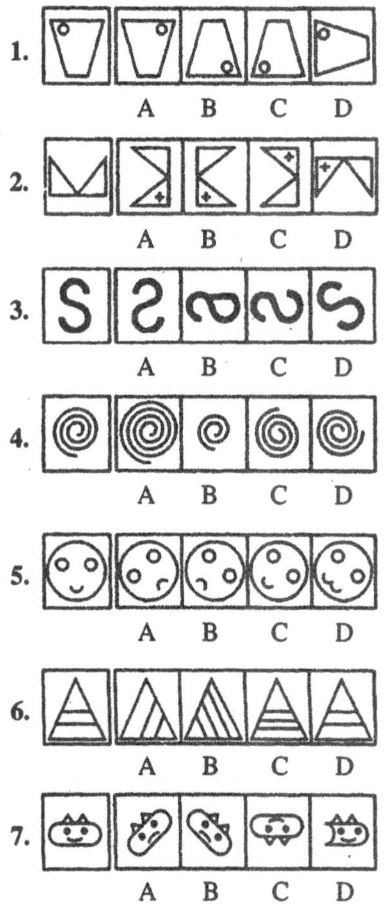

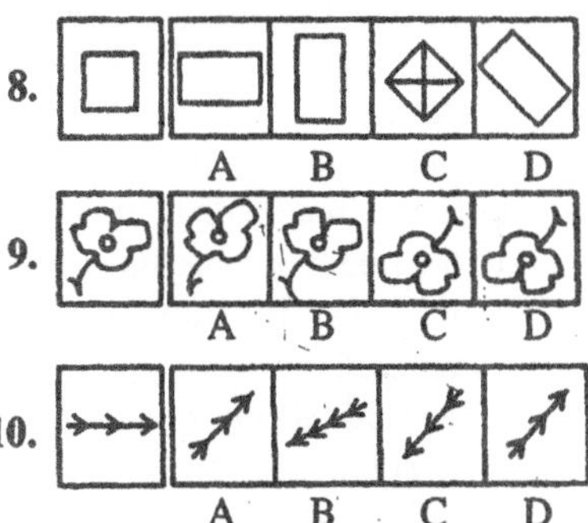

11. Locate the figure from amongst the given five alternatives which would fit the question mark and complete the matrix.

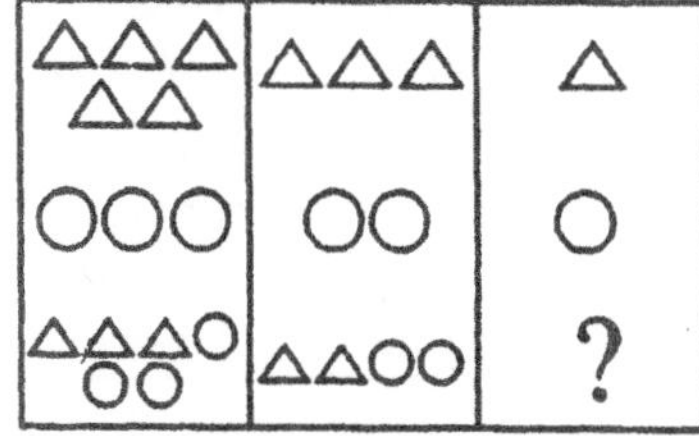

A. △○ B. △△△

C. ○○ D. △△

E. ○○△

12. Which of the figures given in alternatives A, B, C, D and E

would complete the line-drawing given below?

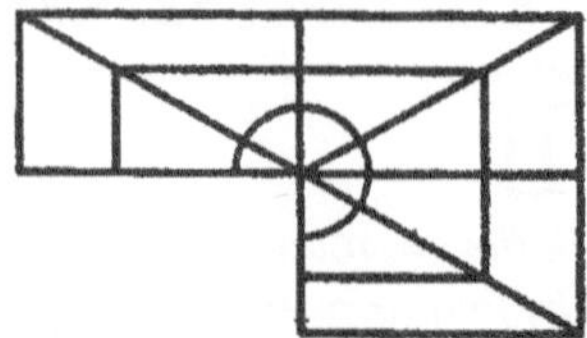

A.  B. 

C.  D. 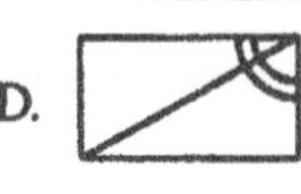

E. 

EXERCISE - 2

Directions (Qs. 1 to 10): *Questions from 1 to 10 is based on the information given below:*

Following are the eligibility conditions for admission in a medical college:

1. The students must have passed the examination of 12th standard.
2. The students must have attained the age of sixteen on or before 1.4.2000.
3. The students must have studied science in 12th class.
4. The students will have to deposit additional fees as under:

Marks obtained in 12th class	*Other than the son or daughter of trustee or staff member of the college*	*Son or daughter of the trustee or staff member of the college*
80% or more	Rs. 20,000	Rs. 10,000
71% to 79%	Rs. 40,000	Rs. 20,000
Less than 71%	Rs. 80,000	Rs. 40,000

If a student has secured more than 90% marks in the 12th standard examination, the case may be referred to the chairman for granting an exemption from payment of additional fees.

5. The student will have to make an instant deposit of the additional fees plus an amount of Rs. 10,000 as annual fee in cash or in the form of Bank Draft at the time of admission.
6. A student belonging to reserve categories will pay only the annual fee if he/she has secured marks 60% or more. If the student has secured marks more than 50% but less than 60%, then he/she will have to deposit an amount equal to one-fourth of the additional fees plus the annual fee. In both the cases the student will have to produce requisite caste certificate in support of his/her claim for fee-relaxation.
7. If the student is in a position to deposit only 50% to 80% of the total amount instantly, then he/she should request the director (admission) for granting an admission in the college who is authorised to grant admission to such a student under certain conditions.
8. If a student is in a position to deposit amount less than 50%, then his/her admission in the college will be cancelled.
9. If a student has secured marks more than 80% but he is not in a

position to deposit the full amount of the fees, then he may get admission in the college on certain conditions.

Based on the information furnished above, find out the possibility of admission of the student in each case as referred to in the following questions. Your answer is (A) if the student is given admission in the college without imposing any condition; if the student is given admission on certain conditions, then your answer is (B); If the student requests the Director (admission) for granting an admission under certain conditions, then your answer is (C); if the case pertaining to admission of the student is referred to the chairman for granting an exemption from payment of additional fees then your answer is (D) and if the student fails to get admission in the college then your answer is (E).

1. Payal, a daughter of the Principal of the College, was sixteen and half years old on 1.3.2001. She studied science in 12th class and passed with 67% marks. She has deposited a draft of Rs. 22,000 for getting admission in the college.
2. Neha attained the age of 16 years on 1.1.2001. She studied science in 12th class and secured 55% marks in the examination. At the time of admission in the college she deposited a draft of Rs. 15,000 and also furnished a caste certificate in favour of her belonging to scheduled caste.
3. Piyush studied science in 12th class and he secured 85% marks. He deposited a draft of Rs. 30,000 for admission in the Medical college.
4. A student studied science in his 12th class and secured 60% in the examination. He deposited a certificate in favour of his belonging to scheduled caste category and a draft amounting to Rs. 20,000 for admission in the Medical College. He was born on 1.1.1983.
5. 17 year old Riya who is daughter of the chairman of the Medical College, had studied science in 12th class. She secured 73% marks in the examination. She deposited a draft of Rs. 30,000 for admission in the Medical College.
6. Aman is the son of Laboratory Assistant of the Medical College. He studied science in 12th class and secured 95% marks in the examination. He was in a position to deposit only annual fee of the Medical College. He was born on 10.1.1984.
7. 17 year old Mridul secured 75% marks in 12th class examination. He was in a position to deposit annual fee plus Rs. 50,000 as additional fees for admission in the Medical College.
8. Anku studied science in 12th class and secured 92% marks in the examination. He was in a position to deposit Rs. 20,000

for admission in the Medical College. On 1.3.2001 he completed his 17 years of age.

9. A student securd 60% in the final examination of class 12th. He was born on 7.12.1985. He studied science in 12th class and he deposited Rs. 10,000 for admission in the Medical College.

10. 18 years old Seema secured 65% marks in 12th class examination. She studied science in 12th class and she deposited Rs. 50,000 for admission in the Medical College.

11. How many digits in the following number series are divisible by 2 and are immediately preceded by digit of 6 and immediately followed by digit of 3?

6656839436736432864682663

A. 3 B. 4
C. 1 D. 2
E. None of these

12. There are 20 balls in a box of which 8 are green, 7 are white and 5 are red. At least how many balls should be picked out from this box so that the picked out collection may definitely contain one ball of each colour?

A. 15 B. 11
C. 16 D. 13

13. In a pile a number of books are kept one above the other. In this pile Book 'A' is third from the top which is regarding contemporary political situation, Book 'B' is sixth from the bottom and it is regarding social scenario in 21st century. This book is fifth book below A. What is the number of total books kept in this pile?

A. 11 B. 15
C. 13 D. 12
E. 14

14. How many digits of 4 in the given number series are immediately followed by 2, 3, 5?

3410842416403457942348946

A. 6 B. 4
C. 3 D. 5
E. 2

15. How many digits of 2 in the following number series are preceded by 5 but not followed by 7?

63527258527294152683

A. 1 B. 4
C. 2 D. 5
E. 3

Directions (Qs. 16 to 20): *Questions from 16 to 20 are based on the following information:*

"The sides of a cube are painted in three different colours, i.e., red, blue and green respectively. None of the two adjacent sides are painted in same colour. This cube is cut into 36 smaller cubes of which 32 are of equal size and remaining 4 cubes are bigger in size. None of these relatively bigger cubes has any face painted in red."

16. How many smaller cubes will be painted on two sides only?

A. 28 B. 16
C. 24 D. 36
E. 32

17. How many smaller cubes will be painted on two or more than two

sides?

A. 16 B. 28

C. 32 D. 36

E. 20

18. How many smaller cubes will be painted on three sides?

A. 20 B. 16

C. 0 D. 32

19. How many cubes will be painted on one face only?

A. 20 B. 8

C. 12 D. 0

E. 8

20. How many cubes will have a face painted in red?

A. 0 B. 8

C. 32 D. 16

E. 20

21. How many digits of 4 in the following number series are immediately followed by 2 or 3 or 5?

3, 4, 10, 8, 4, 2, 4, 1, 6, 4, 0, 3, 4, 5, 7, 9, 4, 2, 3, 4, 8, 9, 4, 6

A. 1 B. 3

C. 2 D. 6

E. None of the above

22. How many digits of 7 are there in the following number series, each of which is immediately preceded by 4 but not immediately followed by 2?

4727235974752479478471

A. 2 B. 3

C. 4 D. 1

E. 5

Directions: *Questions from 23 to 26 are based on the information given below: "A cube with side 3 inches, painted blue on all the faces, is cut into 1 inch cubes."*

23. How many 1 inch cubes are made on cutting the bigger cube?

A. 11 B. 5

C. 9 D. 6

E. 15

24. How many 1 inch cubes will be painted on three sides?

A. 6 B. 9

C. 8 D. 7

E. None of the above

25. How many 1 inch cubes will have no face painted?

A. 1 B. 2

C. 5 D. 4

E. None of the above

26. How many 1 inch cubes will be painted on one face only?

A. 12 B. 4

C. 6 D. 7

E. None of the above

27. I was studying in Allahabad University. In those days I was living with other colleagues in a lodge. One day I received a letter from my father. He was arriving Allahabad by N.E. Express at 6.00 O' clock in the next morning. Next day I reached Allahabad junction at 5.30 A.M. The train was running late. I decided to take breakfast. Puri and Kachodi were being sold in a stall on the junction. Laddoos were also being sold there. I finished my breakfast and after having a cup of coffee, I purchased 4 laddoos. I was about to eat laddoos when a monkey appeared from somewhere and snatched two laddoos from me and ran away. Thinking the monkey as an incarnation of god Hanuman, I perceived that

Hanuman ji also had liking for laddoos. Then I prayed with a view to get his blessings. Can you guess my purpose of visiting Allahabad junction?

A. To get blessings from god Hanuman
B. To have breakfast
C. To welcome father
D. To take coffee

Directions (Qs. 28 to 32): *In each of the questions from 28 to 32, a sentence is given. Read the given sentence carefully and (1) Give answer (A) if the given sentence is a fact; (2) Give answer (B) if the given sentence expresses an opinion; (3) Give answer (C) if the given sentence expresses a firm decision and (4) Give answer (D) if the given sentence is an inference.*

28. Many people in India are illiterate.
A. 1 B. 3
C. 2 D. 4

29. Cent-percent people living in India will get their shelter by the end of 21st century.
A. 2 B. 3
C. 1 D. 4

30. Tamil's problem in Sri Lanka has become grave.
A. 1 B. 3
C. 2 D. 4

31. We have to keep our country secured against attack of enemies at any cost.
A. 4 B. 1
C. 3 D. 2

32. People of Rajasthan are generally superstitious.
A. 4 B. 2
C. 1 D. 3

Directions (Qs. 33 to 41): *In each of the questions from 33 to 41, two words are given in the beginning which indicate some entities. You have to answer the questions given below according to the following instruction.*

1. Give answer (A) if one is made of the other.
2. Give answer (B) if both are made of some other thing.
3. Give answer (C) if one is result of the other.
4. Give answer (D) if one is the need of the other.

33. Unemployment, Poverty
A. 4 B. 1
C. 3 D. 2

34. Bark of a tree, Leaves
A. 1 B. 3
C. 2 D. 4

35. Hunger, Food
A. 2 B. 3
C. 1 D. 4

36. Sympathy, Distressed person
A. 3 B. 1
C. 2 D. 4

37. Delta, River
A. 2 B. 4
C. 3 D. 1

38. Fish, Water
A. 3 B. 1
C. 2 D. 4

39. Cotton, Thread
A. 1 B. 3
C. 2 D. 4

40. Butter, Curd
A. 1 B. 2
C. 3 D. 4

41. Flour, Wheat
A. 1 B. 2
C. 3 D. 4

42. What is the number of triangles in the following figure?

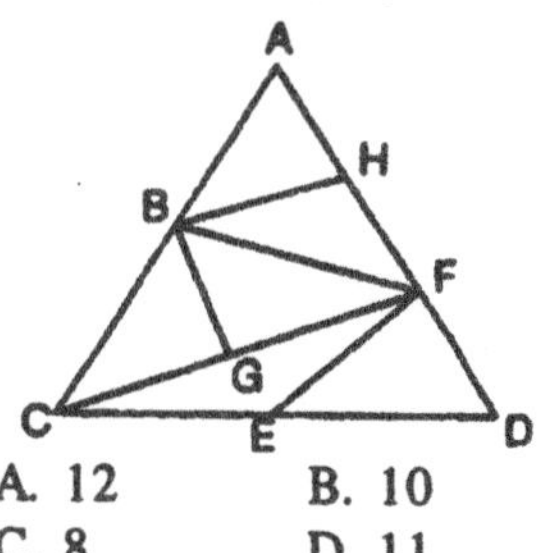

A. 12 B. 10
C. 8 D. 11

43. In the figure given below which one is the shortest route from A to B?

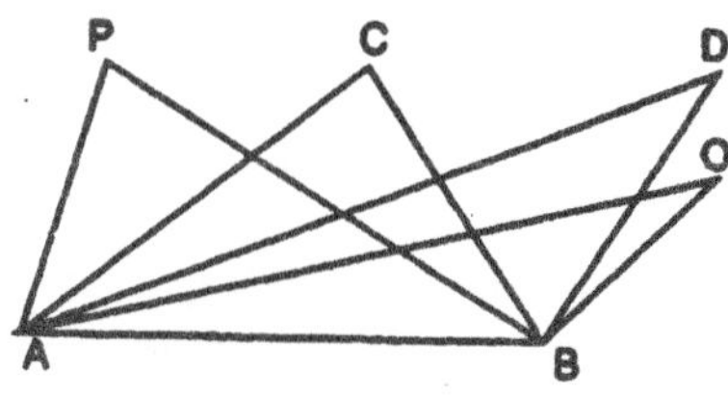

A. ADB B. APB
C. ACB D. None of these

44. In the following figure two fixed dots X and Y have been marked on a solid wheel. Which of the route-diagrams will be formed by X and Y if the wheel moves forward on AB line?

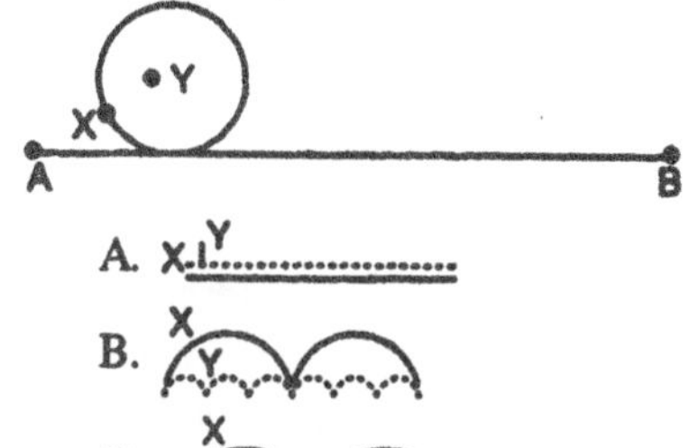

A.
B.
C.
D.

45. What is the number of triangles in the following figure?

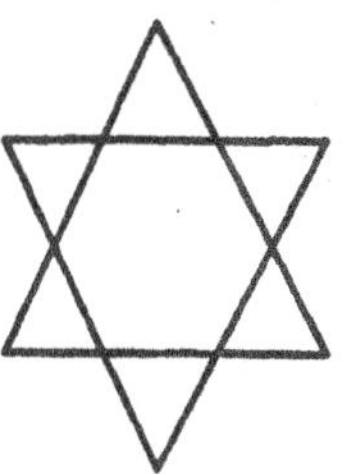

A. 14 B. 8
C. 5 D. 10

46. Three different positions of a cube are shown below. Look carefully their faces and find out the number which will be on the side opposite to 3?

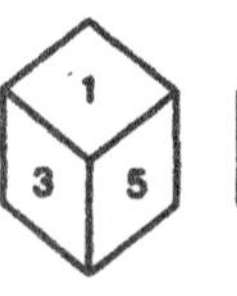

A. 5 B. 6
C. 1 D. 2

47. All the six faces of a solid cube are coloured. This cube is cut into many smaller cubes such that the side of these smaller cubes is one-fourth the side of the bigger cube. How many of these smaller cubes are painted on one face only?

A. 32 B. 16
C. 24 D. 12

48. How many digits of 5 are there in the following number series which are immediately followed by 4 but are not immediately preceded by 6?

25436547859353765446

A. 2 B. 4
C. 3 D. 1

49. Which of the following figures can be drawn in one stretch without raising the pencil in between and none of the lines is left undrawn in the first attempt?

A. A, B, C B. B, C
C. B, D D. A, C and D

50. What is the number of triangles in the following figure?

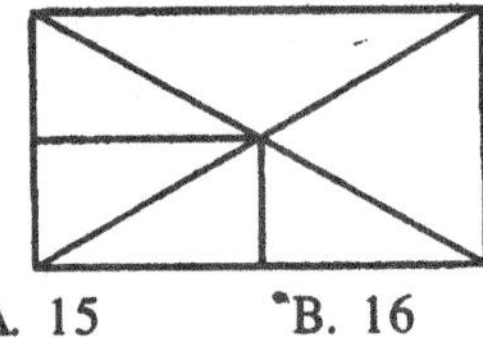

A. 15 B. 16
C. 8 D. 9
E. 12

Directions (Qs. 51 to 55): *In each of the questions from 51 to 55, three words are given in the beginning followed by four alternatives of which you have to select one which best illustrates the general characteristics of the three given words in the beginning.*

51. Drama, Novel, Epic
A. Subject B. Literature
C. Knowledge D. Poetry

52. Jealousy, Deception, Hatred
A. Merit B. Grudge
C. Inhuman D. Destruction

53. Gun, Pistol, Sword
A. Weapon B. Sepoy
C. Bullet D. War

54. Panther, Wolf, Deer
A. Omnivorous
B. Carnivorous
C. Mammal
D. Herbivorous

55. Railway train, Ship, Truck
A. Wheel
B. Rooms
C. Speed
D. Transportation

56. In the figure given below different faces of a cube are shown. Which number will be on the side opposite to 4?

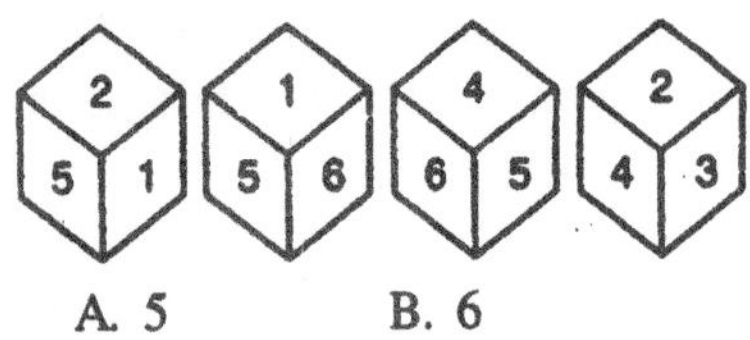

A. 5 B. 6
C. 2 D. 1
E. 3

Directions (Qs. 57 to 66): *Questions from 57 to 66 are based on the PIN CODES given below. Study the given codes carefully before answering the questions.*

112021 306101 113032 506101
306101 404032 112021 112101
403001 112001 112132 504032
504032 113002 503001 306101
112023 112032 712032 712021

57. Difference between total zones and total subzones is:
A. 10 B. 0
C. 7 D. 3
E. 5

58. If third number indicates the assorting zone, then how many assorting zones are there?
A. 4 B. 8
C. 3 D. 6
E. 2

59. What is the number of distributing post offices?
A. 7 B. 8
C. 15 D. 6
E. 20

60. Numerical value of which of the following Pin Codes is maximum?
A. 503001 B. 712021
C. 403001 D. 112023
E. 712032

61. How many Pin Codes have been repeated more than once?
A. 20 B. 5
C. 3 D. 2
E. 4

62. Which of the following distributing post offices will receive maximum mails?
A. 101 B. 032
C. 001 D. 021
E. 002

63. If last three digits indicate distributing post offices then code of how many post offices start from zero?
A. 8 B. 20
C. 7 D. 14
E. 6

64. If first three digits indicate assorting zones, then the number of assorting zones is:
A. 5 B. 6
C. 4 D. 9
E. 2

65. If first two digits indicate sub zones, then the number of sub zones is:
A. 5 B. 20
C. 15 D. 12
E. 8

66. If first digit of the given codes indicates zones, then the number of total zones is:
A. 3 B. 4
C. 8 D. 5

67. In a meeting every member who attended the meeting shook hands with the chairman. If in total hands were shaken 190 times, then the number of members who attended the meeting was:
A. 21 B. 10
C. 20 D. 19
E. None of these

68. What is the number of cubes in the following figure?

A. 13 B. 9
C. 8 D. 10
E. 12

69. In the following number series which digit is being repeated once in the very beginning?
98768564534231O
A. 5 B. 7
C. 9 D. 8

70. A rectangular piece of paper has been cut along the hypotenuse and thus two triangles have been made out of this rectangular piece of paper. Now how many times any of these triangles should be cut to have a quadrangular shape?
A. 1 B. 5
C. 3 D. 6
E. 4

71. How many digits of 5 are there in the following number series each of which is immediately followed by a digit of 4 but not immediately preceded by a digit of 6?
1542654975935476544556

A. 4 B. 2
C. 3 D. 1
E. More than 4

72. In the following number series how many digits of 9 are immediately preceded by digit of 6 but not immediately followed by digit of 3?
693569639269569586669364 6
9196

A. 2 B. 1
C. 4 D. 3
E. None of these

EXERCISE - 3

Directions (Qs. 1 to 4): *Questions from 1 to 4 are based on the following information:*

'Δ' means '–', '□' means '+'; '=' means '>'; '÷' means '<' and '+' means '='.

1. If BC + AD and B = A, then which one of the following is corect?
A. A + B B. D + C
C. C = D D. C ÷ D

2. If AB + CD and B + D, then which one of the following is correct?
A. A + C B. C ÷ A + D
C. C + A D. C ÷ A

3. If AB = CD and B + D, then which of the following is correct?
A. C ≐ A B. B ÷ A
C. A + D D. C ÷ A

4. If A ÷ D and C + D, then which of the following is correct?
A. C + A B. C = A
C. C ÷ A D. C Δ A + B

5. If '+' means '–', '–' means '×', '÷' means '+' and '×' means '÷', then what is the value of 10 × 5 ÷ 3 – 2 + 3?
A. 7 B. $17\frac{2}{3}$
C. $-2\frac{3}{8}$ D. 5
E. None of these

6. How many numbers amongst the numbers 7 to 41 are there which are exactly divisible by 9 but not by 3?
A. 6 B. 7
C. 9 D. 8
E. None of these

7. A man on the bus stop is waiting for a bus of route number 10, 17 or 25. Frequency of the service of route No. 10 is 10 minutes, that of route no. 17 is 20 minutes and of route No. 25 is 40 minutes. If one bus of the above said route numbers had left the bus stop just before the man reached at the bus stop, then calculate the minimum time of waiting of that man on the bus stop.
A. 6 minutes B. 8 minutes
C. 10 minutes D. 4 minutes

Directions (Qs. 8 to 10): *In each of the questions from 8 to 10, a question mark is given which has to be substituted by any one of the five alternatives appended below each question. You have to find out a number from amongst the given alternatives which can be put at the sign of interrogation.*

8. $8 \times 3 + 6 = 72 \div ? + 28 - 6$

A. 9 B. 22
C. 30 D. 8
E. None of the above

9.

14	12	7
8	?	16
11	12	10

A. 6 B. 12
C. 9 D. 10

10. $11 \times 5 + 8 - 3 = 2 \times 2 \times 3 \times ?$

A. 62 B. 12
C. 60 D. 5
E. None of the above

11. If $127 \times 407 = 110$ and $54 \times 86 = 126$, then $125 \times 232 = ?$

A. 116 B. 56
C. 70 D. 121
E. 82

12. 'A' said to 'B' that their uncle Tom had seen them after 13th and before 18th of last month but 'B' said that the uncle had seen them after 16th and before 20th of the last month. On which day had the uncle seen them?

A. 15th B. 16th
C. 17th D. 14th
E. None of these

13. Which one number can be placed at the sign (?) of interrogation?

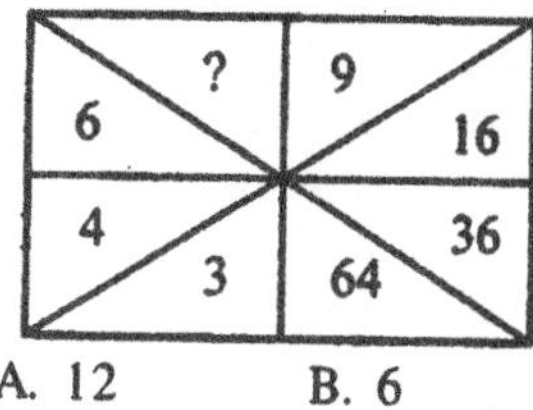

A. 12 B. 6
C. 8 D. 4
E. 3

14. Which one number can be placed at the sign of interrogation?

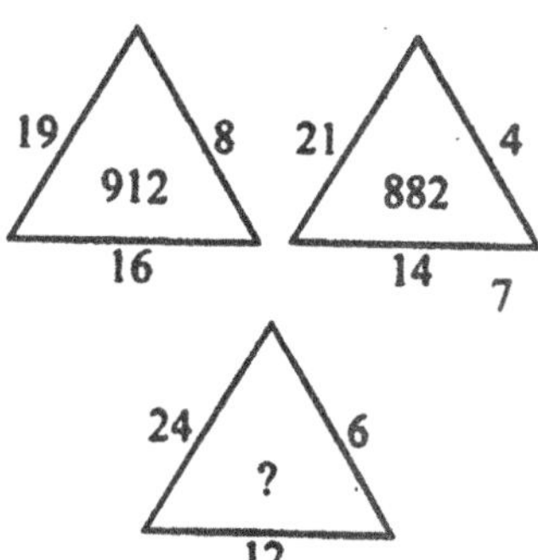

A. 1356 B. 862
C. 1234 D. 864
E. None of the above

15. Select the right option which can be placed at the sign of interrogation?

4	8	20
9	3	15
6	6	?

A. 24 B. 16
C. 20 D. 22
E. 18

16. In a queue Rahul is standing 9th from either end. What is total number of children standing in the queue?

A. 17 B. 16
C. 18 D. 19

17. A man has three packets in his hand. In the first packet he has kept 4 balls of different colours. In the second packet he has kept 5 balls of different colours and in the third packet he has kept 3 balls of different colours. Balls of two specific colours have been kept in first and second packet only and balls of one specific colours have been kept in all the three packets. What is the total number of colours given to these balls?

A. 9 B. 10
C. 8 D. 11
E. 7

18. For an interview, the Managing Director of the company reached in the meeting room 10 minutes before 12.30 P.M. He reached 20 minutes before the arrival of the chairman of the company. The chairman arrived in the meeting room 30 minutes after the fixed time of interview. What was the time fixed for interview in the meeting room?

A. 12.50 P.M. B. 12.00 Noon
C. 12.30 P.M. D. 12.10 P.M.
E. 12.40 P.M.

19. If P stands for division, Q stands for multiplication, R stands for addition and S stands for subtraction, then value of 18 Q 12 P 4 R 5 S 6 is:

A. 65 B. 36
C. 53 D. 59
E. None of the above

20. If in a given number 57124893, we interchange the first and the second digits, the third and the fourth digits and so on, then counting from the left end, which digit will be fourth?

A. 8 B. 2
C. 4 D. 1
E. None of the above

21. In a line of girls Pinki is seventh from the left end and Bhanu is fourth from the right end. If these two girls interchange their places, then Pinki will be standing 15th from the left end. After interchanging what will be the position of Bhanu in the line from right end?

A. Fifteenth B. Eleventh
C. Fourth D. Eighth
E. Twelfth

22. If the number series given below is written in reverse order, what number will be 7th to the right of fourth number from the left end?
1, 8, 3, 9, 7, 4, 10, 6, 2, 11, 13, 5, 14, 16

A. 3 B. 11
C. 9 D. 8
E. 13

23. By using the second, fifth and sixth digits of 46789153, we can have a square number of a two digit number. Which of the following will be the first digit of that square number

A. 8 B. 9
C. 6 D. 1
E. None of the above

24. If digits of each of the three digit numbers given below are written in reverse order and the numbers obtained so are written in descending order, then what will be the digit in the middle of the number placed second from the largest number?
739, 279, 359, 189, 549

A. 8 B. 7
C. 5 D. 3
E. None of the above

25. The capacity of a lift is to carry 12 men or 20 children at a time. What is the number of men who can be accomodated with 15 children in the lift?

A. 3 B. 4
C. 5 D. 6

26. If the price of 15 apples and 20 oranges is equal to the price of 20 apples and 15 oranges, then:

A. Apples are dear and oranges are comparatively cheap in the market
B. Oranges are dear and apples are comparatively cheap in the market
C. Prices of oranges and apples are same in the market
D. Given information is insufficient to distinguish the prices of the two items separately

Directions (Qs. 27 to 30): *You have to select five persons for a team from amongst 5 men P, Q, R, S and T and 4 women A, B, C and D. Some conclusions are as given below:*

R and S will accompany each other.
Q will not accompany B and C.
R and A have to accompany each other.
T will not accompany either A or D.

27. If two lady members are to be taken in the team then which of the following team is not possible to constitute?

A. ACPRS B. ABPRS
C. CDPRS D. BCPST

28. If A is included in the team as a member and 4 other members of the team are men then other members excluding 'A' in the team are:

A. PQST B. PQRS
C. PRST D. QRST

29. If three lady members are to be taken in the team then members of the team will be:

A. ABCDR B. ACDRS
C. BCDPS D. ABCRT

30. If Q is a member incorporated in the team, then other members of the team are:

A. APRS B. ADRS
C. BCPT D. ADPS

31. How many numbers are there between 1 and 100 which are divisible by 8 without leaving any remainder and which consist of digit 8?

A. 4 B. 6
C. 0 D. 8
E. 3

32. In a queue of boys, Shubham was 8th from left end. Changing his place he moved towards his right and thus three more boys came to his left. Now he was 10th from the right end. How many boys were standing in that queue?

A. 19 B. 20
C. 21 D. 18
E. None of these

33. If '+' means '×', '×' mean '–', '–' means '÷' and '÷' means '+', then value of $8 + 4 \times 9 - 3 \div 1 = ?$

A. 32 B. 9
C. 29 D. 41
E. None of the above

34. A goat has been tied to two stakes at point P and Q. If length of each of the rope is 15 meters and P and Q points are 20 metres apart, then which of the following shaded portions will indicate the place of strolling of the goat?

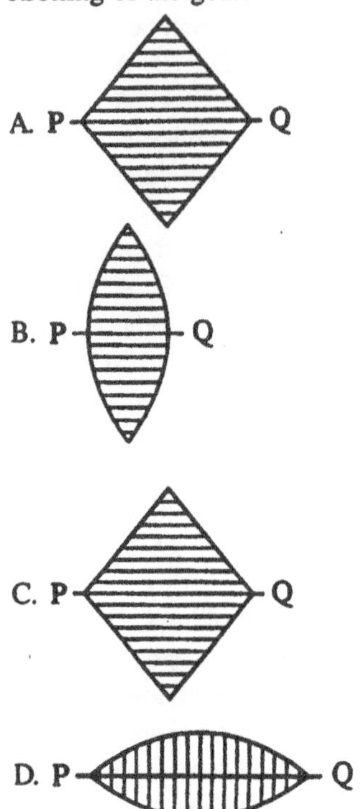

35. In the following figure, a carton is tied with cotton tape. Dimensions of the carton is indicated along its edges. If 10 cms more cotton tape was required to tie a knot then what was the minimum length of cotton tape which was used to tie the carton?

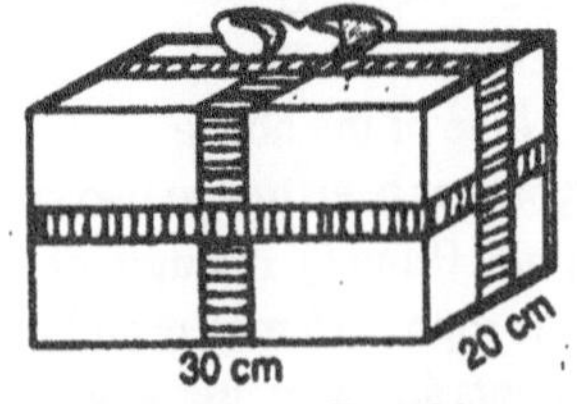

A. 190 cm B. 180 cm
C. 200 cm D. 160 cm

36. Shyam was born in the same year in which Rakesh was awarded with the Degree of B.A. at the age of 18. If Shyam joined, for the first time, in Government Service in 1995 when he was 24 years old, then what will be the age of Rakesh in the year 2004?

A. 51 years B. 45 years
C. 50 years D. 49 years

37. Ramesh, Hari and Monu were playing cards. Ramesh said to Hari, "If you give me two cards then I will have cards double than Monu and if Monu gives you three cards then you will have cards double than Monu". What was the difference between the number of cards possessed by Ramesh and Hari?

A. 8 B. 5
C. 7 D. 6

38. A group of tourists which consists of two fathers and two sons, visited a hotel for dinner. After finishing the dinner, a bill of Rs. 30 was paid. What was the average amount spent on dinner by this group?

A. Rs. 15 B. Rs. 7.50
C. Rs. 10 D. Rs. 17.25

Directions (Qs. 39 to 41): *Questions from 39 to 41 are based on the following information.*

"We are three sisters and two brothers. My father was 25 years old when I was born. My mother is 4 years younger than my father. My two sisters were born when my mother was 25 years and 29 yeas old. My younger brother was born

when my father was 35 years old and my youngest sister was born when I was 12 year old. Now I am 17 years old. ('B'has been used as abbreviation for brother and 'S' has been used as abbreviation for sister)."

39. What will be the age of my youngest sister and my mother two years henceforth?
A. 7 years, 35 years
B. 7 years, 40 years
C. 5 years, 32 years
D. 6 years, 35 years

40. What is my brother's age now?
A. 9 years B. 3 years
C. 7 years D. 5 years

41. In which of the following order my brothers and sisters were born?
A. B, S, S, B, S
B. S, S, S, B, B
C. S, B, S, B, S
D. B, S, B, S, B

42. At a certain place a few cows, a few oxen and 45 hens have been kept. One man has been deputed to look after every 15 animals. Number of oxen is double the number of cows. If the number of total heads (including those of the men deputed) is 186 less than the number of legs, then how many men have been deputed for looking after the animals?
A. 8 B. 6
C. 9 D. 5

43. A straight line is 36 cm long. From both ends on this line you have to put dots in such a manner that the first dot is 1 cm far from the end point, the second dot is 2 cm far from the first dot and so on. If dots put on the end of the line are not taken into account and two coinciding points are counted one, then number of dots will be:
A. 10 B. 13
C. 12 D. 16

44. A man invited a few boys and girls in his son's birthday party. Boys were two less in number than the girls. The man presented a gift check of Rs. 10 to every boy and Rs. 20 to every girl. He thus spent Rs. 280 as the gift amount. What was the number of boys?
A. 8 B. 25
C. 15 D. 10

45. A man travels from P to Q with a speed of 3 kms per hour and from Q to P with a speed of 6 kms per hour. What was his average speed during this journey?
A. 4 kms per hour
B. $4\frac{1}{2}$ kms per hour
C. 5 kms per hour
D. 3 kms per hour

46. Given below three graphs showing the consumption of electricity in three different households. Statement given in which of the following four alternatives is correct?

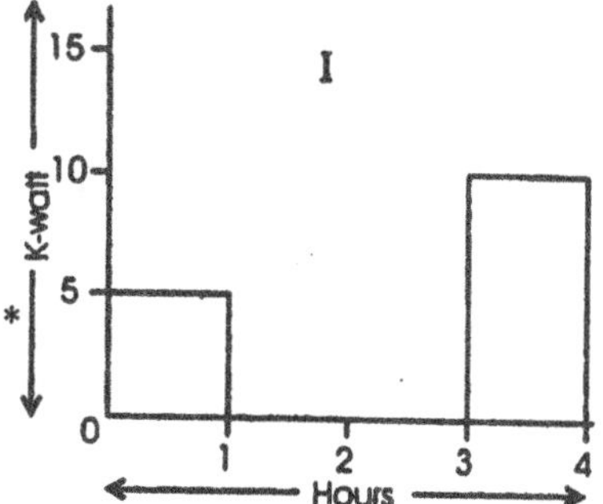

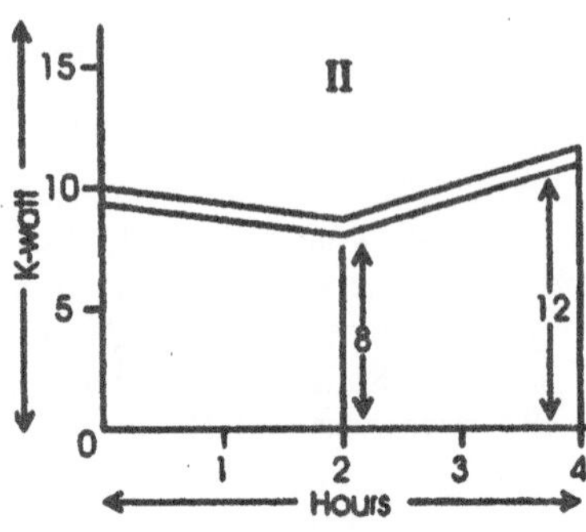

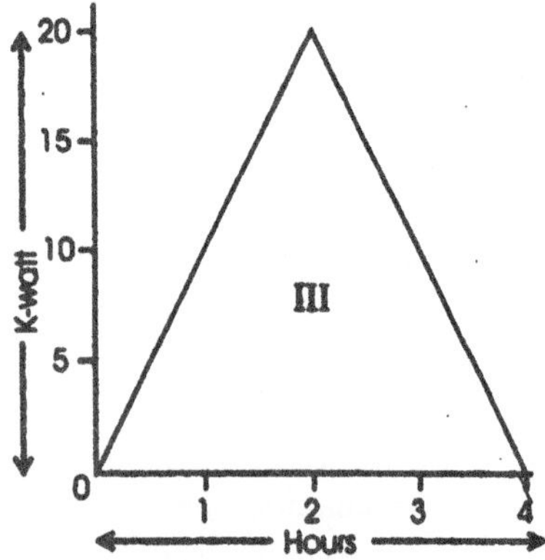

A. Rates of consumption of electricity in all the three households are identical.
B. Consumption of electricity in household-II is more than the other two houses.
C. Consumption of electricity in household-III is in between the consumptions of I & II.
D. Consumption of electricity in household No. I is minimum.

47. If diameter of each of the following circles is 1 m, then area of the shaded part is:

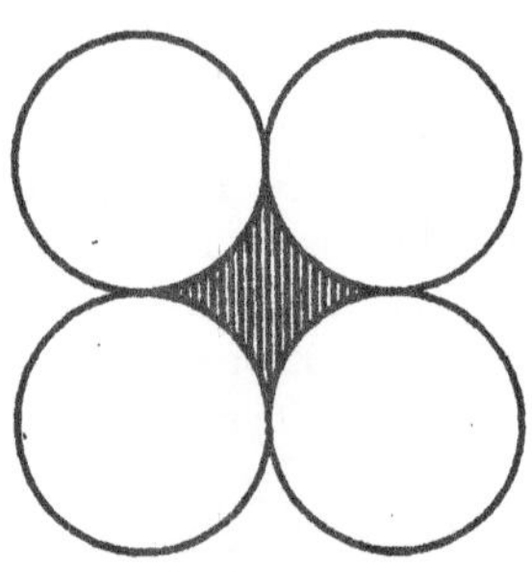

A. (1-π) square meter
B. (4-π) square meter
C. (π-1) square meter
D. (1-π/4) square meter

48. The product of 82540027 and 43253 is:

A. 4272513787834
B. 3470103787833
C. 3570103787831
D. 3570103787832

49. Classes begin at 1.00 P.M. in a school and run upto 3.52 P.M. Four periods are kept during this and before starting each period, 4 minutes time is alloted for shifting from one class-room to another class-room. What is the time duration of one period?

A. 39 minutes
B. 42 minutes
C. 40 minutes
D. 41 minutes

50. If in the following figure, diameter of each of the bigger circle is D, what is the diameter of the smaller circle?

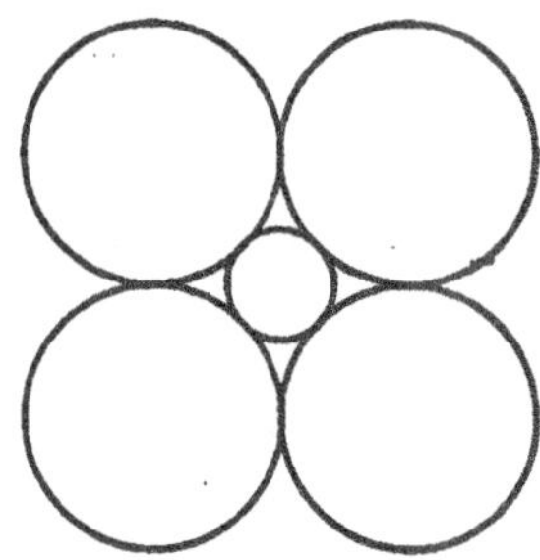

A. D/4 B. D

C. D/2 D. $\left(\sqrt{2}-1\right)$ D

51. Drawn below is a circle of radius r. What is the area of shaded portion?

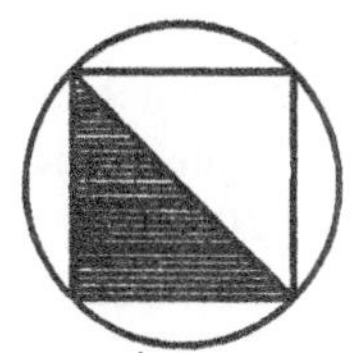

A. $4/r$
B. r^2
C. $4/3r^2$
D. $4r^2$

52. Following two diagrams depict the household expenses of two families A and B. If F denotes expenses on food, C denotes expenses on clothing, R denotes expenses on rent, E denotes expenses on education of the children and M denotes other expenses, then statements given in which of the following alternatives is correct?

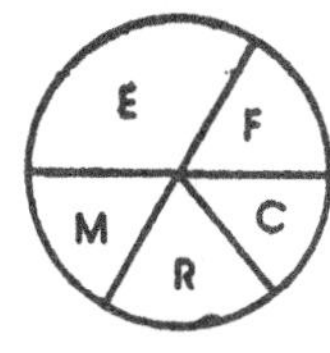

A. Percentage of expenses on education of children in family B is more than that of family A
B. Expenses on food in family A is more than that of family B.
C. We can not determine the exact percentage of expenses on the basis of above diagram
D. Percentage of expenses of both the family on other items is equal to a great exent

53. Aman's mother was 21 years old when his sister was born. His father is 8 years older than his mother. Now Aman is 17 years old and his sister is 3 years older than him. What is the present age of Aman's father?

A. 50 years B. 47 years
C. 46 years D. 49 years
E. None of the above

Directions (Qs. 54 to 58): *In each of the questions below an equation in the beginning followed by four options has been given. You are required to select any one option out of the given options the indicated operations in which if made out in the given equation, the equation would become correct.*

54. $(6 \div 2) \times 3 = 0$

A. Substitute + for × and interchange 2 and 3
B. Substitute – for × and interchange 2 and 3

C. Substitute × for ÷ and interchange 2 and 3

D. Substitute – for × and interchange 2 and 3

55. $4 \times 6 - 2 = 14$

A. Substitute + for × and interchange 4 and 6

B. Substitute × for – and interchange 2 and 6

C. Substitute ± for – and interchange 2 and 6

D. Substitute ÷ for × and interchange 2 and 6

56. $(3 \div 4) + 2 = 2$

A. Interchange the signs + and ÷

B. Interchange the signs + and ÷ and numbers 3 and 4

C. Interchange the signs + and ÷ and numbers 2 and 4

D. Interchange the signs + and ÷ and numbers 2 and 3

57. $6 \times 4 + 2 = 16$

A. Interchange the signs + and × and numbers 4 and 16

B. Interchange the signs + and × and numbers 2 and 16

C. Interchange the signs + and × and numbers 2 and 6

D. Interchange the signs + and × and numbers 4 and 6

58. $3 + 5 - 2 = 4$

A. Interchange the signs + and – and numbers 2 and 4

B. Interchange the signs + and – and numbers 5 and 4

C. Interchange the signs + and – and numbers 3 and 5

D. Interchange the signs + and – and numbers 2 and 3

Directions (Qs. 59 to 63): *In each of the questions from 59 to 63 you are required to find out an equation the signs and numbers of which when changed as per the indication suggested, the equation would become correct.*

59. If the signs – and ×, and numbers 3 and 6 are interchanged:

A. $3 - 6 \times 8 = 10$

B. $6 \times 3 \times 2 = 9$

C. $6 \times 3 - 4 = 15$

D. $3 \times 6 - 4 = 33$

E. $3 - 6 \times 8 = 12$

60. If the signs + and –, and numbers 4 and 8 are interchanged:

A. $4 + 8 - 12 = 12$

B. $4 + 8 - 12 = 16$

C. $8 - 4 + 12 = 8$

D. $8 - 4 - 12 = 20$

E. $4 - 8 + 12 = 10$

61. If the signs + and ×, and numbers 4 and 5 are interchanged:

A. $5 \times 4 + 20 = 100$

B. $5 \times 4 + 20 = 180$

C. $5 \times 4 + 20 = 104$

D. $5 \times 4 + 20 = 40$

62. If the signs + and –, and numbers 4 and 8 are interchanged:

A. $4 - 8 - 2 = 6$

B. $4 - 8 - 6 = 2$

C. $4 - 8 - 6 = 0$

D. $6 - 8 - 4 = 1$

63. If the signs + and ÷, and numbers 2 and 4 are interchanged:

A. $2 + 4 \div 6 = 3$

B. $2 + 4 \div 6 = 8$

C. $4 + 2 \div 6 = 1.5$

D. $4 \div 2 + 3 = 4$

64. On reaching in the conference hall 10 minutes before 11.40 A.M. for attending a meeting, the

Director of a company knew that he had reached 20 minutes before the Joint Director who came 30 minutes late. What was the fixed time of the meeting?

A. 11.20 A.M.
B. 11.40 A.M.
C. 11.50 A.M.
D. 12.10 P.M.
E. 11,30 A.M.

65. Kajal is nine months younger than Rubi while Payal is three months younger than Devi. Payal was a two months baby when Laxmi was born. Now Devi is in the age group of 7 years and Kajal is in the age group of 9 years. Who amongst them is the eldest?

A. Rubi B. Devi
C. Payal D. Laxmi
E. Kajal

66. 8 hours have been fixed as regular working hous in a day and there are five regular working days in a week. A labourer is paid at the rate of Rs. 2.40 per hour for working in regular hours. If he gets Rs. 432 as total remuneration of 4 weeks then what are his total working hours?

A. 180 B. 160
C. 195 D. 175
E. 200

67. I was sitting alone in a park. After a while there came an old man followed by an old lady. They were followed by two couples who were accompanied with a child. Then what was the number of total persons present in the park?

A. 10 B. 9
C. 11 D. 8
E. None of these

68. Hari babu lives in a five storey building. In this building number of steps in the stair constructed for reaching first to second floor is two less than the number of steps in the stair constructed for reaching from ground to first floor. Similarly number of steps in the stair constructed for reaching from second to third floor is two less than the steps in the stair from first to second flour and so on. If one has to ascend 80 steps in total for reaching on the top floor, then what is the number of steps in the top stair?

A. 11 B. 12
C. 18 D. 15
E. 16

69. There are three poles X, Y and Z of different heights. Three spiders A, B and C start climbing up these poles at the same time. In each attempt, spider A climbs up the X pole 5 cms but slips back 1 cm, spider B climbs up the Y pole 6 cms but slips back 3 cms and spider C climbs up the Z pole 7 cms but slips back 2 cms. If each of the spiders make 50 attempts for reaching a top the pole, then what is the height of the shortest pole?

A. 200 cms B. 250 cms
C. 150 cms D. 151 cms
E. 153 cms

70. In the line diagram given below a man reaches from A to O in 5 minutes. He covers the distances from B to O and from O to C each in 3 minutes. If O is the centre of the circle and AB and AC are two tangents of the circle from points B and C, then what time that man will take in reaching from A to C *via* B and O?

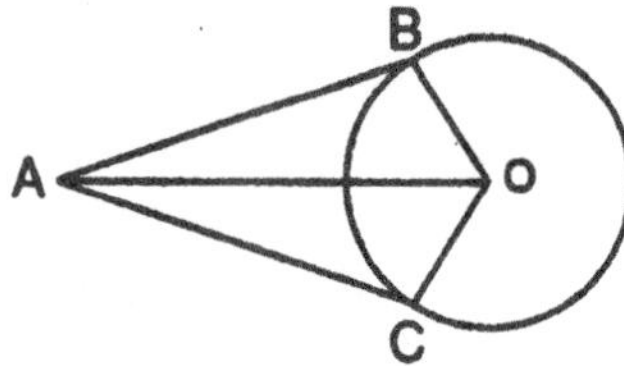

A. 5 minutes
B. 12 minutes
C. 0 minutes
D. 10 minutes
E. 4 minutes

71. In an orchard, trees of mangoes and trees of rose-apples are equal in number. If birds have made their nests on the branches of three-fourth trees of the orchard and monkeys sit on the branches of the trees which are half in number of the total trees in the orchard, then which of the following is the correct statement?

A. Monkeys sit on the branches of all mango trees
B. Monkeys sit on the branches of all rose-apple trees
C. Monkeys sit the branches of at least half mango trees
D. Birds have their nests on the branches of at least half mango trees

72. If '+' means '÷', '÷' means '–'; '–' means '+' and '×' means '–', what will be the value of the following expression?

$8 + 2 \div 1 - 6 \times 4 = ?$

A. 6 B. 2
C. 9 D. 11
E. 5

73. Which one number can be placed at the sign (?) of interrogation?

$3 \times 6 = 18$
$4 \times 7 = 22$
$9 \times 1 = 9$
$5 \times 2 = ?$

A. 3 B. 50
C. 14 D. 7
E. 10

74. If '⊓' means '+'; '⊏' means '–'; '⊐' means '×'; '⊔' means '+'; '∥' means '='; '→' means '>' and '←' means '<', then which of the following expressions is correct?

A. (12 ⊏ 4) ⊐ (5 ⊐ 1) ← (10 ⊓ 20)
B. (20 ⊏ 8) ⊔ (4 ⊏ 1) ∥ (4 ⊓ 1)
C. (10 ⊓ 2) ⊏ (2 ⊔ 2) → (10 ⊔ 2)
D. (18 ⊔ 3) ⊐ (3 ⊓ 1) ⊓ (5 ∥ 120)

75. If in the following figure, area of the square ABCD is A then what will be the area of the whole figure?

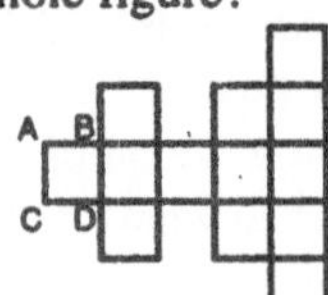

A. 11A B. 13A
C. $13A^2$ D. $11A^2$

76. In the following figure diameter of each of the circles is '*d*'. What is the area of the square ABCD?

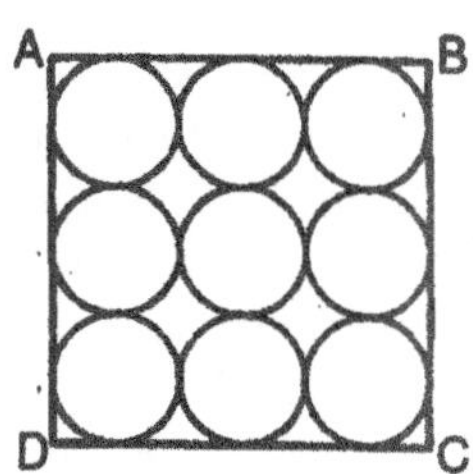

A. $9/4d^2$ B. $3d^2$
C. $9d^2$ D. $9d$

77. If all the faces of the figure given below is to be painted in such a manner that none of the two adjacent faces bear same colour, then how many different colours will be needed?

A. 4 B. 9
C. 2 D. 3

78. If all the six faces of a solid cube are to be painted in such a manner that none of the two adjacent faces bear same colour, then at least how many different colours will be needed?

A. 2 B. 3
C. 4 D. 6

Directions (Qs. 79 to 80): *For answering the questions from 79 to 80, you are required to select a number from amongst the given alternaives which can be placed at the sign (?) of interrogation in the given expressions.*

79. 41 – ? = 14 + 11

A. 18 B. 15
C. 10 D. 11

80. 15 + 20 = 17 + ?

A. 18 B. 14
C. 16 D. 12
E. 15

81. In the following sentences how many ducks float?

1. Two ducks are behind a duck.
2. Two ducks are leading a duck and one duck is in between them.

A. 2 B. 3
C. 5 D. 4

82. Aman, Bunty, Chintu, Dev and Utkarsh distribute among themselves playing cards in such a manner that Aman gets cards one less than Bunty, Chintu gets 5 more than Dev and Utkarsh gets 3 more than Bunty but Dev gets cards equal to Bunty. Who among them got the least number of cards?

A. Dev B. Chintu
C. Bunty D. Aman
E. Utkarsh

83. A wall clock takes the time of 5 seconds in striking 5 bells. What time will it take in striking 9 bells?

A. 7 seconds B. 10 seconds
C. 9 seconds D. 6 seconds
E. 9½ seconds

84. Five students A, B, C, D and E appeared in an examination. C got 5 marks less than B, D got 10 marks more than B but 20 marks less than A. E got 22 marks more than B. If B got total 40 marks then what is the marks of A?

A. 50 B. 60
C. 40 D. 70
E. None of these

85. A child told that number of his sisters is double the number of his brothers. One of this child's sisters told, "Sir, statement of this child is quite amusing because number of my brothers is equal to the number of my sisters". What is the actual number of brothers and sisters in this child's family?

A. Three brothers are three sisters
B. Two brothers and three sisters
C. Three brothers and four sisters
D. Two brothers and two sisters

86. B's age is double the age of A. Age of F is two times the age of B. C's age is half the age of A but age of C is double the age of D. Amongst them who of the following two persons are the eldest and the youngest respectively?

A. B – F B. F – A
C. F – D D. B – D

87. A, B, C, D and E distributed among them a few cards in such a manner that A got one card less than B, C got 5 cards than D, E got 3 cards more than B and D got cards equal in number to the B's cards. Who among them got the least number of cards?

A. B B. D
C. C D. E
E. A

88. If '+' means '×'; '–' means '÷'; '×' means '–' and '–' means '+', then what is the value of following expression?

$6 + 5 \div 5 - 3 \times 6 = ?$

A. $25\frac{2}{3}$ B. $17\frac{2}{3}$

C. $14\frac{1}{3}$ D. $15\frac{2}{3}$

E. $19\frac{1}{3}$

EXPLANATORY ANSWERS

EXERCISE - 1

1. A:

2. A:

3. A: Except 'A', all other figures are quite different from the figure given at the extreme left. Answer figure 'A' is mirror image of the given question figure.

4. C: Only in answer figure C, the Curved line has been turned round thrice.

5. C: Only in answer figure C, a small arch (a line-drawing of nose) is drawn concave toward the two eyes.

6. D: Only in answer figure D, two lines have been drawn in the inside of triangle.

7. C: Only in the answer figure C, the question figure is drawn upside down.

8. C: Except C, all other figures are rectangular in shape.

9. C: In all other figures except C, the small circle drawn inside is being touched by the outer peripheral line of the design.

10. C: Only in the answer figure C, the tip of the arrow is drawn just on the one edge of the line and two other arrows have been drawn.

11. A:

12. C:

EXERCISE - 2

1. E: Payal is daughter of the Principal and she has secured 67% marks. So she is supposed to deposit Rs. 10,000 as annual fee and Rs. 40,000 as additional fee. But she had deposited a draft of Rs. 22,000. Therefore she will not be given admission in the College.

2. E: Neha belongs to Scheduled Caste and she has secured 55% marks, therefore she is supposed to deposit Rs. 10,000 as annual fee and one fourth of Rs. 80,000, *i.e.*, total Rs. 30,000 for getting admission. But she deposited a draft of Rs. 15,000. Therefore she was not granted admission in the College.

3. A: Piyush satisfied all the criteria and got admission in the College.

4. A: The student belongs to scheduled caste and has secured 60% marks. He was granted admission in the Medical College.

5. A: Riya satisfied all the criteria and got admission in the College.

6. D: Aman is not in a position to deposit additional fee. Therefore his case will be referred to the chairman.

7. E: Mridul has not studied science in 12th class. Therefore he will not be granted admission.

8. D: Ankur satisfied all the criteria except one. He was supposed to deposit Rs. 10,000 as annual fee and Rs. 20,000 as additional fee. But he was in a position to deposit only Rs. 20,000 for admission in the Medical College. Therefore his case will be referred to the chairman.

9. E: The student had not attained the age of 16 on 1.4.2000. Therefore he will not be granted admission in the Medical College.

10. C: Seema has secured 65% marks. Therefore she was supposed to deposit Rs. 10,000 as annual fee and Rs. 80,000 as additional fee *i.e.* total Rs. 90,000 for admission in the Medical College. But she was in a position to deposit only Rs. 50,000. This amount is more than 50% of Rs. 90,000. Therefore granting her admission was totally dependant on the Director's sweet will.

11. A:

12. D: After taking out 7 white balls and 5 red balls if 1 more ball is taken out of the box then it will be quite certain that one ball of each colour has been taken out. Therefore at least 13 balls should be taken out from the box.

13. C:

14. C:

15. A:

16. C:

17. C: 8 cubes will be painted on 3 sides and 24 cubes will be painted on 2 sides.

18. E: 8 cubes will be painted on 3 sides.

19. C: 8 cubes will be painted in red on 1 side and 4 cubes of bigger size will be painted on 1 side.

20. C: 16 cubes painted in red on only one face will be got from each opposite side of the cube. Thus total 32 cubes will have a face painted in red.

21. B:

22. C:

23. C:

24. C:

25. A:

26. C:

27. C:

28. A:

29. D:

30. A:

31. C:

32. B:

33. C:

34. D:

35. D:

36. D:

37. C:

38. D:

39. A:

40. B:

41. A:

42. D: Triangles formed in the given figure are:
ACD, ABH, HBF, BGF, BGC, CFE, EFD, AFC, FCD, ABF, BCF

43. D: Shortest route from A to B is AB.

44. C:

45. A:

46. B: It is clear from the positions of the cube that numbers adjacent to 3 are 1, 2, 4 and 5. So, the number on the opposite side to 3 will be 6.

47. C: The solid cube will be cut in the following manner:
"16 smaller cubes will be obtained from one face of the cube of which 4 centre pieces will have only one face painted."
We know that cube has 6 faces. Therefore total 24 smaller cubes will be obtained which will be painted on one face only.

48. A:

49. D:

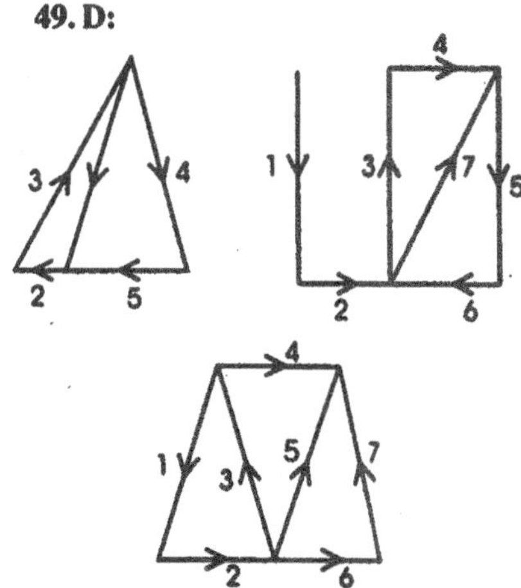

50. E: Triangles formed in the given figure are:
ABC, BCD, CDA, ABD, ABE, BEC, CED, AED, AFE, DEF, DEH, HEL

51. B:

52. C:

53. A:

54. C:

55. D:

56. D: It is clear from the positions of the cube that numbers adjacent to 4 are 5, 6, 2 and 3. So, the number on the opposite side to 4 will be 1.

57. B: Number of total zones = 5.
Number of total subzones = 5
∴ Difference between total zones and total subzones = 5 – 5 = 0

58. A: Third number in the given codes are 2, 3, 4 and 6. Therefore number of assorting zones is 4.

59. D: Distributing Post Offices are 001, 002, 021, 023, 032 and 101. Therefore number of distributing Post offices is 6.

60. E: Numerical value of Pincode 712032 is maximum.

61. C: Pincodes 112021, 306101 and 504032 have been repeated more than once.

62. B: Among the last three digits 032 has been repeated maximum times. Therefore the distributing Post office 032 will receive maximum mails.

63. D: Distributing Post offices have been indicated by last three digits and there are 14 such post offices codes of which start from 0. Therefore number of such post offices is 14.

64. D: Codes formed by first three digits are 112, 306, 403, 504, 404, 113, 503, 712 and 506. Therefore number of assorting zones is 9.

65. A: Codes formed by first two digits are 11, 30, 40, 50 and 71. Therefore number of subzones is 5.

66. D: First digits are 1, 3, 4, 5 and 7. Therefore number of total zones is 5.

67. C: Supposed number of members who attended the meeting is (n).

$$\therefore \quad nC_2 = 190$$

$$\therefore \quad \frac{\underline{|n}}{\underline{|n-2}\,\underline{|2}} = 190$$

$$\therefore \quad \frac{n(n-1)}{2} = 190$$

$$\therefore \quad n^2 - n = 380$$

$$\text{or} \quad n^2 - n - 380 = 0$$

$$\text{or} \quad n^2 - 20n + 19n - 380 = 0$$

$$\text{or} \quad n(n-20) + 19(n-20) = 0$$

$$\text{or} \quad (n-20)(n+19) = 0$$

$$\text{or} \quad n = 20 \text{ or } n = -19$$

Therefore the number of members who attended the meeting was 20.

68. D:

69. D:

70. A: This triangle should be cut along the line bisector of any of the two sides of the triangle

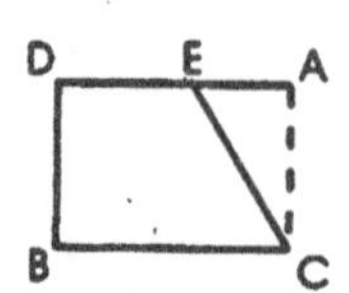

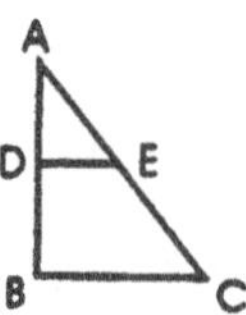

71. B:

72. C:

EXERCISE - 3

1. D: $\because BC = AD$ and $B > A$
$\therefore C < D$

2. C: $\because CD = AB$ and $D = B$
$\therefore A = C$ or $C = A$

3. D: $\because AB > CD$ and $B = D$
$\therefore A > C$ or $C < A$

4. B: $\because A < D$ and $D = C$
$\therefore A < C$ or $C > A$

5. D: On changing the signs of the given expression into indicated signs we get the following expression:
$10 \div 5 + 3 \times 2 - 3 = 2 + 6 - 3 = 5$
(on applying BODMAS rule)

6. E: Number divisible by 9 is also divisible by 3.

7. C: 10 minutes is the least among the three given time intervals.

8. A:

9. C: Sum of the given numbers in line and in column is 33.

10. D:

11. B: $\because 127 \times 407 = 110$
and $54 \times 86 = 126$
$\therefore 125 \times 232 = 56$

12. C: After 13th and before 18th means 14, 15, 16 and 17. But after 16th and before 20th means 17, 18 and 19. Here 17th of the month was the day on which the uncle had seen them.

13. C: $9 = (3)^2$, $16 = (4)^2$, $36 = (6)^2$ and $64 = (8)^2$

14. D: $912 = 19 \times 2\,(16+8)$
$882 = 21 \times 2\,(7 + 14)$
and $? = 24 \times 2\,(6 + 12) = 864$

15. E: $20 = 8 \times 2 + 4$, $15 = 3 \times 2 + 9$
$\therefore\ ? = 6 \times 2 + 6 = 18$

16. A:

17. A:

18. D: The Managing Director reached at 12.20 P.M. The Chairman reached at 12.40 P.M.
Time fixed for interview
= 12.10 P.M.

19. C: 18 Q 12 P 4 R 5 S 6
$= 18 \times 12 \div 4 + 5 - 6$
$= 18 \times 3 + 5 - 6$
$= 54 + 5 - 6 = 53$

20. A: After interchanging the third digit 1 will be fourth.

21. E: Bhanu is standing fourth from the right end, *i.e.*, there are three girls standing to the right of Bhanu. After interchanging the place with Pinki, Pinki will be standing 15th from the left end. In that position there will be 14 girls to the left of Pinki. Thus it is clear that there are 15 girls standing in the line. After interchanging, Bhanu will reach at the place of Pinki and will be seventh from the left end. Therefore after interchanging Bhanu will be 12th from the right end.

22. C: Following number series is obtained on writing given number series in reverse order:
16, 14, 5, 13, 11, 2, 6, 10, 4, 7, 9, 3, 8, 1
In this series fourth number is 13 and 7th number to the right of 13 is 9.

23. D: The second, the fifth and the sixth digits of the given number is 6, 9 and 1 respectively. By using these three digits wer can have 196 which is square of 14. Now first digit of this square number is 1.

24. B: On writing the digits of each of the three digit numbers given in the question in reverse order we find the numbers as 937, 972, 953, 981 and 945. On writing these numbers in descending order we find the following number series:
981, 972, 953, 945, 937.
Digit in the middle of the number placed second from the largest number is 7.

25. A: After accommodating 15 children, 5 more children can be accommodated in the lift.
20 children = 12 men

$\therefore$ 5 children $= \frac{12}{20} \times 5 = 3$ men

26. C: Price of 15 apples and 20 oranges is equal to the price of 20 apples and 15 oranges.
Price of (20 – 15) oranges = Price of (20 – 15) apples
$\therefore$ Price of 5 oranges = Price of 5 apples
$\therefore$ Price of 1 orange = Price of 1 apple

27. C:

28. B:

29. C:

30. A:

31. A: The requisite numbers are 8, 48, 80 and 88.

32. B: Shubham was 8th from left end. After Shubham changed his place 3 more boys came to his left. It means that 10 boys were then standing to the left of Shubham. It is also stated that then he was 10th from right end. Therefore it is clear that total 20 boys were standing in the queue.

33. E: After substituting the symbols the new expression will be:
$8 \times 4 - 9 \div 3 + 1 = 32 - 3 + 1 = 30$

34. B:

35. A: The required length of the cotton tape was:
$2\,(30 + 20) + 2\,(20 + 20) + 10$
$= 190$ cm

36. A: Shyam was 24 years old in 1995. Rakesh is 18 years elder than Shyam. Therefore Rakesh was (24 + 18 = 42) years old in 1995. He will be (42 + 9 = 51) years old in the year 2004.

37. C: Let the number of cards possessed byRamesh, Hari and Monu be x, y and z respectively.
$x + 2 = 2z$

$y+3=2(z-3)$
or $y+3=2z-6$
or $y+3=x+2-6$
or $x-y=3-2+6=7$

38. C: In the group of tourists there were a grand father, a son and a grand son. Therefore total three persons were incuded in the group.
Average amount spent = 30/3 = Rs. 10

For 39 to 41

My present age = 17 years
My father's present age = 42 years
My mother's present age = 38 years
My eldest sister's present age = 13 years
My middle sister's present age = 9 years
My younger brother's present age = 7 years
My youngest sister's present age = 5 years.

39. B:

40. C:

41. A:

42. B: Supposed the number of cows $= x$
Number of Oxen $= 2x$
Number of persons kept for looking after the animals

$$= \frac{x+2x+45}{15}$$

Numer of legs

$$= 4x+8x+90+2\left(\frac{3x+45}{15}\right)$$

Number of heads $= x + 2x + \frac{3x+45}{15} + 45$

Now, $4x+8x+90+2\left(\frac{3x+45}{15}\right) - \left[x+2x+\frac{3x+45}{15}+45\right] = 186$

or $138x = 2070$
$x = 15$

$\therefore$ No. of persons kept

$$= \frac{15+30+45}{15} = 6$$

43. C: Dots from one end will be put at the distances of 1 cm, 3 cm, 6 cm, 10 cm, 15 cm, 21 cm, 28 cm and 36 cm respectively. Similarly dots from the other end will be put at the distances of 35 cm, 33 cm, 30 cm, 26 cm, 21 cm, 15 cm, 8 cm and 0 cm. Dots which are not to be taken into account are the dots put at the distances of 36 cm and 0 cm. Two coinciding points are put at the distances of 15 cm and 21 cm respectively which are to be counted one at each coinciding point.
$\therefore$ No. of requisite dots is $= 8+8-4=12$

44. A: Supposed the number of boys $= x$
$\therefore$ Number of girls $= x+2$
$\therefore$ $10x+20(x+2)=280$
or $30x+40=280$
or $x=8$

45. A: Supposed the distance between points P and Q is x km,
$\therefore$ Time taken in going from P to Q

$= x/3$ hrs. and time taken in going from Q to P $= \frac{x}{6}$ hrs.

Therefore time taken in covering the total distance *i.e.* from P to Q and from Q to P

$$= \frac{x}{3} + \frac{x}{6} = \frac{x}{2} \text{ hrs.}$$

∴ Average speed

$$= \frac{\text{Total Distance}}{\text{time}} = \frac{2x}{\frac{x}{2}}$$

$= 4$ km/hr.

46. D: Consumption of electricity in household I $= 1 \times 5 + 1 \times 10 = 15$ units.

Consumption of electricity in household II

$$= 2 \times 8 + \frac{1}{2} \times 2 \times (8 + 12)$$

$= 36$ units.

Consumption of electricity in household III

$$= \frac{1}{2} \times 4 \times 20 = 40 \text{ units.}$$

Household No. I consumes the least units of electricity.

47. D:

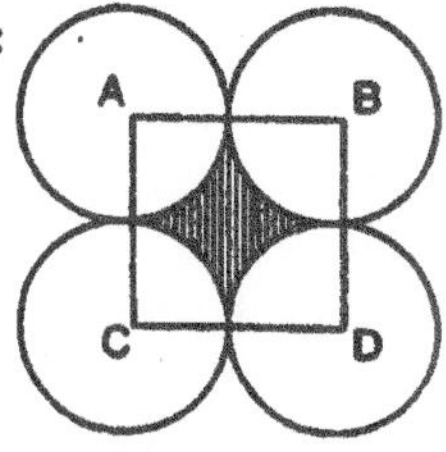

Area of square ABCD $= 1^2 = 1$ square meter

And Area of the 4 sectors

$$= 4 \times \frac{1}{4}\pi\left(\frac{1}{2}\right)^2 = \pi/4 \text{ sq. m.}$$

∴ Area of the Shaded part

$$= \left(1 - \frac{\pi}{4}\right) \text{ square meter}$$

48. C: In the given two numbers, digits at ones place are 7 and 3 respectively and the product of 7 and 3 bears 1 at ones place. Therefore in the product of the given two numbers digit of 1 will be at ones place.

49. C: During the 4 periods 4 minutes time will be excluded thrice from the total time. Therefore time excluded $= 4 \times 3 = 12$ minutes. Time interval from 1.00 P.M. to 3.52 P.M. = 2 hrs 52 minutes = 172 minutes

∴ Time spent during the four periods

$= 172 - 12 = 160$ minutes.

∴ Time duration of 1 period $= 160/4 = 40$ minutes.

50. D:

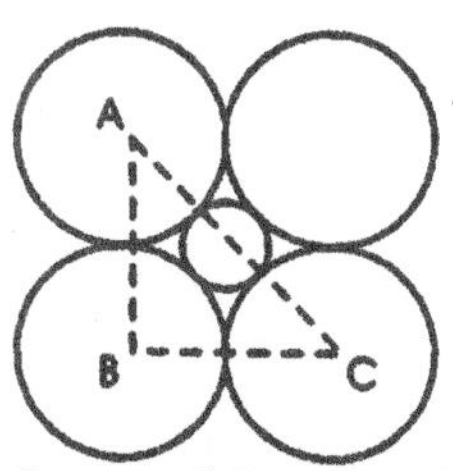

Supposed diameter of the smaller circle $= x$

$$\text{Therefore AC} = x + \frac{D}{2} + \frac{D}{2}\ (x + D)$$

$$\text{And } AC^2 = AB^2 + BC^2$$

$$= D^2 + D^2 = 2D^2$$

$(x + D)^2 = 2D^2$
or $x + D = D\sqrt{2}$
or $x = D\sqrt{2} - D = \left(\sqrt{2-1}\right)D$

51. B: If dimension of one side of the square = l

Area of shaded portion

$= \frac{1}{2}\ l \times l = \frac{l^2}{2}$

Now $l^2 + l^2 = (2r)^2$
or $2l^2 = 4r^2$
or $\frac{l^2}{2} = \frac{4}{2 \times 2} = r^2$

Therefore area of the shaded portion = r^2

52. C: We can not determine the exact percentage of expenses until we know the expenses of A and B families separately.

53. D: Present age of Aman = 17 years
His sister's present age = 20 years
His mother's present age
= 20 + 21 = 41 years
His father's present age
= 41 + 8 = 49 years.

54. B: $(6 \div 3) - 2 = 0$

55. C: $4 \times 2 + 6 = 14$

56. D: $(2 + 4) \div 3 = 2$

57. D: $4 + 6 \times 2 = 16$

58. C: $5 - 3 + 2 = 4$

59. A: $3 \times 6 - 8 = 10$

60. B: $8 - 4 + 12 = 16$

61. C: $4 + 5 \times 20 = 104$

62. A: $8 - 4 + 2 = 6$

63. B: $4 \div 2 + 6 = 8$

64. A:

65. A: Name of the girls in respect of their ages in descending order is: Rubi, Kajal, Devi, Payal, Laxmi

66. A:

67. B:

68. A:

69. E: In 50 attempts distance covered by A = 49 (5 − 1) + 5
= 196 + 5 = 201 cm
Distance covered by B in 50 attempts = 49 (6 − 3) + 6 = 147 + 6
= 153 cm
Distance covered by C in 50 attempts = 49 (7 − 2) + 7 = 245 + 7
= 252 cm
∴ Height of shortest pole is 153 cm

70. D:

71. D:

72. E:

73. C:

74. D:

75. B: Complete figure is divided into 13 squares having equal size. Therefore total area = 13 A

76. C: Length of each side of the square is 3d
∴ Area of the square ABCD
$= (3d)^2 = 9d^2$

77. D:

78. B:

79. C:

80. A:

81. B:

82. D: Suppose the number of cards with Bunty = x
∴ Number of cards with Dev is also x.
Aman got $(x - 1)$ cards, Bunty got $(x + 4)$ cards and Utkarsh got $(x + 3)$ cards.

$(x - 1)$ is the smallest number. Therefore Aman got the least number of cards.

83. B: Time duration in striking 5 bells will be counted after 1st bell is struck. Therefore wall clock took 5 seconds time in striking 4 bells.

$\therefore$ Time taken for striking one bell $= \frac{5}{4}$ seconds

$\therefore$ The clock will take $\frac{5}{4} \times 8 = 10$ seconds in striking 9 bells.

84. D: Suppose marks obtained by A $= x$

$\therefore$ marks obtained by D $= x - 20$

$\because$ marks obtained by B

$= x - 20 - 10 = x - 30$

$x - 30 = 40$

or $x = 40 + 30 = 70$

85. C: Supposed number of brothers $= x$

But that child is one of the brothers.

$\therefore$ Number of his remaining brothers $= x - 1$

$\therefore$ Number of his sisters

$= 2(x - 1) = 2x - 2$

According to a sister of that child, number of her remaining sisters = Number of her brothers.

$\therefore x = 2x - 2 - 1 \quad \therefore x = 3$

$\therefore$ three brothers and four sisters are there in that child's family.

86. C: Suppose A's age$=x$ years

$\therefore$ B's age $= 2x$ years

$\therefore$ F's age $= 4x$ years

$\therefore$ C's age $= \frac{x}{2}$ years

$\therefore$ D's age $= \frac{x}{4}$ years

Therefore F is the eldest and D is the youngest.

87. E: Suppose A got x cards

$\therefore$ Number of B's card $= x + 1$

$\therefore$ Number of D's card $= x + 1$

$\therefore$ Number of F's card $= x + 4$

$\therefore$ Number of E's card $= x + 4$

$\therefore$ Number of C's card $= x + 6$

Therefore A got the least number of cards.

88. A: $? = 6 \times 5 + 5 \div 3 - 6$

$= 6 \times 5 + \frac{5}{3} - 6$

$= 30 + \frac{5}{3} - 6$

$= \frac{77}{3} = 25\frac{2}{3}$

16

TEST ON STATEMENT AND ARGUMENTS

PART-1

In this type of test the candidates are required to decide upon the forcefulness of an argument. They should keep in mind that the argument should not be *(i)* an assumption; *(ii)* generalised (it should be specific); *(iii)* ambiguous; *(iv)* hidden as an implication; *(v)* an example or quotation. Also, the argument should be factually correct and in conformity with the prevailing ideas of truth.

In making decisions about important questions, it is desirable to be able to distinguish between 'strong' arguments and 'weak' arguments so far as they relate to the questions. 'Strong' arguments must be both important and directly related to the question. 'Weak' arguments may not be directly related to the question and may be of minor importance or may be related to the trivial aspect of the given statement. Apart from the information given in the question and the statement, nothing should be assumed or taken for granted.

Statement: Government should make the education free for all.

Arguments I: Yes, this step of the government will make a good number of people living in the country educated.

II: No, due to this step the government will have to suffer a huge amount of deficit in its annual budget.

Explanatory Answer: The lower classes of the people, who are resourceless and otherwise can not get education, will also be able to get education if it is made free by the government. Making the education free for all is beneficial. Therefore the first agument is strong and established the given statement.

Argument II suggests that if education is made free for all, educational institutions will not be able to collect fee and thus they will not contribute to the government's exchequer. This additional burden will affect annual budget of the government and will add to the government's deficit budget. Therefore the second argument is also strong.

EXERCISE - 1

Directions: *In each of the questions given below a statement followed by two arguments numbered I and II has been given. You have to decide which of the given arguments is a 'strong' argument and which is a 'weak' argument. Give answer:*

(A) if only argument I is strong
(B) if only argument II is strong
(C) if either I or II is strong
(D) if neither I nor II is strong
(E) if both I and II are strong

1. Statement: Should colleges be given the status of a University.
Arguments I : Yes, managements of colleges will appreciate it.
II : No, colleges even in western countries have not yet been given such a status.

2. Statement: Should workers be allowed to participate in the management of factories?
Arguments I: Yes, it is one of the demands of workers.
II: No, the management will oppose this idea.

3. Statement: Should promotion of personnel in an organisation be made only on the basis of seniority?
Arguments I: Yes, otherwise senior persons will become disinterested in their work.
II. No, it does injustice to the really deserving persons.

4. Statement: Should octroi be abolished?
Arguments I: Yes, it will eliminate an important source of corruption.
II: No, it would adversely affect government revenue.

5. Statement: Should those who receive dowry, despite the law prohibiting it, be punished?
Arguments I: Yes, because those who violate the law must be punished.
II: No, dowry system is firmly rooted in the society since time immemorial.

6. Statement: Should higher education be restricted only to a few deserving ones?
Arguments I: No, it will increase unemployment in the country.
II: Yes, it will decrease the unnecessary expenditure on higher education upto a maximum possible limit.

7. Statement: should correspondence courses at university level be discontinued?

Arguments I: No, because correspondence courses are being conducted even in developed countries.

II: Yes, this will reduce the work load on Post offices.

8. Statement: Should competitive examinations for selecting candidates for jobs consist of objective tests only?

Arguments I: Yes, the assessment of objective tests is reliable.

II: No, the number of questions to be answered in the objective tests is always very large.

9. Statement: Should religion be taught in our schools?

Arguments I: No, ours is a secular state.

II: Yes, teaching religion helps inculcate moral values among children.

10. Statement: Should computers be indigenously made in India?

Arguments I: Yes, why not?

II: No, we do not have technical know-how.

11. Statement: Should young entrepreneurs be encouraged?

Arguments I: Yes, it will lead to industrial development in our country.

II. Yes, it will help in decreasing unemployment in the country.

12. Statement: Should military training be made compulsory for all?

Arguments I: No, it is against the docrine of non-violence.

II: Yes, all citizens of a country should serve for the safeguard of the country.

13. Statement: Should higher education be restricted only to the most deserving ones?

Arguments I: No, it is against the principle of democracy.

II: Yes, only deserving people are entitled to get higher education.

14. Statement: Should strikes in the field of education be banned?

Arguments I: Yes, it is against professional ethics.

II: Yes, because it affects the students adversely.

15. Statement: Should telecasting feature films be stopped?

Arguments I: Yes, young children are misguided by the feature films.

II: No, this is the only way to educate the masses.

16. Statement: Should state lotteries be banned?

Arguments I: Yes, Government should work to save people from this bad habit of gambling.

II: No, there will be an immense loss of revenue in Government's exchequer.

17. Statement: Should there be one and only are university in entire India?

Arguments I: Yes, this is the only way to bring uniformity in the standard of education.

II: No, this is impossible from the administrative point.

18. Statement: Should intellectuals in India not take part in active politics?

Arguments I: Yes, they are not well versed in politics.

II: No, in a democratic country like India it is against the rights of its citizens.

19. Statement: Should 'mercy killing' be allowed?

Arguments I: Yes, life is futile when all hopes are gone.

II: No, according to the laws in vogue in the country no person has got a right to kill any person.

20. Statement: Should people in India get exemption from paying taxes on personal income?

Arguments I: Yes, this will encourage people to increase their sources of income.

II: No, people should share their earned money with others.

21. Statement: Should sincerity be the only ground of promotion in an organisation?

Arguments I: Yes, because no organisation will be viable without sincerity of the personnels attached with it.

II: No, because it will encourage treachery and discrimination.

22. Statement: Should smoking be prohibited at all public places?

Arguments I: Yes, because this will provide fresh air for breathing to people who do not smoke.

II. No, because this will grab the freedom of the people and they will not be able to smoke at public places.

23. Statement: Should new industries be established at Vadodara?

Arguments I: Yes, it will increase opportunities for new employment.

II: No, it will add to pollution.

24. Statement: Should the students not be assigned with home work at schools?

Arguments I: Yes, because this will relieve the teachers of their responsibilities in respect of checking the home work copies.

II: No, because the students should be able to follow the instructions.

25. Statement: Should employment be kept apart from Degree?

Arguments I: No, because then less qualified persons will also ask for recruitment on posts having greater responsibility and handsome salary.

II: No, because then there will be no enchantment for higher education.

26. Statement: Should sales tax be abolished?

Arguments I: Yes, it will eliminate an important source of corruption.

II: Yes, this will cheapen the goods in the market which will be in the interest of consumers.

27. Statement: Should Government of India dismantle its armed forces?

Arguments I: No, all other countries do not believe in non-violence.

II: Yes, a few Indians believe in non-violence.

28. Statement: Should citizens of the country engage in tax evasion?

Arguments I: Yes, there is a great burden of taxes on citizens.

II: No, it is an anti-national activity.

29. Statement: Should there be a complete ban on non-vegetable food items?

Arguments I: Yes, because the great personalities like Mahatma Gandhi and Lord Bertrand Shaw were vegetarians.

II: Yes, because these are high priced items and a good number of people living in India can not afford.

30. Statement: Should the system of interview for selecting candidates for jobs be completely abolished?

Arguments I: Yes, a lot of time is lost in adopting this unnecesšary system.

II: No, it provides a suitable opportunity for an interaction between the employer and the employee to be recruited before signing a contract for recruitment of the candidate on a certain post.

31. Statement : Should smoking be strictly prohibited at public places?

Arguments I: No, it would adversely affect tobacco industry.

II: No, because many persons who like smoking would express their resentment against this decision.

32. Statement: Should the medium of higher education be English in India?

Arguments I: Yes, even n prosperous countries like England the medium of higher education is English.

II: Yes, because English is being widely used thse days.

33. Statement: Should competitive examinations for selecting candidates for jobs consist of objective tests instead of subjecive tests?

Arguments I: Yes, impartial assessment of the candidate's ability can be made through objecive tests only.

II: No, subjective tests are a better mode of assessment in comparison to objective tests.

34. Statement: Should understanding the given text be given same importance as reading the text?

Arguments I: Yes, we should simultaneously read and understand the given text.

II: No, understanding the given text and reading the given text both are equally important.

35. Statement: Should smoking be prohibited?

Arguments I: Yes, we should not waste our hard earned money on smoking.

II: No, this will throw lakhs of people engaged in tobaco industry out of their employment.

36. Statement: Should India manufacture atom bombs?

Arguments I: Yes, it is imperative

to protect the sovereignty and integrity of the country.

II: No, this will create imbalance in the power of nations in this region.

37. Statement: Should lock out in government organisations be strictly prohibited?

Arguments I: Yes, this is the only way to teach discipline to the government employees.

II: No, this will deprive the citizens of their democratic rights.

38. Statement: Should religion be banned?

Arguments I: Yes, it develops fanaticism in people.

II: No, religion binds people together.

39. Statement: Should there be complete ban on strike by government employees?

Arguments I: Yes, common mass think so.

II: No, this is against the democratic rights of the citizens.

40. Statement: Should the payment of bónus in industries be stopped.

Arguments I: Yes, this will eliminate at least one reason of industrial disputes.

II: No, it will obstruct the ongoing rate of production.

41. Statement: Should efficiency be the basis of promotion in an oranisation?

Arguments I: No, there could be partiality in assessment of efficiency which would be harmful to the career of the capable employees.

II. Yes, it will encourage employees for working more efficiently.

42. Statement: Should military training be made compulsory in India?

Arguments I: Yes, then every able citizen would be able to participate actively for the security of the nation.

II: No, this will lead to civil disobedience.

43. Statement: Should teachers be assessed by the students?

Arguments I: Yes, this will improve the standard of teaching.

II: No, students are not capable of doing so.

44. Statement: Should processions on road organized by

political parties be banned?

Arguments I: Yes, this creates hazards for the traffic.

II: No, this is the only way to show people's protest.

45. Statement: Should India make nuclear weapons?

Arguments I: Yes, because Pakistan is also doing so.

II: No, this will lead to nuclear war in the continent.

46. Statement: Should election for the members of Parliament be held after every 10 years.

Arguments I: Yes, because this will save money allocated for holding election in the five-year plan.

II: No, because the political party in power may misuse the time.

47. Statement: Should a lady be elected for the post of President of India?

Arguments I: Yes, this would stop the atrocities on women.

II: No, a lady is not able to govern over a vast country like India.

48. Statement: Should there be a ban on tabloids?

Arguments I: Yes, tabloids contain sensational news only which spoil the career of youths.

II: No, they should not be banned without any reason.

49. Statement: Should the voting age in India be lowered to 16?

Arguments I: Yes, why should it not be so in India when in some other countries the voting age is 16.

II: No, it will be foolish to do so when even the marriage age for boys is 21.

50. Statement: Should religion be taught in our schools?

Arguments I: Yes, do the parents not wish to develop their wards into matured individuals?

II: No, how can one dream of such a step when we want the young generation to fulfill its role in the twenty-first century.

51. Statement: Should family planning be made compulsory in India?

Arguments I: Yes, looking at the miserable conditions in India, there is no other way.

II: No, in India there are people of various religions and family planning is against the tenets of some of the religions.

52. Statement: Should study through correspondence courses at University level be discontinued in India?

Arguments I: Yes, only interaction between teachers and students and among students while learning helps total development of personality at the University level.

II: No, such a step of discontinuation is the craze of the elite, who have no knowledge of what is meant by poverty.

53. Statement: Should family planning be made compulsory in India?

Arguments I: Yes, because in spite of its industrial and economic growth, India is not able to attain prosperity due to the irrational increase in its population.

II: No, because people of this country will express their resentment against forcible implementation of family planning scheme and to express resentment is their democratic right.

54. Statement: Should the treatment aspect of leprosy be given wide publicity?

Arguments I: Yes, this is being given wide publicity throughout the world.

II: No, we should spend money on research related aspects of leprosy treatment, not on publicity.

55. Statement: Should senior Government officials be elected as vice chancellors of Universities?

Arguments I: Yes, Vice Chancellor of the University deals with administrative issues. So does the senior officer while serving in Government. Therefore senior-government officers can deal with these issues more efficiently.

II: No, University is the highest abode of education and only an educationist can deal with the situations arising in such type of institutions.

56. Statement: Should India stop its nuclear programme?

Arguments I: Yes, there are so many other ways too.

II: No, it will obstruct the research activities relating to the peaceful use of nuclear energy.

57. Statement: Should the caste system in India be abolished?

Arguments I: Yes, then we will behave with people without prejudice of upper caste or lower caste.

II: No, because after caste system is abolished people belonging to lower caste will not be able to take advantages of various welfare schemes of the government being implemented for them.

58. Statement: Should family planning be forcibly implemented in India?

Arguments I: Yes, otherwise country's population will be out of control in next few years.

II: No, instead of implementing forcibly, people of this country should be made aware of its advantages and disadvantages.

Directions (Qs. 59 to 71): *Each question below is followed by two arguments numbered I and II. You have to decide which of the given arguments is a 'strong' argument and which is a 'weak' argument. Give answer:*

(A) if only argument I is strong.

(B) if only argument II is strong.

(C) if either I or II is strong.

(D) if argument I is 'weak' and argument II is 'strong'.

(E) if neither I nor II is strong.

59. Statement: Judiciary should be free from the hold of executive.

Arguments I: Yes, because then unjustifiable steps of the executive will be lessened.

II: No, because then the executive will not take bold steps.

60. Statement: Should mechanised farming be encouraged in a rural country like India?

Arguments I: Yes, production will be increased by doing so.

II: No, it will throw many villagers out of job.

61. Statement: Should strikes be banned in India?

Arguments I: Yes, because strikes adversely affect country's economy.

II: No, because it is worker's democratic right.

62. Statement: Should films be kept under concurrent list?
Arguments I: Yes, views expressed by states will also get concurrence.
II: No, it will decrease the standard of films.

63. Statement: There is a need of computerization in the present banking system.
Arguments I: Yes, because only then there will be a better customer service.
II: No, because it will spoil the mutual relation amongst the bank employees.

64. Statement: Guides published by private agencies should be banned.
Arguments I: Yes, because only then the students will start reading text books.
II: No, because these are of immense help to the weak students in the eleventh hour.

65. Statement: Should taxes on colour television be further increased?
Arguments I: Yes, colour television is a luxury item and only rich people buy them.
II: No, televisions are bought by the poor too.

66. Statement: Should educated people work in villages?
Arguments I: Yes, because they can revolutionize agriculture and revamp rural atmosphere.
II: No, the educated people should be employed in cities.

67. Statement: Should expenditure on central and state legislature elections be incurred by the government?
Arguments I: Yes, it will eliminate corruption in politics.
II: No, it is not so in any other country.

68. Statement: Should the system of marriage be abolished?
Arguments I: Yes, because breach in matrimonial relation has become frequent these days.
II: No, it is essential for living in the society.

69. Statement: Should there be one and only one government in the countries?
Arguments I: Yes, it will cease tension among the countries.
II: No, because then there will be government of only developed countries.

70. Statement: Should health services in the country be nationalized?

Arguments I: Yes, it is so in other countries too.

II: No, because it will further deteriorate the quality of health services in India.

71. Statement: Should the number of political parties be restricted?

Arguments I: Yes, it is essential to educate the politicians.

II: No, it is hazardous for the very spirit of the democracy.

Directions (Qs. 72 to 76): *Each question below is followed by two arguments numbered I and II. You have to decide which of the given arguments is a 'strong' argument and which is a 'weak' argument. Give answer:*

(A) if only argument I is strong
(B) if only argument II is strong
(C) if either I or II is strong
(D) if neither I nor II is strong
(E) if both I and II are strong

72. Statement: Should several service sectors in India be computerised?

Arguments I: No, India is a poor country and therefore we should not spend too much on such aspects.

II: Yes, why should we not do so in India when developed countries are utilizing this facility in various service sectors.

73. Statement: Should training of 'Scout and guide' in schools be made essential?

Arguments I: Yes, this will inculcate discipline among students.

II: No, this will disturb the study of students.

74. Statement: Should the articles of only able writers be published?

Arguments I: Yes, it will save paper because there is scarcity of paper in our country.

II: No, because it is not possible to mark a line between able and unable writers.

75. Statement: Should the industrial sector in India be computerized?

Arguments I: No, it will increase unemployment in India.

II: Yes, it will increase production in industrial sector.

76. Statement: Should the Telephone sector in India be handed over to the private companies?

Arguments I: Yes, because in developed countries, telephone sector has been handed over to private companies.

II: No, handing over this sector to the private companies can not be approved from the security point.

ANSWERS

1	2	3	4	5	6	7	8	9	10
E	E	B	E	A	B	D	A	B	D
11	**12**	**13**	**14**	**15**	**16**	**17**	**18**	**19**	**20**
E	B	A	B	D	D	B	D	D	A
21	**22**	**23**	**24**	**25**	**26**	**27**	**28**	**29**	**30**
D	D	E	B	B	A	D	B	D	B
31	**32**	**33**	**34**	**35**	**36**	**37**	**38**	**39**	**40**
D	B	A	D	A	B	E	E	B	D
41	**42**	**43**	**44**	**45**	**46**	**47**	**48**	**49**	**50**
D	A	E	B	B	D	A	B	B	B
51	**52**	**53**	**54**	**55**	**56**	**57**	**58**	**59**	**60**
D	A	B	B	A	A	E	A	A	D
61	**62**	**63**	**64**	**65**	**66**	**67**	**68**	**69**	**70**
A	E	E	B	D	A	A	B	B	E
71	**72**	**73**	**74**	**75**	**76**				
B	D	A	B	A	D				

PART-II

DEDUCTIVE REASONING

It is a type of logical reasoning in which a logical argument in three propositions is inferred of which two are premises and one is conclusion that follows necessarily from the given premises. Candidates are given two or more than two conclusions based on two premises. They are required to follow the logic and select one of the options as the right choice.

Example: From the given five conclusions (A), (B), (C), (D) and (E), select the conclusion which logically follows from the given statements:

Statements:I. All girls are mothers

II. Some mothers are children

Conclusions: (A) All mothers are girls

(B) Some Children are girls

(C) Some girls are children

(D) All girls are children

(E) None of these

Explanatory Answer (E): When all girls are mothers and some mothers are children, then naturally all girls cannot be children. Therefore conclusion (A) is not correct. Conclusion (B) is also not correct because all girls are mothers and some mothers are children. Conclusion (C) is also incorrect because all girls are mothers and all mothers are not girls. Similarly conclusion (D) is wrong. Therefore conclusion E is correct.

EXERCISE

Directions: *In each of the questions given below two statements followed by a few conclusions are given. You have to take the given statements to be true even if they seem to be at variance with commonly known facts. Read all the conclusions and then decide which of the given conclusions logically follows from the two given statements, disregarding commonly known facts.*

1. **Statement:** Some cups are panthers.
   Some panthers are goats.

   Conclusions:
   I. Some cups are not goats.
   II. No cup is goat.
   III. All cups are goats.
   IV. All goats are cups.
   A. Either conclusion I or IV follows
   B. Either conclusion II or IV follows
   C. Either conclusion I or III follows.
   D. Either conclusion I or II follows
   E. No conclusion is correct.

2. **Statement:** All doors are chairs.
   All chairs are tables.

   Conclusions:
   I. All doors are tables.
   II. All tables are chairs.
   III. Some tables are doors.
   IV. All tables are doors.
   A. only conclusions I and II follow.
   B. only conclusions III and IV follow.
   C. All conclusions are correct.
   D. Only conclusions II, III and IV are correct.
   E. Only conclusions I, II and III are correct.

3. **Statement:** All windows are carpets
   Some carpets are rats.

   Conclusions:
   I. All rats are carpets.
   II. All carpets are windows.
   III. All windows are rats.
   IV. All rats are windows.
   A. Only II, III and IV follow.
   B. Only I, II and IV follow.
   C. All are correct.
   D. Only I, II and III follow.
   E. None of the above.

4. **Statement:** All cats are parrots.
   No parrot is green.

   Conclusions:
   I. No cat is green.
   II. All parrots are cats.
   III. Some parrots are cats.
   IV. Some cats are green.
   A. Only I follows.
   B. All are correct.
   C. Only I and III follow.
   D. Only II and IV follow.

5. **Statement:** Some pens are books.
   All books are rods.

   Conclusions:
   I. All pens are rods.

II. All books are rods.
III. All books are pens.
IV. All rods are pens.
  A. Only II and III follow.
  B. All are correct.
  C. None of the above is correct.
  D. Only I and IV follow.
  E. Only II, III and IV follow.

6. Statement: Quality has a value. India has developed various modes of education.

Conclusions:

I. Quality of education in India is likely to be improved soon.
II. Only money can improve the quality of education.
  A. Only conclusion I follows.
  B. Only conclusion II follows.
  C. Both conclusion I and II follow
  D. None of the above.

7. Statement: Generous people donate generously. Duryodhana had donated enough money. Only due to obdurate attitude of Duryodhana, Pandava was not given even an inch of land. It resulted in war of Mahabharata.

Conclusions:

I. Duryodhana was a generous man.
II. If Duryadhana had a generous feeling, Mahabharata war could be averted.
  A. Only conclusion I follows.
  B. Only conclusion II follows.
  C. Conclusion I and II follow.
  D. None of these.

Directions: *In each question below are given one statement followed by four conclusions A, B, C and D. Read all the conclusions carefully and then decide which one of the given conclusions follows necessarily from the given statement.*

8. If it is false that both A and B are good students then:
  A. 'A' and 'B' both are bad students.
  B. 'A' is bad and 'B' is good student.
  C. 'A' is good and 'B' is bad student.
  D. Either both of them are bad students or one of them is a bad student.

9. "Tolerance is capital of poor persons". It means that:
  A. A poor man is always tolerant.
  B. A poor man has tolerance to earn capital.
  C. A rich man is always tolerant.
  D. A poor man can earn money if he has tolerance.

10. "All men are vertebrate. Some mammals are vertebrate."
  A. All men are mammals.
  B. All mammals are men.
  C. Some vertebrates are mammals.
  D. All vertebrates are men.

11. "Many persons who smoke get cancer."
  A. Many cancer patients are smokers.
  B. Smoking causes cancer.
  C. Generally chain smokers get cancer.
  D. Smoking always results in cancer.

12. "A man is influential if he is rich."
A. John is influential because he is rich.
B. If a man is not rich then he is not influential.
C. Jack is rich and therefore he is influential.
D. Poor man are not influential.

13. "Most of the pens in that shop are costly."
A. None of the pens in that shop is cheap.
B. Some of the pens in that shop are costly.
C. Some of the pens in that shop are cheap.
D. Pens of camlin brand are costly is that shop.

14. "Most of the students are talented"
A. Some students are talented.
B. None of the students is untalented.
C. Some students are dull.
D. All students are talented.

15. "Soldiers serve their country".
A. The person who serve the country, is a soldier.
B. Women do not serve the country because they are not soldiers.
C. Men generally serve the country.
D. Some men who are soldiers, serve the country.

Directions: *In each question below one or two statements followed by four conclusions are given. The candidates have to take the given statements to be true even if they seem to be at variance with commonly known facts. Read the given conclusions carefully and select the one which is correct.*

16. Statements:
I. All types of knowledge are good things.
II. All knowledges are difficult to acquire.

Conclusions:
A. Some good things are difficult.
B. All difficult things are good.
C. All good things are difficult.
D. Easy things do not contain knowledge.

17. Statements:
I. Some teachers are not wise.
II. If it is false, then what is correct?

Conclusions:
A. All teachers are wise.
B. Some learned persons are teachers.
C. Some teachers are wise.
D. All wise men are teachers.

18. Statements:
I. All industrialists are dishonest.
II. All industrialists are fraudulent.

Conclusions:
A. All fraudulent persons are dishonest.
B. Some dishonest persons are fraudulent.
C. Generally fraudulent persons are dishonest.
D. Fraud and dishonesty are closely related with each-other.

19. Statements:
I. Persons belonging to P group were killed during the skirmish.
II. Rahul belonging to P group was cured after treatment in Civil hospital.

Conclusions:

A. All remaining persons belonging to 'P' group were killed.

B. None of the persons belonging to 'P' group was a warrior.

C. All people belonging to 'P' group were not killed.

D. Persons belonging to 'P' group went underground.

20. Statement:

I. Some professors of the college are not football players.

Conclusions:

A. None of the football players is a professor of the college.

B. Some professors of the college may be football players.

C. Some football players may be professors of the college.

D. Mr. Raghava, who plays chess, can not be a Professor of the college.

21. Statements:

I. All ships are boats.

II. All combinations of logs are ships.

Conclusions:

A. All combinations of logs are boats.

B. Some ships are combinations of logs.

C. None of the combinations of logs is a boat.

D. Some boats are combinations of logs.

E. None of the above

22. Statements:

I. All bicycles are two wheelers.

II. Some two wheelers are cars.

Conclusions:

A. All bicycles are cars.

B. Some bicycles are cars.

C. All two wheelers are bicycles.

D. Some cars are bicycles.

E. None of the above

23. Statements:

I. All teachers are fathers.

II. All boys are teachers.

Conclusions:

A. All boys are fathers.

B. Some teachers are boys.

C. None of the boys is a father.

D. Some fathers are boys.

E. None of the above

24. Statements:

I. Some circles are figures.

II. Some circles are squares.

Conclusions:

A. All circles are not figures.

B. Some figures are squares.

C. Some circles are neither figures nor squares.

D. All circles are either figures or squares.

E. None of the above

25. Statements:

I. All children are chairs.

II. All cats are children.

Conclusions:

A. All cats are chairs.

B. Some children are cats.

C. None of the cats is a chair.

D. Some chairs are cats.

E. None of the above

26. Statements:

I. Some roots are fruits.

II. Some roots are trees.

Conclusions:

A. All roots which are not fruits, are trees.

B. Some fruits are trees.
C. There are some roots which are neither fruits nor trees.
D. All roots are either fruits or trees.
E. None of the above

27. Statements:

I. All girls are mothers.
II. Some mothers are children.

Conclusions:

A. All girls are children.
B. Some girls are children.
C. Some mothers are girls.
D. Some children are girls.
E. None of the above

28. Statements:

I. Some men are sensible.
II. Some men are rich.

Conclusions:

A. All men are not sensible but all of them are rich.
B. Some sensible men are rich.
C. Some men are neither sensible nor rich.
D. All men are either sensible or rich.
E. None of the above

29. Statements:

I. Manish is a player.
II. All players are tall.

Conclusions:

A. All tall persons are players.
B. Manish is not tall.
C. Tall persons are not players.
D. Manish is tall.
E. None of the above

30. Statements:

I. All guides are books.
II. Some books are valuable collections.

Conclusions:

A. All guides are valuable collections.
B. Some guides are valuable collections.
C. All books are guides.
D. Some valuable collections are books.
E. None of the above

31. Statements:

I. All cats are choleric.
II. All cats are black.

Conclusions

A. All black cats are choleric.
B. Some choleric cats are black.
C. Some black cats are choleric.
D. Some choleric cats are not animals.
E. None of the above

32. Statements:

I. All boys are handsome creatures.
II. All handsome creatures look nice.

Conclusions:

A. All boys look nice.
B. Some boys look nice.
C. Some creatures who look nice are boys.
D. All handsome creatures do not look nice.
E. None of the above

EXPLANATORY ANSWERS

1	2	3	4	5	6	7	8	9	10	11	12	13	14	15
E	E	E	C	A	A	B	D	D	C	C	C	C	C	D

16. A:

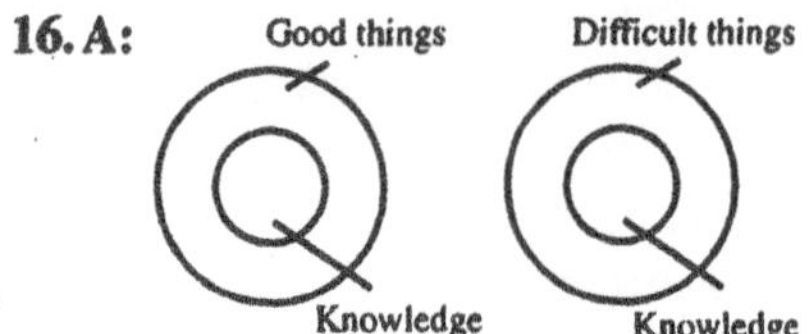

17. D:

18. B:

19. C: During the skirmish all persons belonging to 'P' group were killed but it was a chance that Rahul belonging to 'P' group was cured after the treatment. Then conclusion that "all persons belonging to 'P' group were not killed" is correct.

20. B: Some professors of the college are not football players. Then remaining some professors of the college may be football players. Therefore conclusion 'B' is correct.

21. A:

22. E:

23. A:

24. E:

25. A:

26. E: None of the given conclusions is correct.

27. E:

28. E:

29. D:

30. E: Correct conclusion can not be drawn.

31. C:

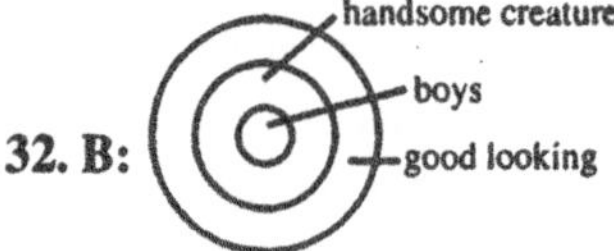

32. B:

handsome creatures
boys
good looking

17

STATEMENT AND ASSUMPTIONS

In this section each of the questions asked contains a statement followed by two assumptions numbered I and II. An assumption is something that can be taken as true without examination or proof. It is a presumption of a fact derived from known facts. An assumption is always derived from the implied meanings of the given statement. Thus an assumption is one type of implication, *i.e.*, a fact that is implicit. The candidates are required to consider the statement and the following assumptions and decide which of the assumptions is implicit in the statement.

Example: Consider the statement and the assumptions given below and decide which of the assumptions is implicit.

Statement: Go by air to reach Mumbai from Bangalore quickly.

Assumptions:

I. Except aeroplane, there is no other means of transport for going from Bangalore to Mumbai.

II. Bangalore and Mumbai are connected by air (route).

Explanatory Answer: It has been stated that to reach quickly from Bangalore to Mumbai one should go by air. It is clear from the statement that Bangalore and Mumbai are connected by air (route). Therefore assumption II is implicit. Assumption I is not implicit because there may be other means of transport for reaching Mumbai from Bangalore but they may take longer time.

EXERCISE

Directions (Qs. 1 to 11): *In each of the questions from 1 to 11, a statement followed by two assumptions numbered I and II has been given. An assumption is something supposed or taken for granted. You are required to consider the statement and the following assumptions and decide which of the assumptions is implicit in the statement.*

Give answer (A) if only assumption I is implicit.

Give answer (B) if only assumption II is implicit.

Give answer (C) if either assumption I or assumption II is implicit.

Give answer (D) if neither assumption I nor assumption II is implicit.

Give answer (E): if both the assumptions are implicit.

1. **Statement:** "You should read this book if you are curious to know about the cultural aspect of India". A teacher says to his students.

Assumptions:

I. Students are curious to know about the cultural aspect of India.

II. The teacher does not know about any other book on this subject.

2. **Statement:** "I watch television for the news at 8.30 P.M. in order to remain acquainted with the latest informations." – a candidate answered before the Interview Board.

Assumptions:

I. The candidate does not read newspapers.

II. Latest informations can be obtained from television only.

3. **Statement:** "During the return journey you can avail the route via Rajkot because it is the shortest one." — a travel agent said to a couple.

Assumptions:

I. The couple want to return through the shortest route.

II. The couple does not want to know about length of the route.

4. **Statement:** "This drink could be taken either directly or after blending with ice-cubes." — an advertisement.

Assumptions:

I. People have different tests.

II. A few people will like this drink because it can be taken directly.

5. **Statement:** "Go and bring the file". The officer instructed his assistant.

Assumptions:

I. The file is confidential.

II. The assistant does not know the whereabout of the file.

6. Decide which of the assumptions is implicit in the statements given below:

Statements:

I. All girls are flowers.

II. All girls are plants.

Assumptions:

I. Plants yield flowers.

II. All flowers look beautiful.

A. Only assumption I is implicit.
B. Only II is implicit.
C. Either I or II is implicit.
D. Neither I nor II is implicit.
E. Both I and II are implicit.

7. **Statement:** Please inform me on telephone because I want to get your approval as early as possible.

Assumptions:

I. We can not hear clear tone on telephone.

II. Detailed messages should be passed on telephones.

8. **Statement:** Efficient workers should be encouraged otherwise they will lose their spirit.

Assumptions:

I. Encouragement enhances the efficiency.

II. A few persons give better result than others.

9. **Statement:** Despite heavy rains railway traffic has not been disturbed this year.

Assumptions:

I. Railway traffic is disturbed only during rainy season.

II. Heavy rains generally disturbs the railway traffic.

10. **Statement:** None of the season ticket holders has registered any

complaint in spite of insufficient services.

Assumptions:

I. People generally do not bear with insufficient services.

II. Sometimes services are improved on registering complaints.

11. Statement: For wide publicity this should be advertised in all leading national newspapers.

Assumptions:

I. In a spcific region number of readers of a particular newspaper is more than the number of readers of other newspapers.

II. People generally do not advertise in local newspapers.

Directions (Qs. 12 to 46): *In each question below is given a statement followed by two assumptions. You are required to decide which of the assumptions is implicit in the statement. Give answer:*

A. if only assumption I is implicit.
B. if only assumption II is implicit
C. if either I or II is implicit
D. if neither I nor II is implicit
E. if both I and II are implicit

12. Statement: According to the new education policy wide changes have been envisaged in the system of education.

Assumptions:

I. Present system of education is not suitable to meet the national requirements.

II. Changes are required in the present sysem of education.

13. Statement: "If you are beautiful, we shall appreciate you and if you are not, we shall beautify you." — an advertisement from a photo studio.

Assumption:

I. Photographer is always beautiful whether the people visiting the photo studio is beautiful or not.

II. People generally wish that others should appreciate their beauty.

14. Statement: "If you are beautiful, we shall appreciate you and if you are not, we shall beautify you". — an advertisement from a photo studio.

Assumptions:

I. "How would they look beautiful" — it is the problem of youths.

II. No body wishes to look beautiful.

15. Statement: I am such a fool that I believed a cunning person like Sahib.

Assumptions:

I: Cunning persons are not believable.

II: It is foolish to have belief in a cunning person.

16. Statement: I am such a fool that I believed a cunning person like Shubham.

Assumptions:

I. Shubham is not believable.

II. I am a fool.

17. Statement: Finance Minister appealed to the officers, field staffs and insurance agents of Life Insurance Corporation to work for making the schemes of insurance popular among people, especially those living in rural and suburban areas.

Assumptions:

I: Generally the insurance is not popular among people.

II: People living in rural and suburban areas are against the insurance.

18. Statement: "Sleep well with X mosquito coils", an advertisement.

Assumptions:

I. In comparison to other brands of mosquito coils, X brand mosquito coils are the best.

II. If is essential to have a sound sleep during nights.

19. Statement: According to the press communique issued last Friday, the Government has procured 1.4 lakhs quintal cotton under the Cotton Procurement Scheme.

Assumptions:

I. Cotton Procurement Scheme is quite progressive.

II. Now the procurement of cotton on government account should be stopped.

20. Statement: The leader of the opposition said to the audience in a meeting of all opposition parties, "it is the high time when all opposition parties having identical ideology should come under a single banner and work for throwing this corrupt government out of power."

Assumptions:

I. Opposition parties having identical ideology should come under a single banner only when they are going to work for throwing the corrupt government out of power.

II. Opposition parties are not corrupt.

21. Statement: Finance Minister appealed to the officers, field staffs and insurance agents of Life Insurance Corporation to work for making the schemes of insurance popular among people, especially those living in rural and suburban areas.

Assumptions:

I. Officers and insurance agents of Life Insurance Corporation are capable of making the insurance schemes popular among people.

II. Officers and insurance agents of Life Insurance Corporation have never made all out efforts for making the insurance schemes popular among people.

22. Statement: Of all the newspapers published in Meerut, 'The Time and Space' has the largest number of readers.

Assumptions:

I. Volume of readership of all the newspapers in Meerut is known.

II. No newspaper in Meerut other than 'The Time and Space' has large readership.

23. Statement: Apart from the entertainment value of television, its educational value cannot be ignored.

Assumptions:

I. People take the television to be means of entertainment only.

II. The educational value of television is not realised properly.

24. Statement: In Mumbai, railway trains are indispensable for people in the suburbs to reach their places of work on time.

Assumptions:

I. Railway trains are the only mode of transport available in the suburbs of Mumbai.

II. Only railway trains run punctually.

25. Statement: The mangoes are too cheap to be good.

Assumptions:

I. When the mango crop is abundant, the prices go down.

II. The lower the selling price, the inferior is the quality of the commodity.

26. Statement: Ten candidates who were on the waiting list could finally be admitted to the course.

Assumptions:

I. Wait-listed candidates get admission with difficulty.

II. A large number of candidates were on the waiting list.

27. Statement: Present examination system requires thorough revision.

Assumptions:

I. Present examination system has lost its significance.

II. An improvement could be brought about by thorough revision.

28. Statement: Contact an estate agent whenever you want to purchase an immovable property for yourself.

Assumptions:

I. It is not essential to hire an estate.

II. Estate agent is an important person.

29. Statement: Every one likes "Time" Magazine.

Assumptions:

I. Time magazine contains quite informative materials.

II. It is not essential that a magazine should be liked by the people who read them.

30. Statement: If someone enquires about your tailor, then take for granted that you wear a finely sewn suit.

Assumptions:

I. Some one enquires about the tailor only when the suit worn is either good or bad.

II. People want to know the criterion of a finely sewn suit.

31. Statement: If you are a Mechanical Engineer, we have a challenging job for you.

Assumptions:

I. You are a Mechanical Engineer.

II. We require the services of a Mechanical Enginer.

32. Statement: A few persons think that on somebody's recommendation one can achieve success undoubtedly.

Assumptions:

I. It is not a right way to achieve success on somebody's recommendation.

II. It is quite difficult to get a favourable recommendation.

33. Statement: In spite of increased facilities, rent of this flat has not been enhanced.

Assumptions:

I. Rent is based on facilities.

II. Rent is not related to the facilities provided.

34. Statement: Every one wants to read 'Popular Magazine".

Assumptions:

I. None wants to read another magazine.

II. It is desirable that a magazine is liked by many persons.

35. Statement: Government should enhance taxes to compensate the deficit in budget.

Assumptions:

I. At present rate of taxes is low.

II. Deficit in budget can not be compensated without increasing the rate of taxes.

36. Statement: "Wanted an unmarried really beautiful, matriculate, capable of speaking English fluently, age between 19 to 22 years as trainees for recruitment to the post of receptionist." — an advertisement.

Assumptions:

I. It is essential that a good receptionist should speak English fluently.

II. Height is not a criterion for recruitment to the post of receptionist.

37. Statement: 'Smoking prohibited' - a notice in a railway compartment.

Assumptions:

I. Some persons like to smoke in the compartment.

II. Some persons smoke in the compartment.

38. Statement: A friend in need is a friend indeed.

Assumptions:

I. Relatives are of no help in difficult circumstances.

II. Taking help from a friend is desirable.

39. Statement: When in Chennai, stay at Hotel X for comfort and good service, because my best friend has recommended it.

Assumptions:

I. My best friend is trustworthy.

II. Comfort and good service cannot be expected from all hotels.

40. Statement: A friend in need is a friend indeed.

Assumptions:

I. A person needs help from others on certain occasions.

II. A friend is expected to help when needed.

41. Statement: 'Smoking prohibited' — a notice in a railway compartment.

Assumptions:

I. Generally, people expect a notice.

II. Smoking is injurious to health.

42. Statement: For every error committed in the past, our country had to meet with serious consequences.

Assumptions:

I. Our countrymen had committed errors in the past.

II. It is a difficult task to work out the consequences at national level.

43. Statement: If you hasten in your taskwork then your speed will be increased but your task will not accomplish.

Assumptions:

I. Speed is the most important element of efficiency.

II. Ideal situation is the one in which speed is increased and simultaneously the taskwork is accomplished.

44. **Statement:** Indian farmers need better quality of seeds besides adequate arrangement for irrigation of their fields.

Assumptions:

I. Condition of Indian farmers can not get improved unless they are provided with adequate arrangement for irrigation of their fields.

II. For enhancing the production, need of better quality seed is still not being felt by the Indian farmers.

45. **Statement:** In the present phase of development, India should take better decision on every issue, as far as possible, with one accord.

Assumptions:

I. In India it is essential to bring a change in present policy of decision-making.

II. Decisions taken with one accord are always better.

46. **Statement:** Indian farmers are suffering from inadequate supply of fertilizers despite the new technical know-how to manufacture is available.

Assumptions:

I. Supply of fertilizers was not adequate before the availability of new technical know how.

II. Increase in the supply of fertilizers was envisaged with the availability of new technical know-how.

Directions (Qs. 47 to 64): *In each question below is given a statement followed by two assumptions. You have to decide which of the assumptions is implicit in the statement. Give answer:*

(A) if assumption I is implicit

(B) if assumption II is implicit

(C) if either I or II is implicit

(D) if neither I nor II is implicit

(E) if both I and II are implicit.

47. **Statement:** "If you are a good painter, then we have a job for you" — an advertisement.

Assumptions:

I. You are a painter.

II. The advertiser needs the services of a painter.

48. **Statement:** Sledge is a cart having two wheels which you can purchase whenever you like.

Assumptions:

I. Sledge is a good cart having two wheels.

II. People wish to purchase a very good cart having two wheels.

49. **Statement:** You know that your suit is excellent when people ask about your tailor who tailored the suit.

Assumptions:

I: People do not ask about your tailor if your suit is not good.

II: People want to know the criterion of an excellent suit.

50. **Statement:** Use 'XYZ' tubes only because these tubes have 5 years longer life than any other.

Assumptions:

I. People prefer only those tubes which are durable.

II. Other tubes are not durable.

51. **Statement:** A successful man has the ability to judge himself correctly.

Assumptions:

I. To judge others is of no use to a successful man.

II. A successful man cannot make a wrong judgement.

52. **Statement:** Despite rains this year's Kharif crops are not expected to yield more.

Assumptions:

I. Prior to the rain it was expected that yield from the Kharif crops would be better.

II. There was a hope of improvement in the crop situation after the rain.

53. **Statement:** In hurry, use of "the book digest" is indispensable.

Assumptions:

I. One should use 'book digest' when there is shortage of time.

II. If enough time in hand, one should not use 'book digest'.

54. **Statement:** This book is aimed at teaching 'Yoga' even in the absence of a yoga teacher.

Assumptions:

I. We can not always find a teacher for teaching yoga.

II. Yoga can be learnt with the help of a book.

55. **Statement:** Rebate in railway fair for hill stations has been withdrawn because people do not necessarily visit hill stations for spendng holidays.

Assumptions:

I. Rebate in Railway fair in India should be given only to the deserving people.

II. Indian Railway should not encourage people to spend their holidays at hill stations.

56. **Statement:** "To stop train pull chain. Penalty for use without reasonable and sufficient cause fine upto Rs. 1,000 and/or imprisonment upto one year."

Assumptions:

I. A few persons are naughty.

II. People travelling in the train want to stop the running train in case of emergency.

57. **Statement:** We should stiffen the qualification criteria to curtail the number of candidates.

Assumptions:

I. At present qualification criteria have been fixed at very low level.

II. A large number of candidates is not desirable.

58. **Statement:** We should work hard for success in examination.

Assumptions:

I. It is desirable to be successful in the examination.

II. Fruit of success is tasted by the pupils who work hard.

59. **Statement:** "Neighbour's envy and owner's pride" – an advertisement on television.

Assumptions:

I. People are envious of neighbour's good things.

II. People want to provoke their neighbour's envy.

60. Statement: Young boys will think many a times before asking for admission in colleges if employment is kept apart from Degree.

Assumptions:

I. Girls do not try to seek employment.

II. Degree is not correlated with employment.

61. Statement: Changes are desirable in the present communication system.

Assumptions:

I. Effecting a total change will bring improvement in the present communication system.

II. Present communication system has become old.

62. Statement: Apart from the informative value of newspapers, their recreational value can not be ignored.

Assumptions:

I. People read newspapers for getting information.

II. People have started realizing the recreational value of newspapers.

63. Statement: Ten persons who were on the waiting list could finally be given reservation in Frontier Mail.

Assumptions:

I. Generally, Wait listed passengers get reservation in Frontier Mail with difficulty.

II. Number of berths available in Frontier Mail is relatively less than the other trains.

64. Statement: Of all the television sets in India, television sets of 'Solar' brand find a ready sale.

Assumptions:

I. Volume of sale of all the television sets manufactured in India is known.

II. Number of other television sets manufactured in India is less than that of Solar television sets.

Directions (Qs. 65-66): *Consider the given statement and the following assumptions in the questions from 65 - 66 and decide which of the assumptions is implicit in the statement.*

65. Statement: In today's economic crisis only the ideals of limited family and hard labour in the field of education can lead India towards prosperity.

Assumptions:

I. Ideals of limited family and hard labour in the field of education are correlated with India's prosperity.

II. A large family faces difficulty in bearing the expenses on education.

A. Only assumption I is implicit

B. Only assumption II is implicit.

C. Both assumptions I and II are implicit.

D. Neither assumption I nor II is implicit.

66. Statement: A pen is more powerful than the sword.

Assumptions:

I. Pen is made of a metal which is harder than the metal used for making the sword.

II. Mental power is more effective than the physical power.

A. Only assumption I is implicit.

B. Only assumptions II is implicit.

C. Both the assumptions I and II are implicit.

D. Neither assumption I nor II is implicit

Directions (Qs. 67 to 69): *In each questions below is given a statement followed by three assumptions numbered I, II and III. An assumption is something supposed or taken for granted. You have to consider the statement and the following assumptions and decide which of the assumptions is implicit in the statement. Select your answer from amongst the five alternatives given.*

67. Statement: "To revitalise the company there is an urgent need to curtail the number of employees and also to mobillise money from financing institutions" — A view of the company adviser.

Assumptions:

I. Financing institutions lend money for such activities.

II. There is marketability for this company's product.

III. Workers of this company are incapable.

A. Only asumptions II and III are implicit.

B. All of the above three assumptions are implicit.

C. None of the above three assumptions are implicit.

D. Only assumptions I and II are implicit.

E. Only assumptions I and III are implicit.

68. Statement: Finding himself unable to meet his expenses, Tamas joined another company.

Assumptions:

I. Working conditions in the new company is better.

II. In the earlier company salary of Tamas was less.

III. New company pays more salary to all the employees.

A. All of the above three assumptions are implicit.

B. None of the above three assumptions is implicit.

C. Only assumption II is implicit

D. only assumptions II and III are implicit

E. None of the above

69. Statement: 'A' says to 'B', "I want to give Aayush on his birthday a novel written by Premchand".

Assumptions:

I. Aaush may not have any novel written by Pemchand.

II. Book is a good birthday gift.

III. 'A' will be invited by Aayush on his birthday.

A. Only assumptions I and II are implicit.

B. Only assumptions I and III are implicit.

C. None of the above three assumptions is implicit

D. Only assumption II is implicit.

E. All of the above three assumptions are implicit.

EXPLANATORY ANSWERS

1. D:	**2. D:**	**3. A:**	**4. E:**	**5. E:**	**6. E:**	**7. D:**
8. A:	**9. B:**	**10. D:**	**11. E:**	**12. E:**	**13. E:**	**14. D:**
15. E:	**16. E:**	**17. A:**	**18. E:**	**19. D:**	**20. B:**	**21. A:**
22. A:	**23. E:**	**24. B:**	**25. E:**	**26. D:**	**27. D:**	**28. B:**
29. A:	**30. A:**	**31. B:**	**32. D:**	**33. B:**	**34. D:**	**35. B:**
36. A:						

37. E: Both the assumption I and assumption II are implicit. If people had neither liked to smoke in the compartment nor they had even smoked then such a notice had no significance.

38. D:

39. E: The best friend would be trustworthy. If comfort and good service could be availed from all hotels then there was no need for the friend to give such a suggestion.

40. B:

41. B:

42. A: Our countrymen had committed errors in the past for which our country had to meet with serious consequences.

43. B:

44. A:

45. B:

46. E:

47. B: If a person is a good painter then the advertiser certainly has a job for him. Therefore the advertiser needs the services of a painter.

48. D: Nothing has been expressed about a good or very good cart in the statement. Therefore none of the assumptions is implicit.

49. B: Only assumption II is implicit. Perfection or excellence arouses curiosity.

50. E: Both assumptions I and II are implicit. The degree of comparison 'Longer Life' is indicative of the fact that other tubes are not durable and people prefer better quality products.

51. E: Both assumpions I and II are implicit. "Judge himself correctly" emphasises the implicity of the assumptions.

52. B: Despite rains yield from the crop was not expected to be better. It means crop situation was not good even before the rains. There was a hope of improvement in the situation after the rain but it was foiled.

53. A: When shortage of time, 'book digest' should be read. Assumption I is implicit.

54. E:

55. A:

56. E:

57. B: In the statement stiffening the qualification criteria has been envisaged to curtail the number of candidates. It means a large number of candidates are not desirable. Therefore assumption

II is implicit. Assumption I is not implicit in the statement because one can not think of very low level of qualification criterion when emphasis is laid on the number of candidates.

58. E:

59. A:

60. B:

61. B: "Changes are desirable in the present communication system" because 'present communication system has become old'. It does not mean that this change will bring improvement in the system.

62. E: Both assumptions I and II are implicit.

63. A:

64. A:

65. C:

66. B:

67. D:

68. D:

69. E: Both assumptions I and II are implicit.

PART-II

In this section a passage is given which is followed by several possible inferences which can be drawn from the facts stated in the passage. Candidates are required to examine each inference separately in the context of the passage and decide upon its degree of truth or falsity.

Example: Read the following passage and drawn the inferences carefully and examine each inference separately in the context of the passage to decide upon its degreė of truth or falsity. Mark answer:

(A) if the inference is 'definitely true'

(B) if the inference is 'probably true'

(C) if the 'data are inadequate'

(D) if the inference is 'probably false'

(E) if the inference is 'definitely false'

"India is an independent country but it is poor. Its poverty is not a matter of today and can not be alleviated within a day or two. India remained under the reign of foreigners for centuries and a grand country which once exported clothes to the countries of Asia, Africa Europe and even America, was squeezed severely under the shackles of slavery. Since independence emphasis has been laid on industrialization in this country and it is expected that this great country which has remained under the shackles of slavery for years would be able to fulfil its losses and would once again become as grand and as great as it was before."

Inference: India, which is a great country, is trying to alleviate its poverty.

Explanatory Answer (B): This inference is true in the context of the passage. But, there is no direct reference to this. Therefore the inference though not definitely true in the light of the facts given, it is probably true.

EXERCISE

Directions: *Given below are 18 passages, each followed by several possible inferences which can be drawn from the facts stated in the passage. You have to examine each inference separately in the context of the passage and decide upon its degree of truth or falsity. Mark answer:*

(A) if the inference is 'Definitely true', *i.e.*, it properly follows from the statement of facts given in the passage.

(B) if the inference is 'probably true' though not 'definitely true' in the light of the facts given.

(C) if the 'data are inadequate', *i.e.*, from the facts given one can not say whether the inference is likely to be true or false.

(D) if the inference is 'probably false' though not definitely false in the light of the facts given.

(E) if the inference is 'Definitely false', *i.e.*, it can not possibly be drawn from the facts given or it contradicts the given facts.

PASSAGE-1

Wind is an inexhaustible source of energy. Wind Electric Generators are used to convert wind energy into electrical energy. Nothing more could be done in this field though surveys conducted have revealed that extensive scopes of development exist in this field. There are four components of wind survey: direction, duration, speed and distribution. Keeping in view these four components, it has been found that hilly regions of Uttar Pradesh are the most suitable locations for establishing Wind Electric Generators. As many as 58 locations have been identified for establishing these Generators in the hilly regions of Uttar Pradesh.

1. These surveys were conducted in the aegis of Government of Uttar Pradesh.
2. Wind energy is comparatively a new field of energy which has come up due to surveys conducted in this field.
3. Except the hilly regions of Uttar Pradesh, no other locations have been found suitable for establishing the Wind Electric Generators.
4. Only the surveys of hilly regions of Uttar Pradesh were conducted to set up the Wind Electric Generators.
5. 58 locations which have been identified for establishing Wind Electric Generators are not electrified.

PASSAGE-2

Condition of primary education in Bihar is not good. In more than 50% schools, classes are conducted in Open Air even during rainy season. More than 6 million children of the families belonging to low income group are left illiterate. Out of 63,000 primary schools, not even 1% schools are provided with facilities like furnitures, lavatories, drinking water and play grounds. In the current financial year 3,113 new teachers have been selected for recruitment in primary schools out of which 2747 are ladies. Each of the 13,220 primary schools has at least two teachers.

6. Most of the primary schools in Bihar do not have their own building.
7. Six million families belong to low income group in Bihar.
8. Large number of schools and school teachers are there in Bihar.
9. 50% children in Bihar are illiterate.
10. 90% teachers in Bihar are ladies.
11. 630 primary schools in Bihar are provided with facilities like furnitures, lavatories, drinking water and play grounds

PASSAGE-3

Consumer movement in India is yet to get full swing. Consumer organisations are working in metropolitan areas but their role to exercise control over the adulteration is quite limited. The situation is worst in villages where providers of consumer services take advantage of ignorance of rural consumers without hesitation. Rules made in this regard by the government is not adequate because these are unable to safeguard consumer's interest. These rules do not encourage people to take part in consumer movement. In addition to this industrial units and other enterprises have been encouraged to earn more and more profit by giving them liberty to levy additional local taxes.

12. People of India never took any interest in schemes formulated by the Government.
13. In other countries consumer movement is at its peak and rules in this regard are adequate to safeguard consumer's interest.
14. Consumer organisations are quite essential because they exercise control over adultration of consumable items.
15. Government has never attempted to arrest the persons indulged in immoral trade practices.
16. Light of consumer movement has not reached in the villages.

PASSAGE-4

We can emphasize that the competence and pace of implementing new techniques in underdeveloped countries could be attributed to the pattern of education and its standard to a great extent. In many underdeveloped countries much resources are spent on higher education of theoretical type and very few resources are spent on creation of able administrators, engineers and technicians.

17. Pattern of education in underdeveloped countries has not been designed according to their requirements.
18. New techniques being adopted in developed countries are not suitable for underdeveloped countries.
19. There is paucity of able administrators, doctors and engineers in underdeveloped countries.

20. Standard of education in developed countries is quite high.
21. Theoretical education is very useful in the process of development

PASSAGE-5

The serious accident in which a person was run over by a car yesterday has again focussed attention on the most unsatisfactory state of street lighting. No one expects side roads to be provided with the same standard of lighting as a main road, but unless the council is prepared to make good its promises as regards road lighting, it will only be a question of time before there are further and perhaps fatal accidents.

22. The accident occurred at night.
23. Several accidents have so far taken place because of unsatisfactory lighting.
24. The accident that occurred was fatal.
25. There will not be a single accident on roads if they are satisfactorily illuminated.
26. It seems that the council has promised to improve the state of lighting on side roads.

PASSAGE-6

Much of our knowledge about ailments caused by cold are regarding how do they spread *i.e.* either by personal contact or by unanimated things. Virologists have found that those who frequently undertake a journey are generally caught by cold because they come in contact with various species of viruses. Those who generally suffer from cold may possibly have problems of physical distortions. For instance, blocking up of eustachian tubes or keeping mouth open while asleep due to which pellicle of the skin in inner mouth gets dried and a good number of viruses enter into body.

27. Virologists have made more efforts to know as to how the ailments of cold spread than to know the reasons of these ailments.
28. People are caught by cold when they come in contact with more than one species of viruses.
29. People who keep their mouth open while asleep may possibly have problems of physical distortion.
30. One can catch cold any time.
31. The reason of ailments of cold is still unknown.

PASSAGE-7

At what extent the medicine administered to protect from an ailment is effective, this is revealed to the medical science only when a post-mortem examination of the body is carried. There is no way available with the medical science to ascertain as to what effect is being produced by a certain medicine on the organs of body until cells and tissues, of which the living body is made, are examined minutely. No doubt, the tests carried on animals in laboratories are helpful but this is to a certain extent only because results obtained by such tests are not completely applicable in the case of human beings.

32. In many cases effect of certain medicine on animals and on human beings is similar.
33. New medicines are tested on animals before they are administered to human beings.
34. Post-mortem examination of the body is a process to examine the cells and tissues of human body.
35. Without a post-mortem examination of the body one can not know as to what extent the medicine administered has produced its effect on the body.
36. Medicines produce effect on cells and tissues of the body.

PASSAGE-8

Gujarat has hardly 8.5 per cent of its total area under forest. Of this, a considerable portion is covered by wild grass and marshes. Denuded of thick forests, fauna have disappeared from many places. Mandvi, for instance, had its share of fauna once. The state government has imposed a total ban on cutting of trees for five years from this year. The imminent destruction of over 40,000 hectares of forest land by the Narmada project has led to nation wide strong protest.

37. A dam on the Narmada river is planned.
38. Once there was thick forest in Mandvi.
39. Government of Gujarat is quite conscious of the need of conservation of forests.
40. There is thick forest in 8.5 per cent of the total area of Gujarat.
41. Gujarat is the first state in India to impose a total ban on cutting of trees.

PASSAGE-9

Text books published in India are generally full of errors. Technical glossaries are either incomplete or they do not contain adequate explanations. Books on Sanskrit literature written by foreign scholars are suitable for those boys studying in universities who are expected to work hard for a better career. Tough explanations and complex sentences are commonly found in text-books published in India.

42. Indian scholars can write books only for weak students.
43. Text-books which have been written by foreign scholars but published in India are generally full of errors.
44. Foreign scholars can not write books for students studying at school level.
45. Text books written by foreign scholars contain tough explanations and complex sentences.
46. Technical glossaries compiled by foreign scholars are inferior to those compiled by Indian scholars.

PASSAGE-10

It is not expected that one should remember bitter experiences of life. We can easily find many persons full of bitter memories of their past—pertaining to their youth or to their childhood—even in their old age. Bitter memories take away our much precious time and lessens our capabilities. These bitter memories of past bear no importance in one's life. We just drag these memories unto our life. Some of them are quite boring and if we retrospect, it would be clear that most of these memories are quite exaggerated and we could cast away them without any problem.

47. Children are punished when they are found guilty.

48. Generally all aged persons waste their valuable time and capability in remembering a few bitter experiences which they had come across during their childhood.

49. A few persons try to retrospect the errors committed in their childhood.

50. None can get rid of the guilty conscious for the errors once committed during childhood or during youth.

51. Some persons find themselves guilty for the errors committed during their childhood.

PASSAGE-11

The smaller pesticide formulation units in India operate under heavy constraints such as obsolete technology, small scale of operation and dependence on larger units for raw materials. In view of the loss of expensive material by the smaller units, it is important to either eliminate or reduce losses to the extent possible through innovative and sustainable waste minimisation techniques. Operating profit margins of the units are very low and small adverse conditions land these companies in trouble. Maximum losses suffered by these units are through poor house keeping, sub-optional operating practices and lack of proper opportunities for recycling wastes.

52. Smaller units should be operationally self-sufficient so as to minimise losses.

53. Recycling of wastes through modern techniques can set off large part of the losses incurred by the smaller units.

54. Pesticide units should necessarily be on a large scale to make them economically viable.

55. Lack of funds compels smaller units to ignore house keeping.

56. Waste management process in India needs modernisation.

PASSAGE-12

Data collected from 24 countries reveal that rate of death caused by stomach cancer is minimum in USA. In Australia, Canada and New Zealand also, where people like dry cereals for their consumption, this rate is at a lower level. In European countries, where food preservatives are not used, this rate of death is found at a higher side. Snacks, Coffee, Butter rolls and Jam are their ideal food stuffs.

57. Europeans are not conservative as regards their eating habits.

58. Coffee, butter rolls and jam add to stomach cancer.

59. Europeans do not like cereals.

60. Cereals save from stomach cancer.

61. Cereals add to stomach cancer besides other kinds of cancer.

PASSAGE-13

To use force in defence against unlawful atrocities of a tryant is not against the ethics of law. It is not required to ascertain whether or not the force used in defence is proper but what is required is to ascertain whether the force was used to check the crime or not.

62. If a man wants to enter into another man's house forcibly and the house owner uses force to stop that man from entering into the house responding which that man beats the house owner severely due to which the house owner becomes unconscious. This act of that man is according to law.

63. To beat the dacoits who have picketed at the house of a businessman with a view to commit robbery in his house is according to law.

64. If a person wants to get into the bus and for this he pushes in other travellers then to reprehend him is according to law.

65. If a father beats his son mercilessly then the man standing nearby has right to save the child from his father's cruelty.

66. To spank on a friend's waist is a crime.

PASSAGE-14

A major scheme of providing mid-day food to the school going children is being implemented in the state of Tamil Nadu only. Although serving only the mid-day food does not fulfil the requirements of nutrition, it actuates the parents to send their wards to school.

67. In Tamilnadu school going children do not require much nutrition.

68. Providing mid-day food will increase the number of school going children.

69. The scheme of providing mid-day food to the school going children in Tamil Nadu has gained success.

70. The scheme of providing mid-day food to the school going children has fulfilled the nutritive requirements of school going children only to a certain extent.

71. In no other state of India except Tamilnadu, the scheme of providing mid-day food to school going children is being implemented.

PASSAGE-15

Various novel ideas evolve in our minds. Idea is a creative power. All types of ideas, whether creative or destructive, simultaneously give birth to so many other ideas. Evolution of an idea is a process of mind which, like sail of a ship, makes us float on waves. Unless our ideas are creative and well considered and at the same time controlled by our strong will power, we shall keep floating on waves and shall be drowned at last.

72. Morning is the high time for evolution of good ideas.

73. Mere ideas without a strong will power are just good for nothing.

74. Good ideas bring prosperity.
75. Evolution of ideas is a process of our body.
76. All of us should have a definite idea of what we want in our life.

PASSAGE-16

As is the case of absolute number of illiterates, the actual number of illiterate females is also increasing with time and faster than the number of male illiterates. More so in the backward states, in the rural areas, and among scheduled castes and scheduled tribes. The correlation between female illiteracy and infant mortality is quite confirmed. It is found that mortality is higher in the case of illiterate mothers both in urban and rural areas but much higher in the latter.

77. In backward states, the population of scheduled castes and scheduled tribes is more than that in other states.
78. Infant mortality is almost same in urban and rural areas.
79. In terms of absolute numbers, there are more male illiterates than female illiterates.
80. Infant mortality is correlated more with the illiteracy of males than with that of females.
81. The illiteracy rate is higher among females as compared to that of males.

PASSAGE-17

Toss has suggested that in the vicinity of the solar system an emission of comparatively brighter light is taking place from orion's outer ring. Scientists are of the view that orion seems to be an extensive cloud of gas and dust and its mass is approximately equal to that of the sun. Its extensive ring is like that of the saturn. According to the scientists study of the high emitting extensive ring of orion would be helpful in revealing the mystery of origin and development of very bright stars which form orion's belt.

82. American scientists are studying about orion.
83. An extensive ring is not seen around the sun as is seen around orion.
84. The sun is not so large as is the orion.
85. Scientists do not have much knowledge about stars.
86. Orion is the nearest star from the earth.

Directions (Qs. 87 to 91): *Read the passage given below carefully and based on the facts stated in this passage, select right answer in each of the questions.*

PASSAGE-18

A steep rise in the demand of castor oil in foreign markets would bring a significant change in the castor-seed economy in the state of Gujarat. This state is emerging as a potential state for production of castor oil and a good number of enterprises concerning castor seed and castor oil are being contained in this particular state. Export of castor oil has now kept under the category of 'price supported product' with a view to encourage its export. Expectations in this field is so high that so many castor oil crushing units have been established in the state and it is hoped that many more will be established in future.

87. More surplus is expected in the sale of castor oil as compared to castor seed.
A. Probably false
B. Probably true
C. Definitely true
D. Data are inadequate
E. Definitely false

88. Production of castor oil is quite profitable.
A. Probably true
B. Probably false
C. Definitely false
D. Data are inadequate
E. Definitely true

89. India can produce adequate quantity of castor seed to meet its domestic requirements as well as requirements for export.
A. Probably true
B. Probably false
C. Definitely false
D. Data are inadequate
E. Definitely true

90. Gujarat is the only castor seed producing state in India.
A. Definitely false
B. Data are inadequate
C. Probably false
D. Definitely true
E. Probably true

91. Gujarat has supplied castor seeds to the castor oil producing units even in the past.
A. Definitely true
B. Probably true
C. Definitely false
D. Probably false
E. Data are inadequate

ANSWERS

1	2	3	4	5	6	7	8	9	10
C	A	C	C	D	B	A	A	C	C
11	12	13	14	15	16	17	18	19	20
E	B	C	A	B	B	A	C	A	C
21	22	23	24	25	26	27	28	29	30
D	A	B	B	D	A	A	D	A	B
31	32	33	34	35	36	37	38	39	40
E	B	A	A	E	B	A	A	B	E
41	42	43	44	45	46	47	48	49	50
E	E	D	E	B	C	C	D	B	E
51	52	53	54	55	56	57	58	59	60
A	B	A	C	E	A	C	C	B	A
61	62	63	64	65	66	67	68	69	70
C	E	A	A	A	C	E	A	A	A
71	72	73	74	75	76	77	78	79	80
A	D	A	A	E	C	A	E	E	E
81	82	83	84	85	86	87	88	89	90
A	C	C	B	A	B	D	E	E	B
91									
A									

PART-III

Directions (Qs. 1 to 6): *In the following questions some statements are followed by one or more inferences. The inference or inferences may be wrongly or correctly drawn. Select one of the alterantives which contains the correctly drawn inference or inferences.*

1. Statements:

Foreigners in Jordan without a valid work permit will be deported. A few Indian employees in the building industry in Jordan do not possess valid work permits.

Inferences:

I. All Indians engaged in building industry in Jordan will be deported to India.

II. A few Indians in building industry in Jordan will be deported.

III. A bulk of Indians in Jordan will be deported to India.

IV. Indian employees in building industry without work permit will be deported from Jordan.

The inferences correctly drawn are:

A. I and III

B. III and IV

C. II and IV

D. I and II

2. Statements:

All scientists working in America are talented. Some Indian scientists are working in America.

Inferences:

I. All talented scientists are Indian.

II. None of the Indian scientists is talented.

III. Some Indian scientists are talented

IV. Some talented Indian scientists are working in America.

The inferences correctly drawn are:

A. I and III B. III and IV

C. II and IV D. I and II

3. Statements:

Aman and Shyam are friends. Shyam is friendly with all. Aman has many enemies. Rahul and Aman do not like each other.

Inferences:

I. Aman and Rahul are both friends of Shyam.

II. Shyam is friendly with Aman's friends.

III. Rahul and Shyam are friends.

IV. Aman, Rahul and Shyam form a clique.

The inferences correctly drawn are:

A. I and III

B. II and III

C. III and IV

D. I, II and III

4. Statements:

I. Freedom fighters are awarded with 'medals'.

II. Kanak was a freedom fighter.

Inferences:

He was awarded a 'medal'.

The inference drawn is:

A. Logical

B. Illogical

C. Probably false

D. Irrelevant

5. Statements:

1. Water boils at 100°C
2. Water freezes into ice at 0°C.

Inferences:

Water boils at low pressure and low temperature.

The inference drawn is:

A. True
B. False
C. Either true or false
D. Irrelevant

6. Statements:

All watches sold in that shop are of high standard. Some of the HMT watches are sold in that shop.

Inferences:

I. All watches of high standard were manufacutred by HMT
II. Some of the HMT watches are of high standard.
III. None of the HMT watches is of high standard.
IV. Some of the HMT watches of high standard are sold in that shop.

The inferences correctly drawn are:

A. I and III
B. II and IV
C. I and IV
D. II and III

Directions (Qs. 7 to 56): *In the following questions, each question has a statement followed by two conclusions. Taking the statement to be true, decide which of the given conclusions definitely follows from the given statement. Indicate your answer as:*

(A) if only conclusion I follows
(B) if only conclusion II follows
(C) if either I or II follows
(D) if both I and II follow
(E) if neither I nor II follows

7. Statement:

If a youngman agrees to marry a girl only on terms of dowry, he defiles women's honour and commits a crime against humanity.

Conclusions:

I. Those who take dowry for marrying a girl, should be excommunicated from the society.
II. Those who do not take dowry in marriage, confer honour to women.

8. Statement:

Government of India has recently declared an average increase of fifteen per cent in the price of steel due to which Steel Authority of India which is a large Public Sector Enterprise, will have to incur loss to the tune of 350 crores during this year.

Conclusions:

I. After effecting increase in the price of steel, Public Sector Enterprise will have to incur loss.
II. Steel Authority of India is presently incurring loss on its performance.

9. Statements:

The road distance between Mumbai and Zafarabad is 900 kms. This distance will be decreased by 280 kms if adopted seaway and thus Rs. 7.92 crores per annum would be saved on fuel.

Conclusions:

I. Transportation by road is costly than that by sea way.

II. We should save expenditure on fuel as much as possible.

10. Statement:

Candidates should be in the age group of 27 years and 32 years and they should be youthful, energetic and dynamic.

Conclusions:

I. People below the age of 27 years are not energetic.

II. People above the age of 32 years are not youthful.

11. Statement:

For construction work sealed tenders should be invited from experienced and able contractors.

Conclusions:

I. Tenders should be invited from experienced contractors only.

II. It is difficult to get able tenderers for construction work.

12. Statement:

Although he is quite sensible, he is not popular among his companions.

Conclusions:

I. Only sensible conduct is not required for gaining popularity.

II. People do not like sensible persons.

13. Statement:

Scientists in some developed countries are working to find extra-solar planets that could harbour life.

Conclusions:

I. There are extra-solar planets potentially able to support life.

II. Existence of such extra-solar planets is impossible which could have evolved life.

14. Statement:

He was promoted despite he was not an efficient worker.

Conclusions:

I. Efficiency and promotion do not have any correlation.

II. Efficiency is essential for getting promotion.

15. Statement:

The manager behaved disgracefully with Mayank when many colleagues of Mayank were present there.

Conclusions:

I. Manager does not like Mayank.

II. Mayank is not popular among his colleagues.

16. Statement:

Good books are like friends because these are always helpful.

Conclusions:

I. One should be very cautious in selecting friends.

II. Books give us permanent delight and satisfaction.

17. Statement:

"Education is a subject under 'concurrent list.' Therefore state governments can not bring improvement readily in the standard of education without getting permission from the central government."

Conclusions:

I. State and central governments are not interested in bringing improvement in the standard of education.

II. If we want to bring improvement in the standard of education readily, then education should be brought under state list.

18. Statement:

Water supply will be affected to the tune of 25% on Sunday in 'A' and 'D' zones of the city due to some maintenance work in a few major water supply lines.

Conclusions:

I. People should not face difficulties due to such maintenance work.

II. Such declarations are essential for the people.

19. Statement:

"In the whole third world, as compared to males, females are more actively involved in production, storage and sale of food products." –a report from FAO.

Conclusions:

I. If we want to increase the production from agriculture in the third world then as compared to males more stress should be given on females for imparting training in respect of new technical know-how of agriculture.

II. As compred to males, females are more devoted workers.

20. Statement:

Water supply will be affected to the tune of 25% on Wednesday in A and D zones of the city due to some maintenance work in a few major water supply lines.

Conclusions:

I. Residents of these zones should avoid excessive use of water on Wednesday.

II. Residents of these zones should store water of their use a day before Wednesday.

21. Statements:

The Minister said, "the view recently expressed by International Labour Organization was, to a great extent, directed only towards the welfare of labours engaged in organised sector. This will not be helpful for the developed countries where maximum number of labours are engaged in unorganised sectors.

Conclusions:

I. International Labour Organization should formulate schemes for the welfare of the labours engaged in unorganised sectors also. Thus this organization would become helpful for the developed countries too.

II. Developed countries are incapable in formulating schemes for the welfare of labours engaged in unorganised sectors.

22. Statement:

The Supreme Court has decided that it will be against the provisions of the Constitution if school authorities make the recitation of national song essential for the students when a few students have objection on the basis of religion.

Conclusions:

I. School authorities should check

whether their major decisions are according to the provisions of the Constitution or not.

II. Schools can not make the recitation of national song essential for their students.

23. Statement:

Although he has strongly denied that Income tax officers have raided his house, it is in the air all over the town.

Conclusions:

I. Income tax officers have raided his house.

II. Income tax officers have not raided his house.

24. Statement:

The knowledge of subject does not matter much, what matters is whether one can orally express it or not.

Conclusions:

I. Any of the subjects is equally important if one has knowledge about the subject.

II. It is essential to know about the subject if one wants to impress others.

25. Statement:

If a young man gets ready to marry a woman on terms of dowry, he loses his honour and shows his disrespect towards women.

Conclusions:

I. Dowry system should be abolished.

II. Those who do not take dowry in marriage, honour women.

26. Statement:

According to a recent decision of Supreme Court any one can attempt suicide without any fear of conviction in the court of law.

Conclusions:

I. Men should behave according to the Surpeme Court's decision.

II. Before Supreme Court's recent decision suicidal attempt was regarded an act against the ethics of law.

27. Statement:

Even an evil-minded person can cite an example from holy books to serve his purpose.

Conclusions:

I. Evil-minded persons also stick to some principles.

II. A real scholar can be found only in holy books.

28. Statement:

A new fashion is becoming so rapidly old that it requires change in every six months.

Conclusions:

I. Fashion designers do not perceive people's demand.

II. People, in general, readily accept new fashions in place of old one.

29. Statement:

The new fades and the old endures.

Conclusions:

I. Change is the law of nature.

II. People do not like to follow old systems.

30. Statement:

The knowledge of content does not matter much, what matters is whether you can orally express it or not.

Conclusions:

I. Art of delivery and knowledge of content are not necessarily interdependent.

II. Oral expression is an acquired skill.

31. Statement:

I am an ignorant and know none of the facts.

Conclusions:

I. The orator of the above statement knows very few.

II. World of knowledge is so vast that a man can not explore its dimensions in his full life-span.

32. Statement:

To give or take divorce is quite easy in America

Conclusions:

I. People, in general, give or take divorce in America.

II. Indians should go America for giving or taking divorce.

33. Statement:

Apples are very costly.

Conclusions:

I. Poor can not buy apples.

II. Only rich men can buy apples.

34. Statement:

All girls in the class are laborious.

Conclusions:

I. Even a single boy does not read in the class.

II. All boys of the class are dull.

35. Statement: X is a poor country.

Conclusions:

I. Inhabitants of X country are beggars.

II. Inhabitants of X country do not work.

36. Statement:

Go by rail to reach Pune from Dehradun.

Conclusions:

I. Dehradun and Pune are far from each other.

II. Dehradun and Pune are connected by rail.

37. Statement:

Apart from the informative value of newspapers, their recreational value can not be ignored.

Conclusions:

I. People subscribe to a newspaper with a view to acquire information.

II. People have now started realising the recreational value of newspapers.

38. Statement:

Ten passengers who were on the waiting-list, finally got reservation in Frontier Mail.

Conclusions:

I. Wait-listed passengers get reservation in Frontier Mail with difficulty.

II. Number of berths in Frontier Mail is comparatively less.

39. Statement:

As compared to other T.V. sets manufactured in India "Solar" T.V. finds a ready sale in the market.

Conclusions:

I. Volume of sale of all the T.V. sets manufactured in India is known.

II. Compared to other TV sets manufactured in India, 'Solar' TV sets, find a ready sale in the market.

40. Statement:

These high priced apples can not be of inferior quality.

Conclusions:

I. When the supply of apples in the market is not adequate to meet its demand, the prices go high.

II. The higher the selling price, the superior is the quality of the commodity.

41. Statement:

Camel is an indispensable mode of transport in desert.

Conclusions:

I. Camel is the only cheapest mode of transport in desert.

II. Camels are abundantly found in desert.

42. Statement:

Our present education system needs thorough amendment.

Conclusions:

I. Thorough amendment brings improvement.

II. Present education system has become obsolete.

43. Statement:

Decisions are not taken on superficial ostentations.

Conclusions:

I. Superficial ostentations could be deceitful.

II. Every one can take decision.

44. Statement:

Without practical acquaintance with the problem of life, only bookish knowledge is of no use.

Conclusions:

I. All books contain practical aspects of life.

II. One should have practical acquaintance with the problems of life.

45. Statement:

According to the 42nd amendment to the Constitution passed by the parliament, President of India is bound to comply with cabinet's decisions.

Conclusions:

I. The president of India never complied with cabinet's decision prior to introduction of 42nd Amendment Bill.

II. Prior to introduction of 42nd Amendment Bill, the President was not accustomed to consider the views expressed by cabinet.

46. Statement:

It is advisable to go by aeroplane if one wants to reach Mumbai from Meerut quickly.

Conclusions:

I. Meerut and Mumbai are connected by aeroplane service.

II. There is no other means of going from Meerut to Mumbai.

47. Statement:

In the present circumstances inhabitants of this country do not require specialists of various diseases who are available in quite insufficient number. What they require are the general practioners who are proficient in their profession.

Conclusions:

I. Extension in the scope of primary medical education is

urgently needed in this country.

II. Specialists of various specific diseases are, in general, not capable of safeguarding general health conditions of the people living in this country.

48. Statement:

He aroused doubt on the utility of current research schemes and suggested that schemes being implemented in the identified sectors of national importance should be replaced by new ones.

Conclusions:

I. Research schemes should be discontinued.

II. Research schemes should be related with the sectors of national importance.

49. Statements:

In a certain group of people only widows do not put bindi on their forehead. Rachna belongs to that group and she put bindi on her forehead.

Conclusions:

I. Rachna is an unmarried girl.

II. Rachna is a married woman.

50. Statements:

Oceans are huge reserviors of almost all minerals including Uranium. But unlike other minerals, Uranium also is found very sparingly in the ocean water, *i.e.*, approximately 3 gms in every 1000 tons of water.

Conclusions:

I. Oceans are not very high costing source of Uranium.

II. Danger of radiation always exists in the water of oceans.

51. Statement:

The profession in which you have engaged yourself does not matter much, what matters is whether you like your profession or not.

Conclusions:

I. Any profession is good so far as it is interesting.

II. Type and quality of a profession do not bear any importance.

52. Statements:

The radiation risk of nuclear power plants is barely one per cent of the total radiation we have to endure. 99 per cent of the average dose received by people working in industrial habitats is from sources other than nuclear energy power plants.

Conclusions:

I. No industrial habitat should be allowed.

II. All nuclear radiations should be banned by law.

53. Statements:

The commission while examining cases of insurance in India found that the detailed terms and conditions of an insurance proposal were either not drawn up at all or delayed for several months. The result was that on receipt of a claim the interpretation of terms and conditions gave the officers an opportunity to show either undue favour or to cause harassment to the party.

Conclusions:

I. There is a need for revamping all

the procedures of the insurance companies.

II. Anybody wanting insurance should himself see that the terms and conditions of the insurance are noted in detail.

54. Statements:

The radiation risks of nuclear power plants is barely one percent of the total radiation we have to endure. 99 per cent of the average dose received by people working in industrial habitat is from sources other than nuclear energy power plants.

Conclusions:

I. Anti-nuclear lobby in the world protesting against nuclear plants should stop their protest marches.

II. All nuclear power plants should be closed to avoid nuclear radiation risks.

55. Statements:

The commission while examining cases of insurance in India found that the detailed terms and conditions of an insurance proposal were either not drawn up at all or delayed for several months. The result was that on receipt of a claim that interpretation of terms and conditions gave the officers an opportunity to show either undue favour or to cause harassment to the party.

Conclusions:

I. Officers of the insuracne companies should always interpret the terms and conditions of any claim favourably.

II. A team of officers of insurance companies should be sent to one of the advanced countries to study the working of the insurance companies there.

56. Statement:

Last month, even premier issues in the capital market were not fully subscribed by public. The Government of India is also worried and wants to revive confidence in the capital market.

Conclusions:

I. Government financial institutions should subscribe if there is a shortfall in public subscription.

II. Government should ask the companies to postpone the issue of public issues for public subscription until stability returns in the capital market.

Directions (Qs. 57 to 66): *In each of the following questions a statement has been given followed by two conclusions. Mark your answer as:*

(A) if only the first conclusion is true

(B) if only the second conclusion is true

(C) if both conclusions are true

(D) if none of the conclusions is true.

57. Statements:

All teachers are good.

Some women are teachers.

Conclusions:

I. All good teachers are women.

II. Some women are good.

58. Statements:

All businessmen are hard-working.

No hard-working men are superstitious.

Conclusions:

I. No businessman is superstitious.

II. Some superstitious are businessmen.

59. Statements:

All clerks are lazy.

Some women are clerks.

Conclusions:

I. All lazy are women.

II. Some women are lazy.

60. Statements:

All students in my class are intelligent.

Rahul is not intelligent.

Conclusions:

I. Rahul is not a student of my class.

II. Rahul must work hard.

61. Statements:

All pilots are brave men.

All astronauts are pilots.

Conclusions:

I. All astronauts are brave men.

II. Some pilots are astronauts.

62. Statement:

The percentage of the national income shared by the top 10 per cent of households in India is 35.

Conclusions:

I. When an economy grows fast, concentration of wealth in certain pockets of population takes place.

II. The national income is unevenly distributed in India

63. Statement:

Crime is a function of criminal's biological make-up and his family relations.

Conclusions:

I. The incidence of crime is higher in identical twins than in fraternal twins.

II. Families in which parents lack in warmth and affection fail to build in children a moral conscience.

64. Statement:

In India, the fruits of development have not been equitably distributed between our rural and urban sectors.

Conclusions:

I. Rural poverty is substantially higher than urban poverty.

II. A large family size in India may be a consequence rather than a cause of poverty.

65. Statement:

The increase in adult literacy will lead to country's development and progress.

Conclusions:

I. The educated persons offer less resistance to new innovations.

II. The literacy rate is higher in developed countries.

66. Statement:

The use of non-conventional sources of energy will eliminate the energy crisis in the world.

Conclusions:

I. Modern technology is gradually replacing the conventional sources of energy.

II. The excessive exploitation of environment has led to the depletion of the conventional sources of energy

Directions (Qs. 67 to 76): *In each of the following questions a statement has been given followed by two conclusions. Mark your answer as:*

(A) if only the first conclusion is true
(B) if only the second conclusion is true
(C) if both conclusions are true
(D) if either the first or the second conclusion is true
(E) if none of the conclusions is true

67. Statement:

Executive powers of the state are vested in the Governor of the State who is nominated by the President of India and discharges his duties according to the desires of the President.

Conclusions:

I. Governor of a state is nominated by the President of India.

II. Governor is personally responsible for all administative affairs of the state.

68. Statement:

Despite difficulties, all developing countries of the world are implementing schemes to achieve zero percent rate of increase in the population of their countries

Conclusions:

I. Zero percent rate of increase in the population of all developing countries can never be achieved.

II. Developing countries have achieved this goal.

69. Statement:

There is no doubt that Mrs. Indira Gandhi had friendly alliance with at least one-third countries of the world. It has been found that non-aligned countries always expected her charismatic leadership.

Conclusions:

I. Non-aligned countries never expected Mrs. Gandhi's charismatic leadership.

II. Non-aligned countries had accepted the charismatic leadership of Mrs. Indira Gandhi.

70. Statement:

Indian voters are generally illiterates.

Conclusions:

I. Irregularities faced during elections are generally caused by illiterates.

II. Voters are not capable of electing persons who are able and bear a well-marked personality.

71. Statement:

Candidates going to appear in the Probationary Officers entrance test are required to labour hard and sincerely follow the prescribed courses of study.

Conclusions:

I. To get through the Probationary Officers entrance test is not an easy task.

II. Candidates should labour hard for other tests also.

72. Statement:

Parliamentary ethics is not a sense of responsibility which evolves naturally.

Conclusions:

I. Sense of responsibility evolves in our minds.

II. Parliamentarians should be imparted training of parliamentary ethics.

73. Statement:

God has created man and man, according to the ideology of the society, has categorised himself among castes.

Conclusions:

I. System of castes has been developed by the man himself.

II. God has created many differences among men by formulating the system of castes.

74. Statement:

Do you think a person who has gone crazy, is not a fool even if he behaves like a fool.

Conclusions:

I. Craze and foolishness are seen together

II. A normal man behaves wisely.

75. Statement:

If we observe government's approach towards rural and urban sectors then the differences between the levels of development in rural and urban areas would be clear to us.

Conclusions:

I. Government has laid more stress on rural development as compared to urban development.

II. Government has laid less stress on rural development as compared to urban development.

76. Statement:

After this amendment to the Constitution, no child below the age of 14 will work in factories, mines or other hazardous units.

Conclusions:

I. Before this amendment, children below the age of 14 were working in the factories, mines or hazardous units.

II. All employer have started refusing the children below the age of 14 for employment after this amendment to the Constitution.

Directions (Qs. 77 to 86): *A statement is given followed by two conclusions numbered I and II. You have to take the given statement to be true even if it seems to be at variance with commonly known facts and then decide which of the given conclusions logically follows from the given statement. Mark your answer as:*

(A) if only conclusion I follows.

(B) if only conclusion II follows.

(C) if either I or II follows

(D) if neither I nor II follows

(E) if both I and II follow

77. Statement:

They have emphatically said that this is the need of the hour that the existing system of examination should be replaced by some other means to judge the students caliber.

Conclusions:

I. System of examination should be abolished.

II. Existing system of examination is not suitable for assessing the student's caliber.

78. Statement:

As compared to the crude oil indigeneously produced in the country, its demand in the domestic market is increasing very rapidly.

Conclusions:

I. Crude oil should be imported in our country.

II. Demand of the crude oil in domestic market should reduce.

79. Statements:

The byproducts obtained from animals such as hairs, skins, horns, etc. contain at least 50 per cent food protein. American scientists have developed methods to segregate 45 per cent of this protein. They have used enzymes developed in Japan to get soya-protein.

Conclusions:

I. It is difficult to prepare enzymes for the Americans.

II. Structure of protein obtained from byproducts of animals is same as that of soya-protein.

80. Statement:

A careful study of the history of ancient India reveals that in ancient times even in India teachers and their disciples both gave more importance to the standard and quality of education than the volume of education.

Conclusions:

I. It is quite substandard to give importance to the volume of education.

II. In ancient India teachers and their disciples both had equal respect for educational values.

81. Statement:

Oceans are vast reservoirs of almost all minerals including Uranium. But like other minerals, Uranium is very sparingly found in the water of ocean, *i.e.*, 3 gms Uranium in every 1000 tons of ocean water.

Conclusions:

I. We can get gold in the water of ocean.

II. Radiation emitted from ports is dangerous.

82. Statements:

To get quality one has to pay its cost. Various modes of teaching have been evolved in India.

Conclusions:

I. Quality of teaching in India will get improved shortly.

II. We can improve the quality of teaching only by spending more money.

83. Statement:

New experiments have revealed that small pimples erupt on our skin only due to malfunctioning of our liver.

Conclusions:

I. To get rid of pimples one should go for treatment of liver.

II. It is useless to apply creams, ointments etc. on our skin.

84. Statements:

Development in the standard of any society brings inequality among the members of the society. It is never justified to stop the process of development to remove inequality.

Conclusions:

I. Inequality among the members of a society should be maintained to secure development.

II: Inequality and development can not be achieved simultaneously.

85. **Statements:**

The byproducts obtained from animals such as hairs, skins, horns, etc. contain at least 50 per cent food protein. Indian scientists have developed methods to segregate 45 per cent of this protein. They have used an enzyme developed in Russia for destruction of soya-protein

Conclusions:

I. Indian scientists can not develop enzymes.

II. If a suitaable method involving less cost is developed then many more food proteins would be obtained.

ANSWERS

1	**2**	**3**	**4**	**5**	**6**	**7**	**8**	**9**	**10**
C	B	D	A	D	B	E	B	B	E
11	**12**	**13**	**14**	**15**	**16**	**17**	**18**	**19**	**20**
A	A	C	A	D	B	D	B	A	E
21	**22**	**23**	**24**	**25**	**26**	**27**	**28**	**29**	**30**
A	B	C	D	E	B	B	C	B	A
31	**32**	**33**	**34**	**35**	**36**	**37**	**38**	**39**	**40**
C	A	D	A	B	C	A	C	B	C
41	**42**	**43**	**44**	**45**	**46**	**47**	**48**	**49**	**50**
E	E	A	E	E	A	B	B	C	D
51	**52**	**53**	**54**	**55**	**56**	**57**	**58**	**59**	**60**
E	D	E	A	B	B	B	A	B	A
61	**62**	**63**	**64**	**65**	**66**	**67**	**68**	**69**	**70**
A	B	D	A	E	A	A	E	B	E
71	**72**	**73**	**74**	**75**	**76**	**77**	**78**	**79**	**80**
A	C	A	A	D	C	B	C	D	B
81	**82**	**83**	**84**	**85**					
A	A	A	E	A					

PART-IV

In this type of test each question contains two statements. Each of these two statements is followed by a conclusion. You have to take the given statements to be true even if they seem to be at variance with commonly known facts and then decide which of the given conclusions can be logically drawn from the statement to which it follows.

Example: Each of the given two statements 'P' and 'Q' is followed by a conclusion. Decide which of the two conclusions can be logically drawn from its statement. Mark your answer as:

(A) if both conclusions are true.
(B) if both conclusions are false.
(C) if conclusion drawn in (P) is true and in (Q) is false.
(D) if conclusion drawn in (P) is false and in (Q) is true.

–(P) water boils at 100°. Liquid X also boils at 100°. Therefore this liquid X is water.

–(Q) All green labelled bottles contain fruit juice. Drinking fruit juice is not injurious to health. Therefore drinking the liquid contained in all green labelled bottles is not injurious to health.

Explanatory Answer (D): It is not clear from (P) that liquid which boils at 100° will certainly be water. Therefore conclusion in 'P' is false. In (Q) it has been stated that green labelled bottles contain fruit juice which is not harmful. Therefore drinking the liquid contained in these green labelled botles is not injurious. Therefore (Q) is true.

EXERCISE

Directions (Qs. 1 to 5): *In each of the questions below two statements 'P' and Q have been given. Each of these two statements is followed by one conclusion. You have to decide whether the conclusion that follows in each statement is correctly drawn from the statement or not. Mark your answer as:*

(A) if only the conclusion drawn in (P) is true.
(B) if only the conclusion drawn in (Q) is true.
(C) if conclusions drawn in (P) and (Q) both are true.
(D) if conclusions drawn in (P) and (Q) both are false.

1. P: Some crows are jackals. No fox is a crow. Therefore no fox is a Jackal.

Q: All crows are not jackals. All foxes are jackals. Therefore some crows are foxes.

2. P: Some philosophers are wise. All philosophers are men. Therefore some men are wise.

Q: Some books can read. All books are pencils. Therefore no pencil can read.

3. P: All balls are bats or rackets or wickets. Some trees are balls but they are neither bats nor rackets. Therefore some trees are wickets.

Q: All bats are balls. Therefore some trees are neither bats nor rackets.

4. P: All types of gold glitter. All types of silver glitter. Therefore all types of gold are silver.

Q: All types of gold glitter. All types of silver glitter. Therefore all those glitter are either gold or silver.

5. P: All workers wear hats. All hats are red. Therefore all workers do not wear red hat.

Q: All wives are ladies. Kajal is a lady. Therefore Kajal is a wife.

Directions (Qs. 5 to 10): *In each of the questions below two statements numbered I and II have been given. You have* *to take the given statements to be true even if they seem to be at variance with commonly known facts and then decide the truth or falsity of the statements. Mark your answer as:*

(A) if both statements I and II are true.
(B) if both statements I and II are false.
(C) if statement I is true and II is false.
(D) if statement I is false and II is true.

6. I: Some singers are not rich. All singers have melodious voice. Therefore all persons having melodious voice are rich.

II: All singers are rich. No rich man has melodious voice. Therefore singers do not have melodious voice.

7. I: All fishes can fly. Some fishes are wild animals. Therefore some wild animals can fly.

II: Some fishes are birds. All birds are wild animals. Therefore some fishes are wild animals.

8. I: Some tables are boxes. All stools are boxes. Therefore all tables are stools.

II: Jackals live in forests. Towns are located in forests. Therefore jackals live in towns.

9. I: Some mangoes are apples. All grapes are mangoes. Therefore all apples are grapes.

II: Some mangoes are apples. All apples are grapes. Therefore some mangoes are grapes.

10. I: Cups play cards. Playing cards is a difficult game. Therefore cups play a difficult game.

II: Radha is a girl. All girls are timid. Therefore Radha is timid.

ANSWERS

1	2	3	4	5	6	7	8	9	10
D	A	C	D	D	D	A	B	D	A

PART-V

In this type of test three statements are given of which two are premises and third is a conclusion that necessarily follows from the two premises. The candidates are asked to decide upon the degree of truth or falsity of the conclusion drawn.

Example 1: Given below are two statements followed by a conclusion drawn from them. Read the two statements and following conclusion carefully and state whether the conclusion is true or false. Mark your answer as:

(A) if the conclusion is definitely true.
(B) if the conclusion is probably true though not definitely true.
(C) if the conclusion is irrelevant.
(D) if the conclusion is probably false though not definitely false.
(E) if the conclusion is definitely false or it contradicts the given facts.

Statements I: This is an insect
II: Some insects are yellow

in colour

Conclusion: Therefore this insect should be yellow in colour.

Explanatory Answer (B): Some insects are yellow and this is an insect. Therefore this insect might be yellow in colour but we can not certainly say that this is yellow in colour. Therefore conclusion is though not definitely true, it is probably true.

Example 2: Given below are two statements followed by a conclusion. You have to examine the conclusion drawn in the light of the facts stated in the given statements. Mark your answer as:

(A) if first statement affirms the conclusion.

(B) if second statement affirms the conclusion.

(C) if both statements affirm the conclusion.

(D) if none of the two statements affirms the drawn conclusion.

Statements: I. For intelligence it is not essential that one should bear a good character.

II. Mala bears a good character.

Conclusion:

Mala is not intelligent.

Explanatory Answer (D): "For intelligence it is not essential that one should bear a good character" does not imply that no intelligent person bears a good character. The second statement also does not imply that Mala is not intelligent. Therefore none of the two statements affirms the drawn conclusion.

Directions (Qs. 1 to 22): *In each of the following questions two statements followed by a conclusion have been given. Read the two statements and following conclusion carefully and state if the conclusion is true or false. Mark you answer as:*

(A) if the conclusion is definitely true.

(B) if the conclusion is definitely false or it contradicts the given facts.

(C) if the conclusion is true to a certain extent and at the same time false to a certain extent.

(D) if the conclusion is not related with the statements.

1. **Statements:**

I: One who reads newspaper can do well in the examination.

II: Bittu does not read newspaper regularly.

Conclusion:

Bittu could not do well in the examination.

A. definitely true
B. Probably true
C. definitely false
D. Probably false

2. **Statements:**

I: I know a lecturer of the University.

II: He has beard.

Conclusion:

All lecturers of the university have beard

3. **Statements:**

I: One should adopt the norm of three children.

II: Rahul has three children.

Conclusion:

Rahul is a rich man.

4. Statements:

I: This bus plies on route number 10.

II: A large number of buses plying on route number 10 go to the stadium.

Conclusion:

This bus goes to the stadium.

5. Statements:

I: We can maintain a good health if we get up early in the morning.

II: Minku generally gets up early in the morning.

Conclusion:

Minku bears a good health.

6. Statements:

I: Mammals suckle their young ones.

II: Rabbit suckles its young ones.

Conclusion:

Rabbit is a mammal.

7. Statements:

I: L is the brother of K.

II: K is the friend of M.

Conclusion:

K is the enemy of M.

8. Statements:

I: P is standing behind M and N.

II: Q is standing behind P.

Conclusion:

Q is standing behind M.

9. Statements:

I: Rats eat Cheese.

II: Cheese is used in Omelet.

Conclusion:

Rats can prepare Omelet.

10. Statements:

I: Climate is cold at high altitude.

II: At high altitude atmospheric pressure is low.

Conclusion:

We feel cold if atmospheric pressure is low.

11. Statements:

I: Neighbour's dog barks.

II: Barking dogs are alert.

Conclusion:

It is the responsibility of the neighbour to keep his dog alert.

12. Statements:

I: Birds generally fly in the air.

II: Fishes swim in water.

Conclusion:

Elephants move on land.

13. Statements:

I: Metals are generally malleable and ductile.

II: X is neither malleable nor ductile.

Conclusion:

X is not a metal.

14. Statements:

I: He is either glad or sad.

II: He is sad.

Conclusion:

Yesterday he was sad.

15. Statements:

I: Glass is brittle.

II: This substance is not brittle.

Conclusion:

This substance is not glass.

16. Statements:

I: Rahul hates Mehul.

II: Mehul hates Rupam.

Conclusion:

Rahul hates Rupam

17. Statements:

I: All workers wear hats.

II: All hats are green.

Conclusion:

All workers wear green hats.

18. Statements:

I: All wives are ladies.

II: She is a lady.

Conclusion:

She is a wife.

19. Statements:

I: Generally murderers leave some or other clue at the site of murder.

II: Some one had murdered Mr. Sharma.

Conclusion:

That murderer will certainly be caught.

20. Statements:

I: "Career correspondence" is useful for people.

II: Anyone can be awarded diploma without studying in class.

Conclusion:

To read in school for such type of diploma is to waste time.

21. Statements:

I: Several Hindus and Sikhs go on a pilgrimage to Pakistan.

II: Several Muslims from Pakistan come India for visiting "Dargah-e-Shareif".

Conclusion:

India and Pakistan have mutual understanding.

22. Statements:

I: A summit conference is being organised shortly.

II: In this summit conference several countries are participating.

Conclusion:

Summit conferences should be organised keeping in view the interests of nations.

Directions (Qs. 23 to 28): *In each of the following questions a few statements have been given followed by one conclusion. You have to examine the conclusion in the context of the statements and decide upon its degree of truth or falsity. Mark your answer as:*

(A) If the conclusion is definitely true in the light of the statements.

(B) If the conclusion is exaggerated.

(C) If statements do not affirm the conclusion.

(D) If conclusion is probably false or true.

(E) If none of the above is correct.

23. Statements:

I: All boys like to play games.

II: X does not like to play games.

Conclusion:

X is not a boy.

24. Statements:

I: Very few people have courage to purchase those houses which are haunted by evil spirits.

II: No body purchased houses located in the vicinity of this Old fort.

Conclusion:

Houses located in the vicinity of the Old fort are haunted by evil spirits.

25. Statements:

I: 'Textile Designers' have a better knowledge of colours.

II: They also possess a better knowledge of painting.

Conclusion:

People who have studied 'Textile Designing', possess better sense of asthetics.

26. **Statements:**

I: Peacock has a long beautiful tail.

II: Peacock dances with great pride.

III: Ostritch also dances with great pride.

Conclusion:

Ostritch has a long beautiful tail.

27. **Statements:**

I: Courageous warriors generally do not marry.

II: Dara Singh is courageous warrior

Conclusion:

Dara Singh is unmarried.

28. **Statements:**

I: People living in temperate climate generally suffer from malaria.

II: Bijnore district of Uttar Pradesh has temperate climate.

III: Two thousand people die every year in the district of Bijnore.

Conclusion:

People in Bijnore are dying due to Malaria.

Directions (Qs. 29 to 33): *In each of the following questions two statements have been given followed by one conclusion. Mark your answer as:*

(A) if the conclusion is true.

(B) if the conclusion is false.

(C) if the conclusion is true to a certain-extent.

(D) if the conclusion is contradictry.

29. **Statements:**

I: Cats drink milk.

II: Cats are very wise.

Conclusion:

All those animals who drink milk are wise.

30. **Statements:**

I: Generally boys like to fly a kite.

II: Generally girls like to play with dolls.

Conclusion:

Girls are wise as compared to boys.

31. **Statements:**

I: Carbohydrate helps in building up of new cells in our body.

II: Growing children require nutrition.

Conclusion:

Carbohydrate is essential for growing children.

32. **Statements:**

I: Lala Lajpat Rai was born in Punjab.

II: Bhagat Singh was also born in Punjab.

Conclusion:

All freedom fighters were born in Punjab.

33. **Statements:**

I: Level of water in the river Ganga is increasing.

II: Some persons live on the bank of the river Ganga.

Conclusion:

Persons who live on the bank of the river Ganga, are afraid of being washed away.

Directions (Qs. 34 to 41): *In each of the following questions two statements have been given followed by a conclusion. Mark your answer as:*

(A) if only statement I affirms the conclusion.

(B) if only statement II affirms the conclusion.

(C) if both statements I and II affirm the conclusions.

(D) if statement I affirms the conclusion but statement II is contradictionary.

(E) None of the statements affirms the conclusion.

34. Statements:

I: Rate of increase in the population of India is quite high.

II: Excessive increase in population blocks the economic development of a country.

Conclusion:

Dense population in India obstructs economic development of the country.

35. Statements:

I: Some vegetables are fruits.

II: Fruits are good for health.

Conclusion:

Some vegetables are good for health.

36. Statements:

I: All rocks are mountains.

II: All rocks are trees.

Conclusion:

Some mountains are trees

37. Statements:

I: All boys are students.

II: No student is a boy.

Conclusion:

Some students are boys.

38. Statements:

I: Miserable condition of economy is responsible for increase in the price of consumer goods.

II: Miserable condition of economy obstructs development of a country.

Conclusion:

Economic prosperity is essential for development of a country.

39. Statements:

I: Climate of Kango forest is moisturous.

II: Moisturous climate is harmful to the health of men.

Conclusion:

Moisturous climate of Kango forest is harmful to the health of persons living there.

40. Statements:

I: All toys are beautiful.

II: All toys provide recreation.

Conclusion:

There is not such toy which is not beautiful.

41. Statements:

I: Some games are exercise.

II: Exercise is useful to health.

Conclusion:

Some games are useful to health.

EXPLANATORY ANSWERS

1. B:

2. B: It is wrong that all lecturers of the university keep beard because I know only one lecturer.

3. D: The word 'rich' is not related with the given statement.

4. C: A large number of buses plying on route number 10 go to the stadium, so there may be some buses which do not go to the stadium. Therefore it is not essential that this bus will certainly go to the stadium.

5. C: It is not essential that Minku certainly bears a good health but it is obvious from the given two statements that Minku bears a good health to a certain extent.

6. A:

7. D: Word 'enemy' does not have any significance in the given statement

8. A: P is standing behind M and N. Q is standing behind P. Therefore Q will be standing behind M.

9. B: Cheese is used in Omelet and rats eat cheese. But rats can not prepare Omelet.

10. A: Both statements are affirming the conclusion drawn. Therefore conclusion is definitely true.

11. D: The word 'neighbour' is not related with the statement.

12. D: The word 'elephant' is not related with the statement.

13. C: From the statement I we can say that there are some metals which are neither malleable nor ductile. But X is neither malleable nor ductile. Therefore we can not affirm that X is not a metal.

14. D: The word 'yesterday' is not related with the given statement.

15. A: Both statements affirm the conclusion drawn. Therefore conclusion is true.

16. B: Rahul hates Mehul and Mehul hates Rupam. But it is not true that Rahul hates Rupam.

17. A: Both statements affirm the conclusion drawn.

18. C: All wives are ladies. But we can not say that all ladies are wives. There are some ladies who are not wives.

19. D:

20. B: Both statements do not affirm the conclusion drawn.

21. A:

22. A:

23. A:

24. D:

25. B:

26. C: In the given statements the parity of the dance performances of Peacock and Ostritch is obvious. But conclusion has been drawn that Sstritch also possesses a long beautiful tail. This is not true.

27. D:

28. D:

29. B: Cats drink milk because cats are very wise. Therefore all those animals who drink milk are wise. This is not a part of the statement. Therefore 'B' is the correct answer.

30. B: In the statements boys are related with kite and girls arc related with dolls. In the conclusion girls are said to be more wise as compared to boys. The drawn conclusion is not related with the statements.

31. A: Conclusion has been drawn that carbohydrate is essential for growing children. Statements-I asserts that carbohydrate is helpful in building up of our body and growing children require nutrition. The two statements affirm the conclusion. Therefore 'A' is the correct answer.

32. C: All freedom fighters were born in Punjab. This statement is not completely correct. Therefore conclusion is partially true. 'C' is correct answer.

33. A:

34. C: Drawn conclusion confirms both statements.

35. C:

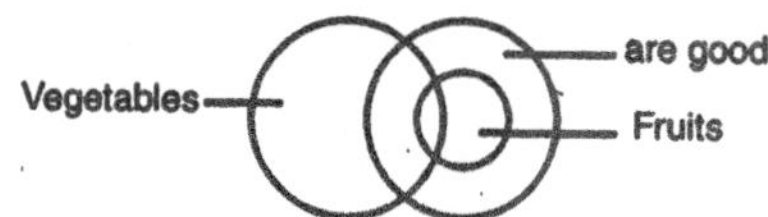

Drawn conclusion is based on statements I and II.

36. C:

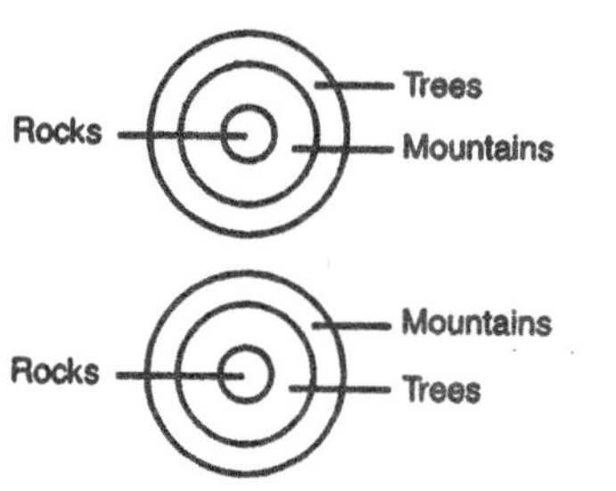

Conclusion is based on the statements I and II.

37. D: All boys are students. Therefore some students are certainly boys. Conclusion is confirmed from statement I while it is contradictory to the statement II.

38. C: Both statements affirm the conclusion.

39. C: 'Moisturous climate of Kango forest is harmful the health of persons living there'. This conclusion is based on both the given statements.

40. A: Conclusion drawn is based on statement I. Therefore 'A' is the correct answer.

41. C: The conclusion is based on both the statements.

18

TEST ON COURSE OF ACTION

In this type of test one statement followed by two courses of action is given. A course of action is a step or administrative decision to be taken for improvement, follow-up or further action with regard to the problem, policy etc. on the basis of the information given in the statement. Everything in the statement is assumed to be true and then it is decided as to which of the two given/suggested courses of action logically follows for pursuing.

Example: In the question given below a statement is followed by two courses of action numbered I and II. The candidates have to assume everything in the statement to be true, then decide which of the suggested courses of action logically follows for pursuing. Mark your answer as:

(A) if only I follows.
(B) if only II follows.
(C) if either I or II follows.
(D) if neither I nor II follows.
(E) if both I and II follow.

Statement: India's performance in the last Olympic Games was very poor. Not even a single medal could be bagged by the players. Government of India had spent Rs. 5 crores in training and deputing a team of players to participate in the Olympic Games on behalf of the country.

Courses of Action:

I. India should stop sending its players to the future Olympic Games.
II. Government should immediately set up an inquiry commission to find out the reasons for India's dismal performance.

Explanatory Answer (B): First course of action is not appropriate because it would affect the good will of Indian players and people would start boycotting games in India. Second course of action is appropriate because thus the reasons of bad performance will be known which could be utilized to remove the flaws.

EXERCISE

Directions (Qs. 1 to 10): *In each question below is given a statement followed by two courses of action numbered I and II. You have to assume everything in the statement to be true and then decide which of the given/suggested courses of action logically follows for pursuing. Mark your answer as:*

(A) if only I follows
(B) if only II follows

(C) if either I or II follows
(D) if neither I nor II follows
(E) if both I and II follow

1. Statement:

Although the Indian economy is still heavily dependent on agriculture, its share in global agricultural trade is less than the share of agricultural exports to total exports.

Courses of Action:

I: Efforts should be made to increase our agricultural production.

II: The exports of non-agricultural commodities should be reduced.

2. Statement:

About 30 to 40 percent of children who are enrolled, do not attend school on any given day.

Courses of Action:

I: More schools should be started.

II: Reasons for this absenteeism should be found out.

3. Statement:

Air export volumes have increased substantially over the past decade causing backlogs and difficulties for air cargo agents because of increased demand for space and service.

Courses of Action:

I: Airlines and air cargo agents should jointly work out a solution to combat the problem.

II: The reasons for the increase in the volume of air export should be found out.

4. Statement:

Huge amount of resources are required to develop tourist places in a country like India which is endowed with vast coastal lines, rivers, forests, temples, etc.

Courses of Action:

I: More tourist-resorts along the coastal line only should be developed.

II: The tourist-potential of India should be exploited

5. Statement:

The world conference on 'Education for All' took place in Thailand in 2000. Widely attended conference endorsed the Frame-work on Action for Meeting the Basic Learning Needs of all children.

Courses of Action:

I: India should suitably implement the Action points of this conference.

II: India should also immediately organise such type of conference.

6. Statement:

The 'expert group' constituted to go into the flaws of existing education system has found that lack of commercialization in our education system is the main factor responsible for 'problem of unemployment' in our country.

Courses of Action:

I: Government should provide funds to the institutions then by the government for conducting commercial courses.

II: Government should provide funds to the educational institutes run by the government for conducting commercial courses.

7. **Statement:**

Central Ministry of Civil Aviation & Tourism has fixed a target of achieving an income of Rs. 10,000 crores per year through tourism by the end of this decade.

Courses of Action:

I: With a view to achieve this target more tourist-resorts are not needed to be developed.

II: Ministry should prepare attractive packages for foreign tourists with a view to achieve this target.

8. **Statements:**

More than 500 villages of Uttar Pradesh are heavily flood-affected and a relief work by the Government has put an additional burden of Rs. 150 crores on the Government's exchequer. The inundation has caused a huge loss to the Khareef crops also.

Courses of Action:

I: To reduce this additional burden government should levy relief tax on the corporate sector.

II: The government will have to explore the means and ways to stop recurrence of flood in this area.

9. **Statement:**

The committee has suggested that such Duty Free Technical Parks should be established at various places all over the country where foreign companies would set up their units to manufacture electronic and hardware goods.

Courses of Action:

I: Government should immediately implement this suggestion of the committee with a view to enhance its stock of foreign currency by export of these goods.

II: Government should not implement this suggestion of the committee because this will bring impediments before the indigeneous production of hardware goods

10. **Statement:**

More than 1200 industrial units situated in Mayapuri Industrial Area of West Delhi, in which about 2,00,000 work forces are employed, are suffering from grave situation of power cut.

Courses of Action:

I: These Industrial Units should be closed immediately.

II: Government should immediately take steps to restore adequate power supply to these industrial units.

Directions (Qs. 11 to 20): *In each of the following questions a statement has been given which is followed by three courses of action numbered I, II and III. A course of action is a step or administrative decision to be taken for improvement, follow-up or further action in regard of the problem, policy etc. on the basis of the information provided. You have to assume everything in the statement to be true, then decide which of the given/suggested courses of action logically follows for pursuing. Select your answer from amongst the* *given alternatives (A), (B), (C), (D) and (E).*

11. Statement:

A further increase in the pollution level of the city due to industrial wastes and automobiles, will produce a grave environmental problem for city dwellers.

Courses of Action:

I: All factories of the city should be stopped immediately.

II: Automobiles in the city should not be allowed to ply for more than 4 hours in a day.

III: Government should restrict permitting new licences to the factories and automobiles.

A. Only III follows
B. All follow
C. Only II follows
D. None follows
E. Only I follows

12. Statement:

Every year thousands of able students, both in rural as well as in urban areas, can not get admission in colleges despite passing the last certificate examination of their schools.

Courses of Action:

I: More colleges should be established in rural as well as in urban areas.

II: Number of schools in rural as well as in urban areas should be decreased.

III: A good number of schools should conduct vocational courses. So that students could start their profession after completing the school education.

A. Only I follows
B. Only II and III follow
C. All follow
D. Only I and III follow
E. None of the above

13. Statements:

Due to heavy rainfall during the last few days the river is in spate which has caused overflowing and several parts of the city are waterlogged. The river bottom is full of silt and mud.

Courses of Action:

I: People living on the river bank should be shifted to safe places.

II: People should be informed about the flood situation on radio and television.

III: Immediately after flood is subsided, the river bottom should be cleaned of silt and mud.

A. Only I and II follow.
B. Only II and III follow.
C. None follows.
D. All follow.
E. Only I and III follow.

14. Statement:

A few species of mosquitoes have developed antibodies against chloroquine which is a widely used medicine for treatment of malaria.

Courses of Action:

I: Sale of chloroquine should be banned.

II: Medical scientists should develop new medicines for treatment of patients suffering from parasitical infection caused due to bite of such species of mosquitoes.

III: All patients suffering from malaria should be tested for detecting these species of mosquitos.

A. None follows.
B. Only I and III follow.
C. Only II and III follow.
D. All follow.
E. Either I or II follows.

15. Statement:

Without active co-operation from the mill owner and the workers, the mill can not remain profitable for long

Courses of Action:

I: Mill should be closed.

II: Workers should be asked to co-operate with mill owner.

III: Mill owner should also co-operate with workers.

A. Only I and II follow.
B. None follows.
C. All follow.
D. Only II and III follow.
E Neither II nor III follows.

16. Statement:

If the faculty members also join the strike, there is going to be a serious problem.

Courses of Action:

I: The faculty members should be persuaded not to go on strike.

II: Those faculty members who join the strike should be suspended.

III: The management should not worry about such trivial issues.

A. Only I follows.
B. Only I and II follow.
C. Only II and III follow.
D. None follows.
E. All follow.

17. Statement:

Higher disposal costs encourages those who produce waste to look for cheaper ways to get rid of it.

Courses of Action:

I: The disposal costs should be made higher.

II: The disposal costs should be brought down.

III: A committee should be set up to study the details in this respect.

A. Only I follows.
B. Only II follows.
C. Only III follows.
D. Only II and III follow.
E. None follows.

18. Statement:

Over 27,000 bonded labourers identified and freed are still awaiting rehabilitation.

Courses of Action:

I: More cases of bonded labourers should be identified.

II: Till the proper rehabilitation facilities are available, the bonded labourers should not be freed.

III: The impediments in the way of speedy and proper rehabilitation of bonded labourers should be removed.

A. Only I follows
B. Only II follows
C. Only III follows
D. Only II and III follow
E. None follows

19. Statement:

Faced with a serious resource

crunch and a depressing overall economic scenario, Orissa is unlikely to achieve the targetted percent compound annual growth rate during the 9th Plan.

Courses of Action:

I: The target growth should be reduced for the next Plan.

II: The reasons for the failure should be studied.

III: Orissa's performance should be compared with that of other states.

A. Only I follows.

B. Only I and II follow.

C. Only II and III follow.

D. None follows.

E. All follow.

20. Statement:

The army has been alerted in the district following floods triggered by incessant rains.

Courses of Action:

I: Relief to flood affected people should be arranged.

II: Supply of food stuff should be arranged.

III: Adequate medical facilities should be arranged.

A. Only I follows.

B. Only II follows.

C. Only I and II follow.

D. None follows.

E. All follow.

ANSWERS

1	2	3	4	5	6	7	8	9	10
A	B	A	B	E	E	B	E	C	B
11	**12**	**13**	**14**	**15**	**16**	**17**	**18**	**19**	**20**
D	D	D	D	D	A	D	C	C	E

19

TEST ON TWO STATEMENTS AND TWO CONCLUSIONS

In this type of test each of the questions asked contains two statements followed by two conclusions. Candidates have to take the two given statements to be true even if they seem to be at variance with commonly known facts and then decide which of the given conclusions logically follows from the given statements. These questions are easy to solve with Venn diagram. The items represented by the diagrams may be individuals, a particular group/class of people (items), etc. On the basis of statements more and more venn diagrams are drawn and then that diagram is selected which most appropriately represents the required conclusion.

Example 1:

I: Some men are thieves.

II: No boy is a thief.

Conclusions:

(a) Some thieves are not men.

(b) Some men are not boys.

Explanatory Answer: On the basis of the two statements following five Venn diagrams can be possibly drawn.

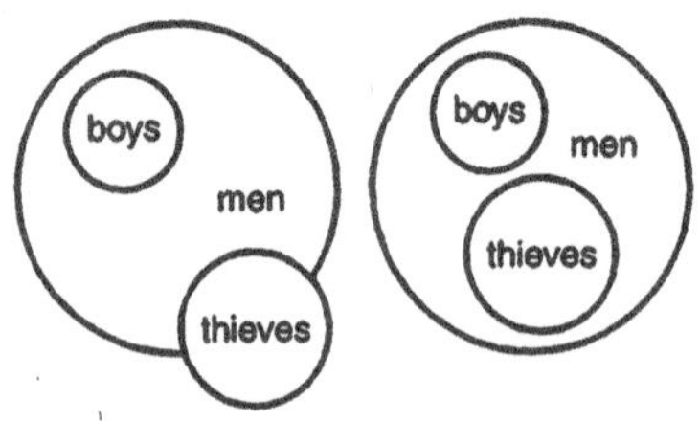

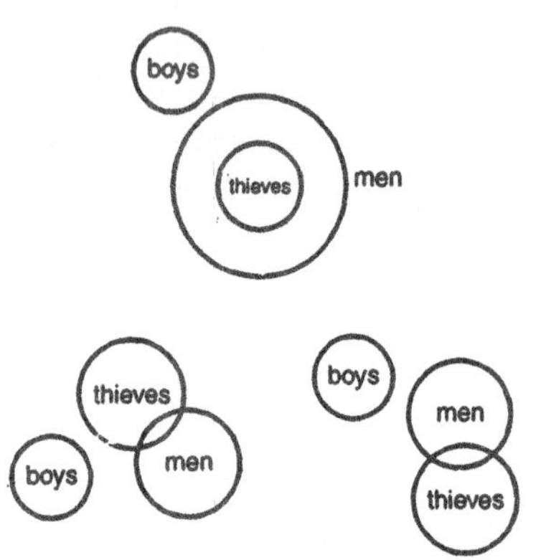

It is obvious from the above five Venn diagrams that circles representing men and boys are separately drawn. Therefore it is affirmed that 'Some men are not boys'. It is also obvious that in some diagrams circle representing 'thieves' is separated from the circle representing 'men' and in some other diagrams it is not so. Therefore the second conclusion is correct.

Directions (Qs. 1 to 49): *In each question below are given two statements followed by two conclusions marked (a) and (b). You have to take the given statements to be true and then decide which of the given conclusions logically follows from the two given statements. Read the two statements and following conclusions carefully and mark your* *answer as:*

(A) if only conclusion *(a)* follows.
(B) if only conclusion *(b)* follows.
(C) if both conclusions *(a)* and *(b)* follow.
(D) if either *(a)* or *(b)* follows.
(E) if none of the conclusions follows.

1. Statements:
I: Some men are wolves.
II: Some hungry persons are wolves.
Conclusions:
(a) All men are hungry wolves.
(b) All those who are hungry, are called wolves.

2. Statements:
I: Some dogs bite.
II: All dogs bark.
Conclusions:
(a) Those also bite who are not dogs.
(b) It is not essential that those dogs who do not bark should bite.

3. Statements:
I: All passengers are men.
II: All men are graduates.
Conclusions:
(a) All men are passengers.
(b) All passengers are graduates.

4. Statements:
I: Some books are birds.
II: Some birds are fingers.
Conclusions:
(a) Some fingers are books.
(b) Some fingers are birds.

5. Statements:
I: All books are bushes.
II: All trees are bushes.
Conclusions:
(a) Some bushes are books.
(b) Some bushes are trees.

6. Statements:
I: All nails are ears.
II: Some ears are eyes.
Conclusions:
(a) All ears are nails.
(b) Some eyes are nails.

7. Statements:
I: All Surahis are tumblers.
II: No Surahi is cup.
Conclusions:
(a) All tumblers are cups.
(b) Some tumblers are cups.

8. Statements:
I: All authors are teachers.
II: All teachers are ladies.
Conclusions:
(a) Some teachers are authors.
(b) All ladies are teachers.

9. Statements:
I: All watches are handles.
II: All handles are bricks.
Conclusions:
(a) All handles are watches.
(b) All watches are bricks.

10. Statements:
I: All potatoes are birds.
II: Some potatoes are books.
Conclusions:
(a) All books are potatoes.
(b) All birds are books.

11. Statements:
I: All lemons are swans.
II: No swan is a carpet.
Conclusions:
(a) No lemon is a carpet.
(b) All swans are lemons.

12. Statement:
I: Some ants are trees.
II: All actors are trees.

Conclusions:

(*a*) All ants are trees.

(*b*) All trees are actors.

13. Statements:

I: All mirrors are eggs.

II: All eggs are bats.

Conclusions:

(*a*) All mirrors are bats.

(*b*) All bats are mirrors.

14. Statements:

I: Some pens are birds.

II: All cats are birds.

Conclusions:

(*a*) Some cats are pens.

(*b*) Some birds are pens.

15. Statements:

I: All apples are parrots.

II: No parrot is green.

Conclusions:

(*a*) No apple is green.

(*b*) Some parrots are apples.

16. Statements:

I: All dogs are chairs.

II: All chairs are tables.

Conclusions:

(*a*) All dogs are tables.

(*b*) All tables are chairs.

17. Statements:

I: Some oranges are crows.

II: Some crows are apples.

Conclusions:

(*a*) Some oranges are apples.

(*b*) Some apples are crows.

18. Statement:

I: All dogs are chairs.

II: All chairs are tables.

Conclusions:

(*a*) Some tables are chairs.

(*b*) Some tables are dogs.

19. Statements:

I: All doctors are ladies.

II: No lady is literate.

Conclusions:

(*a*) No doctor is literate.

(*b*) No man is doctor.

20. Statements:

I: Some negroes are men.

II: All whites are men.

Conclusions:

(*a*) All negroes are men.

(*b*) Some men are whites.

21. Statements:

I: All men are politicians.

II: All politicians are flatterers.

Conclusions:

(*a*) All men are flatterers.

(*b*) All flatterers are men.

22. Statements:

I: All vegetables are fruits.

II: All fruits are pears.

Conclusions:

(*a*) All fruits are vegetables.

(*b*) All vegetables are pears.

23. Statements:

I: All buffaloes are birds.

II: All buffaloes graze at night

Conclusions:

(*a*) All who grazes at night are buffaloes.

(*b*) All birds graze at night.

24. Statements:

I: All roads are aeroplanes.

II: All aeroplanes are parrots.

Conclusions:

(*a*) All roads are parrots.

(*b*) All aeroplanes are roads.

25. Statements:

I: Some boys are clouds.

II: Guman is a boy.

Conclusions:

(*a*) Guman is a cloud.

(*b*) Some clouds are not boys.

26. Statements:

I: All chairs are mangoes.

II: Some mangoes are tables.

Conclusions:

(a) Some mangoes are chairs.

(b) Some tables are not apples.

27. Statements:

I: All roads are aeroplanes.

II: All aeroplanes are parrots.

Conclusions:

(a) All parrots are roads.

(b) All parrots are aeroplanes.

28. Statements:

I: Some boys are clouds.

II: Govind is a boy.

Conclusions:

(a) Some clouds are boys.

(b) Some boys are not clouds.

29. Statements:

I: Some hats are tables.

II: Some tables are chairs.

Conclusions:

(a) Some tables are hats.

(b) Some chairs are hats.

30. Statements:

I: All poets are clerks.

II: Some clerks are not wise.

Conclusions:

(a) No poet is wise.

(b) All clerks are poets.

31. Statements:

I: All books are chairs.

II: All chairs are pens.

Conclusions:

(a) All books are pens.

(b) All pens are books.

32. Statements:

I: Some eagles are horses.

II: All horses are dogs.

Conclusions:

(a) All dogs are horses.

(b) Some dogs are eagles.

33. Statements:

I: All coats are bags.

II: Some bags are toys.

Conclusions:

(a) Some bags are coats.

(b) Some toys are coats.

34. Statements:

I: All cows are dancers.

II: Some buffuloes are dancers.

Conclusions:

(a) All dancers are not cows.

(b) Some dancers are not buffaloes.

35. Statements:

I: All children are boys.

II: All boys are players.

Conclusions:

(a) All children are players.

(b) All boys are children.

36. Statements:

I: Some mangoes are sweet.

II: Some sweets are fruits.

Conclusions:

(a) Some mangoes are fruits.

(b) Some fruits are mangoes.

37. Statements:

I: All vehicles are cars.

II: No car is costly.

Conclusions:

(a) All cars are vehicles.

(b) No Vehicle is costly.

38. Statements:

I: All flowers are girls.

II: Some girls are beautiful.

Conclusions:

(a) All flowers are beautiful.

(b) Some flowers are beautiful.

39. Statements:

I: All tables are ants.

II: Some ants are chairs.

Conclusions:

(a) All ants are tables.

(b) Some chairs are not ants.

40. Statements:

I: All tables are ants.

II: Some ants are chairs.

Conclusions:

(a) Some tables are chairs.

(b) Some chairs are tables.

41. Statements:

I: All watches are roads.

II: All watches are eagles.

Conclusions:

(a) All roads are eagles.

(b) All watches are roads.

42. Statements:

I: Sagar is a good player.

II: Players are generally healthy.

Conclusions:

(a) All healthy persons are players.

(b) Sagar is healthy.

43. Statements:

I: Some birds are clouds.

II: Horse is a bird.

Conclusions:

(a) Horse is a vehicle.

(b) Horse is not cloud.

44. Statements:

I: Some birds are clouds.

II: Horse is a bird.

Conclusions:

(a) Some clouds are birds.

(b) Horse is not cloud.

45. Statements:

I: Some crows are dogs.

II: All dogs are faithful animals.

Conclusions:

(a) All faithful animals are dogs.

(b) Some crows are faithful animals.

46. Statements:

I: Some jackals are deers.

II: Some deers are leopards.

Conclusions:

(a) Some jackals are leopards

(b) All deers are jackals.

47. Statements:

I: All trucks fly.

II: Some scooters fly.

Conclusions:

(a) All trucks are scooters.

(b) Some scooters do not fly.

48. Statements:

I: All spoons are plates.

II: All plates are trays.

Conclusions:

(a) All spoons are trays.

(b) Some trays are Spoons.

49. Statements:

I: Some apples are yellow.

II: Sunehary is an apple.

Conclusions:

(a) Some apples are green.

(b) Sunehary is yellow.

Directions (Qs. 50 to 84): *In each of the questions two statements have been given followed by two conclusions marked as (a) and (b). Based on the facts stated in the statements you have to decide which of the conclusions is correct. Mark your answer as:*

(A) if conclusion *(a)* is true.

(B) if conclusion *(b)* is true.

(C) if both conclusions *(a)* and *(b)* are true.

(D) if *(a)* is true and *(b)* is false.

(E) if both *(a)* and *(b)* are false.

50. Statements:

I: Some crows are cows.

II: Some cows are cats.

Conclusions:

(a) Some crows are cats.

(b) All crows are cats.

51. Statements:

I: All cats are dogs.

II: Some dogs are black.

Conclusions:

(a) Some cats are black.

(b) All crows are cats.

52. Statements:

I: All poets are authers.

II: All singers are authers.

Conclusions:

(a) All singers are poets.

(b) Some authers are not Singers.

53. Statements:

I: All tables are horses.

II: All horses are rivers.

Conclusions:

(a) All tables are rivers.

(b) All rivers are tables.

54. Statements:

I: Some authers are painters.

II: All painters are honest.

Conclusions:

(a) All honest persons are painters.

(b) Some authers are honest persons.

55. Statements:

I: Some intelligent men are angry persons.

II: All angry persons are intelligent men.

Conclusions:

(a) Some intelligent men are unhappy.

(b) Some angry persons are intelligent men.

56. Statements:

I: Some soldiers are followers.

II: Some soldiers are decision makers.

Conclusions:

(a) Some soldiers are either followers or decision makers.

(b) Some soldiers are neither followers nor decision makers.

57. Statements:

I: All men are prisoners.

II: No prisoner is educated.

Conclusions:

(a) All prisoners are educated.

(b) No man is educated.

58. Statements:

I: All eggs are rotten.

II: All rotten eggs are kept in that good looking carton.

Conclusions:

(a) All rotten things are not eggs.

(b) All eggs are kept in good looking carton.

59. Statements:

I: Some essayists are poets.

II: All poets are playwrights.

Conclusions:

(a) All poets are essayists.

(b) Some essayists are playwrights.

60. Statements:

I: No policeman is idle.

II: Only idle persons have fatty physique.

Conclusions:

(a) Those policeman who have fatty physique, do not look nice.

(b) No policeman has fatty physique.

61. Statements:

I: Some men wear traditional Dhoti-Kurta.

II: Some men wear excellent dresses according to their social status.

Conclusions:

(*a*) Rahul, who is a famous industrialist, should wear Dhoti-Kurta.

(*b*) He should wear excellent dresses.

62. Statements:

I: Only those guests drink soup who drink tea.

II: All those who drink tea, do not drink coffee

Conclusions:

(*a*) The guests who drink soup, also drink coffee.

(*b*) The guests who drink tea, neither drink coffee nor soup.

63. Statements:

I: Shirts are less costly than gowns but they are as costly as shoes.

II: Shoes are more costly than sweaters but less costly than handkerchieves.

Conclusions:

(*a*) Sweaters are cheapest.

(*b*) Sweaters are less costly than handkerchieves.

64. Statements:

I: Those who rise early in the morning do not sleep late at night.

II: Those who sleep late at night, can not rise early in the morning.

Conclusions:

(*a*) Those who sleep late at night, rise early in the morning.

(*b*) Those who rise early in the morning, sleep early at night.

65. Statements:

I: Milk is a complete food.

II: Egg is also a complete food.

Conclusions:

(*a*) Milk and eggs can provide complete nutrition to the body.

(*b*) Components of milk and eggs are identical.

66. Statements:

I: B is the uncle of A.

II: C is the only brother of A.

Conclusions:

(*a*) A is the only sister of C.

(*b*) A is a boy.

67. Statements:

I: Some birds do not make their nests.

II: Cuckoo is a bird.

Conclusions:

(*a*) Cuckoo makes her nest.

(*b*) Cuckoo does not make her nest.

68. Statements:

I: All actresses are beautiful.

II: Some Sindhi women are also beautiful.

Conclusions:

(*a*) Some Sindhi women are not beautiful.

(*b*) Those Sindhi women who are beautiful, can get opportunities to become film actresses.

69. Statements:

I: Mutual resentment is a general cause of battle.

II: Battle affected people get compensation.

Conclusions:

(*a*) Opposite parties pay compensation

(*b*) We can always find some persons who are battle affected.

70. Statements:

I: Some cooks are naughty.

II: All boys are naughty.

Conclusions:

(*a*) Some boys are cooks.

(*b*) Some cooks are boys.

71. Statements:

I: Some men are wolves.

II: Some wolves are hungry.

Conclusions:

(*a*) All men are hungry wolves.

(*b*) All those who are hungry, are wolves.

72. Statements:

I: All dogs bite.

II: Some dogs bark.

Conclusions:

(*a*) Those dogs who bark, also bite.

(*b*) Those dogs should not essentially bite who do not bark.

73. Statements:

I: All passengers are men.

II: All men are graduates.

Conclusions:

(*a*) All men are passengers.

(*b*) All passengers are graduates.

74. Statements:

I: All radios are transistors.

II: Some transistors are foreign made.

Conclusions:

(*a*) All radios are foreign made.

(*b*) All transistors are not radios

75. Statements:

I: Some poets are fools.

II: All fools are goats.

Conclusions:

(*a*) Some poets are goats.

(*b*) Some fools are poets.

EXPLANATORY ANSWERS

1. E: **2. B:** **3. B:** **4. B:** **5. E:**
6. B: **7. D:** **8. A:** **9. B:** **10. D:**
11. A: **12. D:** **13. A:** **14. C:** **15. E:**
16. A: **17. D:** **18. E:** **19. A:** **20. B:**

21. A: All men are politicians and all politicians are flatterers. Therefore conclusion (*a*) *i.e.* 'All men are flatterers is true.

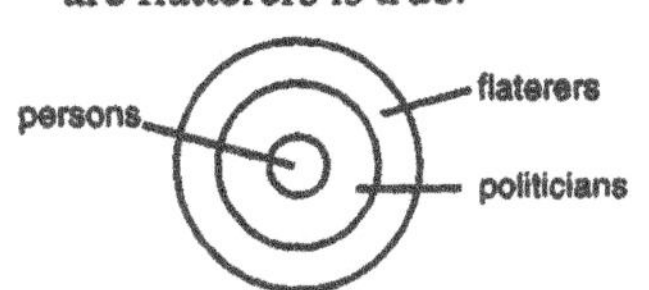

22. B: **23. D:** **24. A:** **25. D:** **26. D:**
27. D: **28. D:** **29. D:** **30. A:**

31. E: Conclusions (*a*) and (*b*) are true as is obvious from the following diagram.

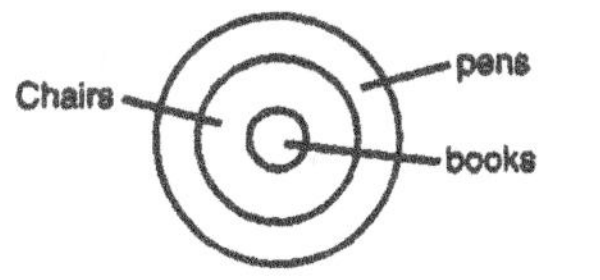

32. B: **33. D:** **34. E:**

35. A: Conclusion (*a*) is true.

36. D: **37. B:** **38. D:** **39. E:** **40. E:**
41. E: **42. E:** **43. E:** **44. E:** **45. B:**
46. E:

47. B: Some scooters fly. Therefore there are some scooters which do not fly.

48. C: Plate is wider than spoon and tray is wider than plate. Similarly all spoons can be kept in a tray. Therefore conclusion (*a*) is true. In the diagram, circle representing spoon is within the circle representing tray. Therefore at least one tray is spoon. Therefore conclusion (*b*) is also true.

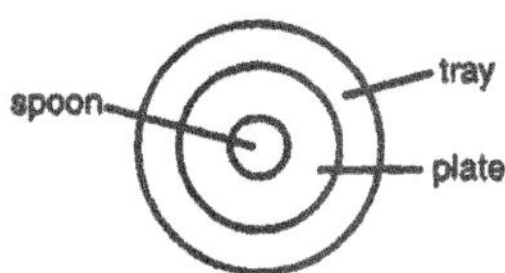

49. E: Conclusion *(a)* is irrelevant from the facts stated in the statements. Conclusion *(b)* is not definitely true.

50. E: 51. E:

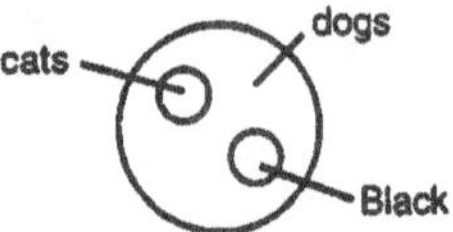

52. E:

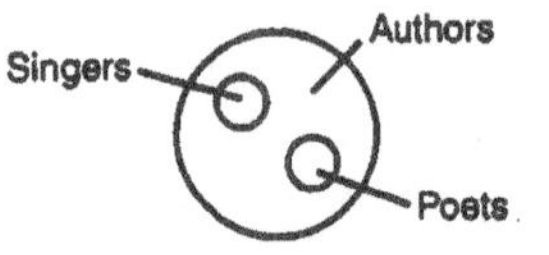

53. C: In the Venn diagram, the circumference of rivers is wider than that of horses and circumference of horses is wider than that of the tables. Therefore conclusion *(a)* 'all tables are rivers' is true. In the same way at least one river is certainly table. Therefore conclusion *(b) i.e.,* 'Some rivers are tables' is also correct. Therefore both conclusions *(a)* and *(b)* are correct.

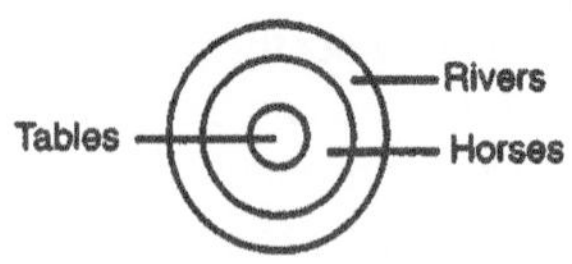

54. B:

55. A: Conclusion *(a)* follows.

56. D: Both conclusions are contradictory to each other *i.e.,* conclusion *(a)* is true and conclusion *(b)* is false.

57. B: According to statement I 'all men are prisoners' and according to statement II 'No prisoner is educated'. Therefore all men are uneducated. Conclusion *(a)* is false and *(b)* is true.

58. B:

59. B: In statement I, some eassayists are poets. Therefore some poets are not essayists. So conclusion *(a)* is false and conclusion *(b)* is true.

60. B: 61. D:

62. E: Only those guests drink soup who drink tea and all those who drink tea do not drink coffee. Therefore those who drink soup and tea, do not drink coffee. Both conclusions and false.

63. C: 64. E:

65. A: Milk and egg both are complete foods.

66. D: 67. D:

68. C: Some Sindhi women are beautiful and some are not beautiful. All actresses are beautiful. Therefore those Sindhi women, who are beautiful, can become actresses. Both conclusions are true.

69. B: 70. D: 71. D: 72. A: 73. B: 74. D: 75. A:

Printed by BoD™ in Norderstedt, Germany

9 789350 127766